Professional Examinations

PART 1

Paper 1.1

Preparing Financial Statements

(International Stream)

ACCA Textbook

ACCA Official Publisher

FOULKS LYNCH PUBLICATIONS

M. Imran Asghar

British Library Cataloguing-in-Publication Data

A catalogue record for this book is available from the British Library.

Published by Foulks Lynch Ltd
4, The Griffin Centre
Staines Road
Feltham
Middlesex
TW14 0HS

ISBN 0 7483 6274 6

Printed and bound in Great Britain

Acknowledgements

We are grateful to the Association of Chartered Certified Accountants, the Chartered Institute of Management Accountants and the Institute of Chartered Accountants in England and Wales for permission to reproduce past examination questions. The answers have been prepared by Foulks Lynch Ltd.

Contents

Introduction

This Textbook is the ACCA's official text for Paper 1.1 *Preparing Financial Statements (International Stream)*, and is part of the ACCA's official series produced for students taking the ACCA examinations.

This new edition, updated for 2004 exams, has been produced with direct guidance from the examiner. It covers the syllabus and study guide in great detail, giving appropriate weighting to the various topics. Targeted very closely on the examination, this textbook is written in a way that will help you assimilate the information easily. Numerous practice questions and exam type questions at the end of each chapter reinforce your knowledge.

DEFINITION

- **Definitions.** The text defines key words and concepts, placing them in the margin, with a clear heading, as on the left. The purpose of including these definitions is to focus your attention on the point being covered.

KEY POINT

- **Key points**. In the margin you will see key points at regular intervals. The purpose of these is to summarise concisely the key material being covered.

ACTIVITY 1

- **Activities**. The text involves you in the learning process with a series of activities designed to catch your attention and make you concentrate and respond. The feedback to activities is at the end of each chapter.

SELF-TEST QUESTIONS

- **Self-test questions**. At the end of each chapter there is a series of self-test questions. The purpose of these is to help you revise some of the key elements of the chapter. All the answers to these questions can be found in the text.

EXAM-TYPE QUESTIONS

- **End of chapter questions**. At the end of each chapter we include examination-type questions. These will give you a very good idea of the sort of thing the examiner will ask and will test your understanding of what has been covered.

Syllabus and study guide

CONTENTS

Objectives of the study guide

This study guide is designed to help you plan your studies and to provide a more detailed interpretation of the syllabus for Paper 1.1 *Preparing Financial Statements (International Stream)*. It contains both the syllabus and the study guide, which you can follow when preparing for the examination.

The syllabus outlines the content of the paper. The study guide takes the syllabus content and expands it into study sessions of similar length. These sessions indicate what the examiner expects of candidates for each part of the syllabus, and therefore gives you guidance in the skills you are expected to demonstrate in the examinations.

Syllabus content

1 GENERAL FRAMEWORK

a Types of business entity – incorporated entities, partnerships and sole traders.

b Forms of capital and capital structures in incorporated entities.

c The role of the International Accounting Standards Board (IASB).

d Application of International Accounting Standards (IASs) to the preparation and presentation of financial statements.

e The IASB's Framework for the Preparation and Presentation of Financial Statements (paragraphs 1 to 46 only).

2 ACCOUNTING CONCEPTS AND PRINCIPLES

a Basic accounting concepts and principles as stated in the IASB's Framework for the Preparation and Presentation of Financial Statements and IAS 1 Presentation of Financial Statements.

b Other accounting concepts i historical cost

ii money measurement

iii entity

iv dual aspect

v time interval.

3 DOUBLE-ENTRY BOOKKEEPING AND ACCOUNTING SYSTEMS

a Double-entry bookkeeping and accounting systems

i form and content of accounting records (manual and computerised)

ii books of original entry, including journals

iii sales and purchase ledgers iv cash bookv general ledger

vi trial balance

vii accruals, prepayments and adjustments

viii asset registers

ix petty cash.

b Confirming and correcting mechanisms

i control accounts

ii bank reconciliations

iii suspense accounts and the correction of errors.

c General principles of the operation of a sales tax.

d Computerised accounting systems.

4 ACCOUNTING TREATMENTS

a Non-current assets, tangible and intangible

i distinction between capital and revenue expenditure

ii accounting for acquisitions and disposals

iii depreciation – definition, reasons for and methods, including straight line, reducing balance and sum of digits

iv research and development

v elementary treatment of goodwill.

b Current assets

i inventory

ii accounts receivable, including accounting for bad and doubtful debts

iii cash.

c Current liabilities and accruals.

d Shareholders' equity.

e Events after the balance sheet date.

f Contingencies.

5 FINANCIAL STATEMENTS

a Objectives of financial statements.

b Users and their information needs.

c Key features of financial statements

i balance sheet

ii income statement
iii cash flow statement
iv notes to the financial statements (examined to a limited extent – see d (iii) below).

d Preparation of financial statements for:
i sole traders, including incomplete records techniques
ii partnerships
iii limited liability companies, including income statements and balance sheets for internal purposes and for external purposes in accordance with IAS 1 Presentation of Financial Statements and preparation of basic cash flow statements in accordance with IAS 7 for limited liability companies (excluding group cash flow statements). The following notes to the financial statements will be examinable and no others:
- Statement of changes in equity
- Non-current assets
- Unusual and extraordinary items
- Events after the balance sheet date
- Contingent liabilities and contingent assets
- Research and development expenditure

iv groups of companies – preparation of a basic consolidated balance sheet for a company with one subsidiary.

6 INTERPRETATION

a Ratio analysis of accounting information and basic interpretation.

Excluded topics

The syllabus content outlines the area for assessment. No questions will be asked on: clubs and societies, partnerships other than the preparation of financial statements for partnerships.

Key areas of the syllabus

The objective of Paper 1.1, Preparing Financial Statements, is to ensure that candidates have the necessary basic accounting knowledge and skill to progress to the more advanced work of Paper 2.5 Financial Reporting. The two main skills required are:

- The ability to prepare basic financial statements and the underlying accounting records on which they are based.
- An understanding of the principles on which accounting is based.

The key topic areas are as follows:

- preparation of financial statements for limited liability companies for internal purposes or for publication£ preparation of financial statements for partnerships and sole traders (including incomplete records)
- basic group accounts – consolidated balance sheet for a company with one subsidiary
- basic bookkeeping and accounting procedures
- accounting conventions and concepts
- interpretation of financial statements
- cash flow statements
- accounting standards – IASs 1, 2, 7, 8, 10, 16, 18, 35 (see note 1 below), 37 (see note 2 below) and 38 (see note 3 below).

Notes

1 The following paragraphs of IAS 35 are examinable: 27, 31, 41 (provisions relating to discontinuance previously in IAS 8).

2 The following paragraphs of IAS 37 are examinable in so far as they relate to contingent liabilities and contingent assets: 10, 27-35, 85-92, Appendices A and B.

3 The following paragraphs of IAS 38 are examinable in so far as they relate to research and development: 7, 39-47, 55, 79, 88, 107, 115.

Additional information

Candidates need to be aware that questions involving knowledge of new examinable regulations will not be set until at least six months after the last day of the month in which the regulation was issued.

The Study Guide provides more detailed guidance on the syllabus. Examinable documents are listed in the 'Exam Notes' section of the Students' Newsletter.

Study guide

1 INTRODUCTION TO ACCOUNTING

Syllabus reference 1a, b, c, d, e; 5a and b

- Define accounting – recording, analysing and summarizing transaction data.
- Explain types of business entity
  - sole trader
  - partnership
  - limited liability company
- Explain users of financial statements and accounting information.
- Explain the main elements of financial statements:
  - balance sheet
  - income statement
- Explain the purpose of each of the main statements.
- Explain the nature, principles and scope of accounting.
- Identify the desirable qualities of accounting information and the usefulness of each (See also Session 14).
- Explain the regulatory system:
  - International Accounting Standards Board (IASB)
- Explain the difference between capital and revenue items.

2 BASIC BALANCE SHEET AND INCOME STATEMENT

Syllabus reference 2a, b, 5c i and ii

- Explain how the balance sheet equation and business entity convention underlie the balance sheet.
- Define assets and liabilities.
- Explain how and why assets and liabilities are disclosed in the balance sheet.
- Draft a simple balance sheet in vertical format.
- Explain the matching convention and how it applies to revenue and expenses.
- Explain how and why revenue and expenses are disclosed in the income statement.
- Illustrate how the balance sheet and income statement are interrelated.
- Draft a simple income statement in vertical format.
- Explain the significance of gross profit and the gross profit as a percentage of sales.

3–4 BOOKKEEPING PRINCIPLES

Syllabus reference 3a and c

- Identify the main data sources and records in an accounting system
- Explain the functions of each data source and record.
- Explain the concept of double entry and the duality concept.
- Outline the form of accounting records in a typical manual system.
- Outline the form of accounting records in a typical computerised system.
- Explain debit and credit.
- Distinguish between asset, liability, revenue and expense accounts.
- Explain the meaning of the balance on each type of account.
- Illustrate how to balance a ledger account.
- Record cash transactions in ledger accounts.
- Record credit sale and purchase transactions in ledger accounts.
- Explain the division of the ledger into sections.
- Record credit sale and purchase transactions using day books.
- Explain sales and purchases returns and their recording.
- Explain the general principles of the operation of a sales tax and the consequent accounting entries.
- Explain the need for a record of petty cash transactions.
- Illustrate the typical format of the petty cash book.
- Explain the importance of using the imprest system to control petty cash.
- Extract the ledger balances into a trial balance.
- Prepare a simple income statement and balance sheet from a trial balance.
- Explain and illustrate the process of closing the ledger accounts in the accounting records when the financial statements have been completed.

5 THE JOURNAL; LEDGER CONTROL ACCOUNTS; BANK RECONCILIATIONS.

Syllabus reference 3b

- Explain the uses of the journal.
- Illustrate the use of the journal and the posting of journal entries into ledger accounts.
- Explain the types of error which may occur in bookkeeping systems, identifying those which can and those which cannot by detected by preparing a trial balance.
- Illustrate the use of the journal in correcting errors, including the use of a suspense account.
- Explain the preparation of statements correcting the profit for errors discovered.
- Explain the nature and purpose of control accounts for the accounts receivable and accounts payable ledgers.
- Explain how control accounts relate to the double entry system.
- Construct and agree a ledger control account from given information.
- Explain the purpose of bank reconciliation statements and the
- need for entries in the cash book when reconciling.
- Draft a bank reconciliation statement.

6 COMPUTERISED ACCOUNTING SYSTEMS

Syllabus reference 3d

- Compare manual and computerised accounting systems.
- Identify the advantages and disadvantages of computerised systems.
- Describe the main elements of a computerised accounting system.
- Describe typical data processing work.
- Explain the use of integrated accounting packages.
- Explain the nature and use of micro-computers.
- Explain other business uses of computers.
- Explain the nature and purpose of spreadsheets.
- Explain the nature and purpose of database systems.

7 THE FINANCIAL STATEMENTS OF A SOLE TRADER 1; INVENTORY, ACCRUALS AND PREPAYMENTS.

Syllabus reference 5d i, 4b i

- Revise the format of the income statement and balance sheet from Sessions 1 and 2.
- Explain the need for adjustments for inventory in preparing financial statements.
- Illustrate income statements with opening and closing inventory.
- Explain how opening and closing inventory are recorded in the inventory account.
- Discuss alternative methods of valuing inventory.
- Explain the provisions of IAS2 Inventories.
- Explain the use of continuous and period end inventory records.
- Explain the need for adjustments for accruals and prepayments in preparing financial statements.
- Illustrate the process of adjusting for accruals and prepayments in preparing financial statements, emphasising the effects in both the income statement and the balance sheet.
- Prepare financial statements for a sole trader including adjustments for inventory, accruals and prepayments.
- Explain how to calculate the value of closing inventory from given movements in inventory levels, using FIFO (first in first out), LIFO (last in first out) and AVCO (average cost).

8 THE FINANCIAL STATEMENTS OF A SOLE TRADER 2: DEPRECIATION AND BAD AND DOUBTFUL DEBTS **Syllabus reference 4a i to iii; 4b ii**

- Revise the difference between non- current assets and current assets.
- Define and explain the purpose of depreciation as stated in IAS 16 Property, Plant and Equipment.
- Explain the advantages, disadvantages and calculation of the straight line, reducing balance and sum of the digits methods of depreciation.
- Explain the relevance of consistency and subjectivity in accounting for depreciation.
- Explain how depreciation is presented in the income statement and balance sheet.
- Explain how depreciation expense and accumulated depreciation are recorded in ledger accounts.
- Explain the inevitability of bad debts in most businesses.
- Illustrate the bookkeeping entries to write off a bad debt and the effect on the income statement and balance sheet.
- Illustrate the bookkeeping entries to record bad debts recovered.
- Explain the difference between writing off a bad debt and making an allowance for a doubtful debt.
- Explain and illustrate the bookkeeping entries to create and adjust an allowance for doubtful debts.
- Illustrate how to include movements in the allowance for doubtful debts in the income statement and how the closing balance of the allowance may appear in the balance sheet.
- Prepare a set of financial statements for a sole trader from a trial balance, after allowing for accruals and prepayments, depreciation and bad and doubtful debts.

9–10 INCOMPLETE RECORDS

Syllabus reference 5d i

- Explain techniques used in incomplete record situations:
  - Calculation of opening capital
  - Use of ledger total accounts to calculate missing figures.
  - Use of cash and/or bank summaries
  - Use of given gross profit percentage to calculate missing figures.
- Explain the calculation of profit or loss as the difference between opening and closing net assets.

11 REVISE ALL WORK TO DATE

12 – 13 PARTNERSHIP ACCOUNTS

Syllabus reference 5d ii

- Define the circumstances creating a partnership.
- Explain the advantages and disadvantages of operating as a partnership, compared with operating as a sole trader or limited company.
- Explain the typical contents of a partnership agreement, including profit- sharing terms.
- Explain the accounting differences between partnerships and sole traders:
  - Capital accounts
  - Current accounts
  - Division of profits
- Explain how to record partners' shares of profits / losses and their drawings in the accounting records and financial statements.
- Explain how to account for guaranteed minimum profit share.
- Explain how to account for interest on drawings.
- Draft the income statement, including division of profit, and balance sheet of a partnership from a given trial balance.

Note: Other aspects of partnership (admission and retirement of partners, amalgamation and dissolution) are not examinable.

14 ACCOUNTING CONCEPTS AND CONVENTIONS; THE IASB'S, FRAMEWORK FOR THE PREPARATION AND PRESENTATION OF FINANCIAL STATEMENTS' (THE FRAMEWORK) AND IAS 1.

Syllabus reference 1d and e; 2a and b;

5a and b

- Explain the need for an agreed conceptual framework for financial accounting.
- Explain the importance of the following accounting conventions (not mentioned in the Framework).
  - Business entity
  - Money measurement
  - Duality
  - Historical cost
  - Realisation
  - Time interval
- Revise the users of financial statements from Session 1.
- Explain the qualitative characteristics of financial statements as described in paras. 24 to 46 of the Framework (Revision from Session 1)
- Explain the principles of revenue recognition as defined in IAS 18 Revenue Recognition.

15 ACCOUNTING FOR LIMITED LIABILITY COMPANIES 1 – BASICS

Syllabus reference 5d iii; 4d

Note: The inclusion of an introductory coverage of company accounts at this point is to enable students to practise the work so far on financial statements using questions on limited companies, and also to facilitate understanding of reserves referred to in the next Session.

- Explain the legal and other differences between a sole trader and a limited liability company.
- Explain the advantages and disadvantages of operation as a limited liability company rather than as a sole trader.
- Explain the capital structure of a limited liability company including:
  - Authorised share capital
  - Issued share capital
  - Called up share capital
  - Paid up share capital
  - Ordinary shares
  - Preference shares
  - Loan notes.
- Explain the nature of reserves and the difference between capital and revenue reserves.
- Explain the share premium account
- Explain the other reserves which may appear in a company balance sheet.
- Explain why accumulated profits (losses) appear in a company balance sheet.
- Explain the recording of dividends paid in ledger accounts and the financial statements and the treatment of proposed dividends.
- Explain the nature of income taxes on company profits and illustrate the ledger account required to record them.
- Explain how income taxes appear in the income statement and balance sheet of a company.
- Draft an income statement and balance sheet for a company for internal purposes.

16 RECORDING AND PRESENTATION OF TRANSACTIONS IN NON-CURRENT ASSETS; LIABILITIES AND PROVISIONS

Syllabus reference 4a i to iii; 4b and c

- Explain and illustrate the ledger entries to record the acquisition and disposal of non-current assets, using separate accounts for non-current assets, using separate accounts for non-current asset cost and accumulated depreciation.
- Explain and illustrate the inclusion of profits or losses on disposal in the income statement.
- Explain that the upward revaluation of an asset cannot constitute a gain which may appear in the income statement.
- Explain how to record the revaluation of a non-current asset in ledger accounts and the effect in the balance sheet.
- Explain why, after an upward revaluation, depreciation must be based on the revised figure, referring to the requirements of IAS16 Property, Plant and Equipment.
- Explain the adjustments necessary if changes are made in the estimated useful life and/or residual value of a non-current asset.
- Explain how non-current asset balances and movements are disclosed in company financial statements in accordance with IAS 16 Property, Plant and Equipment.
- Define and give examples of liabilities.
- Explain the distinction between current and non-current liabilities.
- Explain the difference between liabilities and provisions.
- Explain the requirements of IAS 1 (Revised) Presentation of Financial Statements as regards current assets and current liabilities.

17 GOODWILL, RESEARCH AND DEVELOPMENT

Syllabus reference 4a iv and v

- Define goodwill.
- Explain the factors leading to the creation of non-purchased goodwill.
- Explain the difference between purchased and non-purchased goodwill.
- Explain why non-purchased goodwill is not normally recognised in financial statements.
- Explain how purchased goodwill arises and is reflected in financial statements.
- Explain the need to amortise purchased goodwill.
- Define 'research' and 'development' as in IAS 38 Intangible Assets.
- Classify expenditure as research or development.
- Calculate amounts to be capitalized as development expenditure from given information.
- Disclose research and development expenditure in the financial statements in accordance with IAS 38.

18 EVENTS AFTER THE BALANCE SHEET DATE AND CONTINGENCIES

Syllabus reference 4e and f

- Define an event after the balance sheet date in accordance with IAS 10 Events After the Balance Sheet Date.
- Distinguish between adjusting and non-adjusting events and explain the methods of including them in financial statements.
- Classify events as adjusting or non-adjusting from a given list.
- Draft notes to company financial statements including requisite details of events after the balance sheet date.
- Define 'contingent liability' and 'contingent asset' in accordance with IAS 37 Provisions, Contingent Liabilities and Contingent Assets.
- Explain the different ways of accounting for contingent liabilities and contingent assets according to their degree of probability.
- Draft notes to company financial statements including requisite details of contingent liabilities and contingent assets.

19, 20 and 21 ACCOUNTING FOR LIMITED LIABILITY COMPANIES 2 – ADVANCED

Syllabus reference 5d iii

- Revise the work of Session 15 and the preparation of financial statements for limited liability companies for internal purposes including the treatment of income tax and dividends.
- Revise the work of Session 15 on company capital structure, including equity shares, preference shares and loan notes.
- Outline the advantages and disadvantages of raising finance by borrowing rather than by the issue of ordinary or preference shares.
- Define and illustrate gearing (leverage)
- Define a bonus (capitalisation) issue and its advantages and disadvantages.
- Record a bonus (capitalisation) issue in ledger accounts and show the effect in the balance sheet.
- Define a rights issue and its advantages and disadvantages.
- Record a rights issue in ledger accounts and show the effect in the balance sheet.
- Revise the definition of reserves and the different types of reserves.
- Explain the need for regulation of companies in legislation and accounting standards.
- Explain the provisions of international accounting standards governing financial statements (excluding group aspects):
  - IAS 1 Presentation of Financial Statements:
  - Overall considerations
  - Structure and content
  - Changes in equity
  - Illustrative financial statements:
    - Balance sheet
    - Income statement
    - Statement of changes in equity
    - IAS 8 Net Profit or Loss for the Period, Fundamental Errors and Changes in Accounting Policies.
    - IAS 35 Discontinuing operations (paras 27, 31 and 41 only, previously in IAS 8)
- Explain the notes to financial statements required for the syllabus:
  - Statement of changes in equity
  - Details of non-current assets
  - Details of events after the balance sheet date
  - Details of contingent liabilities and contingent assets (see Session 18)
  - Details of research and development expenditure.
- Prepare financial statements for publication complying with relevant accounting standards as detailed above.

22 REVISE ALL WORK TO DATE.

23 CASH FLOW STATEMENTS

Syllabus reference 5c iii and 5e

- Explain the differences between profit and cash flow.
- Explain the need for management to control cash flow.
- Explain the value to users of financial statements of a cash flow statement.
- Explain the provisions of IAS 7 Cash Flow Statements and the standard format therein (excluding group aspects).
- Explain the inward and outward flows of cash in a typical company.
- Explain how to calculate the figures needed for the cash flow statement including among others:
  - Cash flows from operating activities (indirect method)
  - Cash flows from investing activities (purchases, sales and depreciation of non-current assets).
- Explain how to calculate cash flow from operating activities using the direct method.
- Review of information to be derived by users from the cash flow statement (see also Sessions 25 – 26).
- Prepare cash flow statements from given balance sheets with or without an income statement.

24 BASIC CONSOLIDATED ACCOUNTS

Syllabus reference 5d iv

- Define parent company, subsidiary company and group.
- Explain the provisions of IAS 27 Consolidated Financial Statements and Accounting for Investments in Subsidiaries defining which companies must be consolidated.
- Prepare a consolidated balance sheet for a parent with one wholly-owned subsidiary (no goodwill arising).
- Explain how to calculate the retained profit balance for the consolidated balance sheet.
- Explain how other reserves (share premium account and revaluation reserve) are dealt with on consolidation.
- Introduce the concept of goodwill on acquisition and illustrate the effect on the consolidated balance sheet.
- Explain the need to amortise goodwill and illustrate in the workings.
- Explain a methodical approach to calculating the necessary figures for the consolidated balance sheet.
- Introduce the concept of minority interests in subsidiaries and illustrate the effect on the consolidated balance sheet.
- Explain how the calculation of the minority interest is made in the workings.

25-26 INTERPRETATION OF FINANCIAL STATEMENTS

Syllabus reference 6

- Revise users of financial statements and their information needs.
- Explain the advantages and disadvantages of interpretation based on financial statements.
- Explain the factors forming the environment in which the business operates.
- Explain the uses of ratio analysis.
- Explain the main ratios to be used in interpreting financial statements to appraise:
  - Profitability
  - Liquidity
  - Working capital efficiency
  - Financial risk
  - Performance from an investor's point of view.
- Explain the working capital cycle (or cash operating cycle)
- Explain normal levels of certain ratios.
- Explain how to formulate comments on movements in ratios between one period and another or on differences between ratios for different businesses.
- Explain the factors which may distort ratios, leading to unreliable conclusions.
- Prepare and comment on a comprehensive range of ratios for a business.

27 THE THEORETICAL AND OPERATIONAL ADEQUACY OF FINANCIAL REPORTING

Syllabus reference 2a and b

- Revise the qualitative characteristics of financial information from Sessions 1 and 14.
- Explain the advantages and disadvantages of historical cost accounting (HCA) in times of changing prices.
- Explain in principle the main alternatives to HCA:
  - Current purchasing power accounting (CPP)
  - Current cost accounting (CCA) Note: computational questions on CPP and CCA will not be set.
  - Revise the roles of the IASB in raising standards of financial reporting by setting accounting standards.

28 REVISION

Examinable documents

Prior to each sitting of the examination, the ACCA issues Exam Notes setting out which official documents are examinable.

The documents which are examinable for Paper 1.1 (International Stream) are set out below. We recommend that students read the *Student Accountant* to keep up-to-date.

International Accounting Standards (IASs)

No	*Title*	*Issue date*
1	Presentation of Financial Statements (Revised Aug 1997)	Aug 1997
2	Inventories	Dec 1993
7	Cash flow statements (excluding group and foreign currency)	Dec 1992
8	Net Profit or Loss for the Period, Fundamental Errors and Changes in Accounting Policies	Dec 1993
10	Events after the Balance Sheet Date (Revised May 1999)	May 1999
16	Property, Plant and Equipment (Revised Sept 1998)	Sept 1998
18	Revenue	Dec 1993
27	Consolidatied Financial Statements and Accounting for Investments in Subsidiaries	Jan 1995
35	Discontinuing Operations (Note 2)	June 1998
37	Provisions, Contingent Liabilities and Contingent Assets (Note 4)	Sept 1998
38	Intangible Assets (Note 4)	Sept 1998

Notes:

1 The IASB's Framework for the Preparation and Presentation of Financial Statements is examinable at an introductory level. Detailed guidance is available in the study guide.

2 The following paragraphs of IAS 35 are examinable in so far as they relate to disclosures previously in IAS 8 in relation to Discontinuing Operations: 27, 31, 41.

3 The following paragraphs of IAS 37 are examinable in so far as they relate to contingent liabilities and contingent assets: 10, 27–35, 85–92, appendices A and B. The measurement rules in paragraphs 36–52 are not examinable.

4 The following paragraphs of IAS 38 are examinable in so far as they relate to research and development: 7, 55, 79, 88, 107, 115.

Other Statements

Title	*Issue date*
Framework for the Preparation and Presentation of Financial Statements	July 1989

The examination

CONTENTS

Format of the examination

Paper-based examination

	Number of marks
Section A: 25 compulsory multiple choice questions (2 marks each)	50
Section B: 5 compulsory short form questions (8 – 12 marks each)	50
	100
Total time allowed: 3 hours	

Computer-based examination

	Number of marks
Objective test questions (approximately 50)	100
Total time allowed: 3 hours	

The overall balance in the examination will be approximately 60% computational and 40% non-computational.

Examination tips: paper-based exam

- Spend the first few minutes of the examination **reading the paper**.
- Where you have a **choice of questions**, decide which ones you will do.
- **Divide the time** you spend on questions in proportion to the marks on offer. One suggestion is to allocate 1½ minutes to each mark available, so a 10 mark question should be completed in 15 minutes.
- Unless you know exactly how to answer the question, spend some time **planning** your answer. Stick to the question and **tailor your answer** to what you are asked.
- **Fully explain** all your points but be **concise**. Set out all workings **clearly and neatly**, and state briefly what you are doing. Don't write out the question.
- If you do not understand what a question is asking, **state your assumptions**. Even if you do not answer precisely in the way the examiner hoped, you should be given some credit, if your assumptions are reasonable.
- If you **get completely stuck** with a question, leave space in your answer book and **return to it later.**
- Towards the end of the examination spend the last **five minutes** reading through your answers and **making any additions or corrections**.
- Before you finish, you must fill in the required information on the front of your answer booklet.

Answering the questions

- **Multiple-choice questions**: Read the questions carefully and work through any calculations required. If you don't know the answer, eliminate those options you know are incorrect and see if the answer becomes more obvious. Remember that only one answer to a multiple choice question can be right!
- **Objective test questions** might ask for numerical answers, but could also involve paragraphs of text which require you to fill in a number of missing blanks, or for you to

write a definition of a word or phrase, or to enter a formula. Others may give a definition followed by a list of possible key words relating to that description.

- **Essay questions**: Make a quick plan in your answer book and under each main point list all the relevant facts you can think of. Then write out your answer developing each point fully. Your essay should have a clear structure; it should contain a brief introduction, a main section and a conclusion. Be concise. It is better to write a little about a lot of different points than a great deal about one or two points.

- **Case studies**: To write a good case study, first identify the area in which there is a problem, outline the main principles/theories you are going to use to answer the question, and then apply the principles/theories to the case. Include relevant points only and then reach a conclusion and, if asked for, recommendations. If you can, compare the facts to real-life examples – this may gain you additional marks in the exam.

- **Computations**: It is essential to include all your workings in your answers. Many computational questions require the use of a standard format: company profit and loss account, balance sheet and cash flow statement for example. Be sure you know these formats thoroughly before the examination and use the layouts that you see in the answers given in this book and in model answers. If you are asked to comment or make recommendations on a computation, you must do so. There are important marks to be gained here. Even if your computation contains mistakes, you may still gain marks if your reasoning is correct.

- **Reports, memos and other documents**: Some questions ask you to present your answer in the form of a report or a memo or other document. Use the correct format - there could be easy marks to gain here.

Study skills and revision guidance

CONTENTS

This section aims to give guidance on how to study for your ACCA exams and to give ideas on how to improve your existing study techniques.

Preparing to study

Set your objectives

Before starting to study decide what you want to achieve – the type of pass you wish to obtain. This will decide the level of commitment and time you need to dedicate to your studies.

Devise a study plan

- Determine which times of the week you will study.
- Split these times into sessions of at least one hour for study of new material. Any shorter periods could be used for revision or practice.
- Put the times you plan to study onto a study plan for the weeks from now until the exam and set yourself targets for each period of study – in your sessions make sure you cover the course, course assignments and revision.
- If you are studying for more than one paper at a time, try to vary your subjects, this can help you to keep interested and see subjects as part of wider knowledge.
- When working through your course, compare your progress with your plan and, if necessary, re-plan your work (perhaps including extra sessions) or, if you are ahead, do some extra revision/practice questions.

Effective studying

Active reading

You are not expected to learn the text by rote, rather, you must understand what you are reading and be able to use it to pass the exam and develop good practice. A good technique to use is SQ3Rs – Survey, Question, Read, Recall, Review:

1. **Survey** the chapter – look at the headings and read the introduction, summary and objectives, so as to get an overview of what the chapter deals with.
2. **Question** – whilst undertaking the survey, ask yourself the questions that you hope the chapter will answer for you.
3. **Read** through the chapter thoroughly, answering the questions and making sure you can meet the objectives. Attempt the exercises and activities in the text, and work through all the examples.
4. **Recall** – at the end of each section and at the end of the chapter, try to recall the main ideas of the section/chapter without referring to the text. This is best done after a short break of a couple of minutes after the reading stage.
5. **Review** – check that your recall notes are correct.

You may also find it helpful to reread the chapter and try to see the topic(s) it deals with as a whole.

Note-taking

Taking notes is a useful way of learning, but do not simply copy out the text. The notes must:

- be in your own words
- be concise
- cover the key points
- be well-organised
- be modified as you study further chapters in this text or in related ones.

Trying to summarise a chapter without referring to the text can be a useful way of determining which areas you know and which you don't.

Three ways of taking notes:

- **summarise the key points** of a chapter.
- **make linear notes** – a list of headings, divided up with subheadings listing the key points. If you use linear notes, you can use different colours to highlight key points and keep topic areas together. Use plenty of space to make your notes easy to use.
- **try a diagrammatic form** – the most common of which is a mind-map. To make a mind-map, put the main heading in the centre of the paper and put a circle around it. Then draw short lines radiating from this to the main sub-headings, which again have circles around them. Then continue the process from the sub-headings to sub-sub-headings, advantages, disadvantages, etc.

Highlighting and underlining

You may find it useful to underline or highlight key points in your study text – but do be selective. You may also wish to make notes in the margins.

Revision

The best approach to revision is to revise the course as you work through it. Also try to leave four to six weeks before the exam for final revision. Make sure you cover the whole syllabus and pay special attention to those areas where your knowledge is weak. Here are some recommendations:

- **Read through the text and your notes again** and condense your notes into key phrases. It may help to put key revision points onto index cards to look at when you have a few minutes to spare.
- **Review any assignments** you have completed and look at where you lost marks – put more work into those areas where you were weak.
- **Practise exam standard questions** under timed conditions. If you are short of time, list the points that you would cover in your answer and then read the model answer, but do try and complete at least a few questions under exam conditions.
- Also **practise producing answer plans** and comparing them to the model answer.
- If you are stuck on a topic find somebody (a tutor) to explain it to you.
- **Read good newspapers and professional journals**, especially ACCA's *Student Accountant* – this can give you an advantage in the exam.
- Ensure you **know the structure of the exam** – how many questions and of what type you will be expected to answer. During your revision attempt all the different styles of questions you may be asked.

Chapter 1
INTRODUCTION TO ACCOUNTING

CHAPTER CONTENTS

This chapter introduces some of the principles underlying the preparation of financial statements.

Financial statements are prepared for a variety of users with a variety of needs. In general though, all user groups need information that will be useful for making economic decisions.

You will find it beneficial to return to this chapter later in your studies.

Objectives

By the time you have finished this chapter you should be able to:

- define accounting and the information it provides
- identify the users of financial accounting information
- understand the different types of accounting
- identify the desirable qualities of accounting information
- understand the international regulatory system and in particular the work of the International Accounting Standards Board
- understand the distinction between capital and revenue items.

1 What is accounting?

1.1 Recording and summarising transactions

KEY POINT

Elements of accounting:

- **recording**
- **summarising.**

Accounting can be considered as consisting of two elements, recording and summarising.

Recording

Transactions must be recorded as they occur in order to provide up-to-date information for management. For example, credit sales must be recorded so that statements can be sent to the customers and the money due collected.

KEY POINT

Important summary statements:

- **income statement**
- **balance sheet.**

Summarising

The transactions for a period are summarised in order to provide information about the performance and position of a business to interested parties.

The two most important summary statements produced are the **income statement** and the **balance sheet**. These described in Section 3.

1.2 Business entities

KEY POINT

Business types:

- **sole trader (one person)**
- **partnership (more than one person)**
- **company.**

Companies are owned by **shareholders** or **members.**

Businesses can be organised in several ways.

The simplest form of business is the **sole trader.** This is owned and managed by one person (although there might be any number of employees). A sole trader is fully and personally liable for any losses that the business might make.

The next level of complexity is the **partnership**. A partnership is owned jointly by a number of partners. The partners are jointly and severally liable for any losses that the business might make. Traditionally the big accounting firms have been partnerships, but some (such as KPMG in the UK) are converting their status to limited liability companies.

Companies are owned by **shareholders** or. There can be one shareholder or many thousands of shareholders. Shareholders are also known as **members**. Each shareholder owns part of the business. As a group they elect the **directors** who run the business. Directors often own shares in their companies, but not all shareholders will be directors.

KEY POINT

Companies are almost always **limited** companies.

Shareholders' liabilities are limited to the money they have put into the company.

Companies are almost always **limited** companies. This means that the shareholders will not be personally liable for any losses that the company incurs. Their liability is limited to the nominal value of the shares that they own. Their shares may become worthless, but they will not be forced to make good losses.

This limited liability is achieved by counting the company as a completely separate legal entity.

KEY POINT

Capital: the money put into a business.

For all three types of entity, the money put up by the individual, the partners or the shareholders is referred to as the business **capital.** In the case of a company, this capital is divided into **shares.** The shares have a nominal value (normally $1), but the shareholders may then buy and sell the shares at any price. Shares in quoted companies can be bought and sold on a Stock Exchange.

1.3 Availability of accounting information

KEY POINT

Financial statements:

- **sole traders and partnerships: statements are private**
- **companies: statements sent to shareholders and may also be publicly filed.**

The financial statements of sole traders and partnerships are completely private. Only the owners and the taxman can demand to see them. Banks may also have access to their business customers accounts, say in support of a loan application.

Shareholders receive a copy of the financial statements of their company, and in many countries a copy is held in a central office where they are available for public inspection.

In the next section we look at possible **users** of accounting information.

2 The users of financial accounts and statements

2.1 Introduction

The purpose of accounting is to provide information to users of financial statements. Different users have different needs. The main users and needs are noted below:

2.2 Management

KEY POINT

Managers need financial information for planning and decision-making.

Management need very detailed information in order to control their business and plan for the future. Budgets will be based upon past performance and future plans. These budgets will then be compared with the actual results. Information will also be needed about the profitability of individual departments and products. Management information must be very up-to-date, and it is normally produced on a monthly basis.

2.3 Shareholders and potential shareholders

KEY POINT

Shareholders and potential shareholders need financial information for investment decisions.

This group includes investors and their advisors. They are interested in their potential profits and the security of their investment. Future profits will be based on the target companies past performance as shown in the income statement. The security of their investment will be revealed by the financial strength and solvency of the company as shown in the balance sheet.

Having bought shares, the shareholders are then responsible for (re)electing the Board of Directors. If the reported results are good, then the Directors will be re-elected. If the results are poor, then in theory they should be removed from the Board. In this way the Directors are held to account for their 'Stewardship' of the company. This is where the term 'stewardship accounting' comes from.

The largest and most sophisticated group of investors are the institutional investors, such as pension funds and unit trusts. Many of the new and more complicated accounting standards are aimed at the needs of these investors.

2.4 Employees and their trade union representatives

KEY POINT

Employees and their representatives need financial information to safeguard their jobs and income.

Employees and their representative need to know if their employer can offer secure employment and possible pay-rises. They will also have a keen interest in the salaries and benefits enjoyed by senior management. Information about divisional profitability will also be useful if a part of the business is threatened with closure.

2.5 Lenders

KEY POINT

Lenders need financial information to safeguard loans that they have made or intend to make.

Businesses will owe money to banks (for loans) and suppliers (for payment for goods and services). Both banks and suppliers will need to know if they will be repaid. This will depend on the solvency of the company, which should be revealed by the balance sheet. Long-term loans may also be backed by "security" given by the business over specific assets. The value of these assets will also be indicated in the balance sheet.

2.6 Government agencies

KEY POINT

Government agencies need financial information to monitor the economy and to collect tax.

Governments need to know how the economy is performing in order to plan their financial and industrial policies. Financial statements will be a key source of information for them. The tax authorities also use financial statements as a basis for assessing the amount of tax payable by a business.

2.7 The business contact group

Businesses often have a few key customers or suppliers. They need to monitor the financial viability of these key contacts in order to take early action if one of them appears to be in financial difficulties. Businesses will also use financial statements to compare their own performance against that of their competitors.

2.8 The public

There are many other user groups and interest groups; e.g. members of a local community where the company operates, environmental pressure groups, and so on.

KEY POINT

Financial statements serve a wide variety of user groups, who have different interests.

Financial statements serve a wide variety of user groups, who have different interests and also different levels of financial sophistication. This makes it particularly difficult to produce financial statements that are simple enough for the layman to understand, but also comprehensive enough for the expert.

3 The main financial statements available to users

As we saw above, there are two main financial accounting statements: the balance sheet and the income statement.

3.1 The balance sheet

The balance sheet is a statement of assets and liabilities at a point in time (the balance sheet date). Each asset and liability is valued according to certain accounting conventions. The balance sheet shows the **financial position** of the enterprise.

DEFINITION

An **asset** is any tangible or intangible possession which has value.

Liabilities are the financial obligations of an enterprise.

An **asset** is an item that is **controlled** by a business and which will bring **future economic benefits** to the business. For example, a machine in a factory is controlled by a business and will be used to make products that will be sold for a profit. They are normally owned, but they may also be held under a lease. They may be tangible (physical, like a machine) or intangible (untouchable, like a patent).

Liabilities are the financial obligations of an enterprise, e.g. to suppliers, lenders, and, in the case of a bank loan or overdraft, to a bank.

3.2 The income statement

The income statement summarises income and expenditure over a period of time; if income exceeds expenditure there is a profit, if vice versa there is a loss. Note that again income and expenditure are measured using accounting conventions. The income statement measures **financial performance** over a period of time.

ACTIVITY **1**

How useful do you think that the balance sheet and income statement would be to each of the user groups? Suggest any alternative information that might be useful.

Feedback to this activity is at the end of the chapter.

4 Nature, principles and scope of accounting

4.1 Financial accounting

Financial accounting is mainly concerned with the production of financial statements for external users. It is a report on the Directors' stewardship of the funds entrusted to them by the shareholders.

Financial accounts highlight:

- The way in which company funds have been invested (the balance sheet).
- The return made on those investments (the income statement).
- New funds invested in the business by the shareholders, and funds paid back out to the shareholders as dividends (the statement of changes in equity).
- A cash flow statement is also prepared. This is because businesses can run out of cash even if they are making a profit.

The financial accounts will be prepared annually (and in some countries every six months or quarterly). Because they are public documents they will not reveal details about product profitability.

KEY POINT

Accounts need to meet the requirements of:

- **International Accounting Standards**
- **local legislation.**

Investors need to be able to choose which companies to invest in. Therefore, financial accounts are prepared using accepted accounting conventions and standards. IASs and IFRSs help to reduce the differences in the way that companies draw up their financial statements, but even these standards contain allowed 'alternative treatments'.

Financial accounts will also have to comply with local laws. The mix of accounting standards and local laws gives rise to what is known as *Generally Accepted Accounting Practice* or 'GAAP'. During your studies you are likely to meet 'US GAAP' and 'International GAAP'.

4.2 Management accounting

Managers need much more detailed and up-to-date information in order to control the business and plan for the future. They need to be able to cost out products and production methods, assess profitability and so on.

KEY POINT

Management accounting is used for:

- **strategy**
- **planning and controlling**
- **decision taking**
- **optimising resource use.**

Management accounting is an integral part of management activity concerned with identifying, presenting and interpreting information used for:

- formulation of strategy
- planning and controlling the activities
- decision taking
- optimising the use of resources.

Financial accounting and management accounts can be contrasted as follows:

4.3 Financial Accounting and Management Accounting compared

	Financial accounting		*Management accounts*
(i)	In many instances (e.g. companies) is required by law.	(i)	Records are not mandatory.
(ii)	Accordingly the cost of record keeping is a necessity.	(ii)	Accordingly the cost of record keeping needs to be justified.
(iii)	Objectives and uses of financial accounts are vague and ill-defined.	(iii)	Objectives and uses of management accounts can be laid down by management.
(iv)	Is mainly concerned with profits.	(iv)	Are mainly concerned with cash flow, profits and business management generally.
(v)	Is mainly a historical record.	(v)	Are regularly concerned with predictions.
(vi)	Information should be computed prudently, and in accordance with legal and accounting requirements.	(vi)	Information should be computed as management requires, the key criterion being relevance.

4.4 Financial management

KEY POINT

Financial management covers all the functions of ensuring that financial resources are obtained and used in the most effective way to secure attainment of the objectives of the organisation.

Financial management ensures that financial resources are obtained and used in the most effective way to secure attainment of the objectives of the organisation.

A key part of management is concerned with managing the liquidity of a business. A business must maintain an inflow of cash in order to survive, and a further inflow of funds if it is to expand.

Cash is often referred to as the 'lifeblood of a business'. Profits are important, but without cash the business will fail.

4.5 Auditing

Auditing may be external or internal.

DEFINITION

External audit: the independent examination of, and expression of opinion on, the financial statements of an enterprise.

External audit

This is 'the independent examination of, and expression of opinion on, the financial statements of an enterprise'.

It is normally a legal requirement for companies. The auditors will be appointed by and report to the shareholders. Their "opinion" will be whether or not the financial statements prepared by the Directors show a fair view of the company's position and performance for the year. Without this external audit the shareholders would have no confidence in the truthfulness of the reports sent to them by the Directors.

DEFINITION

Internal audit: an appraisal activity established within an entity as a service to the entity. Its functions include, amongst other things, examining, evaluating and monitoring the adequacy and effectiveness of the accounting and internal control systems.

Internal audit

This is 'an appraisal activity established within an entity as a service to the entity. Its functions include, amongst other things, examining, evaluating and monitoring the adequacy and effectiveness of the accounting and internal control systems.'

There is normally no legal requirement to have an internal audit. (In some countries banks and building societies are required to have formal internal audit procedures.) Internal audit departments are appointed by and report to the Board of Directors. They normally ensure compliance with company procedures and carry out investigations on behalf of senior management.

4.6 The public sector

The basic rules of public sector accounting are the same as for the private sector. Indeed, the public sector is getting more 'commercial' in its approach all the time. The key difference is the way in which the accounting information is used. The objective of the private sector is to make a profit, whereas the public sector is normally obliged to provide a service. The public sector will use accounting information in order to deliver that service as efficiently, economically and effectively as possible.

5 Desirable qualities of accounting information

Having identified the users of financial statements, the problem arises as to what information is useful to them. Some criteria can be identified. They are listed briefly in the table below, and considered in more detail in Chapter 14.

Criteria	*Comment*
Relevance	The information should be relevant to the needs of the users, so that it helps them to evaluate the financial performance of the business and to draw conclusions from it. **Problem**: to identify these needs, given the variety of users.
Reliability	The information should be of a standard that can be relied upon by external users, so that it is free from error and can be depended upon by users in their decisions. **Problem**: the complexities of modern business make reliability difficult to achieve in all cases.
Comparability	Accounts should be comparable with those of other similar enterprises, and from one period to the next. **Problem**: the main problem has been the use of different accounting policies by different enterprises. Accounting standards have reduced, but not eliminated, this problem.
Understandability	The information should be in a form which is understandable to user groups. **Problems**: users have very different levels of financial sophistication; also the very complexity of business transactions makes it difficult to provide adequate disclosure whilst maintaining simplicity.
Completeness	Accounting statements should show all aspects of the business. **Problem**: the resultant volume of the information.
Lack of bias	Accounting statements should not be biased towards the needs of one user; they should be objective. **Problem**: financial statements are prepared by one user group, management. An external audit should remove this bias, but some authorities question the effectiveness of the audit in this respect.

Timeliness	Accounting statements should be published as soon as possible after the year end. **Problem**: there is a conflict between this criterion and that of reliability, in that quicker accounts mean more estimates, and hence reduce reliability.

ACTIVITY **2**

Consider the characteristics of useful information. Make a list of any pair of characteristics that you feel may not be compatible.

Feedback to this activity is at the end of the chapter.

6 The regulatory system

6.1 Introduction

Each country has its own legislation governing accounting and the operation of companies. This local legislation obviously varies considerably from country to country, and the ACCA's International syllabus; for their accountancy examinations do not require a knowledge of it.

KEY POINT

The main source of regulations for the purpose of the ACCA's Preparing Financial Statements examination is the International Accounting Standards Board (IASB).

The main source of regulations for the purpose of the ACCA's Preparing Financial Statements examination is the International Accounting Standards Board (IASB) which has issued a number of authoritative International Accounting Standards (IASs), ten of which are, at the time of writing wholly or partly in that syllabus.

IASs are used as the basis for accounting in a number of countries, and in many countries in which local standard-setting bodies exist, such as the UK, local standards are aligned with International standards as far as possible.

6.2 International Accounting Standards

The International Accounting Standards Committee was set up in 1973. In 2001 it changed its name to the International Accounting Standards Board. The old IASC published 'International Accounting Standards', whereas the new IASB publishes 'International Financial Reporting Standards'.

One of the main aims of the IASB is to achieve global convergence of accounting standards. The European Union (EU) will adopt International standards in 2005 for listed companies. Some changes to existing standards may be made to ease this adoption.

IFRS 1 First time adoption of International Financial Reporting Standards

From 2005, International Financial Reporting Standards dominate UK financial reporting. EU regulations require UK quoted companies to apply international standards for periods beginning on or after January 2005. These companies and their subsidiaries will therefore be first time adopters that year. Non quoted companies have the option to adopt IFRSs but do not have to.

IFRS 1 sets out the procedures for making the transition from national accounting standards to international standards, and applies to all first time adopters for accounting periods beginning on or after 1st January 2004. This means that for companies that have to make the transition, the task has to be started sooner.

6.3 The IASB Constitution

Objectives

The objectives of the IASB are:

- to develop, in the public interest, a single set of high quality, understandable and enforceable global accounting standards that require high quality, transparent and comparable information in financial statements and other financial reporting to help participants in the world's capital markets and other users make economic decisions
- to promote the use and rigorous application of those standards
- to bring about convergence of national accounting standards and International Accounting Standards to high quality solutions.

Structure

The following diagram shows the structure of the IASB.

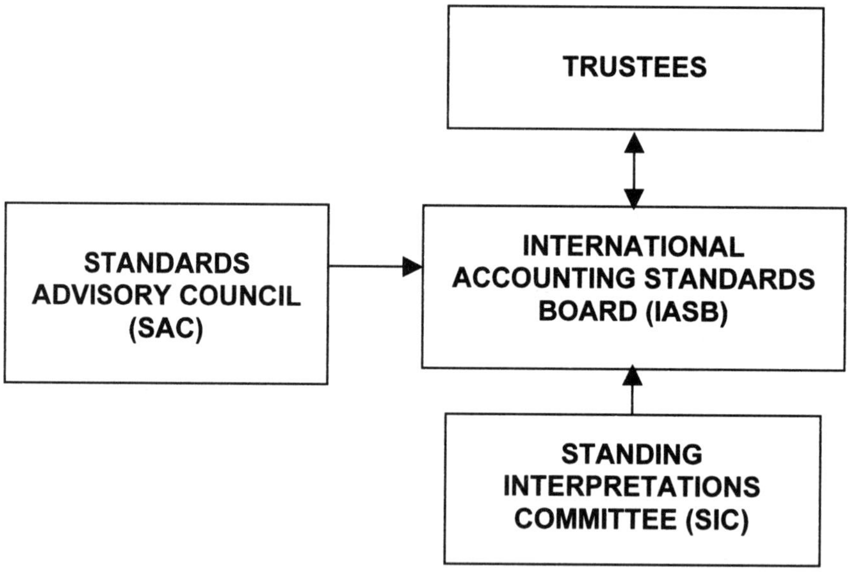

Structure of the International Accounting Standards Board

Trustees

There are 19 trustees, appointed to ensure a wide geographical spread:

- six from North America
- six from Europe
- four from the Asia/Pacific region
- three from any area.

The main duties of the Trustees are:

- fundraising
- appointing the members for the IASB, the SIC and the SAC
- annually reviewing strategy

The trustees have no involvement in technical matters relating to accounting standards.

The Board (IASB)

The Board has 14 members, 12 of whom work full-time. There is no geographical restriction on the appointment of the Board members, but to achieve a balance of perspectives and experience, the following stipulations are made:

- five or more members: practicing auditing background
- three or more members: concerned with preparation of financial statements
- three or more members: users of financial statements
- at least one member: academic background.

The Board has complete responsibility for all technical matters

The first Chairman of the Board is Sir David Tweedie of the United Kingdom.

The Board's procedures in developing Standards

The Board's procedures in developing Standards will normally be:

- form a Steering Committee to advise on major projects
- consult the Standards Advisory Council
- publish a Draft Statement of Principles or other discussion documents, inviting comment from interested parties
- publish an Exposure Draft, again inviting comment
- publish the final International Financial Reporting Standard (IFRS)

Exposure Drafts and IFRSs require the approval of eight of the 14 members of the Board. Other decisions of the Board, including the issuance of a Draft Statement of Principles or Discussion Paper, require a simple majority at a meeting attended by at least 60% of the members of the Board.

Standing Interpretations Committee (SIC)

The SIC's main task is to interpret the application of IASs and IFRSs if difficulties arise. They may issue Draft Interpretations for public comment before finalizing an Interpretation. They report to the IASB and must obtain Board approval for their Interpretations before issue.

Standards Advisory Council (SAC)

The SAC exists to provide the IASB with advice on major standard setting projects and other matters. It has about 30 members including representatives of national standard setters and other interested parties.

6.4 Benchmark and allowed alternative treatments

KEY POINT

Benchmark treatments and **allowed alternative treatments**: the treatments acceptable to the IASB.

An IAS often contains more than one permitted accounting treatment for a transaction or event. One of them may be designated the **benchmark** treatment. The other treatment or treatments, if acceptable, are classified as **allowed alternative treatments**. The IASB tries to limit the number of alternative treatments allowed in an IAS, and thus tries to minimise the number of Standards containing allowed alternative treatments.

KEY POINT

Generally accepted accounting practice (GAAP): the set of accounting practices applied in a given country or context.

6.5 Generally accepted accounting practice (GAAP)

You may come across the expression **generally accepted accounting practice** (GAAP). This means the set of accounting practices applied in a given country or context. For an individual country, GAAP is a combination of legislation, accounting standards, stock exchange requirements and, in areas where detailed rules do not exist, other acceptable accounting practices. Thus one may speak of 'UK GAAP' or 'US GAAP'. In an international context, 'GAAP' means accounting practice as defined in IASs, with each country adding its own local requirements and practices.

7 The difference between capital and revenue items

7.1 Introduction

Receipts and expenditure can be classified as capital or as revenue. This distinction is of more importance to expenditure and thus we concentrate on the distinction from the expenditure point of view.

7.2 Distinction between capital and revenue expenditure

KEY POINT

The distinction between **capital expenditure** and **revenue expenditure** derives from the fact that financial statements are produced on an annual basis.

The life of an enterprise extends over a long period of time. The problem is that reports on the profitability of the business are needed at fairly regular intervals, usually of twelve months. This requirement gives rise to certain problems. For example, how should one treat $5,000 expenditure on an item of plant which is expected to be useful to the enterprise for the next ten years? Such expenditure is referred to as capital expenditure because of the long-term nature of the benefits which are expected to be received.

The distinction between capital expenditure and revenue expenditure derives from the fact that, by convention, financial statements are produced on an annual basis.

Examples

Category	*Types of expenditure included*
Capital expenditure	(a) Expenditure on the acquisition of non-current assets required for use in the business and not for resale. (b) Expenditure on existing non-current assets aimed at increasing their earning capacity.
Revenue expenditure	(a) Expenditure on current assets (e.g. inventory). (b) Expenditure relating to running the enterprise (e.g. administration, selling expenses). (c) Expenditure on maintaining the earning capacity of non-current assets (e.g. repairs and renewals).

7.3 Capital and revenue receipts

DEFINITION

A **capital receipt** is one which relates to an item that would be regarded as capital on the balance sheet.

A **capital receipt** is one which relates to an item that would be regarded as capital on the balance sheet.

A capital receipt may be accounted for through the income statement but not necessarily so. If the receipt represents a profit or loss on the disposal of a non-current asset it represents a gain or loss to the owners of the business and thus should be shown in the income statement (after matching the receipt with the book value of the asset).

A capital receipt will also include additional cash invested in the business by the owner(s) and the raising of a loan from a bank. As these receipts represent sums which need to be paid back at some stage, they are not reported through the income statement.

Conclusion

This chapter has introduced some of the principles underlying the preparation of financial statements and emphasised the reasons why accounting information is prepared.

You should now appreciate some of the problems of preparing financial statements. There is a wide variety of users, each of whom has differing needs and requirements from those financial statements. Financial statements are a method of communicating information about a business entity to those who are interested in it. As such the financial statements should satisfy the generally accepted criteria for useful information.

SELF-TEST QUESTIONS

Users of financial statements

1 Who are the main categories of users of financial statements? (2.2 – 2.8)

2 What are the main requirements of management from financial information? (2.2)

3 What would potential shareholders' interests be in the financial statements? (2.3)

4 What would be the main concerns of long-term lenders concerning an organisation? (2.5)

Nature of accounting

5 What types of accounting are there? (4.1, 4.2)

Qualities of accounting information

6 What is meant by the relevance of information? (5)

7 What is meant by information being reliable? (5)

8 What is one method of removing bias from the financial statements? (5)

9 What are financial statements meant to be comparable with? (5)

The regulatory system

10 How are International Accounting Standards developed? (6.3)

11 What is the difference between a benchmark treatment and an allowed alternative treatment? (6.4)

Capital and revenue

12 What types of expenditure are regarded as:

(a) capital (7.2)

(b) revenue? (7.2)

EXAM-TYPE QUESTION

Financial statements

(a) To whom should information contained in a company's financial statements be communicated? **(4 marks)**

(b) What are the desirable characteristics of information which will satisfy the needs of users? **(4 marks)**

(c) Describe briefly the kind of information needed by two of the groups of people you mentioned in (a). **(2 marks)**

(Total: 10 marks)

For the answer to this question, see the 'Answers' section at the end of the book.

FEEDBACK TO ACTIVITY 1

Management

Historical information is of some use to management as they may be able to learn from it. However, management are the decision-makers and as such require budgets and plans of future costs and revenues as well as historical information in order to take decisions.

Shareholders

Shareholders are likely to be concerned about the current performance of their investment, and therefore the balance sheet and income statement are useful to them. However, they may also be interested in the future plans of the company in order to decide whether to remain as investors.

Potential shareholders

Potential shareholders are likely to be interested in both the historical performance of the company over a number of years as reflected in the income statements for those years but also in the future prospects of the organisation.

Employees

Employees will have some interest in the historical information provided by the balance sheet and income statement but they will also be interested in the future plans of the company.

Lenders

Lenders may either be short-term lenders, such as a bank overdraft or trade suppliers, or longer-term lenders. Long-term lenders will probably have some form of security over the assets of the business. They will therefore be interested in the balance sheet to the extent that it shows up-to-date values for the assets and liabilities of the organisation. Both long and short-term lenders will be concerned about the short-term cash flow prospects of the organisation and some form of cash flow budget would be useful to them.

Government agencies

Government agencies collecting statistical information will probably find the balance sheet and income statement provide most of the information that they need.

Customers

Customers of the business are likely to be interested in the future viability and prospects of the business, which are not clear from the balance sheet and income statement.

The public

The public interest in an organisation will depend upon the reason for the interest and the group concerned.

FEEDBACK TO ACTIVITY 2

Relevance and completeness

If the financial statements show all aspects of the business, there will be much information that is not relevant to the needs of individual users.

Reliability and timeliness

If the financial statements are to be produced quickly after the year end, they may not be totally reliable.

Relevance and timeliness

If financial statements are tailored to the needs of individual users, they may take longer to prepare.

Understandability and completeness

If all aspects of the business are to be shown, this may make the financial statements less comprehensible.

Chapter 2

BALANCE SHEET AND INCOME STATEMENT

CHAPTER CONTENTS

We consider the two main financial statements in this chapter and the relationship between individual accounting transactions and the financial statements. Understanding the relationship is essential in order to understand double entry bookkeeping. The use of the accounting equation or balance sheet equation demonstrates the link.

This is a short chapter but one which needs to be thoroughly understood before proceeding.

Objectives

By the time you have finished this chapter you should be able to:

- understand the typical components of an income statement and balance sheet
- have an awareness of the some of the concepts and principles underlying the preparation of financial statements
- understand the accounting equation and be able to recognise the two effects of a transaction.

1 The balance sheet and the balance sheet equation

1.1 Methods of setting out

KEY POINT

Two ways of setting out the balance sheet:

- **double-sided (or horizontal) format**
- **vertical format.**

The balance sheet attempts to show the financial position of a business at a certain point in time. There are two possible ways of setting out the balance sheet:

- double-sided (or horizontal) format
- vertical format.

1.2 Double-sided format

The vertical format is today the most popular form of presentation, but for illustration both formats will be shown here.

As an example, the balance sheet of a sole trader using the double-sided format might appear as follows:

B Ashton
Balance sheet as at 31 December 20X6

	$	$		$
Non-current assets:			Capital account:	
Motor van		2,400	Balance at 1 January 20X6	5,200
Current assets:			Add: Net profit for year	3,450
Inventory	2,390			
Trade and other				8,650
receivables	1,840		Less: Drawings for year	2,960
Cash at bank	1,704			
Cash in hand	56			5,690
			Current liabilities:	
		5,990	Trade and other payables	2,700
		8,390		8,390

1.3 Definitions of assets, liabilities and capital

The assets of the business are shown on the left-hand side; the capital and liabilities of the business are shown on the right-hand side. Assets and liabilities have already been defined in the previous chapter.

> **DEFINITION**
>
> The **capital** of a business entity is the amount that the business owes its owner.

The **capital** of a business entity is a special liability of the business. It is the amount that the business owes back to the owner of the business.

1.4 The balance sheet equation

The most important point is that the balance sheet shows the position of B Ashton's business at one point in time – in this case at close of business on 31 December 20X6. A balance sheet must always satisfy the basic equation:

> **KEY POINT**
>
> Assets = Proprietor's capital + Liabilities

Assets = Proprietor's capital + Liabilities

This is known as the **balance sheet equation** or the **accounting equation**.

The balance sheet equation underlies the balance sheet in that every transaction of the enterprise affects the balance sheet twice. We will see later in the chapter how this is achieved.

1.5 The business entity convention

> **DEFINITION**
>
> The **business entity** concept states that financial accounting information relates only to the activities of the business entity and not to the activities of its owner.

The **business entity** concept states that financial accounting information relates only to the activities of the business entity and not to the activities of its owner.

Under this concept, accounting is seen as relating to an independent unit, the entity. The entity is seen as being separate from its owners, whatever its legal status. Thus, a company is both legally and for accounting purposes a separate entity distinct from its owners, the shareholders. On the other hand, the business of a sole trader is not a legal entity distinct from its proprietor; however, for accounting purposes, the business is regarded as being a separate entity and accounts are drawn up for the business separately from the trader's own personal financial dealings.

The entity concept is essential in order to be able to account for the business as a separate economic unit. Thus, flows of money between the business and the proprietors may be separately identified from other money flows:

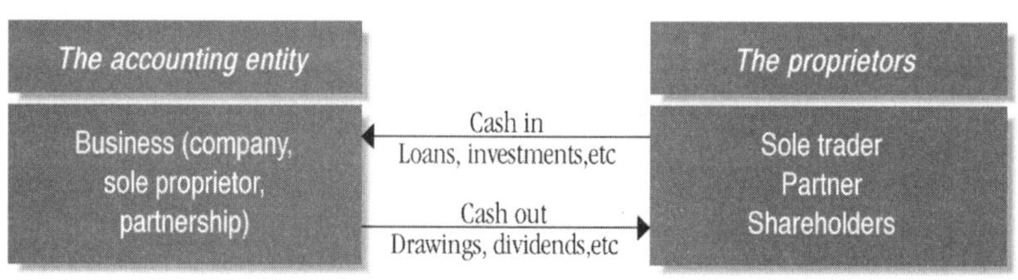

(Other accounting entities could include charities, government departments, nationalised industries and the like.)

Since we will be concerned with business entities, the correct terms for these cash movements should be established:

Cash movement from/to proprietors	*Sole trader, partnership*	*Company*
In	Either 'loans from proprietors' or 'increase in capital'	Share issue proceeds
Out	Either 'drawings' or 'reduction in capital'	Dividends

The key link between the owner and the business is the amount stated as capital. In B Ashton's balance sheet, at the beginning of the year the amount owing to the proprietor was $5,200. During the year, the overall profit of the business of $3,450 increased the amount owing to the proprietor, whereas the cash drawings (cash and goods withdrawn from the business by the proprietor for his own purposes) reduced the amount owing to him.

It may not seem clear why the balance sheet shows the information regarding the capital account. The reason is one of convention: although its key figure is $5,690 (balance at 31 December 20X6), it is useful to show B Ashton why his balance has increased from $5,200 to $5,690.

It is important to appreciate that the *balance*, i.e. the amount that is added to the other balances on the balance sheet, is $5,690. The balance sheet could be presented without the disclosure of information as to the movements in capital during the year as follows:

B Ashton
Balance sheet as at 31 December 20X6

	$	$		$
Non-current assets:				
Motor van		2,400	Capital account:	5,690
Current assets:				
Inventory	2,390		Current liabilities:	
Trade and other receivables	1,840		Trade and other payables	2,700
Cash at bank	1,704			
Cash in hand	56			
		5,990		
		8,390		8,390

1.6 Disclosure of assets and liabilities in the balance sheet

KEY POINT

Book values: the individual amounts making up the assets.

The assets used in the business amount to $8,390. The individual amounts making up the $8,390 are usually referred to as the **book values**. It cannot be assumed that these assets could be sold in the open market for $8,390 – in fact this is very unlikely. The valuation is on a 'historical' not a 'market value' basis.

KEY POINT

Liquid assets: cash and those assets which are close to cash.

As regards the listing of assets in the balance sheet, the least liquid assets are dealt with first, followed by the more liquid assets. The term **liquid assets** refers to cash and those assets which are close to cash. Looking at assets and starting with the least liquid assets:

Non-current assets

DEFINITION

A **non-current asset** is any asset acquired for retention and not held for resale in the normal course of trading.

The motor van is classified as a **non-current asset**.

A non-current asset is any asset tangible or intangible acquired for retention by an entity for the purpose of providing a service to the business, and not held for resale in the normal course of trading.

KEY POINT

Current assets:

- inventory
- accounts receivable
- cash at bank
- cash in hand.

Current assets

- The remaining assets are classified as **current assets**:
- **Inventory** i.e. goods held for resale. When the goods are eventually sold, the business will receive in exchange cash or a claim to cash (usually referred to as an account receivable).
- **Accounts receivable** i.e. amounts owing from customers which will eventually result in the receipt of cash.
- **Cash at bank** i.e. cash on current account at the bank.
- **Cash in hand** i.e. notes and coins.

KEY POINT

Liabilities are claims on the business by outsiders.

Current liabilities are those liabilities payable within 12 months of the balance sheet date.

Liabilities are claims on the business by outsiders. **Current liabilities** are those liabilities which are payable within 12 months of the balance sheet date. Payables are amounts owing in respect of goods and services previously received.

1.7 The vertical format

The balance sheet of the same sole trader using the vertical format would appear as follows:

B Ashton
Balance sheet as at 31 December 20X6

	$	$
Non-current assets:		
Motor van		2,400
Current assets:		
Inventory	2,390	
Accounts receivable	1,840	
Cash at bank	1,704	
Cash in hand	56	
		5,990
		8,390
Capital account:		
Balance at 1 January 20X6	5,200	
Add: Net profit for year	3,450	
	8,650	
Less: Drawings for year	2,960	
		5,690
Current liabilities:		
Accounts payable		2,700
		8,390

KEY POINT

The balance sheet is a statement of the financial position of an entity at a given date.

Unless instructed otherwise, always use this vertical layout for balance sheets.

The balance sheet is a statement of the financial position of an entity at a given date.

ACTIVITY 1

List the following items showing the least liquid items first:

- cash in hand
- inventory of finished goods
- cash at bank
- accounts receivable
- inventory of raw materials.

Feedback to this activity is at the end of the chapter.

2 The income statement

2.1 The matching convention

Assume that Ashton is a retailer and makes his profit from selling goods. In principle there are two steps in calculating his profit:

- deciding what his sales revenue is for the year
- deducting from this figure:
  - the cost of buying goods from his suppliers
  - various expenses such as wages, rent and insurance.

KEY POINT

Matching convention: the comparison of the costs associated with making a sale with the sale proceeds.

The comparison of the costs associated with making a sale with the sale proceeds is known as the **matching convention.**

2.2 Layout of income statement: vertical format

Mr Ashton's income statement might have looked like this:

Mr B Ashton
Income statement for the year ended 31 December 20X6

	$	$
Sales revenue		33,700
Opening inventory	3,200	
Purchases	24,490	
	27,690	
Less: Closing inventory	2,390	
Cost of sales		25,300
Gross profit		8,400
Wages	3,385	
Rent	1,200	
Sundry expenses	365	
		4,950
Net profit		3,450

2.3 Disclosure of revenue and expenses in the income statement

The detailed preparation of balance sheets and income statements will be considered later, but it is useful at this stage to obtain an overall view.

- The first point, in direct contrast with the balance sheet, is that the income statement summarises the trading activities of a business **over a period of time**, usually twelve months.
- Secondly, the figure of $33,700 for sales revenue relates to goods sold during the year, whether or not the cash was actually received during the year.
- Having arrived at a figure for sales revenue, one must deduct the cost of buying these goods. It is quite likely that some of the goods sold at the beginning of the year were goods which were held in inventory at the previous year-end. One must therefore add these onto goods which were actually purchased during the year. However, some of this year's purchases were unsold at 31 December 20X6. These must be deducted from purchases as they will be set off against next year's sales.
- Sales revenue less cost of sales gives gross profit. Net profit is arrived at by deducting expenses from gross profit.

- Note that for convenience the income statement is divided into two parts. The first part shows the calculation of the gross profit and the second, produced by subtracting the expenses from the gross profit, concludes with the net profit.
- Finally, one must be very careful to distinguish between **wages** and **drawings**. Wages relate to payments to third parties (employees) and represent a deduction or charge in arriving at net profit. Amounts paid to the proprietor (even if he calls them 'salary'!) must be treated as drawings. It would be wrong to treat drawings as a business expense as the amounts drawn are not used to further a sale. The whole of the profit belongs to the proprietor, and the drawings are that part of the profit the proprietor chooses to withdraw.

KEY POINT

An income statement summarises the trading transactions of a business entity over a period of time.

An income statement summarises the trading transactions of a business entity over a period of time.

2.4 Relationship between the income statement and the balance sheet

Balance sheets are pictures of the business at particular points in time, while the income statements show the activities of the business in between those balance sheet dates. Therefore the linkage between the accounting statements can be seen as:

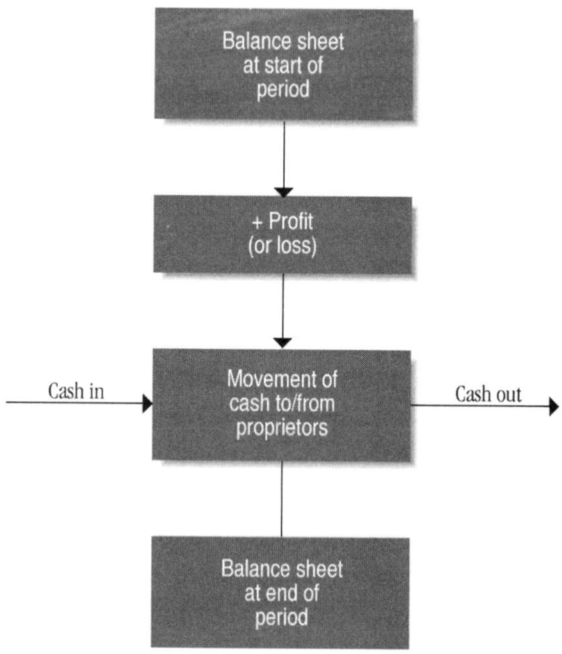

Thus, the balance sheets are not merely isolated statements; they are linked over time by the profit (or loss) as analysed in the income statement, plus movements of cash with the proprietors.

3 The accounting equation in action

3.1 Introduction

DEFINITION

Assets = Liabilities + Proprietor's capital or

Assets – Liabilities = Proprietor's capital.

Assets = Proprietor's capital + Liabilities Assets – Liabilities = Proprietor's capital

The accounting equation is a simple fact that at any point in time the assets of the business will be equal to its liabilities plus the capital of the business.

Each and every transaction that the business makes or enters into has two aspects to it and has a double effect on the business and the accounting equation. This is known as the dual aspect of transactions.

So if a business buys some goods for cash, the two aspects of the transaction are that it now has some goods but it has less cash. Equally, if it sells some goods for cash, the effect is that cash has increased and a sale has been made on which there may have been a profit made.

Example

This example involves a series of transactions using the accounting equation to build up a set of financial statements. The transactions are as follows:

Day 1	Avon commences in business introducing $1,000 cash.
Day 2	Buys a motor car for $400 cash.
Day 3	Buys goods for $200 cash.
Day 4	Sells all the goods bought on Day 3 for $300 cash.
Day 5	Buys goods for $400 on credit.
Day 6	Sells half of the goods bought on Day 5 on credit for $250.
Day 7	Pays $200 to his supplier.
Day 8	Receives $100 from a customer.
Day 9	Proprietor draws $75 in cash.
Day 10	Pays rent of $40 in cash.
Day 11	Receives a loan of $600 repayable in two years.
Day 12	Pays cash of $30 for insurance.

Using the accounting equation, a balance sheet will be drawn up for the end of each day (representing the cumulative effect of transactions to date) and later an income statement will be drawn up for the twelve-day period. For simplicity, the distinction between cash at bank and cash in hand will be ignored. Each day's balance sheet is shown using the horizontal format.

Solution

Day 1: introduction of cash as capital

Balance sheet Day 1

	$		$
Cash	1,000	Capital	1,000

Note carefully that this transaction, like all others, affects two aspects of the balance sheet. The business has $1,000 of cash but also owes $1,000 back to Avon, the capital of the business.

Day 2: purchase of non-current asset for cash

This is merely a change of the form in which the assets are held.

Balance sheet Day 2

	$		$
Motor car	400	Capital	1,000
Cash ($1,000 – $400)	600		
	1,000		1,000

Note: the implication is that the increasing (or the acquiring) of an asset must lead to one of the following:

- reducing another asset by a corresponding amount (as above)
- incurring a corresponding liability (Day 5)
- increasing the capital contributed by the proprietor (Day 1).

Day 3: purchase of goods for cash

Again this is merely a change in the form in which the assets are held. $200 is withdrawn from cash and invested in inventory.

Balance sheet for Day 3

	$		$
Motor car	400	Capital	1,000
Inventory	200		
Cash ($600 – $200)	400		
	1,000		1,000

Day 4: sale of goods at a profit

This is an important new development. It is true that one asset (inventory) is being replaced by another (cash), but the amounts do not correspond.

	$
Cash acquired (sale proceeds)	300
Asset relinquished (inventory)	200
Difference (= profit)	100

DEFINITION

Profit is the difference between purchase price and sale proceeds and it belongs to the proprietor(s) of the business.

Thus total assets have increased by $100. Since there are no liabilities involved, if the fundamental equation is to remain valid the capital must increase by $100.

Profit is the difference between purchase price and sale proceeds and it belongs to the proprietor(s) of the business. It is an increase in the capital of the business.

Balance sheet for Day 4

	$		$	$
Motor car	400	Capital introduced	1,000	
Cash ($400 + $300)	700	Add: Profit	100	
				1,100
	1,100			1,100

Day 5: purchase of goods on credit

It has been indicated that assets can be increased by a corresponding increase in liabilities. This can now be seen in operation.

Balance sheet for Day 5

	$		$	$
Motor car	400	Capital introduced	1,000	
Inventory	400	Add: Profit	100	
Cash	700			
				1,100
		Accounts payable		400
	1,500			1,500

Note that the accounts payable are acting in effect as a source of finance for the business.

Day 6: sale of part of inventory on credit terms

This transaction introduces two new concepts:

- **Sale on credit**. Essentially this is the same as a sale for cash, except that the asset increased is not cash, but accounts receivable.
- Sale of **part** of the inventory. In practice this is the normal situation. The important accounting requirement is to separate:
  - inventory still held as an asset, from
  - cost of inventory sold.

This is best viewed diagrammatically:

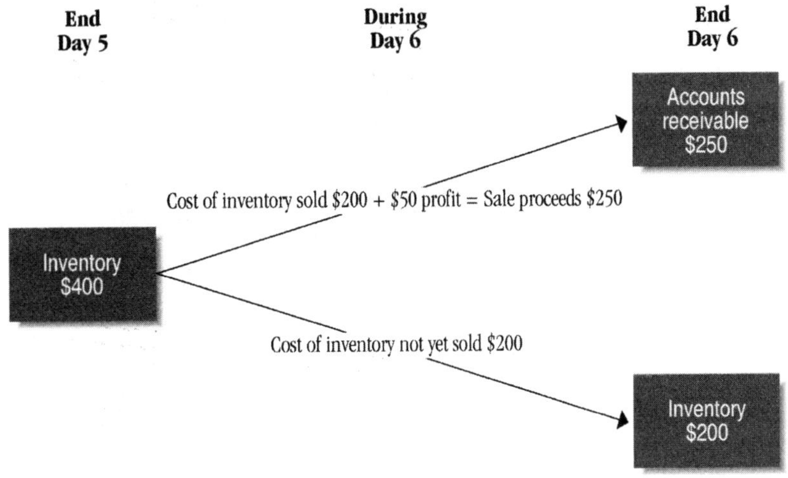

Balance sheet for Day 6

	$			$	$
Motor car	400	Capital introduced		1,000	
Inventory	200	Add:	Profit to date		
Accounts receivable	250		($100 + $50)	150	
Cash	700				
					1,150
		Accounts payable			400
	1,550				1,550

Note that profit is recorded when the sale is made, not when the cash is received. Thus the payment of the accounts payable (Day 7) or the receipt of cash from accounts receivable (Day 8) will not alter the total profit.

It would be useful at this stage to draw up a summary of the profit to date:

Statement of profit for first six days of trading

		$	$
Sales revenue:	Cash		300
	Credit		250
			550
Purchases:	Cash	200	
	Credit	400	
Goods available for sale		600	
Less: Goods not sold (closing inventory)		200	
Cost of goods sold			400
Gross profit			150

Notice that the goods not sold, i.e. the closing inventory, are stated at historical cost (or original purchase price). This is part of the traditional historical cost convention of accounting.

The cost of goods sold is also known as the cost of sales.

Day 7: payment to trade account payable

This is simply the reduction of one liability (accounts payable) and one asset (cash) by a corresponding amount ($200).

Balance sheet for Day 7

	$		$	$
Motor car	400	Capital introduced	1,000	
Inventory	200	Add: Profit to date	150	
Accounts receivable	250			
Cash ($700 – $200)	500			1,150
		Accounts payable ($400 – $200)		200
	1,350			1,350

Day 8: receipt of cash from account receivable

A change in the form in which assets are held:

Balance sheet for Day 8

	$		$	$
Motor car	400	Capital introduced	1,000	
Inventory	200	Add: Profit to date	150	
Accounts receivable ($250 – $100)	150			
Cash ($500 + $100)	600			1,150
		Accounts payable		200
	1,350			1,350

Day 9: cash withdrawal by the proprietor

DEFINITION

Cash or other assets taken out by the owner are called **amounts withdrawn**, or **drawings**.

This arises where the proprietor wishes to withdraw some of his interest in the business i.e. his original capital as increased by profits earned. This shows on the balance sheet as a reduction of capital, and as a reduction of cash.

Cash or other assets taken out of the business by the owner are called 'amounts withdrawn', or 'drawings'.

Balance sheet for Day 9

	$		$	$
Motor car	400	Capital introduced	1,000	
Inventory	200	Add: Profit to date		
Accounts receivable		($150 – $40)	150	
($250 - $100)	150			
Cash ($600 – $75)	525		1,150	
		Less: Amounts withdrawn	75	
				1,075
		Accounts payable		200
	1,275			1,275

Day 10: payment of rent

This is an example of a business expense. The payment of the expense reduces the profit and reduces the cash.

Balance sheet for Day 10

	$		$	$
Motor car	400	Capital introduced	1,000	
Inventory	200	Add: Profit to date		
Accounts receivable	150	($150 – $40)	110	
Cash ($525 – $40)	485			
			1,110	
		Less: Amounts withdrawn	75	
				1,035
		Accounts payable		200
	1,235			1,235

Day 11: medium-term loan received of $600

Balance sheet for Day 11

	$		$	$
Motor car	400	Capital introduced	1,000	
Inventory	200	Add: Profit to date	110	
Accounts receivable	150			
Cash ($485 + $600)	1,085		1,110	
		Less: Amounts withdrawn	75	
				1,035
		Loan		600
		Accounts payable		200
	1,835			1,835

Day 12: payment of insurance

This is a further example of a business expense. The payment reduces both profit and cash.

Balance sheet for Day 12

	$		$	$
Motor car	400	Capital introduced	1,000	
Inventory	200	Add: Profit to date		
Accounts receivable	150	($110 – $30)	80	
Cash ($1,085 – $30)	1,055			
			1,080	
		Less: Amounts withdrawn	75	
				1,005
		Loan		600
		Accounts payable		200
	1,805			1,805

This marks the end of the transactions. The financial statements for the twelve-day period can now be considered.

KEY POINT

After each transaction the accounting equation will always be equal:

Assets = Capital + Liabilities.

After each transaction the accounting equation will always be equal:

Assets = Capital + Liabilities.

3.2 The financial statements

DEFINITION

Gross profit is the difference between sales proceeds and the cost of goods sold.

Net profit is the gross profit less the expenses of the business.

The income statement can be prepared by summarising all the sales, purchases and expenses that have taken place in the 12 day period, not forgetting the closing inventory at the end of the period.

Gross profit is the difference between sales proceeds and the cost of goods sold.

Net profit is the gross profit less the expenses of the business.

It is assumed that both the income statement and the balance sheet are to be presented in vertical form as follows:

Income statement for the twelve days ended … 20..

		$	$
Sales revenue:	Cash		300
Credit			250
			550
Cost of sales: Purchases:	Cash	200	
	Credit	400	
		600	
Less: Closing inventory		200	
Cost of goods sold			400
Gross profit			150
Rent		40	
Insurance		30	
			70
Net profit			80

Balance sheet as at end of Day 12

		$	$
Non-current asset:	Motor car (at cost)		400
Current assets:	Inventory	200	
	Accounts receivable	150	
	Cash	1,055	
			1,405
			1,805
Capital account of Avon:	Capital introduced	1,000	
	Net profit	80	
		1,080	
	Less: Amounts withdrawn	75	
			1,005
Non-current liability:	Loan		600
Current liabilities:	Accounts payable		200
			1,805

Notes

(1) Although the alternative (double-sided) form of balance sheet is acceptable, the above vertical presentation is generally regarded as preferable.

(2) Current liabilities are payable within twelve months of the balance sheet date and cannot therefore include a loan of $600 repayable in two years. Note the presentation of this loan as a non-current liability in the vertical form balance sheet.

(3) The motor car is stated in the balance sheet at its historical (or original) cost of $400. The important subject of depreciation will be considered at a later stage.

3.3 Summary of the effect of each transaction

	Assets	*Capital and liabilities*	*Reference*
Introduction of cash as capital	+ Cash	+ Capital	Day 1
Purchase of asset for cash	+ Asset – Cash	No effect	Days 2 + 3

Purchase of asset on credit	+ Asset	+ Liabilities	Day 5
Sale of inventory at a profit – for cash	– Inventory + Cash	+ Capital	Day 4
Sale of inventory at a profit – on credit	– Inventory + Account receivable	+ Capital	Day 6
Payment of account payable	– Cash	– Liabilities	Day 7
Receipt from account receivable	+ Cash – Account receivable	No effect	Day 8
Drawings by proprietor	– Cash	– Capital	Day 9
Payment of expense in cash	– Cash	– Capital	Days 10 + 12
Cash received as a loan	+ Cash	+ Liabilities	Day 11

KEY POINT

The accounting equation must always balance:

Assets = Capital + Liabilities

or

Assets – Liabilities = Capital

- Every business transaction affects at least two items in the accounting equation.
- The accounting equation must always balance:

  Assets = Capital + Liabilities

  or

  Assets – Liabilities = Capital.
- The net profit for the period is made up of the gross profit less business expenses.
- The gross profit is calculated as sales proceeds less the original cost of the goods sold.

ACTIVITY 2

Explain the effect on the accounting equation of each of the following transactions:

(a) Payment of $200 to a supplier.

(b) Payment of $1,000 by cheque for office furniture.

(c) A sale on credit of $350 (goods sold originally cost $250).

(d) Receipt of $140 from an account receivable.

(e) Taking out of a bank loan of $4,000.

(f) Amounts withdrawn by the owner of $100.

(g) Payment of $40 casual wages.

(h) Purchase of a computer for the office on credit for $1,500.

(i) Sale for cash of $800 (goods sold originally cost $600).

Feedback to this activity is at the end of the chapter.

Conclusion

The two main financial statements have been examined in this chapter and we have looked at how individual transactions are represented in these financial statements using the balance sheet equation. The accounting equation holds true no matter how complex a business seems to be. Every transaction or event of a business has two equal and opposite effects on the business.

We will be reinforcing your knowledge of these areas in later chapters.

SELF-TEST QUESTIONS

The balance sheet and its equation

1 What is meant by the capital of a business? (1.3)

2 What is the definition of a non-current asset? (1.6)

3 What are current liabilities? (1.6)

The income statement

4 Who does the profit of a business belong to? (2.3)

5 What are drawings? (2.3)

6 What is the difference between gross profit and net profit? (2.3)

7 How are the balance sheet and the income statement interrelated? (2.4)

EXAM-TYPE QUESTION

The Frog Shop

Day	*Transaction*
1	Kermit starts a business and introduces $2,000 in cash.
2	He buys for cash a motor van for $1,000 and some shop fittings for $800.
3	He buys some goods from Fozzie costing $500 on credit.
4	He sells one half of the goods to Scooter for $650 cash.
5	He pays $500 to Fozzie.
6	He draws $50 of cash from the business for his own use.
7	He buys goods costing $1,000 on credit terms from Fozzie.
8	He sells goods which cost him $900 to Miss Piggy on credit terms for $1,200.
9	He receives $500 from Miss Piggy.
10	He pays wages of $100 to Rolf, his employee.

You are required to:

(a) prepare the balance sheet of Kermit's business (known as 'The Frog Shop') at the end of each day **(10 marks)**

(b) prepare an income statement for The Frog Shop for the ten days ended above. **(5 marks)**

(Total: 15 marks)

For the answer to this question see the 'Answers' section at the end of the book.

FEEDBACK TO ACTIVITY 1

The correct order is:

- inventory of raw materials
- inventory of finished goods
- accounts receivable
- cash at bank
- cash in hand.

FEEDBACK TO ACTIVITY **2**

(a) Decrease in cash $200.

Effect: Decrease in accounts payable $200

(b) Increase in non-current asset (office furniture) $1,000.

Effect: Decrease in cash $1,000

(c) Increase in accounts receivable $350.

Effect: Decrease in inventory $250

Profit $100

(d) Increase in cash $140.

Effect: Decrease in accounts receivable $140

(e) Increase in cash $4,000.

Effect: Increase in loan $4,000

(f) Decrease in cash $100.

Effect: Decrease in capital $100

(g) Decrease in cash $40.

Effect: Decrease in profit (expense) $40

(h) Increase in non-current assets (computer) $1,500.

Effect: Increase in accounts payable $1,500

(i) Increase in cash $800.

Effect: Decrease in inventory $600

Profit $200

Chapter 3
BOOKKEEPING PRINCIPLES

CHAPTER CONTENTS

In the previous chapter we recorded each transaction immediately into the financial statements. In practice such an approach is neither sensible nor desirable. What is needed is a set of accounting records which can provide information for the day-to-day running of the business and for the periodic preparation of financial statements showing the profit or loss the business has made (income statement) and the position of the business at the end of the period covered by the income statement (balance sheet).

The purpose of this chapter is to explain the main elements of the bookkeeping system which provides this information.

In this chapter, ledger accounts will be introduced and the 'rules' of double entry bookkeeping examined. The process of balancing the ledger accounts and producing a list of account balances will be examined but the actual preparation of financial statements will be dealt with in a later chapter.

Objectives

By the time you have finished this chapter you should be able to:

- understand the principles of double entry bookkeeping
- write up simple transactions in the ledger accounts
- balance off ledger accounts and prepare a trial balance (also called a list of account balances)
- deal with opening balances in ledger accounts
- understand the types of error that may occur in bookkeeping systems and whether they are detected by the trial balance
- understand the recording of cash discounts.

1 The main data sources and their function

1.1 Introduction

Whenever a business transaction takes place there is a need to record the transaction on or in a document.

DEFINITION

A **source document** is an individual record of a business transaction.

A **source document** is an individual record of a business transaction – for example, a sales invoice is a formal record of a sale having occurred.

Since financial statements only need to be prepared at set intervals, not every day, the sufficient first stage is to have a sensible system of source documents which can be used as the raw material for our later entries.

In this section we will examine the type of source documents which exist. Most business transactions revolve around the purchase and sale of goods and services and thus most source documents relate to either of these items.

1.2 Sales and purchase orders

DEFINITION

A **purchase order** is an agreement to purchase goods/services from a business.

DEFINITION

A **sales order** is an agreement to sell goods/services to a business.

A **purchase order** is an agreement to purchase goods/services from a business. It is prepared by the purchaser.

A **sales order** is an agreement to sell goods/services to a business. It is prepared by the seller.

A sales or purchase order is normally the first occasion when an intended transaction is put in writing. It does however record an **intended** rather than an actual transaction and thus a more important document in terms of recording financial transactions is the **invoice**.

1.3 Sales and purchase invoices

When a business sells goods or services to a customer it sends a sales invoice to the customer.

DEFINITION

A **sales invoice** is a formal record of the amount of money due from the customer as a result of the sale transaction.

A **sales invoice** is a formal record of the amount of money due from the customer as a result of the sale transaction.

To the customer, the invoice represents a purchase and thus he will refer to it as a purchase invoice.

The invoice may contain a lot of detailed information about the transaction, e.g.:

- name and address of seller and purchaser
- date of sale
- reference to order
- description of goods
- amount due
- terms of payment.

It is an essential document which provides the information which will be entered into the accounting records of a business.

1.4 Credit and debit notes

KEY POINT

A **credit note** records goods returned by a customer or the reduction of monies owed by a customer.

A credit note records goods returned by a customer or the reduction of monies owed by a customer. The credit note is issued subsequent to a sales invoice and will refer to that invoice. There are many reasons why the original sale may have been incorrect. Faulty goods may have been supplied or the price charged on the invoice was incorrect.

A debit note is sometimes raised by a purchaser of goods and is a formal request for a credit note to be issued by the supplier.

2 Accounting records

2.1 Summary of stages of accounting

KEY POINT

Data in source documents are transferred to books of prime entry.

Accounting records are any listing or book which records the transactions of a business in a logical manner. The source documents above are part of the accounting records of a business, but the information contained in them needs to be more clearly laid out. This is achieved by the use of **books of prime entry**.

The chart below shows the route by which transactions are recorded in the final output of the accounting system: the financial statements.

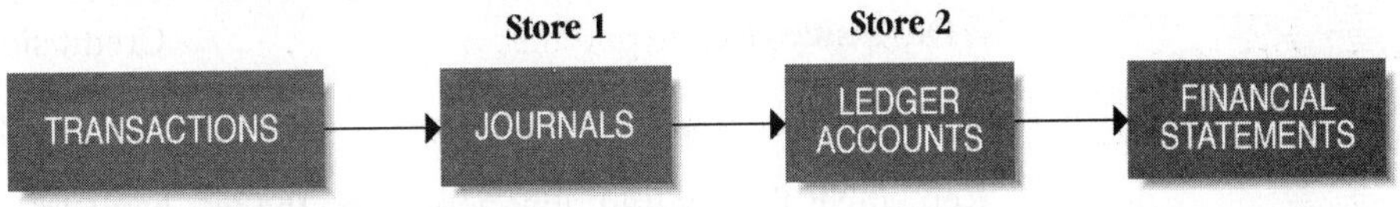

DEFINITION

Journals record the similar transactions of each day.

A **ledger account** or 'T' account is where all transactions of a similar type are recorded.

Journals record the similar transactions of each day. They are used as an initial 'store' of information of the business transactions prior to storing the information in the ledger accounts.

A **ledger account** or 'T' account is where all transactions of a similar type are recorded, e.g. all cash transactions or all purchases of non-current assets. Ledger accounts are pages in a book (the ledger) with a separate page reserved for transactions of the same type.

The form of journals will be considered in a later chapter. The important point to note about them for the moment is that their prime function is to list transactions of a common nature and these listings will be used to make further entries in the accounting system.

For example, a sales journal will list all the sales invoices raised by the business, and will contain sufficient information about each sale so that further entries can be made at a convenient later date without having to refer back to the sales invoices.

Initially *we will assume that journals do not exist* as a better understanding of the double entry system used in operating ledger accounts will be obtained. Transactions will thus be entered direct into the ledger accounts.

2.2 Ledger accounts and double entry

In the previous chapter, an examination was made of the effect on the balance sheet, day by day, of a series of transactions.

KEY POINT

All transactions affect the accounting equation and all transactions could, if we wished, be recorded directly by drawing up a balance sheet.

All transactions affect the accounting equation and all transactions could, if we wished, be recorded directly by drawing up a balance sheet.

The problem with this approach is that it becomes cumbersome in a practical situation involving a large number of transactions. In practice, therefore, it is necessary to summarise all categories of transactions so that the balance sheet need only be produced at intervals of, say, twelve months. The approach used is called the **double entry** system of bookkeeping. This involves the use of journals and ledger accounts.

2.3 The theory of double entry

As has been shown, every transaction affects two items in the balance sheet. To follow the rules of double entry, every time a transaction is recorded, both aspects must be taken into account.

KEY POINT

Debit side entries: Dr

Credit side entries: Cr

Traditionally, one aspect is referred to as the debit side of the entry (abbreviated to Dr) and the other as the credit side of the entry (abbreviated to Cr).

2.4 Ledger accounts

Each aspect is recorded in the relevant ledger account. Any business of reasonable size will have a large number of ledger accounts. Each account has two sides – the **debit side** and the **credit side.**

Ledger account

Debit side (Dr)	$	Credit side (Cr)	$

KEY POINT

Debit side entries: left-hand side

Credit side entries: right-hand side

Remember that by tradition, debit is on the left-hand side, and credit is on the right-hand side.

For each transaction it is now not only necessary to identify the two effects of the transaction and therefore the two ledger accounts to be used, but also to decide which ledger account has the debit entry and which has the credit entry.

The ledger account is usually set out in practice in three columns thus:

	Debit $	*Credit* $	*Balance* $

However, for examination purposes the 'two-sided' ledger account or T-account illustrated above is more convenient.

2.5 Debit and credit and the format of ledger accounts

In bookkeeping, the terms 'debit' and 'credit' have meanings different from those attached to them in ordinary speech.

You will soon get used to their technical meaning in bookkeeping. Here is a table to explain them.

Entries on the DEBIT side	Entries on the CREDIT side
Assets	Liabilities
Expenses	Income
Losses	Profits

KEY POINT

The **cash account** records cash received and paid by the business.

One fundamental ledger account in a bookkeeping system is the **cash account**, recording cash received and paid by the business. The balance of cash in hand, being an asset, is on the debit side of the cash account. If we spend some of this cash, this could be for three reasons:

- to buy an asset
- to pay an expense
- to repay a debt or liability.

The bookkeeping entry to record a payment of cash is on the **credit** side of the cash account (reducing the cash balance) and on the **debit** side of the account recording the other aspect of the transaction:

To buy an asset	Debit the asset account to record the fact that we have more of the asset concerned.

To pay an expense	Debit the expense account to record the fact that we have paid the expense.
To repay a debt or liability	Debit the liability account to record the fact that we owe less as a result of the payment.

The example which follows shows the procedure in action. Note the format of the ledger account, with columns for the date and the details of the transaction.

2.6 Drawing up ledger accounts

In practising the following examples, provide plenty of space between the ledger accounts so that the entries can be made. It is *essential* that the examples are practised by opening ledger accounts and writing down the entries. In this way the practice and theory of double entry will be more quickly understood.

Also allow a full page width for each ledger account. This will enable narrative and figures to be clearly written and also emphasise the 'left-hand' and 'right-hand' nature of the entries.

Example

To illustrate the rules of double entry, the example used in the previous chapter will be used again.

Twelve separate transactions were considered. For convenience these are summarised again below:

Day 1	Avon commences in business introducing $1,000 cash.
Day 2	Buys a motor car for $400 cash.
Day 3	Buys goods for $200 cash.
Day 4	Sells all the goods bought on Day 3 for $300 cash.
Day 5	Buys goods for $400 on credit.
Day 6	Sells half of the goods bought on Day 5 on credit for $250.
Day 7	Pays $200 to his supplier.
Day 8	Receives $100 from a customer.
Day 9	Proprietor draws $75 in cash.
Day 10	Pays rent of $40 in cash.
Day 11	Receives a loan of $600 repayable in two years.
Day 12	Pays cash of $30 for insurance.

Solution

Day 1

Avon introduced cash of $1,000 into the business. What are the two aspects of this transaction? Quite clearly cash (an asset) is increased and so are the claims of the proprietor (his capital). As this is a new business we must open up ledger accounts for cash and capital.

The cash account has the debit entry and the capital account has the credit entry.

Cash account

Date	*Details*	$	*Date*	*Details*	$
(1)	Capital	1,000			

Capital account

Date	*Details*	$	*Date*	*Details*	$
			(1)	Cash	1,000

Note that the items (1) refer to the date of the transaction. The details refer to the other account that is being debited or credited.

On the cash account, the receipt of $1,000 is by convention entered on the left-hand side (the debit side) and its description 'capital' indicates where the other side of the double entry (the other aspect of the transaction) may be found. In the capital account, $1,000 appears on the right-hand side (the credit side) and the description 'cash' shows where the other side of the double entry may be found.

KEY POINT

Whenever a business receives cash there is a debit entry made in the cash account.

Whenever a business receives cash there is a debit entry made in the cash account.

Day 2

On this day the business purchases a motor car (which is a non-current asset) for cash. The payment of cash is a credit in the cash account and the other side of the double entry is a debit in the motor car account. Using the cash account already opened, the transaction appears as follows:

Cash account

Date	*Details*	$	*Date*	*Details*	$
(1)	Capital	1,000	(2)	Motor car	400

Motor car account

Date	*Details*	$	*Date*	*Details*	$
(2)	Cash	400			

KEY POINT

Whenever a business pays out cash there is a credit entry made in the cash account.

An asset (or an increase in an asset) is always a debit entry.

Whenever a business pays out cash there is a credit entry made in the cash account.

An asset (or an increase in an asset) is always a debit entry.

Day 3

The purchase of goods on Day 3 is a cash purchase and so the cash account is credited.

So which account is debited? The temptation may well be to answer 'inventory, of course', but this would be wrong. Inventory is a special case as will be explained later. For the moment the thing to remember is that it is the *purchases account* which is debited.

Cash account

Date	*Details*	$	*Date*	*Details*	$
(1)	Capital	1,000	(2)	Motor car	400
			(3)	Purchases	200

Purchases account

Date	*Details*	$	*Date*	*Details*	$
(3)	Cash	200			

The purchases account contains items which are held for resale by the business or are raw materials which will be used to manufacture goods.

Day 4

The sale of goods for cash involves a receipt of cash and thus a debit to the cash account. What then is credited? Again the answer is *not* inventory but sales revenue account.

Cash account

Date	*Details*	$	*Date*	*Details*	$
(1)	Capital	1,000	(2)	Motor car	400
(4)	Sales revenue	300	(3)	Purchases	200

Sales revenue account

Date	*Details*	$	*Date*	*Details*	$
			(4)	Cash	300

The sales revenue account collects the sales that have been made by the business during the period.

Income to the business is always a credit entry.

KEY POINT

Income to the business is always a credit entry.

The effect of having separate sales revenue and purchases accounts is that profit is not computed when each sale is made as it was in the previous example. As many sales are being made each day, it is not practical to compute profit on each transaction. Profit is instead calculated at the end of the period.

Day 5

This produces a minor problem: cash is not involved!

The transaction involves a purchase of goods (as did the Day 3 transaction). Purchases account is therefore debited.

But what is credited? The answer is a liability account for the supplier of the goods. The credit on his account represents a liability to him. We normally refer to amounts due to creditors as 'accounts payable' or 'payables'.

Purchases account

Date	*Details*	$	*Date*	*Details*	$
(3)	Cash	200			
(5)	Accounts payable	400			

Accounts payable

Date	*Details*	$	*Date*	*Details*	$
			(5)	Purchases	400

A liability (or an increase in a liability) is always a credit entry.

KEY POINT

A liability (or an increase in a liability) is always a credit entry.

Day 6

A similar problem now arises. The transaction is a sale (like Day 4), so the sales revenue account, representing all the sales taking place in the period, is credited.

The debit side of the double entry goes to a debtors account. Debtors are assets – they represent amounts owing to the business, i.e. promises to pay cash at some future date. We normally refer to amounts due from debtors as 'accounts receivable' or 'receivables'.

Sales revenue account

Date	*Details*	$	*Date*	*Details*	$
			(4)	Cash	300
			(6)	Accounts receivable	250

Accounts receivable

Date	*Details*	$	*Date*	*Details*	$
(6)	Sales revenue	250			

The information about only half of the goods being sold does not concern us at this stage. At the end of the period when the financial statements are drawn up, account will be taken of any closing inventory (representing unsold goods).

Day 7

What about the payment of $200 to the account payable? What effect does this have? The two aspects are, firstly, that the asset cash is reduced (a credit) and, secondly, that liabilities or amounts owing are reduced (debit to accounts payable).

Cash account

Date	*Details*	$	*Date*	*Details*	$
(1)	Capital	1,000	(2)	Motor car	400
(4)	Sales revenue	300	(3)	Purchases	200
			(7)	Accounts payable	200

Accounts payable

Date	*Details*	$	*Date*	*Details*	$
(7)	Cash	200	(5)	Purchases	400

Day 8

The receipt of $100 from a debtor increases the asset cash (debit cash) and reduces the asset accounts receivable (credit accounts receivable).

Cash account

Date	*Details*	$	*Date*	*Details*	$
(1)	Capital	1,000	(2)	Motor car	400
(4)	Sales revenue	300	(3)	Purchases	200
(8)	Accounts receivable	100	(7)	Accounts payable	200

Accounts receivable

Date	*Details*	$	*Date*	*Details*	$
(6)	Sales revenue	250	(8)	Cash	100

Day 9

Drawings of cash must clearly be credited to cash. The debit side of the double entry should be taken to a drawings account.

Cash account

Date	*Details*	$	*Date*	*Details*	$
(1)	Capital	1,000	(2)	Motor car	400
(4)	Sales revenue	300	(3)	Purchases	200
(8)	Accounts receivable	100	(7)	Accounts payable	200
			(9)	Drawings	75

Drawings account

Date	*Details*	$	*Date*	*Details*	$
(9)	Cash	75			

Day 11

The loan represents a receipt of cash (debit cash). But the business now owes $600 to a third party (i.e. a liability). A loan account must be credited. Note that a separate account should be opened for each liability (i.e. each third party).

Cash account

Date	*Details*	$	*Date*	*Details*	$
(1)	Capital	1,000	(2)	Motor car	400
(4)	Sales revenue	300	(3)	Purchases	200
(8)	Accounts receivable	100	(7)	Accounts payable	200
(11)	Loan	600	(9)	Drawings	75

Loan account

Date	*Details*	$	*Date*	*Details*	$
			(11)	Cash	600

Days 10 and 12

The payments of rent and insurance represents expenditure. Cash is credited and the respective *expense* accounts debited.

Cash account

Date	*Details*	$	*Date*	*Details*	$
(1)	Capital	1,000	(2)	Motor car	400
(4)	Sales revenue	300	(3)	Purchases	200
(8)	Accounts receivable	100	(7)	Accounts payable	200
(11)	Loan	600	(9)	Drawings	75
			(10)	Rent	40
			(12)	Insurance	30

Rent account

Date	*Details*	$	*Date*	*Details*	$
(10)	Cash	40			

Insurance account

Date	*Details*	$	*Date*	*Details*	$
(12)	Cash	30			

An expense account collects the costs of the various expenses of running the business. These expenses eventually find their way to the income statement.

KEY POINT

Expenses of the business are always a debit entry.

Expenses of the business are always a debit entry.

2.7 Final ledger accounts

The final ledger accounts would appear as follows:

(Note: the totals in brackets are there merely for convenience later in the chapter. They form no part of the double entry.)

Capital account

Date	*Details*	$	*Date*	*Details*	$
			(1)	Cash	1,000

Cash account

Date	*Details*	$	*Date*	*Details*	$
(1)	Capital	1,000	(2)	Motor car	400
(4)	Sales revenue	300	(3)	Purchases	200
(8)	Accounts receivable	100	(7)	Accounts payable	200
(11)	Loan	600	(9)	Drawings	75
			(10)	Rent	40
			(12)	Insurance	30
(Total $2,000)			(Total $945)		

Motor car account

Date	*Details*	$	*Date*	*Details*	$
(2)	Cash	400			

Purchases account

Date	*Details*	$	*Date*	*Details*	$
(3)	Cash	200			
(5)	Accounts payable	400			
(Total $600)					

Sales revenue account

Date	*Details*	$	*Date*	*Details*	$
			(4)	Cash	300
			(6)	Accounts receivable	250
			(Total $550)		

Accounts payable (for each supplier)

Date	*Details*	$	*Date*	*Details*	$
(7)	Cash	200	(5)	Purchases	400

Accounts receivable (for each customer)

Date	*Details*	$	*Date*	*Details*	$
(6)	Sales revenue	250	(8)	Cash	100

Drawings account

Date	*Details*	$	*Date*	*Details*	$
(9)	Cash	75			

Rent account

Date	*Details*	$	*Date*	*Details*	$
(10)	Cash	40			

Loan account

Date	*Details*	$	*Date*	*Details*	$
			(11)	Cash	600

Insurance account

Date	*Details*	$	*Date*	*Details*	$
(12)	Cash	30			

ACTIVITY 1

Summarise the debit and the credit entries for each of the transactions that Avon made.

Can you draw any general conclusions regarding the entries to be made for assets, liabilities, income and expenses?

Feedback to this activity is at the end of the chapter.

2.8 Asset, liability, revenue and expense accounts

The above activity should provide some clues as to the distinction between asset, liability, revenue and expense accounts.

DEFINITION

Asset account: information on assets of a business.

Liability account: information on liabilities of a business.

An **asset account** collects information about particular assets of a business. It mainly consists of debit entries.

A **liability account** collects information about particular liabilities of a business. It mainly consists of credit entries.

Asset and liability accounts appear on the balance sheet at the end of the accounting period.

DEFINITION

Expense account: information on costs of a business.

Revenue account: information on income of a business.

An **expense account** collects information about particular costs of a business. It mainly consists of debit entries.

A **revenue account** collects information about particular income of a business. It mainly consists of credit entries.

Revenue and expenses are transferred to the income statement in order to compute profit for a period. The only revenue account we have come across so far is the sales account.

We will see later that some revenue/expense accounts will also record assets and liabilities – known as accruals and prepayments.

2.9 Usefulness of cash

Only a combination of experience and thought will provide familiarity with double entry techniques. Even experienced accountants occasionally have to ask which account is credited!

It was clear in the previous illustration how useful cash was in establishing one side of the double entry. If cash was received, then cash account was debited and it was a question of deciding what had to be credited. Conversely, a payment of cash involved a credit to cash account and it was then a question of deciding in which ledger account the debit was to appear.

ACTIVITY 2

Harold commenced business on 1 July 20X4. The following transactions took place during the month of July.

1 July	Introduced cash of $4,000 and a car valued at $1,750.
2 July	Bought goods for cash at a cost of $1,130.
8 July	Paid wages of $13 and sundry expenses of $2.
9 July	Sold goods on credit to Victor for $190.
14 July	Sold goods on credit to Susan for $240.

18 July	Bought goods on credit from Williams for $85.
22 July	Bought fixtures and fittings for cash at a cost of $350.
25 July	Paid wages of $38.
26 July	Paid drawings to himself of $80.
31 July	Victor paid the full amount owing.
31 July	Paid rent of $500.

Write up the ledger accounts for the month of July 20X4.

Feedback to this activity is at the end of the chapter.

3 Trial balance

3.1 The nature and purpose of a trial balance

The large number of transactions recorded in ledger accounts means that there is the possibility of errors occurring. Periodically some assurance is required as to the accuracy of the procedures. This can be done by listing all the balances. In the case of a moderate-sized business, although final accounts will usually be prepared annually, a trial balance will be extracted at more frequent intervals (say, monthly).

DEFINITION

A **trial balance** is a *memorandum* listing of all the ledger account balances.

A **trial balance** is simply a *memorandum* listing of all the ledger account balances. In an accounting context 'memorandum' means that the listing is not a part of the double entry.

If the double entry procedures have been carefully followed, then the trial balance should show that the total of the debit balances agrees with the total of the credit balances, because every transaction has been recorded by means of a debit entry and a credit entry.

3.2 Balancing the ledger accounts

Before a trial balance can be drawn up, the ledger accounts must be balanced.

Where there are several entries in a ledger account, the computation of the balance of the ledger account to go onto the list of account balances can be shown in the ledger account by **carrying down** and **bringing down** a balance.

The procedure is as follows:

1 Add up the total debits and credits in the account and make a (memorandum) note of the totals.

  Insert the *higher* total at the bottom of *both* the debits and credits, leaving one line for the inclusion of a **balance c/d** (carried down).

2 The totals should be level with each other and underlined.

3 Insert on the side which has the lower arithmetical total, the narrative 'balance c/d' and an amount which brings the arithmetical total to the total that has been inserted under step 2 above.

4 The same figure is shown on the other side of the ledger account but *underneath* the totals. This is the **balance b/d** (brought down).

  The balance c/d is known as the **closing balance**. The balance b/d is known as the **opening balance.**

KEY POINT

Closing balance: the balance c/d.

Opening balance: the balance b/d.

Example

The cash account from the example Avon is reproduced below:

Cash account

		$			$
(1)	Capital	1,000	(2)	Motor car	400
(4)	Sales revenue	300	(3)	Purchases	200
(8)	Accounts receivable	100	(7)	Accounts payable	200
(11)	Loan	600	(9)	Drawings	75
			(10)	Rent	40
			(12)	Insurance	30
(Total $2,000)			(Total $945)		

Step 1

The arithmetic totals have already been computed.

Step 2

The higher total is inserted, $2,000.

Cash account

		$			$
(1)	Capital	1,000	(2)	Motor car	400
(4)	Sales revenue	300	(3)	Purchases	200
(8)	Accounts receivable	100	(7)	Accounts payable	200
(11)	Loan	600	(9)	Drawings	75
			(10)	Rent	40
			(12)	Insurance	30
		2,000			2,000

Note that credits do not yet add up to $2,000.

Steps 3 and 4

Insert the balances b/d and c/d. The balance can be found from the arithmetical totals $2,000 – $945 = $1,055.

Cash account

		$			$
(1)	Capital	1,000	(2)	Motor car	400
(4)	Sales revenue	300	(3)	Purchases	200
(8)	Accounts receivable	100	(7)	Accounts payable	7200
(11)	Loan	600	(9)	Drawings	75
			(10)	Rent	40
			(12)	Insurance	30
				Balance c/d	1,055
		2,000			2,000
	Balance b/d	1,055			

The $1,055 is known as a *debit* balance because the b/d figure is on the debit side of the account, i.e. the debit entries in the account before it was totalled must have exceeded the credit entries by that amount.

This balance means that there is $1,055 cash left within the business at the end of the period and also at the beginning of the next period.

The carrying down of balances causes problems to some students. However, if the procedure is *practised* it soon becomes second nature. It is helpful to have a clear mental picture of the form of a ledger account when practising examples.

ACTIVITY **3**

Balance off the remaining ledger accounts in the example Avon.

(Note that where there is only one entry in an account, there is no necessity to carry out the balancing procedure as this one entry is the balance c/d and the balance b/d.)

Feedback to this activity is at the end of the chapter.

3.3 Drawing up the trial balance

Once the ledger accounts have all been balanced, the trial balance can be drawn up. This is done by listing each of the ledger account names in the business's books showing against each name the balance on that account and whether that balance is a debit or a credit balance brought down. Note that it is the balance brought down which determines whether the account is said to have a debit or a credit balance.

Example

Continuing the example of Avon, the trial balance at the end of Day 12 would appear as follows:

Trial balance at the end of Day 12

Account	*Debit* $	*Credit* $
Capital		1,000
Cash	1,055	
Motor car	400	
Purchases	600	
Sales revenue		550
Accounts payable		200
Accounts receivable	150	
Drawings by proprietor	75	
Rent	40	
Loan		600
Insurance	30	
	2,350	2,350

ACTIVITY **4**

The debit and the credit totals of the trial balance are equal. Consider why this should be the case.

Feedback to this activity is at the end of the chapter.

3.4 Errors not revealed by the trial balance

The fact that the two totals agree may be reassuring but it is not final proof that the accounts are correct! It is possible for certain types of error to occur and yet the overall effect is that the list of balances still appears to balance. .

DEFINITION

To **post** amounts to a ledger account means to write the amount up in the ledger accounts.

To 'post' amounts to a ledger account means to write the amount up in the ledger accounts.

Such errors include:

1 **Errors of omission** where no entry of a transaction has been made at all.

2 **Errors of commission** where an amount has been correctly posted but to the wrong account, although it is the right type of account, e.g. B Smith, a customer, pays $50 by cheque which is debited to the cash book and then in error posted to the credit of the account of R Smith, another customer.

   Although there will have been a debit and a credit, nevertheless the account of R Smith shows a credit balance of $50 higher than it should be, while the account of B Smith is also $50 out.

3 **Errors of principle**. This occurs where an item is incorrectly classified by the bookkeeper and posted to the wrong type of account, e.g. the sale of surplus office equipment has been classified as sales of goods.

4 **Errors of entry**. This occurs where an incorrect amount is posted to both the accounts in question, e.g. $2.00 is misread as $200 and so entered on both debit and credit sides of the correct accounts.

   Some accountants refer to this error as an error of original entry as it often arises due to the entry originally being recorded in a journal (see later) at the wrong amount.

5 **Compensating errors.** These occur where two or more errors cancel out each other. They are difficult to locate and fortunately tend not to occur frequently.

A trial balance is simply a memorandum listing of all the ledger account balances. It is *not* part of the double entry, e.g. cash is not being credited with $1,055 and the list of balances debited with $1,055. It merely summarises the net result of all the debits and credits that have been made during the period.

4 Ledger accounts – further complications

4.1 Introduction

If a business has been in operation for a number of years, then at the beginning of any accounting period it will have assets and liabilities such as cash, accounts receivable, non-current assets and accounts payable left over from the previous period. Such opening amounts are shown in the ledger accounts as opening balances.

Remember that assets are always debits and therefore the opening balance on an asset account will be a debit entry and as liabilities are credits the opening balance on liability accounts will be credit entries.

ACTIVITY **5**

Draw up the opening position on the ledger accounts for the following items:

	$
Cash opening balance	1,000
Accounts payable opening balance	2,000
Accounts receivable opening balance	2,500
Overdraft opening balance	800
Fixtures and fittings opening balance	3,000

Feedback to this activity is at the end of the chapter.

Example

Elton makes up his accounts to 31 December each year. His balance sheet at 31 December 20X8 showed the following position:

	$	$
Non-current assets:		
Shop		17,600
Current assets:		
Inventory	5,343	
Accounts receivable	4,504	
Cash	2,801	
		12,648
		30,248
Capital account:		
Balance at 1 January 20X8	16,730	
Net profit for 20X8	4,708	
	21,438	
Drawings	4,620	
		16,818
Long-term liability:		
Loan		8,000
Current liabilities:		
Accounts payable		5,430
		30,248

Notes

(a) Accounts receivable consist of:

	$
E	2,600
F	987
G	536
H	381
	4,504

(b) Accounts payable consist of:

	$
M	2,840
N	1,990
O	600
	5,430

The following transactions took place during January 20X9:

3 January	G settled his account in full.
5 January	Paid $847 to N.
8 January	F returned as faulty, goods with an invoice value of $264 and paid off the balance owing on his account.
12 January	Sold goods to G, invoice value $706.
18 January	Purchased goods from P, invoice value $746.
19 January	E paid his account subject to a discount of 2% for prompt payment.
24 January	Paid O subject to 1.5% discount for early settlement.
28 January	Bought goods from O with invoice value $203.
31 January	Returned goods to P, invoice value $76.

The inventory remaining at 31 January totalled $6,100. You are required to prepare:

(a) ledger accounts relating to all the above matters (other than closing inventory)

(b) trial balance at 31 January 20X9.

Solution

Step 1

Open up all of the ledger accounts that have opening balances on them. These are all of the accounts shown in the balance sheet at 31 December 20X8.

Capital account

	$			$
		20X9		
		1 Jan	Balance b/d	16,818

Note that balance b/d is short for balance brought down from the previous period. (Last year's ledger account would have shown all the figures, including drawings of $4,620, leading up to the final balance of $16,818.) Thus the b/d figure records the fact that at the beginning of the accounting period the credits on the capital account exceed the debits by $16,818.

To reinforce this point about balances, the ledger account for *last year* is shown below.

Capital account

20X8		$	*20X8*		$
31 Dec	Drawings	4,620	1 Jan	Balance b/d	16,730
31 Dec	Balance c/d (balancing figure)	16,818	31 Dec	Net profit for year	4,708
		21,438			21,438
			20X9		
			1 Jan	Balance b/d	16,818

Loan account

	$			$
		20X9		
		1 Jan	Balance b/d	8,000

Shop account

20X9		$		$
1 Jan	Balance b/d	17,600		

Inventory account

20X9		$		$
1 Jan	Balance b/d	5,343		

Cash account

		$			$
20X9					
1 Jan	Balance b/d	2,801			

Accounts receivable – E

		$			$
20X9					
1 Jan	Balance b/d	2,600			

Accounts receivable – F

		$			$
20X9					
1 Jan	Balance b/d	987			

Accounts receivable – G

		$			$
20X9					
1 Jan	Balance b/d	536			

Accounts receivable – H

		$			$
20X9					
1 Jan	Balance b/d	381			

Accounts payable – M

		$			$
			20X9		
			1 Jan	Balance b/d	2,840

Accounts payable – N

		$			$
			20X9		
			1 Jan	Balance b/d	1,990

Accounts payable – O

		$			$
			20X9		
			1 Jan	Balance b/d	600

Step 2

Record the transactions for the period in the ledger accounts.

Note: you should look carefully at the following items in particular.

(a) 8 January

Some of the goods sold to F were faulty so he returned them. When the sale was originally made, the double entry was to credit sales and debit F's account.

When goods are returned the debtor's account must be credited with the invoice amount of the goods as the debtor is obviously not going to pay for the goods. The corresponding debit entry is not to sales revenue but instead to a sales returns or returns inwards, account.

DEFINITION

Sales returns are goods returned by a customer because they are unsatisfactory.

Sales returns are goods returned by a customer because they are unsatisfactory.

(b) 19 January

When the goods were originally sold to E, the terms of the sale were that, if he paid his account by a certain date, then he would be entitled to a 2% discount for prompt payment. This is known as a cash or settlement discount. E owes $2,600 but the cash that Elton will receive will be $2,548 (98% of $2,600).

This payment satisfies his liability in full and therefore his debtor account must be cleared. This is done by crediting it with $52, the amount of the discount, and debiting a discount allowed account. The discount allowed is an expense of the business that will appear in the income statement as the business is sacrificing $52 in order to receive the money earlier.

A cash discount allowed is a discount allowed to a customer if he pays by a certain date.

DEFINITION

A **cash discount received** is a discount received from a supplier if the business pays its invoices by a certain date.

(c) 24 January

This is an example of a discount received from a supplier. Elton owes O $600 but as he is evidently paying the invoice early, Elton need only pay $591 (98.5% of $600).

In order to clear the ledger account for O, it must be debited with the $9 of the discount as well as with the cash payment and the $9 is then credited to a discount received account. This $9 will appear as income in the income statement for the period.

(d) 31 January

DEFINITION

Purchases returns are goods returned to a supplier because they are unsatisfactory.

This is an example of a purchase return. Goods purchased from P are being returned and therefore P's ledger account will be debited as the goods will not be paid for. The credit entry is to a purchases returns, or returns outwards, account. .

Purchases returns are goods returned to a supplier because they are unsatisfactory.

Cash account

20X9		$	*20X9*		$
1 Jan	Balance b/d	2,801	5 Jan	N	847
3 Jan	G	536	24 Jan	O	591
8 Jan	F	723			
19 Jan	E	2,548	31 Jan	Balance c/d	5,170
		6,608			6,608
	Balance b/d	5,170			

Sales revenue account

		$	*20X9*		$
			12 Jan	G	706

Sales returns account

20X9		$			$
8 Jan	F	264			

Purchases account

20X9		$			$
16 Jan	P	746			
28 Jan	O	203		Balance c/d	949
		949			949
	Balance b/d	949			

Purchases returns account

		$			$
			20X9		
			31 Jan	P	76

Discount allowed account

		$			$
20X9					
19 Jan	E	52			

Discount received account

		$			$
			20X9		
			24 Jan	O	9

E's account

		$			$
20X9			*20X9*		
1 Jan	Balance b/d	2,600	19 Jan	Cash (98% × $2,600)	2,548
				Discount allowed	52
		2,600			2,600

F's account

		$			$
20X9			*20X9*		
1 Jan	Balance b/d	987	8 Jan	Sales returns	264
				Cash	723
		987			987

G's account

		$			$
20X9			*20X9*		
1 Jan	Balance b/d	536	3 Jan	Cash	536
12 Jan	Sales revenue	706	31 Jan	Balance c/d	706
		1,242			1,242
	Balance b/d	706			

H's account

		$			$
20X9					
1 Jan	Balance b/d	381			

M's account

		$			$
			20X9		
			1 Jan	Balance b/d	2,840

N's account

		$			$
20X9			*20X9*		
5 Jan	Cash	847	1 Jan	Balance b/d	1,990
31 Jan	Balance c/d	1,143			
		1,990			1,990
				Balance b/d	1,143

O's account

20X9		$	20X9		$
24 Jan	Cash (98.5% × $600)	591	1 Jan	Balance b/d	600
	Discount received	9	28 Jan	Purchases	203
31 Jan	Balance c/d	203			
		803			803
				Balance b/d	203

P's account

20X9		$	20X9		$
31 Jan	Purchase returns	76	18 Jan	Purchases	746
31 Jan	Balance c/d	670			
		746			746
				Balance b/d	670

Step 3

Balance off all of the accounts where necessary (see above).

Step 4

Prepare the trial balance.

Trial balance at 31 January 20X9

		Dr	*Cr*
		$	$
1	Capital		16,818
2	Loan		8,000
3	Shop	17,600	
4	Inventory	5,343	
5	Cash	5,170	
6	Sales revenue		706
7	Sales returns	264	
8	Purchases	949	
9	Purchases returns		76
10	Discount allowed	52	
11	Discount received		9
12	E	–	
13	F	–	
14	G	706	
15	H	381	
16	M		2,840
17	N		1,143
18	O		203
19	P		670
		30,465	30,465

ACTIVITY 6

Continue with the example of Elton above and prepare his income statement in vertical form and the balance sheet at the end of January.

Note: the treatment of sales returns and purchases returns is to net them off against sales revenue and purchases respectively in the income statement.

Feedback to this activity is at the end of the chapter.

ACTIVITY 7

Ian Wright owes ABC & Co $2,000 and is owed $3,400 by Templeman Associates. Ian offers a cash discount to his customers of 2.5% if they pay within 14 days and ABC & Co have offered Ian a cash discount of 3% for payment within ten days.

Ian decides to pay ABC & Co within ten days and Templeman Associates take advantage of the cash discount offered to them.

Write up the ledger account for ABC & Co, Templeman Associates, discounts received and discounts allowed.

Feedback to this activity is at the end of the chapter.

KEY POINT

A **discount received** from a supplier is debited to the supplier's account.

A **discount allowed** to a customer is credited to the customer's account.

4.2 Discounts

A discount received from a supplier is debited to the supplier's account in order to clear the amount outstanding and is credited to a discount received account. This is similar to income as it is a reduction in the amount that has to be paid to the supplier. The discount received is shown as income beneath gross profit in the income statement.

A discount allowed to a customer is credited to the customer's account in order to clear the amount outstanding and is debited to a discount allowed account. This is an expense of the business and appears as such in the list of expenses in the income statement.

Conclusion

This has been a long chapter in which you should have grasped the basics of double entry bookkeeping. It is essential material on which many later chapters are based. Do make sure you understand it fully before proceeding. As always, work through the questions below before moving to Chapter 4.

The previous chapter began with the accounting equation which states that:

Assets = Liabilities + Proprietor's capital.

This will always hold true no matter how complex the business seems. This is the case because every transaction or event of the business has two equal and opposite effects on the business.

This brought this chapter on to double entry bookkeeping where the key point is that every transaction or event has two effects on the accounting of the business – one of these effects is recorded as a *debit* entry in a ledger account and the other is recorded as a *credit* entry in a ledger account.

There are a number of helpful rules that can be learnt in order to assist in finding the correct accounts to debit and credit for each transaction, but the key to double entry bookkeeping is practice at writing up ledger accounts.

SELF-TEST QUESTIONS

Accounting records

1 If cash is received by the business, is that a debit or a credit entry in the cash account? (2.5)

2 Are liabilities debit or credit entries in the liability accounts? (2.5)

Account balances

3 What is a trial balance? (3.1)

4 If the debit and the credit totals of the trial balance are equal, what does this mean? (3.1)

5 What is meant by the balance b/d on a ledger account? (3.2)

Ledger accounts – further complications

6 What is the double entry for a sales return? (4.1)

7 What is a return outwards? (4.1)

8 What is a discount allowed? (4.2)

9 What is the double entry for a discount received? (4.2)

EXAM-TYPE QUESTION

Grace

Grace commenced business on 1 June 20X9 with cash of $5,000 and she introduced a car valued at $4,500. The following transactions took place:

1 June Purchased goods for $1,000 cash.

2 June Purchased fixtures and fittings $900.

3 June Purchased goods on credit from Eileen $1,500.

4 June Sold goods for $1,200 cash.

5 June Sold goods on credit to Tom for $900.

8 June Paid wages $100 in cash.

9 June Bought goods from Eric for $850 on credit.

10 June Sold goods to Trevor $800 on credit.

11 June Sold goods on credit to Tom for $1,000.

12 June Paid Eileen all that was owed to her.

15 June Tom paid in full.

16 June Purchased $700 goods for cash.

17 June Sold $500 goods for cash.

18 June Trevor paid $500 on account.

19 June Paid wages $150.

22 June Paid Eric in full.

24 June Loan received from Guy $1,000.

25 June Purchased premises $4,000.

26 June Paid wages $150.

You are required to write up the ledger accounts for the month of June and extract a trial balance. (Ignore dates in the ledger accounts.) **(15 marks)**

For the answer to this question see the 'Answer' section at the end of the book.

FEEDBACK TO ACTIVITY 1

Transaction	*Ledger account* *Debit*	*Credit*
Introduction of cash as capital	Cash	Capital
Receipt of cash as loan	Cash	Loan
Purchase of goods for cash	Purchases	Cash
Purchase of goods on credit	Purchases	Accounts payable
Sale of goods for cash	Cash	Sales revenue
Sale of goods on credit	Sales revenue	Accounts receivable
Purchase of non-current asset for cash	Non-current asset	Cash
Payment of expense in cash	Expense	Cash
Cash withdrawn by proprietor	Drawings	Cash

This can be summarised as:

	Debits	*Credits*
Balance sheet items	Assets	Liabilities
Income statement items	Expenses	Income

FEEDBACK TO ACTIVITY 2

Your accounts should be as follows:

Cash account

20X4 *Jul*	*Details*	$	*20X4* *Jul*	*Details*	$
1	Capital	4,000	2	Purchases	1,130
31	Victor	190	8	Wages	13
			8	Sundry expenses	2
			22	Fixtures and fittings	350
			25	Wages	38
			26	Drawings	80
			31	Rent	500

Capital account

20X4 *Jul*	*Details*	$	*20X4* *Jul*	*Details*	$
			1	Cash	4,000
			1	Motor car	1,750

Motor car account

20X4 *Jul*	*Details*	$	*20X4* *Jul*	*Details*	$
1	Capital	1,750			

Tutorial note: the introduction of capital in a form other than cash has the same double entry as if it were cash, i.e. debit the asset account and credit the capital account.

Purchases account

20X4			20X4		
Jul	*Details*	$	*Jul*	*Details*	$
2	Cash	1,130			
18	Williams	85			

Wages account

20X4			20X4		
Jul	*Details*	$	*Jul*	*Details*	$
8	Cash	13			
25	Cash	38			

Sundry expenses account

20X4			20X4		
Jul	*Details*	$	*Jul*	*Details*	$
8	Cash	2			

Sales revenue account

20X4			20X4		
Jul	*Details*	$	*Jul*	*Details*	$
			9	Victor	190
			14	Susan	240

Accounts receivable – Victor

20X4			20X4		
Jul	*Details*	$	*Jul*	*Details*	$
9	Sales revenue	190	31	Cash	190

Accounts receivable – Susan

20X4			20X4		
Jul	*Details*	$	*Jul*	*Details*	$
14	Sales revenue	240			

Rent account

20X4			20X4		
Jul	*Details*	$	*Jul*	*Details*	$
31	Cash	500			

Accounts payable – Williams

20X4			20X4		
Jul	*Details*	$	*Jul*	*Details*	$
			18	Purchases	85

Fixtures and fittings account

20X4			20X4		
Jul	*Details*	$	*Jul*	*Details*	$
22	Cash	350			

Drawings account

20X4			*20X4*		
Jul	*Details*	$	*Jul*	*Details*	$
26	Cash	80			

FEEDBACK TO ACTIVITY 3

Your accounts should be as follows:

Capital account

Date	*Details*	$	*Date*	*Details*	$
			(1)	Cash	1,000

Motor car account

Date	*Details*	$	*Date*	*Details*	$
(2)	Cash	400			

Purchases account

Date	*Details*	$	*Date*	*Details*	$
(3)	Cash	200		Balance c/d	600
(5)	Accounts payable	400			
		600			600
	Balance b/d	600			

Sales revenue account

Date	*Details*	$	*Date*	*Details*	$
	Balance c/d	550	(4)	Cash	300
			(6)	Accounts receivable	250
		550			550
				Balance b/d	550

Accounts payable

Date	*Details*	$	*Date*	*Details*	$
(7)	Cash	200	(5)	Purchases	400
	Balance c/d	200			
		400			400
				Balance b/d	200

Accounts receivable

Date	*Details*	$	*Date*	*Details*	$
(6)	Sales revenue	250	(8)	Cash	100
				Balance c/d	150
		250			250
	Balance b/d	150			

Drawings account

Date	*Details*	$	*Date*	*Details*	$
(9)	Cash	75			

Rent account

Date	*Details*	$	*Date*	*Details*	$
(10)	Cash	40			

Loan account

Date	*Details*	$	*Date*	*Details*	$
			(11)	Cash	600

Insurance account

Date	*Details*	$	*Date*	*Details*	$
(12)	Cash	30			

FEEDBACK TO ACTIVITY 4

The trial balance has the same debit and credit totals because for every debit entry in the ledger accounts there has been an equal and opposite credit entry.

FEEDBACK TO ACTIVITY 5

Your accounts should be as follows:

Cash

	$		$
Balance b/d	1,000		

Accounts payable

	$		$
		Balance b/d	2,000

Accounts receivable

	$		$
Balance b/d	2,500		

Overdraft

	$		$
		Balance b/d	800

Fixtures and fittings

	$		$
Balance b/d	3,000		

FEEDBACK TO ACTIVITY **6**

Your solution should be as follows:

Income statement for the month of January 20X9

	$	$	$
Sales revenue			706
Less: Sales returns			264
			442
Cost of goods sold:			
Opening inventory		5,343	
Purchases	949		
Less: Purchases returns	76		
		873	
		6,216	
Less: Closing inventory		6,100	
			116
Gross profit			326
Discount received (income)			9
			335
Less: Expenses:			
Discount allowed			52
Net profit			283

Balance sheet as at 31 January 20X9

	$	$
Non-current assets		
Shop		17,600
Current assets:		
Inventory	6,100	
Accounts receivable (706 + 381)	1,087	
Cash	5,170	
		12,357
		29,957
Capital at 1 January	16,818	
Profit for the month	283	
		17,101
Long-term liabilities:		
Loan		8,000
Current liabilities:		
Accounts payable (2,840 + 1,143 + 203 + 670)		4,856
		29,957

FEEDBACK TO ACTIVITY **7**

Your solution should be as follows:

ABC & Co

	$		$
Cash (97% × 2,000)	1,940	Balance b/d	2,000
Discount received	60		
	2,000		2,000

Templeman Associates

	$		$
Balance b/d	3,400	Cash (97.5% × 3,400)	3,315
		Discount allowed	85
	3,400		3,400

Discount received

	$		$
		ABC & Co	60

Discount allowed

	$		$
Templeman Associates	85		

Chapter 4

INVENTORY AND THE PREPARATION OF FINANCIAL STATEMENTS

CHAPTER CONTENTS

Having learnt how to write up the transactions of a business in its ledger accounts, and how to balance off those ledger accounts and prepare a trial balance, it is now necessary to consider how the income statement and balance sheet of the business are prepared.

In order to do this, one further piece of double entry bookkeeping must be considered: how to treat closing inventory. Once the treatment of closing inventory in the ledger accounts is understood, then the preparation of the income statement and balance sheet from the ledger accounts and the trial balance can be tackled.

Objectives

By the time you have finished this chapter you should be able to:

- deal with opening and closing inventory in the ledger accounts of a business
- prepare a simple set of financial statements from the ledger account balances or a trial balance
- explain alternative inventory valuation methods
- understand the main provisions of IAS 2 *Inventories*.

1 Closing inventory

1.1 Introduction

In order to be able to prepare a set of financial statements, it is first necessary to learn how to account for any items of goods held at the end of the year, i.e. closing inventory. (In some countries inventory is referred to as 'stock'.)

Example

A trader starts in business and by the end of his first year he has purchased goods costing $21,000 and he has made sales totalling $25,000. Goods which cost him $3,000 have not been sold by the end of the year.

What profit has he made in the year?

Solution

The goods not sold are referred to as closing inventory. This inventory is deducted from purchases in the income statement.

Gross profit is thus:

	$	$
Sales revenue		25,000
Purchases	21,000	
Less: Closing inventory	3,000	
Cost of sales		18,000
Gross profit		7,000

Closing inventory appears on the balance sheet as an asset.

The situation becomes slightly more complicated when the business has been in existence for more than one year, as will now be seen.

Example

A wholesaler buys goods from a manufacturer at $2 per unit and sells them on credit terms to various retailers at $3 per unit. He has summarised his transactions for 20X7 as follows:

	Units
Opening inventory (1 January 20X7)	500
Purchases (Cost at $2 = $12,400)	6,200
	6,700
Sales revenue (Proceeds at $3 = $17,700)	5,900
Closing inventory (31 December 20X7)	800

How is the gross profit to be calculated?

Solution

Gross profit is sales revenue less cost of sales. This brings us to the idea of matching. Against the revenue from the 5,900 units sold, we must 'match' what it cost to buy those goods in the first place. The purchases figure does not give the answer, since clearly some of the goods sold during the year come from the goods the wholesaler started off with at the beginning of the year (last year's closing inventory) and some from the goods bought during the year (purchases). When comparing sales revenue and cost of sales it is important to make sure that one is comparing like with like.

In the example assume that both opening and closing inventory are valued for accounts purposes at $2 per unit, giving inventory figures of $1,000 and $1,600 respectively.

Gross profit can be calculated as follows:

	$	$
Sales revenue		17,700
Opening inventory (at cost)	1,000	
Purchases (at cost)	12,400	
	13,400	
Less: Closing inventory (at cost)	1,600	
Cost of sales		11,800
Gross profit		5,900

1.2 Ledger accounts for inventory

In considering ledger accounts for inventory, we need to consider the position of the income statement and the balance sheet in the context of the double entry bookkeeping system.

1.3 Income statement

Initially it is critical to appreciate that the income statement is part of the double entry bookkeeping system, whereas the balance sheet is not.

KEY POINT

However it is presented, the **income statement** is simply another 'T' account or ledger account.

It is easy to be put off by the fact that the income statement is set out in vertical form, whereas other ledger accounts are set out in 'T' account form. However, you must remember that, although it is not presented as such, the income statement is a 'T' account and the double entry principles apply here as with any other such account. However it is presented, the income statement is simply another 'T' account or ledger account.

1.4 Balance sheet

KEY POINT

The **balance sheet** is an ordered list of all of the ledger account balances remaining once the income statement has been prepared.

The balance sheet is much more similar to the trial balance, being a balance of the ledger accounts after double-entry has been completed, and requiring that debits must equal credits.

The balance sheet is an ordered list of all of the ledger account balances remaining once the income statement has been prepared.

Example

From the previous example we arrived at a gross profit of $5,900. Let us examine the relevant ledger accounts. We will consider the accounts at two separate points in time:

(a) immediately before extracting a trial balance at 31 December 20X7

(b) immediately after the financial statements have been prepared and the various accounts ruled off.

Solution

(a) Ledger accounts before extracting a trial balance

Inventory account

20X7		$		$
1 Jan	Balance b/d	1,000		

The inventory is an asset and therefore is a debit entry in the inventory account.

Purchases account

20X7	$		$
Various suppliers	12,400		

Sales revenue account

	$	*20X7*	$
		Various customers	17,700

Points to note

- The balance of $1,000 in inventory account originated from last year's balance sheet when it appeared as closing inventory. Remember that last year's closing inventory is this year's opening inventory. This figure remains unchanged in the inventory account until the very end of the year when closing inventory at 31 December 20X7 is considered.
- The closing inventory figure (which is known to be $1,600) is not usually provided to us until after we have extracted the trial balance at 31 December 20X7.
- The purchases and sales figures have been built up over the year and represent the year's accumulated transactions.

(b) Ledger accounts reflecting the closing inventory

Assume that we are told that closing inventory for accounting purposes has been valued at $1,600. What adjustments are required?

Step 1

The income statement forms part of the double entry. At the year end the accumulated totals from the sales and purchases accounts must be transferred to it.

Ref	*Debit*	*Credit*	*With*
1	Income statement	Purchases	$12,400
2	Sales revenue	Income statement	$17,700

These transfers are shown in the ledger accounts below.

Step 2

The opening inventory figure ($1,000) must be transferred to the income statement account in order to arrive at cost of sales.

3	Income statement	Inventory	$1,000

Step 3

The income statement cannot be completed (and hence gross profit calculated) until the closing inventory is included.

4	Inventory	Income statement	$1,600

After summarising and balancing off, the ledger accounts (cross-referenced to the above summaries) then become:

Inventory account

20X7		$	*20X7*		$
1 Jan	Balance b/d	1,000	31 Dec (3)	Income statement	1,000
31 Dec (4)	Income statement	1,600	31 Dec	Balance c/d	1,600
		2,600			2,600
20X8					
1 Jan	Balance b/d	1,600			

Purchases account

20X7		$	*20X7*		$
Various dates	Accounts payable	12,400	31 Dec (1)	Income statement	12,400

Sales revenue account

20X7		$	*20X7*		$
31 Dec (2)	Income statement	17,700	Various dates	Accounts receivable	17,700

Income statement ('T' account form)

20X7		$	*20X7*		$
31 Dec (1)	Purchases	12,400	31 Dec (2)	Sales revenue	17,700
(3)	Inventory	1,000	(4)	Inventory	1,600
	Gross profit c/d	5,900			
		19,300			19,300
				Gross profit b/d	5,900

The key points regarding ledger accounts reflecting the closing inventory are shown below:

- The sales revenue and the purchases accounts are cleared out to and summarised in the income statement.
- Opening inventory is cleared out to the income statement and closing inventory is entered into the inventory account and the income statement.
- The balance on the inventory account remains at the end of the period and is listed in the balance sheet under current assets as inventory.
- The first part of the income statement can be balanced at this stage to show the gross profit figure carried down and brought down.
- The above layout of the income statement is not particularly useful but it assists the appreciation of the actual double entry processes and the realisation that the income statement is part of the double entry.

KEY POINT

The balance on the inventory account remains at the end of the period and is listed in the balance sheet under current assets as inventory.

A more useful (and by now familiar) layout of the first part of the income statement is:

	$	$
Sales revenue		17,700
Opening inventory	1,000	
Add: Purchases	12,400	
	13,400	
Less: Closing inventory	1,600	
Cost of sales		11,800
Gross profit		5,900

1.5 Inventory account

After the financial statements have been completed, it is usual to balance and rule off the various ledger accounts (as shown above). Note particularly the treatment of the inventory account. The balance carried down (c/d) is a balance at the end of the year which will be entered on the balance sheet representing closing inventory. This is brought down (b/d) at the beginning of the following year, representing the opening inventory for the next accounting period. This illustrates two key features in bookkeeping:

- any balance carried down at the end of an accounting period should be included on the balance sheet
- any balance carried down at the end of an accounting period, the closing balance on an account, will become the opening balance here at the beginning of the next accounting period.

KEY POINT

Entries are only ever made to the inventory account at the end of the accounting period.

Entries are only ever made to the inventory account at the end of the accounting period when the opening inventory is transferred to the income statement and the closing inventory is entered into the inventory account.

ACTIVITY 1

The trading position of a simple cash-based business for its first week of trading was as follows:

	$
Capital introduced by the owner	1,000
Purchases for cash	800
Sales for cash	900

At the end of the week there were goods which had cost $300 left in inventory.

Write up the ledger accounts for this first week of trading, including an income statement, and then prepare a vertical income statement as well as a balance sheet.

Feedback to this activity is at the end of the chapter.

ACTIVITY 2

The business described in the previous activity now continues into its second week. Its transactions are as follows:

	$
Sales for cash	1,000
Purchases for cash	1,100

The goods left at the end of this second week originally cost $500.

Write up the ledger accounts for this second week, including the income statement and then prepare a vertical income statement together with a balance sheet at the end of the second week.

Feedback to this activity is at the end of the chapter.

2 Preparation of financial statements

2.1 Approach

The above ledger accounts may appear complex and bewildering. For examination purposes, however, it is not necessary to write up the ledger accounts if the question asks only for the presentation of the financial statements.

For example, the information contained in the first example in this chapter would often be given in the form of a trial balance.

Trial balance as at 31 December 20X7

	$	$
Sales revenue		17,700
Inventory	1,000	
Purchases	12,400	
Other balances	X	X
	XX	XX

Additional information would be given as follows:

Inventory has been valued at 31 December 20X7 as $1,600.

KEY POINT

Remember that the inventory shown on the trial balance is *last year's* inventory.

Remember that the inventory shown on the trial balance is *last year's* inventory as profit has not yet been computed by transferring sales and purchases to the income statement.

This fact should be reinforced by the additional information given concerning closing inventory (which is *not* on the trial balance).

The financial statements can be prepared straight from the information given:

Income statement for the year ended 31 December 20X7 (extract)

	$	$
Sales revenue (from trial balance)		17,700
Opening inventory (from trial balance)	1,000	
Purchases (from trial balance)	12,400	
	13,400	
Closing inventory (from additional information)	1,600	
Cost of sales		11,800
Gross profit		5,900

Balance sheet as at 31 December 20X7 (extract)

	$	$
Current assets		
Inventory (from additional information)	1,600	

Example

The trial balance of Elmdale at 31 December 20X8 is as follows:

	Dr $	*Cr* $
Capital account		8,602
Inventory	2,700	
Sales revenue		21,417
Purchases	9,856	
Rent	1,490	
Drawings	4,206	
Electricity	379	
Shop	7,605	
Accounts receivable	2,742	
Accounts payable		3,617
Cash at bank		1,212
Cash in hand	66	
Sundry expenses	2,100	
Wages and salaries	3,704	
	34,848	34,848

In addition, Elmdale calculates that closing inventory should be valued for accounts purposes at $3,060.

You are required to prepare an income statement for the year ended 31 December 20X8 and a balance sheet at that date.

Solution

Step 1

Inventory figures can be inserted into the financial statements without a working. Inventory in the trial balance is opening inventory and goes to the income statement. Inventory not in the trial balance is closing inventory which goes to the income statement *and* the balance sheet.

For information only the inventory account is reproduced below:

Inventory

	$		$
Per trial balance	2,700	Income statement	2,700
Income statement	3,060	Balance c/d	3,060
	5,760		5,760
Balance b/d	3,060		

Step 2

Deal with the other items on the trial balance.

In the case of income statement items, this entails debiting the relevant accounts and crediting income statement (in the case of income) and debiting income statement and crediting the relevant accounts (in the case of expenses). However, as the ledger accounts are not required in a question like this, the items will simply be put into the vertical income statement.

The remaining balances are balance sheet items that are simply listed in the balance sheet.

Step 3

Prepare the income statement.

Income statement for the year ended 31 December 20X8

	$	$
Sales revenue		21,417
Opening inventory	2,700	
Purchases	9,856	
	12,556	
Closing inventory	3,060	
Cost of sales		9,496
Gross profit		11,921
Rent	1,490	
Electricity	379	
Wages and salaries	3,704	
Sundry expenses	2,100	
		7,673
Net profit		4,248

Step 4

Prepare the balance sheet.

Balance sheet as at 31 December 20X8

	$	$
Non-current assets:		
Shop		7,605
Current assets:		
Inventory	3,060	
Receivables	2,742	
Cash in hand	66	
		5,868
		13,473
Capital account:		
Balance at 1 January 20X8	8,602	
Net profit	4,248	
	12,850	
Less: Drawings	4,206	
		8,644
Current liabilities:		
Accounts payable	3,617	
Overdraft	1,212	
		4,829
		13,473

Notes

- Remember that the closing inventory in the balance sheet must agree with the closing inventory in the income statement
- The balance on the trial balance for cash at bank is a credit balance, a liability, and therefore an overdraft.

It is essential to appreciate that adherence to double entry bookkeeping principles is always necessary in the preparation of financial statements.

KEY POINT

Adherence to double entry bookkeeping principles is always necessary in the preparation of financial statements.

ACTIVITY 3

H Hillman extracted the trial balance below from his ledger on 31 March 20X6 in respect of the year then ended:

Inventory at 31 March 20X6 is valued at $300.

Prepare the financial statements of H Hillman, using the vertical format.

	Dr $	*Cr* $
Light and heat	100	
Sales revenue		6,000
Accounts receivable	2,000	
Wages	600	
Drawings	2,100	
Rent	400	
Postage and stationery	200	
Capital at 1 April 20X5		5,500
Purchases	2,800	
Inventory	400	
Accounts payable		800
Fixtures and fittings	3,500	
Cash	200	
	12,300	12,300

Feedback to this activity is at the end of the chapter.

3 Inventory valuation

3.1 Introduction

So far in examples we have been given the valuations of inventory, normally the opening inventory being found on the list of balances and the closing inventory being given in readiness for the final adjustments to that list of balances.

However, it is anything but a simple procedure to arrive at the valuation placed on closing inventory, because:

- initially the existence of the inventory, and the quantities thereof, have to be ascertained by means of an inventory count, and
- following on from this, a valuation has to be placed on the inventory which, as will be seen, may differ according to which accounting policy a company adopts.

KEY POINT

The valuation of inventory is governed by IAS 2 *Inventories*

The valuation of inventory is governed by IAS 2 *Inventories*.

3.2 Definition of inventory and work in progress

KEY POINT

Partly-finished goods are called **work in progress**.

At any point in time most manufacturing and retailing enterprises will hold several categories of inventory including:

- goods purchased for resale
- consumable stores (such as oil)
- raw materials and components (used in the production process)
- partly-finished goods (usually called **work in progress**)
- finished goods (which have been manufactured by the enterprise).

3.3 The matching and prudence concepts

We considered the concept of matching earlier to justify the carrying forward of purchases not sold by the end of the accounting period, to leave the remaining purchases to be 'matched' with sales.

When it comes to placing a value on the inventory carried forward, we have a further concept to consider: the **prudence concept.**

KEY POINT

The **prudence concept** requires the application of a degree of caution in making estimates under conditions of uncertainty.

If it weren't for this concept we would carry forward inventory at its cost to the business. The prudence concept however, requires the application of a degree of caution in making estimates under conditions of uncertainty.

In the context of the value of inventory, this means that if goods are expected to be sold below cost after the balance sheet date (for example, because they are damaged or obsolete), account must be taken of the loss in order to prepare the balance sheet.

KEY POINT

The amount at which inventory should be stated in the balance sheet is the lower of cost and net realisable value.

The amount at which inventory should be stated in the balance sheet is the lower of cost and net realisable value.

3.4 What is cost?

DEFINITION

Cost includes all the expenditure incurred in bringing the product or service to its present location and condition.

Cost includes all the expenditure incurred in bringing the product or service to its present location and condition.

This includes:

- cost of purchase – material costs, import duties, freight
- cost of **conversion** – this is a rather complicated term. It includes **direct costs** and **production overheads**. These terms are explained in the following example.

Example

Gordano is a small furniture manufacturing company. All of its timber is imported from Scandinavia and there are only three basic products – a dining table, a cupboard and a bookcase. At the end of the year the company has 200 completed bookcases in inventory. For final accounts purposes, these will be stated at the lower of cost and net realisable value. How is 'cost' arrived at?

Solution

'Cost' will include several elements:

- **Cost of purchase.** First of all we must identify the timber used in the manufacture of bookcases (as opposed to dining tables and cupboards). The relevant costs will include the cost of the timber, the import duty and all the insurance and freight expenses associated with transporting the timber from Scandinavia to the factory.
- **Cost of conversion.** This will include costs which can be directly linked to the bookcases produced during the year. This includes labour costs 'booked' and sundry material costs (e.g. hinges and screws). **Production overheads** present particular problems. Costs such as factory heat and light, salaries of supervisors and depreciation of equipment are likely to relate to the three product ranges. These costs must be allocated to these product ranges on a reasonable basis. In particular, any percentage additions to cover overheads must be based on the normal level of production. If this proviso was not made, the inventory could be overvalued at the end of a period of low production, because there would be a smaller number of items over which to spread the overhead cost.

These groups of cost must relate to either:

- bookcases sold during the year, or
- bookcases in inventory at the year-end (i.e. 200 bookcases).

3.5 What is net realisable value?

DEFINITION

Net realisable value (NRV) is the revenue (sales proceeds) expected to be earned when the goods are sold, less any selling costs incurred.

Net realisable value (NRV) is the revenue (sales proceeds) expected to be earned in the future when the goods are sold, less any selling costs incurred.

Each individual item or each group of similar items of inventory should be stated in financial statements at the lower of cost and net realisable value. At the balance sheet date it is necessary to make a reasonable estimate of NRV.

ACTIVITY 4

In what circumstances do you think that the net realisable value of inventories might be lower than their cost?

Feedback to this activity is at the end of the chapter.

3.6 Methods of arriving at cost

With the exception of the unit cost method, the techniques mentioned below are not designed to ascertain the *identity* of individual items of inventory, but make *assumptions* as to which items are deemed to be in closing inventory.

Unit cost

DEFINITION

Unit cost is the actual cost of purchasing identifiable units of inventory.

Unit cost is the actual cost of purchasing identifiable units of inventory.

This method is only likely to be used in situations where inventory items are of high value and individually distinguishable. Examples would include jewellery retailers and art dealers, where in each case the proprietors would need to value each item individually.

FIFO: first-in-first-out

DEFINITION

FIFO assumes that the first items of inventory received are the first items to be sold.

In **FIFO**, the assumption is made for costing purposes that the first items of inventory received are the first items to be sold.

Thus every time a sale is made, the cost of goods sold is identified as representing the cost of the oldest goods remaining in inventory.

LIFO: last-in-first-out

LIFO is the reverse of FIFO.

DEFINITION

LIFO assumes that the last items of inventory received are the first items to be sold.

In **LIFO** the assumption for costing purposes is that the last items of inventory received are the first items to be sold.

Every time a sale is made, the cost of goods sold is identified as representing the cost of the newest goods remaining in inventory.

Contrasting LIFO and FIFO

- In a period of inflation, the newest goods are likely to have cost more than the oldest goods. Hence by matching the cost of the oldest goods with the sales revenues, FIFO will give a lower cost of goods sold figure, a higher closing inventory valuation and have a higher reported profit than LIFO.
- LIFO is not generally encouraged by accounting standards but is permitted by IAS 2. This is because LIFO usually does not give a sufficiently close approximation to the actual cost of the inventory.
- In theory the matching of cost and revenues should be carried out each time a sale is made. In practice some modifications to this are likely.

Average cost

DEFINITION

Weighted average cost formula: the cost of each item is determined from the weighted average of the cost of similar items at the beginning and during the period.

Under the weighted average cost formula, the cost of each item is determined from the weighted average of the cost of similar items at the beginning of the period and the cost of similar items purchased or produced during the period.

This calculation can be carried out periodically, or continuously after every purchase. It is a compromise between the extremes of FIFO and LIFO, but it involves much arithmetic.

3.7 Calculation of inventory and cost of sales under these methods

A business is commenced on 1 January and purchases are made as follows:

Month	*No of units*	*Unit price*	*Value*
		$	$
Jan	380	2.00	760
Feb	400	2.50	1,000
Mar	350	2.50	875
Apr	420	2.75	1,155
May	430	3.00	1,290
Jun	440	3.25	1,430
	2,420		6,510

In June, 1,420 articles were sold for $7,000.

(a) Compute the cost of inventory on hand at 30 June using the following methods:

(i) FIFO

(ii) LIFO

(iii) Average cost.

(b) Show the effect of each method on the trading results for the six months.

Solution

(a) **The cost of inventory on hand at 30 June**

Inventory valuation (inventory in hand 2,420 – 1,420 = 1,000 units)

(i) **FIFO – inventory valued at latest purchase prices**

		$
440	articles at $3.25	1,430
430	articles at $3.00	1,290
130	articles at $2.75	357
1,000		3,077

(ii) **LIFO – inventory valued at earliest purchase prices**

		$
380	articles at $2.00	760
620	articles at $2.50	1,550
1,000		2,310

(iii) **Average cost – inventory valued at average purchase price**

$$\frac{\text{Total value}}{\text{Total no of articles}} = \frac{\$6{,}510}{2{,}420} = \$2.69 \text{ per unit}$$

∴ 1,000 articles at $2.69 = $2,690.

(b) **Effect of different inventory methods on trading results**

	No of units	(i) FIFO		(ii) LIFO		(iii) Average	
		$	$	$	$	$	$
Sales revenue	1,420		7,000		7,000		7,000
Purchases	2,420	6,510		6,510		6,510	
Less: Closing inventory	1,000	3,077		2,310		2,690	
Cost of goods sold	1,420		3,433		4,200		3,820
Gross profit			3,567		2,800		3,180

KEY POINT

The method of inventory valuation chosen must be adhered to from one period to the next, so as to give a meaningful trend of trading results.

Each of the above is a means of determining the cost of closing inventory. As can be seen, they each give rise to different gross profits. It is therefore vital that the method of inventory valuation chosen be adhered to from one period to the next, so as to give a meaningful trend of trading results (i.e. the consistency concept).

4 The provisions of IAS 2 *Inventories*

4.1 Introduction

IAS 2 *Inventories* lays down the rules to be applied when valuing inventory and specifies disclosure requirements for the financial statements.

IAS 2 is the first International Accounting Standard we examine in detail. You should recall from Chapter 1 that many IASs contain 'benchmark' treatments, and 'allowable alternative' treatments. You will see this idea in action in IAS 2.

4.2 The basic principle of IAS 2

KEY POINT

The basic principle of IAS 2 is that inventories should be valued at the lower of cost and net realisable value.

The basic principle of IAS 2 is that inventories should be valued at the lower of cost and net realisable value.

4.3 The requirements of IAS 2 for arriving at cost

The cost of inventories should include all costs of purchase, costs of conversion and other costs incurred in bringing the inventories to their present location and condition.

For goods purchased for resale and for raw materials, arriving at cost is reasonably easy. Cost of purchase includes import duties, other taxes (unless recoverable) and transport costs. Trade discounts are obviously to be deducted.

For manufactured goods or work in progress, the problem becomes more complex. Cost must include direct labour and an allocation of fixed and variable overheads. (Fixed overheads are those that remain fairly constant regardless of the volume of production, like factory rent, while variable overheads are those which vary according to the level of production, such as indirect labour or lubricating oils for plant.)

The allocation of fixed overheads needs to be based on the normal level of production, otherwise the cost of inventory could be higher or lower than it should be, as explained above.

KEY POINT

Overhead expenses which must be *excluded* are:

- **selling costs**
- **storage costs**
- **abnormal wastage**
- **administrative overheads.**

Overhead expenses which must be *excluded* are:

- selling costs (excluded because they relate to goods sold, not those held in inventory)
- storage costs
- abnormal wastage of materials, labour or other production costs
- administrative overheads.

4.4 Measurement of cost

As we saw above, there are several ways of deciding which items are deemed to be held in inventory:

- unit cost
- first-in-first-out (FIFO)
- last-in-first-out (LIFO)
- average cost.

Other possibilities are:

- standard cost
- selling price less gross margin.

Standard cost means the cost taking the normal levels of materials, labour, efficiency and capacity utilisation as determined by the costing system of the business.

Selling price less gross margin may be convenient for retailers for whom the selling price is more accessible than the cost price. The inventory is taken at selling price and then reduced to cost by deducting the appropriate percentage gross margin.

Since the objective is to value inventory at cost or a close approximation of cost, method (a) is required for goods whose costs can be specifically identified. For other goods, IAS 2 nominates FIFO or weighted average as **benchmark** treatments, with LIFO as an allowed alternative. Standard cost, or selling price less gross margin, could only be used if it was clear that the resulting inventory figures approximate to the actual cost.

If LIFO is used, some extra disclosure requirements are added.

4.5 Net realisable value

The comparison between cost and net realisable value must be made item by item, not on the total inventory value. It may be acceptable to consider groups of items together if all are worth less than cost.

4.6 Disclosure requirements

IAS 2 contains a number of disclosure requirements, i.e. information which must be disclosed in the financial statements or in a note to those financial statements.

You will not be required to give notes containing inventory information as additions to computational questions on financial statements, but you could be required to know their contents in a non-computational question on inventories.

Under IAS 2 the financial statements should disclose:

- the accounting policies adopted for measuring inventories, including the cost formula used
- the inventory total, analysed into classifications appropriate to the enterprise
- the amount of inventories included at net realisable value
- the amount of any reversal of a writing down to net realisable value (i.e. inventory valued in the previous balance sheet at net realisable value and reinstated to cost in the current balance sheet), and details of the circumstances leading to the reinstatement
- when LIFO is used, the difference between the balance sheet value of the inventories and either:
  - the value of the inventory if FIFO or weighted average methods had been used (with reduction to net realisable value when necessary); or
  - the current cost at the balance sheet date (again with reduction to net realisable value when necessary)
- cost of inventories recognised as an expense during the period; or

  the operating costs, applicable to revenues, recognised as an expense during the period, classified by their nature.

5 Continuous and period end inventory records

5.1 Introduction

In preparing the financial statements, the calculation of what is in closing inventory can be a major exercise for a business. In the previous section we implied that the business will need to count its inventory at the balance sheet date and, in most businesses, this is the most common method. A formal title for the sheets recording the inventory count is 'period end inventory records'.

An alternative would be to have records which show the amount of inventory at any date, i.e. continuous inventory records. These records may take a variety of forms but in essence, a record of each item of inventory would be maintained showing all the receipts and issues for that item.

The merits of continuous inventory records are as follows:

- better information for inventory control
- avoids excessive build up of certain lines of inventory and having insufficient inventory of other lines
- there is less work to be done to calculate inventory at the end of the accounting period.

The merits of period end inventory records are as follows:

- cheaper in most situations than the costs of maintaining continuous inventory records
- even if there is a continuous inventory record, there will still be a need to check the accuracy of the information on record by having a physical check of some of the inventory lines.

Conclusion

In this chapter the preparation of financial statements, the income statement and balance sheet, was considered. In order to prepare the income statement it is necessary to appreciate that the statement itself is in fact a ledger account and it is important to understand the accounting entries that are necessary for inventory at the end of each accounting period.

Inventory is a major adjustment required to the information stored in the ledger accounts and summarised in the list of balances in order to prepare the income statement and balance sheet.

SELF-TEST QUESTIONS

Closing inventory

1 Which accounting concept influences the calculation of gross profit? (1.1)

2 Is it the income statement or the balance sheet that is an account in the double entry accounting system? (1.3)

3 Is opening inventory a debit or a credit balance on the inventory account? (1.5)

4 What is the double entry for closing inventory? (1.5)

Preparation of financial statements

5 Is an overdraft an asset or a liability? (2.1)

Inventory valuation

6 What is the general definition for the cost of inventory? (3.4)

7 What are production overheads? (3.4)

8 Will FIFO or LIFO give a higher cost of sales figure when prices are rising? (3.6)

IAS 2 *Inventories*

9 What items need to be disclosed under IAS 2 in the balance sheet? (4.6)

MULTIPLE-CHOICE QUESTIONS

Question 1

IAS 2 *Inventories* defines the items that may be included in computing the value of an inventory of finished goods manufactured by a business.

Which one of the following lists consists only of items which may be included in the balance sheet value of such inventories according to IAS 2?

A Foreman's wages, carriage inwards, carriage outwards, raw materials

B Raw materials, carriage inwards, costs of storage of finished goods, plant depreciation

C Plant depreciation, carriage inwards, raw materials, foreman's wages

D Carriage outwards, raw materials, foreman's wages, plant depreciation.

Question 2

The closing inventory of X amounted to $116,400 excluding the following two inventory lines:

- 400 items which had cost $4 each. All were sold after the balance sheet date for $3 each, with selling expenses of $200 for the batch.
- 200 different items which had cost $30 each. These items were found to be defective at the balance sheet date. Rectification work after the balance sheet amounted to $1,200, after which they were sold for $35 each, with selling expenses totalling $300.

Which of the following total figures should appear in the balance sheet of X for inventory?

A $122,300

B $121,900

C $122,900

D $123,300

For the answers to these questions, see the 'Answers' section at the end of the book.

EXAM-TYPE QUESTIONS

Question 1: Blabbermouth

Blabbermouth extracted the list of account balances below from his ledger on 31 March 20X7.

Inventory at 31 March 20X7 is valued at $5,200.

You are required to prepare the income statement and balance sheet of Blabbermouth, using the vertical format. **(12 marks)**

	Dr	*Cr*
	$	*$*
Light and heat	100	
Trade receivables	8,250	
Sales revenue		25,375
Wages	8,237	
Drawings by proprietor	3,500	
Rent	500	
Postage and stationery	727	
Capital at 1 April 20X6		18,250
Purchases	17,280	
Inventory	4,100	
Trade payables		7,247
Fixtures and fittings	2,100	
Cash	6,078	
	50,872	50,872

Question 2: Alpha

From the following balances taken from the books of Alpha and the additional information given, **you are required** to prepare the income statement for the year ended 31 December and a balance sheet as at that date:

	$
Sales revenue	39,468
Insurance	580
Plant repairs	110
Rent	1,782
Motor van	980
Plant	2,380
Purchases	27,321
Inventory at 1 Jan (opening)	3,655
Wages	3,563
Discount allowed to customers	437
Motor van expenses	1,019
Shop fittings	1,020
General expenses	522
Capital account – balance 1 Jan (opening)	2,463
Receivables	3,324
Payables	4,370
Cash on hand	212
Personal drawings by proprietor	2,820

Additional information:

(1) The difference in the list of balances is the bank balance at 31 December.

(2) Inventory at 31 December amounted to $3,123.

(3) Adjust for cost of goods taken by Alpha for personal use amounting to $220.

(15 marks)

For the answer to these questions, see the 'Answers' section at the end of the book.

FEEDBACK TO ACTIVITY **1**

Step 1

Record the transactions for the week in the ledger accounts.

Cash

	$		$
Capital	1,000	Purchases	800
Sales revenue	900		

Capital

	$		$
		Cash	1,000

Purchases

	$		$
Cash	800		

Sales revenue

	$		$
		Cash	900

Step 2

Balance off the accounts. Note that as only the cash account has more than one transaction, this is the only one that needs to be balanced. The total on the remaining accounts is simply the single transaction.

Cash

	$		$
Capital	1,000	Purchases	800
Sales revenue	900	Balance c/d	1,100
	1,900		1,900
Balance b/d	1,100		

Step 3

The sales and purchases should be transferred to the income statement.

Sales revenue

	$		$
Income statement	900	Cash	900

Purchases

	$		$
Cash	800	Income statement	800

Income statement

	$		$
Purchases	800	Sales revenue	900

Step 4

As this is the first week of trading for this business there is no opening inventory but the closing inventory must be accounted for by debiting the inventory account (an asset) and crediting the income statement.

The income statement can then be balanced off to give the figure for gross profit.

Inventory

	$		$
Income statement	300		

	$		$
Purchases	800	Sales revenue	900
Gross profit c/d	400	Closing inventory	300
	1,200		1,200
		Gross profit b/d	400

Step 5

The income statement can be prepared in vertical form simply by rearranging the ledger account.

Income statement for week one

	$	$
Sales revenue		900
Cost of goods sold:		
Purchases	800	
Less: Closing inventory	300	
		500
Gross profit		400

Step 6

The balance sheet can then be prepared by listing all of the remaining balances from the ledger accounts.

Balance sheet at the end of week one

	$
Inventory	300
Cash	1,100
	1,400
Capital	1,000
Profit for the week	400
	1,400

FEEDBACK TO ACTIVITY 2

Step 1

Write up the ledger accounts for the second week. Remember that at the end of week one there was $1,100 of cash remaining and this will be shown as the opening balance on the cash account. (Opening balances will be dealt with in more detail later in this chapter.)

There are no opening balances on the sales revenue or purchases accounts as these were cleared out to the income statement at the end of week one.

Once the ledger entries have been written up the cash account can be balanced off.

Cash

	$		$
Balance b/d	1,100	Purchases	1,100
Sales revenue	1,000	Balance c/d	1,000
	2,100		2,100
Balance b/d	1,000		

Sales revenue

	$		$
		Cash	1,000

Purchases

	$		$
Cash	1,100		

Step 2

Transfer the balances on the sales and purchases account to the income statement.

Sales revenue

	$		$
Income statement	1,000	Cash	1,000

Purchases

	$		$
Cash	1,100	Income statement	1,100

Income statement

	$		$
Purchases	1,100	Sales revenue	1,000

Step 3

Remember that this time, as well as there being some closing inventory, there is also some opening inventory, i.e. the closing inventory at the end of week one. This will still be a balance on the inventory account at the end of week one and must be transferred to the income statement.

Inventory

	$		$
Balance b/d	300	Income statement	300

Income statement

	$		$
Purchases	1,100	Sales revenue	1,000
Opening inventory	300		

Step 4

The closing inventory at the end of week two must then be accounted for by debiting the inventory account and crediting the income statement.

Inventory

	$		$
Balance b/d	300	Income statement	300
Income statement	500		

Income statement

	$		$
Purchases	1,100	Sales revenue	1,000
Opening inventory	300	Closing inventory	500
Gross profit c/d	100		
	1,500		1,500
		Gross profit b/d	100

Step 5

Prepare a vertical income statement.

Income statement for week two

	$	$
Sales revenue		1,000
Cost of goods sold:		
Opening inventory	300	
Purchases	1,100	
	1,400	
Less: Closing inventory	500	
		900
Gross profit		100

Step 6

List the remaining balances in the balance sheet.

	$
Inventory	500
Cash	1,000
	1,500
Capital at start of week two	1,400
Profit for week two	100
	1,500

Note: the capital at the beginning of week two is the total capital from the end of week one, that is the opening capital of $1,000 plus the $400 of profit made in week one.

FEEDBACK TO ACTIVITY 3

Your solution should be as follows:

Income statement for the year ended 31 March 20X6

	$	$
Sales revenue		6,000
Opening inventory	400	
Purchases	2,800	
	3,200	
Less: Closing inventory	300	
		2,900
Gross profit		3,100
Wages	600	
Rent	400	
Postage and stationery	200	
Light and heat	100	
		1,300
Net profit		1,800

Balance sheet as at 31 March 20X6

	$	$
Non-current assets:		
Fixtures and fittings		3,500
Current assets:		
Inventory	300	
Accounts receivable	2,000	
Cash	200	
		2,500
		6,000
Capital employed:		
Capital at 1 April 20X5	5,500	
Net profit for year	1,800	
	7,300	
Less: Drawings	2,100	
		5,200
Current liabilities:		
Accounts payable		800
		6,000

FEEDBACK TO ACTIVITY 4

NRV may be relevant in special cases, such as where goods are slow-moving, damaged or obsolete. However, most items of inventory will be stated at cost.

Chapter 5

ACCRUALS, PREPAYMENTS, CASH AND LIABILITIES

CHAPTER CONTENTS

In this chapter the expenses and miscellaneous income of a business will be examined.

The aim with expenses is to ensure that the correct amount is being included in the income statement as the expense for the period, and that any payables or amounts paid in advance for expenses are recognised and shown in the balance sheet.

The aim with items of miscellaneous income is to ensure that the correct amount of income is included in the income statement for the period and that any receivables or amounts received in advance are recognised and shown in the balance sheet.

Such year-end adjustments to expense items can take the form of an entire examination question themselves or more regularly form part of a larger question on some other topic, such as the financial statements of a sole trader, company or partnership.

Objectives

By the time you have finished this chapter you should be able to:

- explain the meaning of the accruals concept
- understand the practical implications of the accruals concept for items of expense and miscellaneous income
- calculate the amounts that should appear in the income statement and balance sheet where there are accruals or prepayments of expenses and items of income
- carry out the double entry required to account for accrued and prepaid expenses and miscellaneous income.

1 The accruals concept

1.1 A fundamental accounting concept

KEY POINT

Income and expenses should be **matched together** and dealt with in the income statement for the period to which they relate, regardless of the period in which the cash was actually received or paid.

The accruals concept has already been introduced. It is identified as a fundamental accounting concept by IAS 1 *Presentation of Financial Statements*. The concept is that income and expenses should be matched together and dealt with in the income statement for the period to which they relate, regardless of the period in which the cash was actually received or paid. Therefore, all of the expenses involved in making the sales for a period should be matched with the sales income and dealt with in the period in which the sales themselves are accounted for.

Examples

Sales revenue

The sales revenue for an accounting period is included in the income statement when the sales are made. This means that when a sale is made on credit, it is recognised in the income statement when the agreement is made and the invoice is sent to the customer rather than waiting until the cash for the sale is received. This is done by setting up an account receivable in the balance sheet for the amount of cash that is due from the sale (debit accounts receivable and credit sales revenue).

Purchases

Similarly purchases are matched to the period in which they were made by accounting for all credit purchases when they took place and setting up an account payable in the balance sheet for the amount due (debit purchases and credit accounts payable).

Cost of sales

The major cost involved in making sales in a period is the actual cost of the goods that are being sold. As well as including purchases in the cost of goods sold, it was explained in the section on inventories that the cost of the items sold are matched to the actual sales by carrying forward the cost of any closing items of inventory at the end of an accounting period to the following period to be matched with the actual sales of those items. Equally, any items of inventory that were not sold in the previous period are brought forward as opening inventory in the income statement to be matched against their sale in the current period by adding their cost to the cost of the purchases for the period.

Expenses

This leaves the expenses of the period that the business has incurred in making its sales, such as rent, electricity, telephone, etc. These must also be matched with the sales for the period and this means that the actual expense incurred in the period should be included in the income statement rather than simply the amount of the expense that has been paid for in cash.

- If the rental due on a business's factory is $5,000 every quarter, then the annual rental expense will be $20,000 whatever the pattern of cash payments for the rental is.
- If a business has an accounting year to 31 December 20X1 and during that year has paid $1,000 of electricity bills and has outstanding a bill for the quarter from 1 October to 31 December 20X1 of $300 then the electricity expense incurred by the business is $1,300 for the year to 31 December 20X1.
- If in the previous example the outstanding bill had been for the period from 1 November 20X1 to 31 January 20X2 then an estimate of the electricity expense for the period to 31 December 20X1 would be:

  $$\$1{,}000 + \left(\tfrac{2}{3} \times 300\right) = \$1{,}200$$

- If a business with an accounting year end of 31 December 20X1 pays for 18 months of insurance on its buildings on 1 January 20X1 at a total cost of $3,000 then the insurance expense for the year to 31 December 20X1 would be:

  $$\frac{12}{18} \times \$3{,}000 = \$2{,}000$$

ACTIVITY 1

Calculate the appropriate expense for the accounting period in the following examples:

(a) For the year to 30 September 20X5 a business paid heating bills of $2,700. At 30 September 20X5, the year end, there was an unpaid bill outstanding of $600 for the three months to 30 November 20X5.

(b) A business paid its rent for the six months to 31 March 20X3 $1,200, for the six months to 30 September 20X3 $1,800 and for the six months to 31 March 20X4 $1,800. If the business's year end is 31 December 20X3, what is the rent expense for that accounting year?

Feedback to this activity is at the end of the chapter.

2 Accrued expenses

2.1 The nature and purpose of an accrual

DEFINITION

An **accrued expense** is an item of expense that has been incurred during the accounting period but has not yet been paid for.

An **accrued expense** is an item of expense that has been incurred during the accounting period but has not yet been paid for.

In order to ensure that the full expenses of the period have been included in the income statement, the accountant must ensure that the expense accounts include not only those items that have been paid for during the period but any outstanding amounts due for expenses. In some instances a bill or invoice will have been received for any outstanding amounts but in other instances when the accounts are prepared any additional expense items will need to be estimated from previous years and earlier bills or invoices.

Example with no opening accrual

John Simnel's business has an accounting year end of 31 December 20X1. He rents factory space at a rental cost of $5,000 per quarter payable in arrears. During the year to 31 December 20X1 his cash payments of rent have been as follows:

	$
31 March (for quarter to 31 March 20X1)	5,000
29 June (for quarter to 30 June 20X1)	5,000
2 October (for quarter to 30 September 20X1)	5,000

The final payment due on 31 December 20X1 for the quarter to that date was not paid until 4 January 20X2.

It should be quite clear that the rental expense for John Simnel's business for the year to 31 December 20X1 is $20,000 (4 × $5,000) even though the final payment for the year was not made until after the year end. It should also be noted that at 31 December 20X1 John Simnel's business owes the landlord $5,000 of rental for the period from 1 October to 31 December 20X1.

Solution

Step 1

In order to account for this situation, the cash payments would first be entered into the Factory rent account.

Factory rent

20X1	$	*20X1*	$
31 Mar Cash	5,000		
29 June Cash	5,000		
2 Oct Cash	5,000		

Step 2

The charge to the income statement that is required at 31 December 20X1 is $20,000 and this is entered into the account on the credit side (the debit is the expense in the income statement).

Factory rent

20X1	$	*20X1*	$
31 Mar Cash	5,000		
29 June Cash	5,000		
2 Oct Cash	5,000		
		31 Dec Income statement	20,000

Step 3

In order for the account to balance, a further debit entry of $5,000 is required:

- this is in fact the balance carried down on the account
- the double entry is to debit the account above the total with $5,000 and show a credit in the account below the total
- this gives a brought down credit balance representing the amount owed to the landlord for the final quarter's rent.

Factory rent

20X1	$	*20X1*	$
31 Mar Cash	5,000		
29 June Cash	5,000		
2 Oct Cash	5,000		
31 Dec Bal c/d	5,000	31 Dec Income statement	20,000
	20,000		20,000
		20X2	
		1 Jan Bal b/d	5,000

By this method the correct expense has been charged to the income statement under the accruals concept, $20,000, and the amount of $5,000 owed to the landlord has been recognised as a credit balance on the account.

This credit balance would be listed in the balance sheet under the heading of current liabilities and described as an accrued expense.

Example with an opening accrual

During the year to 31 December 20X2 John Simnel's rental charge remained the same and his payments were as follows:

	$
4 January (for quarter to 31 December 20X1)	5,000
28 March (for quarter to 31 March 20X2)	5,000
28 June (for quarter to 30 June 20X2)	5,000
4 October (for quarter to 30 September 20X2)	5,000
23 December (for quarter to 31 December 20X2)	5,000

The first step in accounting for these transactions is to enter the cash payments in the Factory rent account. Note that there is already a brought down balance on the account at 1 January 20X2 being the accrued expense of $5,000, a creditor and therefore a credit balance, at 31 December 20X1.

Factory rent

20X2	$	*20X2*	$
4 Jan Cash	5,000	1 Jan Bal b/d	5,000
28 Mar Cash	5,000		
28 June Cash	5,000		
4 Oct Cash	5,000		
23 Dec Cash	5,000		

Even though $25,000 has been paid in cash during the year, the income statement expense is still only $20,000 (4 × $5,000); if this transfer to the income statement is made then the account will balance at 31 December 20X2, as there is no accrued expense to be carried forward this year since the amount due for the final quarter of the year was paid before the year end.

Factory rent

20X2		$	*20X2*		$
4 Jan	Cash	5,000	1 Jan	Bal b/d	5,000
28 Mar	Cash	5,000			
28 June	Cash	5,000			
4 Oct	Cash	5,000			
23 Dec	Cash	5,000	31 Dec	Income statement	20,000
		25,000			25,000

KEY POINT

Accounting treatment of an **accrued expense**:

- debit the expense account
- carry the balance forward as an accrued expense.

The accounting treatment of an accrued expense is to debit the expense account, thereby increasing the expense in the income statement, and carry this balance forward as an account payable, an accrued expense, in the balance sheet.

ACTIVITY **2**

A business has paid the following electricity bills during the year to 31 December 20X6.

	$
28 Feb: For the three months to 28 February 20X6	300
31 May: For the three months to 31 May 20X6	540
31 Aug: For the three months to 31 August 20X6	220
30 Nov: For the three months to 30 November 20X6	360

It is estimated that the electricity used in December 20X6 totalled $120.

Write up the electricity account for the year ended 31 December 20X6.

Feedback to this activity is at the end of the chapter.

3 Prepaid expenses

3.1 The nature and purpose of a prepayment

DEFINITION

A **prepaid expense** is an item of expense that has been paid during the current accounting period but relates to the next accounting period.

A **prepaid expense** is an item of expense that has been paid during the current accounting period but relates to the next accounting period.

As well as ensuring that all of the expenses incurred in the period appear in the income statement, the accountant must also ensure that no items of expense that relate to future periods, but have already been paid for, are shown as expenses of the current period.

Example with no opening prepayment

John Simnel also pays insurance on the factory that he rents and this is paid in advance. His payments during 20X1 for this insurance were as follows:

	$
1 January (for three months to 31 March 20X1)	800
28 March (for six months to 30 September 20X1)	1,800
2 October (for six months to 31 March 20X2)	1,800

The insurance expense for the year to 31 December 20X1 can be calculated as follows:

	$
1 January to 31 March 20X1	800
1 April to 30 September 20X1	1,800
1 October to 31 December 20X1 ($\frac{3}{6}$ × 1,800)	900
	3,500

The remaining $900 that was paid on 2 October, which is not to be charged to the income statement for the year to 31 December 20X1, is a prepaid expense. It is an amount that has been paid in advance to the insurance company and as such it has the characteristics of an account receivable, the insurance company effectively owing the $900 back to John Simnel at 31 December 20X1.

Solution

Step 1

In order to account for the insurance expense, again the cash payments should be entered first into the Factory insurance account.

Factory insurance

20X1	$	20X1	$
1 Jan Cash	800		
28 Mar Cash	1,800		
2 Oct Cash	1,800		

Step 2

- The charge to the income statement calculated above as $3,500 is then entered in the account and in order for the account to balance a further credit entry of $900 is required.
- The double entry is to credit the account above the total with $900 and put the debit entry in below the total at 1 Jan 20X2.
- This is the prepayment that is to be carried down and will appear as a brought down debit balance.

Factory insurance

20X1	$	20X1	$
1 Jan Cash	800		
28 Mar Cash	1,800	31 Dec Income statement	3,500
2 Oct Cash	1,800	31 Dec Bal c/d	900
	4,400		4,400
20X2			
1 Jan Bal b/d	900		

- This has given the correct charge to the income statement of $3,500 for the year to 31 December 20X1 and has recognised that there is a receivable or prepayment of $900 at 31 December 20X1.
- The $900 balance will appear in the balance sheet as a current asset under the heading of prepayments or prepaid expenses.

Example with opening prepayment

In writing up expense accounts, care must be taken to remember to include any opening balances on the account which were accruals or prepayments at the end of the previous year. For example, John Smith pays his annual rent of $4,000 in two equal instalments of $2,000 each on 1 April and 1 October each year. His rent account for the year to 31 December 20X1 would therefore look like:

Rent

20X1		$	*20X1*		$
1 Jan	Bal b/d ($\frac{3}{6}$ × 2,000)	1,000			
1 April	Cash	2,000	31 Dec	Income statement	4,000
1 Oct	Cash	2,000	31 Dec	Bal c/d ($\frac{3}{6}$ × 2,000)	1,000
		5,000			5,000

Note that at 1 January there is an opening debit balance on the account of $1,000. This is the three months rent from 1 January 20X1 to 31 March 20X1 that had been paid for on 1 October 20X0. You were not specifically told this opening balance but would be expected to work it out from the information given.

KEY POINT

Prepaid expense:

- credit the expense account with the amount of the prepayment
- carry the balance forward as a prepayment.

The treatment of a prepaid expense is to credit the expense account with the amount of the prepayment, thereby reducing the expense to be charged to the income statement, and to carry the balance forward as a prepayment, in the balance sheet.

4 Examination-style problems

Some examination questions can be more complicated than the examples given above, having both brought down and carried down accruals and prepayments. An example might use a telephone expense, as the telephone bill will tend to be made up of two elements. There will be a charge for the actual rental of the telephones and lines which will normally be paid in advance, and a further charge for the actual calls made paid in arrears.

Example

The details of John Simnel's telephone bills for 20X1 are as follows:

	$
Quarterly rental payable in advance on 1 February, 1 May, 1 August and 1 November each year	60
Calls paid in arrears for previous three months:	
1 February 20X1	120
1 May 20X1	99
1 August 20X1	144
1 November 20X1	122
1 February 20X2	132

His telephone account for the year to 31 December 20X1 is to be written up.

Solution

Step 1

Any opening balances for accruals or prepayments at the beginning of the year should be calculated and then entered into the account.

- The opening debit balance represents the prepayment of the rental at 31 December 20X0. On 1 November 20X0 a payment of $60 would have been made to cover the period from 1 November 20X0 to 31 January 20X1. The amount of the 20X1 expense paid in 20X0 is therefore $\frac{1}{3}$ × $60 = $20.

- The opening credit balance represents the calls made in November and December 20X0 that were not paid for until 1 February 20X1. This can be approximated as $\frac{2}{3} \times \$120 = \$80$.

Telephone

20X1		$	*20X1*		$
1 Jan	Bal b/d	20	1 Jan	Bal b/d	80

Step 2

The cash payments made during the year should be entered into the account.

Telephone

20X1		$	*20X1*		$
1 Jan	Bal b/d	20	1 Jan	Bal b/d	80
1 Feb	Cash – rental	60			
1 Feb	Cash – calls	120			
1 May	Cash – rental	60			
1 May	Cash – calls	99			
1 Aug	Cash – rental	60			
1 Aug	Cash – calls	144			
1 Nov	Cash – rental	60			
1 Nov	Cash – calls	122			

Step 3

Any closing accruals and prepayments should be calculated and entered into the account.

- There is a closing prepayment of telephone rental. $60 was paid on 1 November 20X1 for the following three months rental. This covers November and December 20X1 as well as January 20X2. The prepayment is the amount that relates to January 20X2
$\frac{1}{3} \times \$60 = \$20$.

- The accrued expense at 31 December 20X1 is for November and December's calls that will not be paid for until 1 February 20X2. These can be estimated as $\frac{2}{3} \times \$132 = \$88$.

- Finally the income statement charge can be entered as the balancing figure in the account.

Telephone

20X1		$	*20X1*		$
1 Jan	Bal b/d	20	1 Jan	Bal b/d	80
1 Feb	Cash – rental	60			
1 Feb	Cash – calls	120			
1 May	Cash – rental	60			
1 May	Cash – calls	99			
1 Aug	Cash – rental	60			
1 Aug	Cash – calls	144			
1 Nov	Cash – rental	60			
1 Nov	Cash – calls	122	31 Dec	Income statement (bal fig)	733
31 Dec	Bal c/d (accrual)	88	31 Dec	Bal c/d (prepayment)	20
		833			833
20X2			20X2		
1 Jan	Bal b/d	20	1 Jan	Bal b/d	88

Step 4

The income statement expense that was included in the account as a balancing figure could be proved, although this is not generally necessary in actual questions.

	$
Rental charge for 1 January to 31 December 20X1 (4 × 60)	240
Calls:	
1 January to 31 January 20X1 ($\frac{1}{3}$ × 120)	40
1 February to 30 April 20X1	99
1 May to 31 July 20X1	144
1 August to 31 October 20X1	122
1 November to 31 December 20X1 ($\frac{2}{3}$ × 132)	88
	733

5 Miscellaneous income

So far all of the examples have concerned expenses of the business as these are the most common areas for accruals and prepayments to occur. However, some organisations also have sources of miscellaneous income which may also be prepaid or accrued.

Example

John Simnel sublets part of his factory space for a quarterly rental in advance of $900. The payments are due on 1 March, 1 June, 1 September and 1 December each year and are always paid on time. The rental receivable account for the year to 31 December 20X1 will show both an opening and a closing prepayment of rental of ($\frac{2}{3}$ × $900) = $600. However the account is showing income (rather than an expense) and therefore income received in advance is effectively a creditor. The opening prepayment will therefore be a credit balance brought down and the closing prepayment a debit balance carried down and credit balance brought down on 1 January 20X2.

The cash entries are also cash receipts and therefore will be credit entries in the rental income account (debit in the cash account).

The income which will be credited to the income statement (debit the rental income account) will be $3,600 (4 × $900).

Rental income

20X1		$	*20X1*		$
			1 Jan	Bal b/d	600
			1 Mar	Cash	900
			1 June	Cash	900
31 Dec	Income statement	3,600	1 Sept	Cash	900
31 Dec	Bal c/d	600	1 Dec	Cash	900
		4,200			4,200
			20X2		
			1 Jan	Bal b/d	600

The $600 credit balance brought down at 31 December 20X1 would be shown in the balance sheet as a payable and described as **income received in advance** or **deferred income** or **deferred revenue.**

ACTIVITY 3

Have a go at this short example before looking at the solution.

A business receives rental income in cash of $2,000 on 30 June 20X4, and at its year end of 30 September 20X4 there is another $1,500 of rental income due which has not yet been received. Write up the ledger account for rental income for the year ended 30 September 20X4.

Feedback to this activity is at the end of the chapter.

6 Liabilities and cash

6.1 Definition and examples of liabilities

DEFINITION

Liabilities are the financial obligations of an enterprise.

Liabilities are the financial obligations of an enterprise. They may arise as a result of a trading transaction or may represent the obligation to repay monies borrowed by the enterprise.

Examples are trade accounts payable, loans from a bank, and accruals made at the year end before an invoice has been received.

6.2 Distinction between current and non-current liabilities

It is conventional to distinguish current and non-current liabilities when preparing a balance sheet. The distinction is useful information to a user of the accounts as he can better determine the ability of the business to pay the liabilities when they become due for payment.

DEFINITION

A **current liability** is a liability which is payable within 12 months of the balance sheet date.

A **current liability** is a liability which is payable within 12 months of the balance sheet date. A **non-current liability** is any other liability.

This rule is precisely applied. If a liability is due for payment after 12 months and one day, it is shown as a non-current liability.

6.3 Disclosure of liabilities on the balance sheet

Liabilities are disclosed under the two headings: current and non-current. Other terms may be used for non-current, such as 'long-term'.

It is mainly loans which are shown under the heading 'non-current'. Most other liabilities are due for payment quite quickly, e.g. trade accounts payable typically have a 30 day settlement and bank overdrafts are technically repayable on demand (i.e. when the bank asks for the money back).

6.4 Bank and cash balances in a balance sheet

Bank and cash balances are the most liquid item that a business possesses. As such it is conventional to show them as the last item under current assets. Cash at the bank and cash in hand (i.e. actually in the form of cash at the balance sheet date) are often shown as one item in the balance sheet under the heading 'cash at bank and in hand'.

A business may have more than one type of bank account, even with the same bank. A current account for example will deal with all the trading transactions, and a deposit account may be used to store temporary surpluses of money so that interest can be received. When some of the cash is required to pay for trading transactions it will be transferred back from the deposit account to the current account. It can happen that such transfers are not made in time with the consequence that the current account becomes overdrawn. If this happens at the balance sheet date, it is important to show the overdraft as a current liability and the deposit account as a current asset, i.e. the two amounts should not be netted off.

Conclusion

This chapter introduces the accruals concept and its practical implications. It is a very important chapter – examiners' reports on candidates' performance frequency refer to weakness in this area, so study it well before proceeding to the next chapter.

SELF-TEST QUESTIONS

The accruals concept

1 What is meant by the accruals concept? (1.1)

2 Which International Accounting Standard introduces the accruals concept? (1.1)

3 When a sale is made on credit what is the other side of the double entry? (1.1)

4 How is the cost of sales expense matched to the sales for the period? (1.1)

Accrued expenses

5 What is the definition of an accrued expense? (2.1)

Prepaid expenses

6 What is the definition of a prepaid expense? (3.1)

Miscellaneous income

7 If income is received in advance, will this be shown as an asset or a liability in the balance sheet? (5)

EXAM-TYPE QUESTIONS

Question 1: Dundee Engineering

Dundee Engineering has a number of motor vehicles that are used within the business. The expenses of running these vehicles are recorded in the Motor expenses and insurance account. At 1 May 20X7 there were garage bills accrued of $478 and insurance that had been prepaid of $290. During the year to 30 April 20X8 the transactions shown below took place.

	$
30 June 20X7 paid garage bills	698
1 September 20X7 paid insurance for half of the motor vehicles for the year to 30 August 20X8	3,480
1 December 20X7 paid insurance for remaining motor vehicles for the year to 30 November	3,900

At 30 April 20X8 there were garage bills unpaid totalling $356.

You are required to write up the Motor expenses and insurance account for the year ended 30 April 20X8. **(10 marks)**

Question 2: Heilbronn Properties

Heilbronn Properties has purchased a number of different properties over the years that it has been in business by way of a variety of loans. Some of the interest on the loans is paid in arrears and some in advance.

A number of these properties are rented out to tenants some of whom pay their rent in advance and some in arrears.

Interest payable and prepaid and rental due and received in advance at the beginning and end of Heilbronn Properties' accounting year are as follows:

	31 July 20X4	*31 July 20X5*
	$	$
Interest payable	12,000	14,500
Interest prepaid	8,000	6,400
Rental due from tenants	15,000	19,000
Rental received in advance from tenants	3,000	2,500

During the year to 31 July 20X5 the amount of interest payable charged to the income statement was $56,000 and the cash collected from rental tenants was $116,000.

You are required to write up the Interest payable account and the Rental income account for the year ended 31 July 20X5. **(12 marks)**

For the answers to these questions, see the 'Answers' section at the end of the book.

FEEDBACK TO ACTIVITY 1

The solutions are as follows:

(a) $2,700 + ($\frac{1}{3}$ × 600) = $2,900

(b)

	$
Rent for 1 January to 31 March 20X3 ($\frac{3}{6}$ × 1,200)	600
Rent for 1 April to 30 September 20X3	1,800
Rent for 1 October to 31 December 20X3 ($\frac{3}{6}$ × 1,800)	900
Rent expense for the year to 31 December 20X3	3,300

FEEDBACK TO ACTIVITY 2

Step 1

- Calculate the opening accrual as at 31 December 20X5. If the bill for the three months to 28 February 20X6 is $300 then the amount that relates to December 20X5 (the opening accrual) is $\frac{1}{3}$ × $300 = $100.
- Enter the opening accrual in the ledger account.

Electricity

20X6		$	*20X6*		$
			1 Jan	Bal b/d	100

Step 2

Enter the cash payments in the ledger account.

Electricity

20X6		$	*20X6*		$
28 Feb	Cash	300	1 Jan	Bal b/d	100
31 May	Cash	540			
31 Aug	Cash	220			
30 Nov	Cash	360			

Step 3

- Calculate and enter the closing accrual (in this instance the amount for December 20X6 is given as $120).
- Enter the income statement transfer as a balancing figure.

Electricity

20X6		$	20X6		$
28 Feb	Cash	300	1 Jan	Bal b/d	100
31 May	Cash	540			
31 Aug	Cash	220			
30 Nov	Cash	360			
31 Dec	Bal c/d	120	31 Dec	Income statement	1,440
		1,540			1,540
			1 Jan	Bal b/d	120

FEEDBACK TO ACTIVITY 3

Your solution should be as follows:

Rental income

20X4		$	20X4		$
			30 June	Cash	2,000
30 Sept	Income statement	3,500	30 Sept	Bal c/d	1,500
		3,500			3,500
1 Oct	Bal b/d	1,500			

The income to the income statement is increased by crediting the rental income account with the $1,500 due but not yet received. The $1,500 is also carried down as a debit balance, a receivable for rental due which would be shown under current assets in the balance sheet.

Chapter 6
RECEIVABLES AND BAD DEBTS

CHAPTER CONTENTS

In this chapter consideration will be given to the situation where a debtor of the organisation either does not pay his debt or there is some doubt about the eventual payment of all or part of that debt. Both the ledger accounting entries for these situations and the presentation of the financial statements will be examined.

Objectives

By the time you have finished this chapter you should be able to:

- understand the meaning of the terms bad debt and doubtful debt
- explain the accounting treatment of a bad debt written off
- explain the ledger entries for setting up an allowance for doubtful debts and for both increasing and decreasing that allowance
- explain the ledger entries for a bad debt recovered
- understand the financial statement presentation for bad debts and doubtful debt allowances.

1 Sales and accounting concepts

1.1 Definition of a trade account receivable

When a sale is made, it might be a sale for cash or it might be a sale on credit. If the sale is for cash then the customer pays for the goods immediately when the sale is made. If the sale is on credit terms then the customer will probably take the goods with him or arrange to have them delivered but he will not pay for the goods at that time. Instead, the customer will be given or sent an invoice detailing the goods and their price and the normal payment terms. This will tell the customer when he is expected to pay for those goods.

1.2 Accruals concept

KEY POINT

Under the accruals concept, a sale is included in the ledger accounts at the time that it is made.

Under the accruals concept, a sale is included in the ledger accounts at the time that it is made. For a cash sale, this will be when the cash or cheque is paid by the customer and the double entry will be:

Dr Cash account
Cr Sales revenue account.

For a sale on credit, the sale is made at the time that the invoice is sent to the customer and therefore the accounting entries are made at that time as follows:

Dr Account receivable account
Cr Sales revenue account.

When the customer eventually settles the invoice the double entry will be:

Dr Cash account
Cr Account receivable account.

This then clears out the balance on the customer's account.

1.3 Realisation concept

KEY POINT

The **realisation concept** allows gains or profits to be accounted for at the time that the transaction is made.

The **realisation concept** allows gains or profits, such as those made on sales, to be recognised and accounted for at the time that the transaction is made and the receipt of cash from that transaction is reasonably certain. Therefore, under the realisation concept there is no necessity to wait until the cash from a credit sale is received before the sale is recognised. Thus, the double entry shown above, setting up an account receivable at the time that the invoice is sent out, is appropriate.

1.4 Collectability of debts

The problem that businesses face with credit sales is that of the collectability of the amounts owing on sales invoices. If a customer is fraudulent and disappears without trace before payment of the amount due, then it is unlikely that such amounts will ever be recovered. If a customer is declared bankrupt, then again it is unlikely that he will be able to pay the amounts due. If a customer is having financial difficulties or is in liquidation, then there is likely to be some doubt as to his eventual ability to pay.

KEY POINT

Bad debt: when it is highly unlikely that the amount owing by a customer will be received.

Doubtful debt: when there is some doubt about the reliability of the debtor.

If a business is faced with a situation where it is highly unlikely that the amount owing by a customer will be received, then this debt is known as a **bad debt**. As it will probably never be received, it is written off by writing it out of the ledger accounts completely.

If the eventual receipt of cash from a customer is possible but there is some doubt about the reliability of the debtor, then such a debt is known as a **doubtful debt**. It is still hoped that such a debt will be received and therefore it will remain in the ledger accounts. However, in order to be prudent, such a debt will be allowed for. This means that the possible loss from not receiving the cash will be accounted for immediately, whilst the amount of the original debt will still remain in the ledger account just in case the customer does eventually pay.

2 Bad debts

2.1 Introduction

DEFINITION

A **bad debt** is a debt which is, or is considered to be, uncollectable.

A **bad debt** is a debt which is, or is considered to be, uncollectable.

If a debt is considered to be uncollectable then it would be prudent to remove it totally from the accounts and to charge the amount as an expense to the income statement. The original sale remains in the accounts as this did actually take place. The debt is, however, removed as it is now considered that the debt will never be paid and an expense is charged to the income statement for bad debts.

The double entry required to achieve these effects is:

Dr Bad debts expense account

Cr Accounts receivable.

2.2 Example

Abacus & Co have total accounts receivable at the end of their accounting period of $45,000. Of these it is discovered that one, Mr James Scott who owes $790, has been declared bankrupt, and another who gave his name as Peter Campbell has totally disappeared owing Abacus & Co $1,240.

2.3 Solution

Step 1

Enter the opening balance in the accounts receivable account. As accounts receivable are an asset, then this will be on the debit side of the ledger account.

Accounts receivable

20XX	$	*20XX*	$
Opening balance	45,000		

Step 2

As the two debts are considered to be irrecoverable, they must be removed from accounts receivable by a credit entry and a corresponding debit entry to a bad debts expense account.

Accounts receivable

20XX	$	*20XX*	$
Opening balance	45,000	Bad debts expense – J Scott	790
		Bad debts expense – P Campbell	1,240

Bad debts expense

20XX	$	*20XX*	$
Receivables – J Scott	790		
Receivables – P Campbell	1,240		

Step 3

The accounts receivable account must now be balanced and the closing balance would appear in the balance sheet as the accounts receivable figure at the end of the period.

Accounts receivable

20XX	$	*20XX*	$
Opening balance	45,000	Bad debts expense – J Scott	790
		Bad debts expense – P Campbell	1,240
		Balance c/d	42,970
	45,000		45,000
Balance b/d	42,970		

$42,970 would appear in the balance sheet as the figure for accounts receivable under current assets at the end of the accounting period.

Step 4

Finally, the bad debts expense account should be balanced and the balance written off to the income statement as an expense of the period.

Bad debts expense

20XX	$	*20XX*	$
Receivables – J Scott	790	Income statement	2,030
Receivables – P Campbell	1,240		
	2,030		2,030

Note that the sales revenue account has not been altered and the original sales of $790 to James Scott and $1,240 to Peter Campbell remain. This is because these sales actually took place and it is only after the sale that the expense of not being able to collect these debts has occurred.

KEY POINT

When a debt is considered to be bad then it is **written out** of the accounts completely.

When a debt is considered to be bad, then it is written out of the accounts completely by removing it from receivables and charging the amount as an expense to the income statement in the period in which the debt was determined as bad.

3 Doubtful debts

3.1 Introduction

DEFINITION

A **doubtful debt** is an amount owing to the business concerning which there is some doubt as to its collectability.

A **doubtful debt** is an amount owing to the business concerning which there is some doubt as to its collectability.

A doubtful debt is one about which there is some cause for concern but which is not yet definitely irrecoverable. Therefore, although it is prudent immediately to recognise the possible expense of not collecting the debt in the income statement, it would also be wise to keep the original debt in the accounts in case the debtor does in fact pay up.

This is achieved by the following double entry:

Dr Bad debts expense account

Cr Allowance for doubtful debts account.

3.2 The difference between a bad debt written off and a doubtful debt allowance

As with the example of a bad debt, the expense is written off in the bad debts expense account but this time the debt is *not* removed from receivables. Instead, an allowance is set up which is a credit balance. This is netted off against trade receivables in the balance sheet to give a net figure for receivables that are probably recoverable.

3.3 Types of doubtful debt

KEY POINT

Use a **specific allowance** where a customer is known to be in financial difficulties.

Use a **general allowance** for all doubtful recoverables other than the specific cases.

There are two types of amount that are likely to be considered as doubtful debts in an organisation's accounts:

- There will be some specific debts where the customer is known to be in financial difficulties and therefore the amount owing may not be recoverable. The allowance for such a debt is known as a **specific allowance**.
- The past experience and history of a business will indicate that not all of its trade receivables will be recoverable in full. It may not be possible to indicate the precise debtors that will not pay but an estimate may be made that a certain percentage is likely not to pay. The allowance made against this percentage of receivables is known as a **general allowance**.

3.4 Example – general allowance for doubtful debts

On 31 December 20X1 Jake Williams had receivables of $10,000. From past experience Jake estimated that 3% of these customers were likely never to pay their debts and he therefore wished to make a general doubtful debt allowance for this amount.

During 20X2 Jake made sales on credit totalling $100,000 and received cash from his customers of $94,000. He still considered that 3% of the receivables were doubtful and should be allowed for.

During 20X3 Jake made sales of $95,000 and collected $96,000 from his debtors. At 31 December 20X3 Jake still considered that 3% of his receivables were doubtful and should be allowed for.

3.5 Solution

Step 1

Enter the balance on the receivables account at 31 December 20X1.

Receivables

20X1	$	*20X1*	$
31 Dec	10,000		

Step 2

Set up an allowance for 3% of $10,000, $300, by debiting the bad debts expense account and crediting the allowance for doubtful debts account.

Bad debts expense

20X1	$	*20X1*	$
31 Dec Allowance for doubtful debts	300		

Allowance for doubtful debts

20X1	$	*20X1*	$
		31 Dec Bad debts expense	300

Step 3

Balance off the three accounts.

Receivables

20X1	$	*20X1*	$
31 Dec	10,000	31 Dec Bal c/d	10,000
	10,000		10,000
20X2			
1 Jan Bal b/d	10,000		

This balance of $10,000 will appear in the balance sheet under current assets as the receivables at 31 December 20X1.

Bad debts expense

20X1	$	*20X1*	$
31 Dec Allowance for doubtful debts	300	Income statement	300
	300		300

This is the expense for the period to be included in the income statement.

Allowance for doubtful debts

	$		$
20X1		*20X1*	
31 Dec Bal c/d	300	31 Dec Bad debts expense	300
	300		300
		20X2	
		1 Jan Bal b/d	300

This credit balance of $300 is included in the balance sheet under current assets and netted off against the receivables at the end of 20X1 in order to indicate the amount of receivables that are doubtful.

An extract from the balance sheet would be as follows:

	$	$
Current assets		
Trade receivables	10,000	
Less: Allowance for doubtful debts	300	
		9,700

Step 4

Write up the receivables account for 20X2 and balance it off to find the receivables figure at 31 December 20X2.

Receivables

	$		$
20X2		*20X2*	
1 Jan Bal b/d	10,000	31 Dec Cash	94,000
31 Dec Sales revenue	100,000	31 Dec Bal c/d	16,000
	110,000		110,000
20X3			
1 Jan Bal b/d	16,000		

Step 5

Set up the allowance required of 3% of $16,000, $480. Remember that there is already an opening balance on the allowance account of $300. Therefore in order to end 20X2 with a total balance on the allowance account of $480 only a further $180 will need to be charged to the bad debts expense account for the period and thus to the income statement.

Bad debts expense

	$		$
20X2		*20X2*	
31 Dec Allowance for doubtful debts	180	31 Dec Income statement	180
	180		180

Allowance for doubtful debts

20X2	$	*20X2*	$
		1 Jan Bal b/d	300
31 Dec Bal c/d	480	31 Dec Bad debts expense	180
	480		480
		20X3	
		1 Jan Bal b/d	480

Step 6

The extract from the balance sheet at 31 December 20X2 would be as follows:

	$	$
Current assets:		
Trade receivables	16,000	
Less: Allowance for doubtful debts	480	
		15,520

KEY POINT

Allowance for doubtful debts:

- Year 1: allow full amount
- Later years: allow required increase.

When an allowance for doubtful debts is first made, then the full amount of the allowance is charged to the income statement for the period. In subsequent years, if the allowance required increases, then it is only necessary to charge the increase in allowance over the period to the income statement.

Step 7

Write up the receivables account for 20X3. Balance off the account to find the receivables at 31 December 20X3.

Receivables

20X3	$	*20X3*	$
1 Jan Bal b/d	16,000	31 Dec Cash	96,000
31 Dec Sales revenue	95,000	31 Dec Bal c/d	15,000
	111,000		111,000
20X4			
1 Jan Bal b/d	15,000		

Step 8

Set up the allowance required at 31 December 20X3 of 3% of $15,000, $450. This time there is already an opening balance on the allowance for doubtful debts account of $480.

The allowance is to be reduced and this is done by debiting the allowance account with the amount of the decrease required ($480 – $450 = $30) and crediting the bad debts expense account.

The credit on the bad debts expense account is transferred to the income statement for the period as an item of sundry income or a negative expense and is described as 'decrease in doubtful debts allowance'.

Allowance for doubtful debts

20X3	$	*20X3*	$
31 Dec Bad debts expense	30	1 Jan Bal b/d	480
31 Dec Bal c/d	450		
	480		480
		20X4	
		1 Jan Bal b/d	450

Bad debts expense

20X3	$	*20X3*	$
31 Dec Income statement	30	31 Dec Allowance for doubtful debts	30
	30		30

Step 9

The extract from the balance sheet at 31 December 20X3 would be as follows:

	$	$
Current assets:		
Trade receivables	15,000	
Less: Allowance for doubtful debts	450	
		14,550

KEY POINT

To **decrease allowance** for doubtful debts:

- debit decrease to allowance for doubtful debts
- credit decrease to bad debts expense account.

If the allowance for doubtful debts is to be decreased from one period end to another, then the allowance for doubtful debts account will be debited with the amount of the decrease and the bad debts expense account will be credited.

ACTIVITY 1

John Stamp has opening balances at 1 January 20X6 on his trade receivables account and allowance for doubtful debts account of $68,000 and $3,400 respectively. During the year to 31 December 20X6 John Stamp makes credit sales of $354,000 and receives cash from his debtors of $340,000.

At 31 December 20X6 John Stamp reviews his receivables listing and acknowledges that he is unlikely ever to receive debts totalling $2,000. These are to be written off as bad. John also wishes to allow for 5% of his remaining receivables after writing off the bad debts.

You are required to write up the receivables account, allowance for doubtful debts account and the bad debts expense account for the year to 31 December 20X6.

Feedback to this activity is at the end of the chapter.

3.6 Disclosure of trade receivables in the balance sheet after bad debts and a doubtful debt allowance

Note that the bad debt does not appear on the balance sheet but the allowance does.

The relevant extract from the balance sheet at 31 December 20X6 would be as follows:

	$	$
Current assets:		
Trade receivables	80,000	
Less: Allowance for doubtful debts	4,000	
		76,000

3.7 The corresponding charges or credits in the income statement

The income statement records the combined effect of the bad debts written off and the movement in the allowance.

Income statement for the year ended 31 December 20X6 (extract)

Expenses	$
Bad debts	2,600

Example – specific allowance for doubtful debts

Steven Saunders has accounts receivable of $11,200 at his year end of 31 May 20X4. Of these he decides that there is some doubt as to whether or not he will receive a sum of $500 from Peter Foster and he also wishes to allow for the possibility of not receiving 2% of his remaining receivables.

At 1 June 20X3 Steven Saunders had a balance on his allowance for doubtful debts account of $230.

Solution

Step 1

Calculate the allowance for doubtful debts required at 31 May 20X4.

	$
Specific allowance against Peter Foster's debt	500
General allowance against remaining balances (($11,200 – 500) × 2%)	214
Total allowance required	714

Step 2

Write up the allowance for doubtful debts account, putting in the opening balance of $230 and the closing balance required of $714. The difference, the increase in allowance required, is the expense to the bad debts expense account and subsequently to the income statement.

Allowance for doubtful debts

20X3/4	$	*20X3/4*	$
		1 June Bal b/d	230
31 May Bal c/d	714	31 May Bad debts expense	484
	714		714
		20X4/X5	
		1 June Bal b/d	714

Bad debts expense

20X3/4	$	*20X3/4*	$
31 May Allowance for doubtful debts	484	31 May Income statement	484
	484		484

4 Bad debts recovered

4.1 Introduction

There is a possible situation where a debt is written off as bad in one accounting period, perhaps because the debtor has been declared bankrupt, and the money, or part of the money, due is then unexpectedly received in a subsequent accounting period.

4.2 Double entry

When a debt is written off the double entry is:

Dr Bad debts expense account (an expense in the income statement)

Cr Customer's account (removing the debt from the accounts).

The full double entry for the cash being received from that customer in a subsequent accounting period is:

Dr Receivables account (to reinstate the debt that had been cancelled when it was written off)

Cr Bad debts recovered account (unexpected sundry income credited to the income statement)

and

Dr Cash account

Cr Receivables account.

Note that this second entry is the usual double entry for cash received from a customer.

This double entry can be simplified to:

Dr Cash account

Cr Bad debts recovered account

as the debit and the credit to the receivables account cancel each other out. However, it may be useful to pass the transaction through the customer's account so that the fact that the debt was eventually paid, or partly paid, is recorded there.

ACTIVITY 2

Celia Jones had receivables of $3,655 at 31 December 20X7. At that date she wrote off a debt from Lenny Smith of $699. During the year to 31 December 20X8 Celia made credit sales of $17,832 and received cash from her customers totalling $16,936. She also received the $699 from Lenny Smith that had already been written off in 20X7.

Write up these transactions in Celia Jones's ledger accounts for 20X7 and 20X8.

Feedback to this activity is at the end of the chapter.

Conclusion

Having studied this chapter you should now understand the reason for considering the collectability of debts and the accounting concepts that are relevant to this area: accruals, realisation and prudence. Note that this topic is very frequently examined.

SELF-TEST QUESTIONS

Sales and accounting concepts

1 What is the double entry for a sale on credit? (1.2)

2 How is the realisation concept relevant to the accounting for credit sales? (1.3)

3 Which accounting concept would require an allowance for doubtful debts to be set up? (1.4)

Bad debts

4 What is the definition of a bad debt? (2.1)

5 What is the double entry for writing off a bad debt? (2.1)

Doubtful debts

6 What is an allowance for doubtful debts? (3.1)

7 What is the double entry required when an allowance for doubtful debts is initially set up? (3.1)

8 What is a specific allowance for doubtful debts? (3.3)

9 If there is to be a decrease in the allowance for doubtful debts over a period, will this result in a debit or a credit entry in the income statement? (3.5)

Bad debts recovered

10 What is the full double entry required to account for cash received from a debt that had been written off in a previous accounting period? (4.2)

EXAM-TYPE QUESTION

Harry Evans

Harry Evans set up in business on 1 January 20X0 as a violin maker. At the end of his first year of trading, 31 December 20X0, the amounts owing to him from customers totalled $6,570. After some consideration, Harry decided that of these debts a total of $370 was unlikely ever to be received and should be written off as bad. Of the remaining balances he decided to be prudent and allow against 4%.

By 31 December 20X1 Harry's receivables had increased to $8,400 and of these $1,500 were considered to be bad. Harry decided that his allowance for doubtful debts could be reduced to 2% of the remaining receivables.

At 31 December 20X2 Harry's receivables totalled $6,250. There were no debts that were considered bad but a specific allowance was to be made against one debt of $350 and a general allowance of 2% was to be continued on the remaining receivables.

You are required:

To write up the allowance for doubtful debts account and the bad debts expense account for the years ended 31 December 20X0, 20X1 and 20X2. **(12 marks)**

For the answer to this question, see the 'Answers' section at the end of the book.

FEEDBACK TO ACTIVITY 1

Step 1

Write up the receivables account showing the opening balance, the credit sales for the year and the cash received.

Receivables

20X6		$	*20X6*		$
1 Jan	Bal b/d	68,000	31 Dec	Cash	340,000
31 Dec	Sales revenue	354,000			

Step 2

Write off the bad debts for the period:

Dr Bad debts expense account

Cr Receivables account.

Bad debts expense

		$			$
20X6			*20X6*		
31 Dec	Receivables	2,000			

Receivables

		$			$
20X6			*20X6*		
1 Jan	Bal b/d	68,000	31 Dec	Cash	340,000
31 Dec	Sales revenue	354,000	31 Dec	Bad debts expense	2,000

Step 3

Balance off the receivables account to find the closing balance against which the allowance is required.

Receivables

		$			$
20X6			*20X6*		
1 Jan	Bal b/d	68,000	31 Dec	Cash	340,000
31 Dec	Sales revenue	354,000	31 Dec	Bad debts expense	2,000
			31 Dec	Bal c/d	80,000
		422,000			422,000
20X7					
1 Jan	Bal b/d	80,000			

Step 4

Set up the allowance required of 5% of $80,000, $4,000. Remember that there is already an opening balance on the allowance for doubtful debts account of $3,400, therefore only the increase in allowance required of $600 is credited to the allowance account and debited to the bad debts expense account.

Bad debts expense

		$			$
20X6			*20X6*		
31 Dec	Receivables	2,000			
31 Dec	Allowance for doubtful debts	600	31 Dec	Income statement	2,600
		2,600			2,600

Allowance for doubtful debts

		$			$
20X6			*20X6*		
			1 Jan	Bal b/d	3,400
31 Dec	Bal c/d	4,000	31 Dec	Bad debts expense	600
		4,000			4,000
			20X7		
			1 Jan	Bal b/d	4,000

Note that only the one bad debts expense account is used both to write off bad debts and to increase or decrease the allowance for doubtful debts. There is no necessity to use separate accounts for each type of expense.

FEEDBACK TO ACTIVITY 2

Step 1

Write up the receivables account and bad debts expense account at 31 December 20X7.

Receivables

20X7		$	*20X7*		$
31 Dec	Bal b/d	3,655	31 Dec	Bad debts expense	699
			31 Dec	Bal c/d	2,956
		3,655			3,655
20X8					
1 Jan	Bal b/d	2,956			

Bad debts expense

20X7		$	*20X7*		$
31 Dec	Receivables	699	31 Dec	Income statement	699
		699			699

Step 2

Write up the receivables account for 20X8 showing the credit sales and cash received from debtors.

Receivables

20X8		$	*20X8*		$
1 Jan	Bal b/d	2,956	31 Dec	Cash	16,936
31 Dec	Sales revenue	17,832			

Step 3

Continue with the receivables account and put through the entries for the bad debt recovered:

Dr Receivables account

Cr Bad debts recovered account

and

Dr Cash

Cr Receivables account.

Receivables

20X8		$	*20X8*		$
1 Jan	Bal b/d	2,956	31 Dec	Cash	16,936
31 Dec	Sales revenue	17,832	31 Dec	Cash	699
31 Dec	Bad debts expense	699			

Bad debts recovered

20X8		$	*20X8*		$
			31 Dec	Receivables	699

Step 4

Balance off the receivables account and transfer the balance on the bad debts expense account to the income statement. Note that the two entries of $699 in the receivables account cancel each other out. The remaining entries are a debit to the cash account for cash received and a credit in the bad debts recovered account that is transferred to the income statement as sundry income.

Receivables

20X8		$	*20X8*		$
1 Jan	Bal b/d	2,956	31 Dec	Cash	16,936
31 Dec	Sales revenue	17,832	31 Dec	Cash	699
31 Dec	Bad debts expense	699	31 Dec	Bal c/d	3,852
		21,487			21,487
20X9					
1 Jan	Bal b/d	3,852			

Bad debts recovered

20X8		$	*20X8*		$
31 Dec	Income statement	699	31 Dec	Receivables	699
		699			699

It is best to show the bad debts recovered separately in the income statement. If they are netted off against bad debts written off in the year, the total cost of bad debts is obscured.

Chapter 7

NON-CURRENT ASSETS AND DEPRECIATION

CHAPTER CONTENTS

When a non-current asset is purchased by a business, the double entry is to debit a non-current asset account and credit either cash or a payable account. The asset then remains in the balance sheet of the business until it is disposed of. There are, however, two problems with this:

- The non-current asset is earning revenue for the business that will be recognised in the income statement but no part of the cost of the non-current asset is being charged to the income statement.
- The non-current asset remains in the balance sheet at its original cost until it is disposed of. However, it is highly unlikely that the non-current asset's value will remain that of its original cost over the years; it is likely to decrease in value as it is used and ages.

The process of depreciation deals with both of these problems and is explained in this chapter. Depreciation is a method of charging a proportion of a non-current asset's original cost to the income statement each year to match with the revenues that the asset earns. The depreciation charge for each year also creates an accumulated depreciation account which is used to net off against the original cost of the asset in the balance sheet.

Objectives

By the time you have finished this chapter you should be able to:

- define and explain the purposes of depreciation
- calculate the annual depreciation charge for a non-current asset under a variety of methods
- account for depreciation in the ledger accounts and financial statements
- account for the disposal of a non-current asset
- account for the revaluation of non-current assets
- understand the provisions of IAS 16 *Property, Plant and Equipment.*

1 Non-current assets and depreciation

DEFINITION

A **non-current asset** is an asset intended for use on a continuing basis in the business.

KEY POINT

Tangible assets are plant, buildings, motor vehicles, etc.

Intangible assets are goodwill, patents, trademarks, etc.

1.1 Definition of a non-current asset

A **non-current asset** is an asset intended for use on a continuing basis in the business.

Non-current assets can be sub-divided into **tangible** assets (plant, buildings, motor vehicles, etc.) and **intangible** assets (goodwill, patents, trademarks, etc.). Both types of non-current assets are depreciated, and the following comments will apply to both tangible and intangible assets. At this stage you may be unsure as to what is meant by goodwill, but this will be explained in a later chapter.

1.2 What is depreciation?

DEFINITION

Depreciation is the systematic allocation of the depreciable amount of a non-current asset over its useful life.

Depreciation is the systematic allocation of the depreciable amount of a non-current asset over its useful life. ('Depreciable amount' means book value less residual value). This may arise from:

- **use**, e.g. plant and machinery or motor vehicles
- **physical wear and tear**
- **passing of time**, e.g. a ten-year lease of property
- **obsolescence** through technology and market changes, e.g. plant and machinery of a specialised nature
- **depletion**, e.g. the extraction of material from a quarry.

1.3 Purpose of depreciation

Assume an item of plant cost $5,000 and that it has a nil scrap value at the end of ten years. Since expenditure on the asset will benefit the revenues of the next ten years, the matching concept requires us to match the $5,000 costs against all of those revenues. The simplest way is to use the straight line method (discussed below) and charge one-tenth (i.e. $500) against the revenue of each year.

KEY POINT

Under historical cost accounting the purpose of depreciation is to allocate the cost of an asset over its expected life.

Under historical cost accounting, the purpose of depreciation is to allocate the cost of $5,000 over the expected life of the asset of ten years. The income statement for each year is charged with part of the cost of the asset.

1.4 The relationship between depreciation and asset replacement

Note that depreciation is not intended to provide a fund for the replacement of the asset. It is simply a method of allocating the cost of the asset over the periods estimated to benefit from its use. In our example it is unlikely that an equivalent replacement asset will cost $5,000 in ten years' time, due to inflation, and in any event depreciation does not provide the funds to replace it.

KEY POINT

Depreciation applies the matching concept to the cost of non-current assets. It does not provide for replacement of the asset.

Depreciation is a method of applying the matching or accruals concept to the cost of non-current assets. It is not a method of providing for, or saving up for, replacement of non-current assets.

2 Methods of calculating depreciation

2.1 Introduction

There are several possible methods of calculating depreciation. The methods below are included in the syllabus:

- straight line method
- reducing balance method
- sum of the digits method
- revaluation method.

Examiners will normally specify which method is to be used. If they do not, the straight line method should generally be adopted as it is the easiest to compute.

2.2 Straight line method

KEY POINT

Under the **straight line method**, the depreciation charge is constant over the life of the asset.

This is the simplest and most popular method of calculating depreciation. Under this method the depreciation charge is constant over the life of the asset. To calculate the depreciation charge, we require three pieces of information:

- the original (historical) cost of the asset
- an estimate of its useful life to the business
- an estimate of its residual value at the end of its useful life.

The depreciation charge is then calculated as follows.

$$\text{Annual depreciation charge} = \frac{\text{Original - Residual value}}{\text{Estimated useful value}}$$

Example – Straight line method

Mead is a sole trader with a 31 December year-end. He purchased a car on 1 January at a cost of $12,000. He estimates that its useful life is four years, after which he will trade it in for $2,400. The annual depreciation charge is to be calculated using the straight line method.

Solution – Straight line method

$$\text{Depreciation charge} = \frac{(\$12{,}000 - \$2{,}400)}{4} = \$2{,}400 \text{ p.a.}$$

Notes

1 Depreciation is often expressed as a percentage of original cost, so that straight line depreciation over four years would alternatively be described as straight line depreciation at 25% p.a.

2 If the car had been purchased on 30 September 20X3, strictly speaking we should only charge three months' depreciation in 20X3. The depreciation charged each year would be:

	$
20X3	600
20X4	2,400
20X5	2,400
20X6	2,400
20X7	1,800

You should follow this approach unless the question specifies that a full year's depreciation should be charged in the year of purchase, irrespective of the date of purchase.

3 Frequently, residual value is not specified, in which case you should assume it to be zero and the whole original cost will be written off over the life of the asset.

2.3 Reducing balance method

DEFINITION

Under **the reducing balance method**, the depreciation charge is higher in the earlier years of the life of the asset.

Under this method the depreciation charge is higher in the earlier years of the life of the asset. If examiners require this method, they will usually give you a percentage to apply. In the first year the percentage is applied to cost but in subsequent years it is applied to the asset's **net book value** (alternatively known as **written down value**).

The **net book value** (NBV) or **written down value** (WDV) of a non-current asset is its original cost less the accumulated depreciation on the asset to date.

DEFINITION

The net book value (NBV) of a non-current asset is its original cost less the accumulated depreciation on the asset to date.

Example – Reducing balance method

A trader purchased an item of plant for \$1,000. The depreciation charge for each of the first five years is to be calculated, assuming the depreciation rate on the reducing balance to be 20% p.a.

Solution – Reducing balance method

Year	*% × NBV = Depreciation charge*	*Depreciation charge* \$	*Cumulative depreciation* \$
1	20% × \$1,000	200	200
2	20% × \$(1,000 – 200)	160	360
3	20% × \$(1,000 – 360)	128	488
4	20% × \$(1,000 – 488)	102	590
5	20% × \$(1,000 – 590)	82	672

Notice how this method results in higher depreciation charges in earlier years and also that a much higher annual rate is required than for the straight line method if the asset is to be written off over the same period.

2.4 Percentage formula

In the above example the fixed depreciation percentage was given. To derive this percentage the following formula can be used:

$$Dp = \left(1 - \sqrt[N]{R/C}\right) \times 100\%$$

Where Dp = depreciation percentage
N = useful life of asset (years)
R = residual value of the asset
C = cost of the asset.

There are problems in using the formula:

- if there is no residual value, Dp becomes 100%
- if residual value is small relative to cost, Dp becomes a very high percentage.

For these reasons, a 'reasonable' percentage is often used in the reducing balance method which does not result in the NBV equalling the residual value at the end of the useful life but does achieve the main purpose of providing a higher depreciation charge in the earlier years.

In the examination, the depreciation percentage is usually given and does not therefore have to be calculated.

ACTIVITY 1

What type of non-current asset might the reducing balance method of depreciation be most useful for?

Feedback to this activity is at the end of the chapter.

2.5 Sum of the digits method

This is a variation on the reducing balance method and, as with that method, the aim is to show a higher depreciation charge in the early years of the life of an asset.

Example – Sum of the digits method

Cost of asset	\$4,200
Scrap value	\$200
Estimated useful life	Four years

Solution – Sum of the digits method

Sum of digits: 4 years + 3 years + 2 years + 1 year = 10

Year		*Depreciation charge*	*Cumulative depreciation*
		$	$
1	4/10 × $(4,200 – 200)	1,600	1,600
2	3/10 × $4,000	1,200	2,800
3	2/10 × $4,000	800	3,600
4	1/10 × $4,000	400	4,000

The method is sometimes referred to as the rule of 78 method, being so called because calculating for one year on a monthly basis the sum of the digits would be 12 months + 11 months + 10 months... + 1 month = 78. (This method is sometimes used for charging interest on a monthly basis.)

Formula for sum of the digits

A formula which gives the sum of the digits for any number of years is:

$$\frac{n(n+1)}{2}$$

Where n = number of years.

Thus the sum of the digits for four years is:

$$\frac{4(5)}{2} = 10$$

If the life of an asset is fifteen years:

$$\frac{15(16)}{2} = 120$$

ACTIVITY 2

A non-current asset originally cost $12,000 and is estimated to have a scrap value of $2,000 after the eight years of its estimated useful life.

What is the depreciation charge in year two of the asset's life under

(a) the straight line method

(b) the reducing balance method using an annual rate of 20%.

Feedback to this activity is at the end of the chapter.

3 Accounting for depreciation

3.1 Ledger accounts

Whichever of the methods is used (other than the revaluation method), the bookkeeping remains the same.

(a) On acquisition of the non-current asset:

Debit	*Credit*	*With*
Non-current asset – cost	Cash	Cost of the asset

(b) At the end of each year make the adjustment for depreciation:

Debit	*Credit*	*With*
Income statement – depreciation	Non-current asset – accumulated depreciation	Depreciation charge

This entry sets up the depreciation on the asset.

Note that the depreciation is not recorded by an entry in the non-current asset account. The non-current asset account is retained at cost and the depreciation charge is credited to a separate account. The reason for this is that we want to show the net book value in the balance sheet by disclosing cost minus the **accumulated** depreciation over the years since the asset was acquired, as shown in 3.2 below.

Example

A trader buys a motor car on 1 January 20X3 for £12,000. It is to be depreciated on the straight line basis over 4 years with an assumption of a residual value of £2,400.

Show the ledger accounts for the first three years, together with the effect on the financial statements. Take the date of purchase to be 1 January.

Solution

Step 1 Set up a 'motor car – cost' account and a 'motor car – accumulated depreciation' account.

Step 2 Account for the purchase of the car by debiting the motor car – cost account with $12,000 on 1 January 20X3.

Step 3 At 31 December 20X3 carry down the cost of the car on the motor car cost account.

Step 4 At 31 December 20X3 account for the first year's depreciation charge of $2,400 by debiting the income statement and crediting the motor car – accumulated depreciation account. Carry down the balance on the motor car – accumulated depreciation account.

Step 5 Repeat steps 3 and 4 at 31 December 20X4 and 20X5. Note how the balance on the motor car – accumulated depreciation account increases each year as this is the total of the depreciation charged to date on that motor car.

Motor car – cost account

		$		$
20X3			*20X3*	
1 Jan	Cash	12,000	31 Dec Balance c/d	12,000
20X4			20X4	
1 Jan	Balance b/d	12,000	31 Dec Balance c/d	12,000
20X5			20X5	
1 Jan	Balance b/d	12,000	31 Dec Balance c/d	12,000
20X6				
1 Jan	Balance b/d	12,000		

Motor car – accumulated depreciation account

		$			$
20X3			*20X3*		
31 Dec	Balance c/d	2,400	31 Dec	Income statement	2,400
20X4			20X4		
31 Dec	Balance c/d	4,800	1 Jan	Balance b/d	2,400
			31 Dec	Income statement	2,400
		4,800			4,800
20X5			20X5		
31 Dec	Balance c/d	7,200	1 Jan	Balance b/d	4,800
			31 Dec	Income statement	2,400
		7,200			7,200
			20X6		
			1 Jan	Balance b/d	7,200

Alternative solution

An alternative approach, which is normally used in more complex situations, is to open an additional account for depreciation expense. The overall effect will be exactly the same, as can be shown if we consider the year 20X3 in the example above.

Motor car – cost account

		$			$
20X3			*20X3*		
1 Jan	Cash	12,000	31 Dec	Balance c/d	12,000
20X4					
1 Jan	Balance b/d	12,000			

Motor car – accumulated depreciation account

		$			$
20X3			*20X3*		
31 Dec	Balance c/d	2,400	31 Dec	Depreciation (income statement)	2,400
			20X4		
			1 Jan	Balance b/d	2,400

Depreciation expense account

		$			$
20X3			*20X3*		
31 Dec	Motor car accumulated depreciation	2,400	31 Dec	Income statement	2,400

KEY POINT

The annual charge for depreciation is made by debiting either a depreciation expense account or the income statement directly, and crediting the accumulated depreciation account.

The annual charge for depreciation is made by debiting either a depreciation expense account or the income statement directly, and crediting the accumulated depreciation account.

3.2 Disclosure in the financial statements

The non-current asset will be shown in the financial statements as follows:

1 Income statement

Year	*Depreciation charge* $
20X3	2,400
20X4	2,400
20X5	2,400

2 Balance sheet

		20X3	*20X4*	*20X5*
		$	$	$
Non-current asset:				
Motor car:	Cost	12,000	12,000	12,000
	Depreciation	2,400	4,800	7,200
	Net book value	9,600	7,200	4,800

KEY POINT

The balance on the accumulated depreciation account is netted off against the cost of the non-current asset in the balance sheet each year to give the net book value of the non-current asset.

The balance on the accumulated depreciation account is netted off against the cost of the non-current asset in the balance sheet each year to give the net book value of the non-current asset.

3.3 Summary of the effect of depreciation

- Without depreciation the full cost of the asset would appear on the balance sheet each year.
- With depreciation the value of the asset on the balance sheet is reduced by the amount of the cumulative annual depreciation charges.
- The annual depreciation charge appears in the income statement each year thereby charging the income statement with a proportion of the cost of the non-current asset each year in accordance with the matching or accruals concept.

ACTIVITY 3

S Telford purchases a machine for $6,000. He estimates that the machine will last for eight years and its scrap value then will be $1,000.

Prepare the ledger accounts for the first three years of the machine's life and show the balance sheet extract at the end of each year, charging depreciation on the straight line method.

Feedback to this activity is at the end of the chapter.

4 Sale of non-current assets

4.1 Introduction

When a non-current asset is sold, the cost of that asset together with the related accumulated depreciation should be transferred to a non-current asset disposals account. The profit or loss on disposal is calculated by comparing:

- the net book value of the asset at the date of sale (i.e. cost less accumulated depreciation), and
- the proceeds of sale.

4.2 Ledger account entries

Summary of the bookkeeping entries:

Ref	*Debit*	*Credit*	*With*
1	Disposals account	Non-current asset – cost account	Original cost of asset
2	Non-current asset – accumulated depreciation	Disposals account	Accumulated depreciation up to the date of disposal
3	Cash	Disposals account	Proceeds of sale
4A or	Disposals account	Income statement	Profit on sale
4B	Income statement	Disposals account	Loss on sale

Example

The motor car used in the previous example was sold on 7 January 20X6 for proceeds of $5,100. Show the entries in the relevant ledger accounts.

Solution

Step 1

The profit on sale can be calculated arithmetically or derived from the use of the disposals account. The arithmetic computation is:

	$
Proceeds of sale	5,100
Less: Net book value at date of sale $(12,000 – 7,200)	4,800
Profit on sale	300

Step 2

Write up the ledger accounts.

Motor car – cost account

20X6		$	*20X6*		$
1 Jan	Balance b/d	12,000	7 Jan	(1) Disposals	12,000

Motor car – accumulated depreciation

20X6		$	*20X6*		$
7 Jan	(2) Disposals	7,200	1 Jan	Balance b/d	7,200

Motor car – disposals account

20X6		$	*20X6*		$
7 Jan	(1) Motor car – cost	12,000	7 Jan	(2) Depreciation	7,200
31 Dec	(4A) Income statement (bal fig)	300		(3) Cash	5,100
		12,300			12,300

(Numbers in brackets refer to the reference numbers in the summary chart above.)

4.3 Presentation

A final point: How should the $300 be presented in the income statement? There are two possibilities:

1 Show the profit on sale of $300 as a separate item of miscellaneous income below gross profit.

2 Describe the $300 as depreciation over-provided and deduct it from the total depreciation charge for the year.

KEY POINT

When a non-current asset is sold, the cost and accumulated depreciation are cleared to the disposal account and compared with the sale proceeds.

Both these presentations are acceptable, though the first is probably easier and clearer.

When a non-current asset is sold the cost and accumulated depreciation are cleared to the disposal account and compared with the sale proceeds. This will give a profit/loss on sale or over/under depreciation provided.

5 Revaluation of non-current assets

5.1 Reasons for revaluation

During a period of inflation, the current monetary value of non-current assets, such as land and buildings, may be much in excess of their net book value (historical cost less depreciation). A business may wish to reflect the current worth of such assets on its balance sheet. This is particularly the case with large companies who wish to show to the users of their financial statements, the current worth of significant assets in the company.

KEY POINT

Revaluation reserve: Account holding the difference between the revalued amount and the previous net book value.

The difference (usually a surplus) between the revalued amount and the previous net book value needs to be credited to an account separate from the income statement as the gain is not realised (i.e. there is no intention of turning the asset into cash by selling it). The account is known as a **revaluation reserve.**

IAS 16 *Property, Plant and Equipment* requires that when an item of property, plant or equipment is revalued, the entire class of property, plant or equipment to which the asset belongs must be revalued.

5.2 Depreciation of a revalued asset

When a non-current asset has been revalued, the charge for depreciation should be based on the revalued amount and the remaining useful economic life of the asset. Therefore, because of the revaluation, the depreciation is higher than previously. This may appear strange; an upward revaluation has resulted in a higher depreciation charge to the income statement. However, it should be remembered that the prime function of depreciation is to write off the 'cost' of an asset over its expected life. If the 'cost' is increased, the depreciation to be charged increases.

The accounting treatment of non-current asset revaluations can be seen in the following example.

Example

A company revalues its buildings and decides to incorporate the revaluation into the books of account. The following information is relevant

(a) **Extract from the balance sheet at 31 December 20X7**

	$
Buildings:	
Cost	1,500,000
Depreciation	450,000
	1,050,000

(b) Depreciation has been provided at 2% per annum on the straight line basis.

(c) The building is revalued at 30 June 20X8 at $1,380,000. There is no change in its remaining estimated future life.

You are required to show the relevant extracts from the final accounts at 31 December 20X8.

Solution

Income statement – depreciation charge

	$
Based on original cost	30,000
Based on increase in valuation	5,000
Total	35,000

Balance sheet

	$
Buildings:	
Valuation 30 June 20X8	1,380,000
Accumulated depreciation	20,000
	1,360,000

Workings **(a)**

Buildings account (NBV)

		$			$
20X8			*20X8*		
1 Jan	Balance b/d	1,050,000	30 Jun	Income statement: depreciation first half year	15,000
30 Jun	Revaluation surplus (bal fig)	345,000	30 Jun	Balance c/d	1,380,000
		1,395,000			1,395,000
30 Jun	Balance b/d	1,380,000	31 Dec	Income statement: depreciation second half year	20,000
			31 Dec	Balance c/d	1,360,000
		1,380,000			1,380,000

Tutorial note: there are two important points to appreciate. First, depreciation must continue to be charged on original cost until the date of the revaluation. Secondly, the accumulated depreciation on the old cost is effectively 'cleared out' when the gain is transferred to the revaluation reserve. Thus accumulated depreciation at the year end only consists of the depreciation charged on the revalued amount.

Workings **(b) Depreciation calculations**

	$
First half year $0.5 \times 2\% \times 1{,}500{,}000$	15,000
Second half year $0.5 \times \frac{1{,}380{,}000}{34.5^{**}}$	20,000
	35,000

Had this building not been revalued, the charge for the year would have been $30,000.

** This is arrived at as follows

			Years
Total number of years before building fully depreciated			50.0
Less: Depreciation in years to 31 December 20X7	$\frac{450,000}{30,000}$	15.0	
Depreciation 1 January 20X8 to 30 June 20X8		0.5	
			15.5
Number of years for depreciation to run			34.5

6 The provisions of IAS 16 *Property, Plant and Equipment*

6.1 Introduction

The provisions of IAS 16 are mainly relevant in relation to company financial statements.

You may prefer to leave a detailed study of this section until you have studied company financial statements in Chapters 19 and 20.

6.2 IAS 16 *Property, Plant and Equipment*

IAS 16 deals with depreciation of tangible non-current assets, but also with their recognition, measurement and revaluation.

Recognition

The conditions for recognition of a tangible non-current asset are that:

1 It is probable that future benefits will flow to the enterprise from the asset.

2 The cost of the asset can be measured reliably.

Measurement

The initial measurement of the value of a tangible non-current asset should be cost or, if the asset was obtained by an exchange, fair value at the time of the exchange.

Revaluation

The benchmark treatment in IAS 16 is that non-current assets should be carried at cost less depreciation. Revaluation is an allowed alternative, but if assets are once revalued, the valuation should be repeated whenever the fair value differs from the carrying amount. On revaluation the usual way of dealing with the accumulated depreciation is to eliminate it against the gross carrying amount of the asset. That means that accumulated depreciation after the revaluation is only that since the date of the revaluation. This treatment was illustrated above.

An upward revaluation should be credited to revaluation reserve, unless it reverses a previous downward revaluation which was charged as an expense.

A downward revaluation should be charged as an expense, unless it reverses a previous upward revaluation, when it may be charged against the revaluation surplus for that same asset.

If one asset in a class is revalued, all assets of that class must be revalued. This is to prevent selective revaluation of only those assets that have increased in value. Also, revaluations must be kept up to date.

Depreciation

Depreciation should be allocated on a systematic basis over the useful life of the asset so as to eliminate the 'depreciable amount' – cost or valuation less residual value, and should reflect the rate at which the benefits of the asset are used over its life.

The factors to be considered in determining useful life are:

1 rate of usage

2 expected wear and tear

3 technical obsolescence

4 legal or other limits on the use of the asset, such as the expiry of a lease.

Land normally has an unlimited life and so does not require depreciation, but buildings should be depreciated.

Review of useful life

The useful life of assets should be periodically reviewed, and if they have changed materially the depreciation charge should be adjusted.

Review of depreciation method

The depreciation methods used should also be reviewed periodically, and changed if the existing methods no longer reflect the rate of usage of the asset. If the depreciation method is changed, this affects current and future periods, with no adjustment to past period depreciation.

Impairment

The carrying amount of assets should be reviewed periodically, and if the future value of the asset (the recoverable amount) is estimated to be less than that carrying amount, the asset should be immediately written down to the recoverable amount through the income statement.

Disposals

Gains or losses on disposals are recognised as income or expense in the income statement. When assets are exchanged, the initial value of the new asset is taken to be the fair value of the old asset plus the cash paid, if any. (See Chapter 8 below for an example.)

6.3 The disclosure requirements of IAS 16

IAS 16 contains a number of disclosure requirements. Here are the main ones:

1 The measurement bases used for arriving at the carrying amount of the asset (e.g. cost or valuation). If more than one basis has been used, the amounts for each basis must be disclosed.

2 Depreciation methods used, with details of useful lives.

3 The gross amount of each asset heading and its related accumulated depreciation (aggregated with accumulated impairment losses) at the beginning and end of the period.

4 A reconciliation of the carrying amount at the beginning and end of the period, showing:

- additions

- disposals
- revaluations
- depreciation

Illustrations of the layout of this reconciliation are in Chapter 20 below, where company financial statements are covered.

5 Any commitments for future acquisition of property, plant and equipment.

Conclusion

Having completed this chapter you should be able to discuss the reasons for the depreciation of non-current assets and the various methods of calculating the annual depreciation charge that are available. Once the depreciation charge for the year is calculated then it is entered into the accounts by debiting either the income statement directly or via a depreciation expense account and crediting an accumulated depreciation account.

The balance on the accumulated depreciation account is netted off against the original cost of the asset in the balance sheet each year in order to arrive at the net book value of the asset.

It is also necessary to be able to account for the disposal of a non-current asset by clearing out the cost and the accumulated depreciation to date on that asset to the disposal account and comparing this net book value to the proceeds of sale. This will give either a profit on sale, which is effectively an over-depreciation of the asset, or a loss on sale, which is an under-depreciation of the asset. The profit or loss on sale can either be shown as a separate item in the income statement or included with the depreciation charge for the year.

SELF-TEST QUESTIONS

Non-current assets and depreciation

1 What is the definition of depreciation? (1.2)

Methods of calculating depreciation

2 What is the formula for calculating the annual depreciation charge using the straight line method of depreciation? (2.2)

3 What is the net book value of a non-current asset? (2.3)

4 What is the formula for deriving the fixed depreciation percentage to be used with the reducing balance method? (2.4)

5 What is the formula for calculating the sum of the digits for any number of years? (2.5)

Accounting for depreciation

6 How should non-current assets be shown in the balance sheet of an organisation? (3.2)

Sale of non-current assets

7 What is the double entry required to account for the disposal of a non-current asset? (4.2)

8 What are the two alternative presentations for a profit on sale of a non-current asset? (4.3)

Revaluation of non-current assets

9 How is depreciation calculated when an asset is revalued? (5.2)

MULTIPLE-CHOICE QUESTION

B acquired a lorry on 1 May 2000 at a cost of $30,000. The lorry has an estimated useful life of four years, and an estimated resale value at the end of that time of $6,000. B charges depreciation on the straight line basis, with a proportionate charge in the period of acquisition.

What will the depreciation charge for the lorry be in B's ten month accounting period to 30 September 2000?

A $3,000

B $2,500

C $2,000

D $5,000

For the answer to this question, see the 'Answers' section at the end of the book.

EXAM-TYPE QUESTIONS

Question 1: Depreciation 1

Explain the purpose of providing for depreciation and give details of one method of computing the annual depreciation on an asset. **(8 marks)**

Question 2: Depreciation 2

A firm has the following transactions with motor cars:

20X4

1 Jan Purchased car for $8,000 (Car 'A')

1 Jul Purchased additional car for $12,000 (Car 'B')

20X5

1 Jul Car 'A' sold for $6,000

The firm's accounting year ends on 31 December in each year, and the following amounts of depreciation have been calculated as being relevant to those years:

Accounting year ending 31 December 20X4 Car 'A' $1,600

Accounting year ending 31 December 20X4 Car 'B' $1,200

Accounting year ending 31 December 20X5 Car 'A' $800

Accounting year ending 31 December 20X5 Car 'B' $2,400

Accounting year ending 31 December 20X6 Car 'B' $2,400

You are required to show the motor cars accounts for each of the three accounting years, together with the entry for motor cars in the balance sheet at 31 December 20X5. **(12 marks)**

Question 3: Grasmere

Grasmere has been trading for many years, making up his accounts to 31 December.

On 1 July 20X2 he purchased a van for $2,400. He estimates that its useful life is five years, with a $300 residual value. He provides depreciation on a straight line basis on all his non-current assets.

Grasmere sold the van on 1 April 20X4 for proceeds of $1,800.

You are required to enter the above transactions in the relevant ledger accounts and to show the effect on the financial statements for each year. **(12 marks)**

For the answers to these questions, see the 'Answers' section at the end of the book.

FEEDBACK TO ACTIVITY **1**

The type of non-current asset that loses a large proportion of its value in the early years of its life and a lesser proportion in later years, such as a new car. It is also sometimes argued that assets that require little maintenance in the early years of their life but much more as they get older should be depreciated using the reducing balance method as the total of depreciation and maintenance costs each year should then be evened out. However, depreciation is usually regarded as an allocation of cost, not an attempt to value the asset.

FEEDBACK TO ACTIVITY **2**

(a) **Straight line method**

$$\frac{\$12{,}000 - 2{,}000}{8} = \$1{,}250$$

(b) **Reducing balance method**

Year	*NBV*	*Depreciation charge*
	$	$
1	12,000	(12,000 × 20%) = $2,400
2	(12,000 – 2,400) = 9,600	(9,600 × 20%) = $1,920

IAS 16 *Property, Plant and Equipment* requires that the depreciation method used should reflect the pattern in which the asset's economic benefits are consumed by the enterprise.

FEEDBACK TO ACTIVITY **3**

Straight line method

Annual depreciation

$$= \frac{\text{Cost} - \text{Scrap value}}{\text{Estimated life}}$$

$$= \frac{\$6{,}000 - \$1{,}000}{8 \text{ years}}$$

= $625 p.a.

Machine account cost

	$		$
Year 1:			
Cost	6,000		

Accumulated depreciation

		$			$
Year 1:			Year 1:		
	Balance c/d	625		Income statement	625
Year 2:			Year 2:		
	Balance c/d	1,250		Balance b/d	625
				Income statement	625
		1,250			1,250
Year 3:			Year 3:		
	Balance c/d	1,875		Balance b/d	1,250
				Income statement	625
		1,875			1,875
			Year 4:		
				Balance b/d	1,875

Note: a depreciation account (i.e. an **expense** account) could also have been shown. The function of a depreciation account is to store the information regarding charges for depreciation made for the **current** year until it is closed off to the income statement.

Balance sheet extract

	Non-current asset	*Cost*	*Accumulated depreciation*	*Net book value*
		$	$	$
Year 1	Machine	6,000	625	5,375
Year 2	Machine	6,000	1,250	4,750
Year 3	Machine	6,000	1,875	4,125

Chapter 8
FROM TRIAL BALANCE TO FINANCIAL STATEMENTS

CHAPTER CONTENTS

At this stage the main areas of double entry bookkeeping have been covered. The purpose of this chapter is to introduce you to the type of question that you might meet in an examination where all that has been learned so far must be applied. This type of question is where students are given a trial balance and a series of other information regarding such items as accruals and prepayments, depreciation, inventory and bad and doubtful debts. All of the information must be assimilated and a full set of financial statements prepared. .

The large example in this chapter will bring together the double entry covered in the previous chapters as well as introducing some new items into the accounts such as carriage inwards and outwards and customs duties.

As well as being concerned with the accounting involved in this type of question, it is also important to take note of the points of presentation and approach that will be emphasised throughout the chapter.

Objectives

By the time you have finished this chapter you should be able to:

- draw up a set of financial statements from a trial balance plus additional information
- understand the different accounting presentation of carriage inwards and carriage outwards
- account for the disposal of a non-current asset that is traded in for a new non-current asset
- handle the approach necessary for more complex examination-type questions.

1 Trial balance-type questions

1.1 Example

The trial balance of Tyndall at 31 May 20X6 is shown on the next page.

You ascertain the following information:

1. Closing inventory has been valued for accounts purposes at $8,490.
2. The motor van was sold on 31 August 20X5 and traded in against the cost of a new van. The trade-in price was $1,400 and the cost of the new van was $3,600. No entries have yet been made for this transaction apart from debiting the $2,200 cash paid to New delivery van account.
3. Depreciation on the straight line basis is to be provided at the following annual rates:

Motor vans	25%
Furniture and equipment	10%
4. 5% of the closing receivables total is estimated to be doubtful.
5. An accrual of $372 is required in respect of light and heat.

6 A quarter's rent to 30 June 20X6 amounting to $900 was paid on 2 April 20X6. Insurance for the year to 31 March 20X7 amounting to $1,680 was paid on 16 April 20X6.

	$	$
Capital account		15,258
Drawings by proprietor	5,970	
Purchases	73,010	
Returns inwards	1,076	
Returns outwards		3,720
Discounts	1,870	965
Credit sales		96,520
Cash sales		30,296
Customs duty	11,760	
Carriage inwards	2,930	
Carriage outwards	1,762	
Salesman's commission	711	
Salesman's salary	3,970	
Office salaries	7,207	
Bank charges	980	
Loan interest	450	
Light and heat	2,653	
Sundry expenses	2,100	
Rent	3,315	
Insurance	4,000	
Printing and postage	2,103	
Advertising	1,044	
Bad debts	1,791	
Doubtful debts allowance		437
Inventory	7,650	
Receivables	10,760	
Payables		7,411
Cash at bank	2,634	
Cash in hand	75	
New delivery van (less trade-in)	2,200	
Motor expenses	986	
Furniture and equipment:		
Cost	8,000	
Depreciation at 1 June 20X5		2,400
Old delivery van:		
Cost	2,000	
Depreciation at 1 June 20X5		1,000
Loan account at 9% (repayable in five years)		5,000
	163,007	163,007

You are required to prepare:

1 An income statement for the year ended 31 May 20X6.

2 A balance sheet as at 31 May 20X6.

1.2 Solution

Step 1 Inventory

The closing inventory figure of $8,490 is identified for the financial statements. No working is required.

Step 2 Non-current assets and depreciation

This is the most difficult part of the question. Considering the motor vehicles initially, the approach should be in three stages:

(i) Depreciation on the old vehicle up to the point of sale: 25% × 3/12 × \$2,000 = \$125.

(ii) To record the trade-in we need to have regard to the provisions of IAS 16 *Property, Plant and Equipment*. IAS 16 requires us to treat the cost of the new van as being the fair value of the old van at the time of the trade-in plus the cash paid. The cost of the new van is calculated as:

	\$
Fair value of old van	1,400
Cash paid	2,200
	3,600

(iii) Depreciation on the new vehicle from the date of purchase to the year end: 25% × 9/12 × \$3,600 = \$675.

The ledger accounts will show:

Old delivery van – cost

	\$		\$
Per trial balance	2,000	Old delivery van – disposal	2,000

Old delivery van – accumulated depreciation

	\$		\$
Old delivery van – disposal	1,125	Per trial balance	1,000
		Depreciation expense	125
	1,125		1,125

New delivery van – cost

	\$		\$
Cash (from trial balance)	2,200	Balance c/d	3,600
Old delivery van – disposal	1,400		
	3,600		3,600

Old delivery van – disposal

	\$		\$
Old delivery van – cost	2,000	Old delivery van – accumulated depreciation	1,125
Profit on disposal	525	New delivery van – fair value	1,400
	2,525		2,525

New delivery van – accumulated depreciation

	$		$
Balance c/d	675	Depreciation expense	675

Depreciation expense – motor vans

	$		$
Old delivery van – accumulated depreciation account	125	Income statement – depreciation	800
New delivery van – accumulated depreciation account	675		
	800		800

In this case, depreciation has been provided on the old van up to the date of disposal, and on the new van from the date of acquisition. In practice and in examination questions, the assumption may be made to charge no depreciation on an asset in the year in which it is sold, and to charge depreciation for a whole year on a new asset regardless of the date in the year on which it was purchased.

KEY POINT

If the dates of the purchase and sale are given, take proportional depreciation.

For examination purposes, the clue is to check whether the dates of the purchase and sale are given. If they are, take proportional depreciation. If they are not, you really have no alternative but to make the simplifying assumption stated above.

Depreciation on the furniture and equipment is much more straightforward.

Furniture and equipment – accumulated depreciation

	$		$
Balance c/d	3,200	Per trial balance	2,400
		Depreciation expense ($8,000 × 10%)	800
	3,200		3,200

Step 3 Bad debts

Careful scrutiny of the trial balance will reveal two accounts of importance here:

- bad debts – a debit balance of $1,791 representing bad debts already written off in the year
- doubtful debts allowance – a credit balance of $437 representing the current allowance against doubtful debts.

Bad debts

	$		$
Per trial balance	1,791	Income statement	1,892
Doubtful debts allowance	101		
	1,892		1,892

Allowance for doubtful debts

	$		$
Balance c/d (5% × $10,760)	538	Per trial balance	437
		Bad debts (bal fig)	101
	538		538

KEY POINT

The increase in the doubtful debts allowance is charged to the income statement through the bad debts account.

The increase in the doubtful debts allowance is charged to the income statement through the bad debts account.

Step 4 Light and heat

A straightforward accrual.

Light and heat

	$		$
Per trial balance	2,653	Income statement (bal fig)	3,025
Balance c/d	372		
	3,025		3,025

KEY POINT

The accrual increases the expense shown in the income statement and also appears in the balance sheet as a current liability.

The accrual increases the expense shown in the income statement and will also appear in the balance sheet as a current liability.

Step 5 Rent

Rent prepaid ($\frac{1}{3}$ × $900) = $300

Rent

	$		$
Per trial balance	3,315	Income statement (bal fig)	3,015
		Balance c/d	300
	3,315		3,315

KEY POINT

The prepayment of rent reduces the expense to the income statement and will appear in the balance sheet as a current asset.

The prepayment of rent reduces the expense to the income statement and will appear in the balance sheet as a current asset.

Insurance prepaid: 10/12 × $1,680 = $1,400

Insurance

	$		$
Per trial balance	4,000	Income statement (bal fig)	2,600
		Balance c/d	1,400
	4,000		4,000

Step 6 Prepare the income statement and balance sheet.

(a) Income statement for the year ended 31 May 20X6

	$	$	$
Sales revenue:			
Credit sales			96,520
Cash sales			30,296
			126,816
Less: Sales returns			1,076
			125,740
Opening inventory		7,650	
Purchases	73,010		
Less: Purchase returns	3,720		
	69,290		
Carriage inwards	2,930		
Customs duty	11,760		
		83,980	
		91,630	
Closing inventory		8,490	
Cost of sales			83,140
Gross profit			42,600
Discount received			965
Profit on sale of van			525
			44,090
Less: Expenses:			
Depreciation:			
Van (Step 2)		800	
Equipment		800	
Bad debts (Step 3)		1,892	
Light and heat (Step 4)		3,025	
Rent (Step 5)		3,015	
Insurance		2,600	
Discount allowed		1,870	
Carriage outwards		1,762	
Salesman's commission		711	
Salesman's salary		3,970	
Office salary		7,207	
Bank charges		980	
Loan interest		450	
Sundry expenses		2,100	
Printing and postage		2,103	
Advertising		1,044	
Motor expenses		986	
			35,315
Net profit			8,775

(b) Balance sheet at 31 May 20X6

	Cost	*Acc dep'n*	
	$	$	$
Non-current assets:			
Motor van	3,600	675	2,925
Furniture and equipment	8,000	3,200	4,800
	11,600	3,875	7,725
Current assets:			
Inventory		8,490	
Receivables	10,760		
Less: Allowance for doubtful debts	538		
		10,222	
Prepayments (rent and insurance)		1,700	
Cash at bank		2,634	
Cash in hand		75	
			23,121
			30,846
Capital account:			
Balance at 1 June 20X5		15,258	
Net profit		8,775	
		24,033	
Less: Drawings by proprietor		5,970	
			18,063
Non-current liabilities:			
Loan			5,000
Current liabilities:			
Trade payables		7,411	
Accrued expenses		372	
			7,783
			30,846

1.3 Notes on presentation

1 The gross profit calculation in the income statement includes all expenditure incurred in bringing the goods to their present location and condition. This includes:

- purchase cost including import duty
- carriage inwards and freight costs.

In contrast, carriage outwards is treated as an expense of selling and is included with all the other expenses. Note that both carriage inwards and carriage outwards are debits (i.e. expenses).

Carriage means transport costs.

Inwards refers to the cost of bringing in raw materials from suppliers. Carriage outwards is thus delivery charges incurred in supplying goods to customers.

DEFINITION

Carriage means transport costs.

KEY POINT

Inwards refers to the cost of bringing in raw materials from suppliers.

Returns inwards are the same as sales returns.

2 'Returns' often causes difficulties. Returns inwards are the same as sales returns. Since sales are credits, sales returns are debits. For presentation purposes, sales returns are deducted from sales. In the same way purchase returns are deducted from purchases. In more advanced examples you will simply show the net sales and purchases without showing the returns separately.

3 The discounts are shown as one line in the list of balances with both a debit and a credit balance. Remember that expenses are debit balances, and income, credit balances. Therefore the discount allowed is the debit balance and the discount received the credit balance. These figures should not be netted off.

4 In examinations the answers should precede the workings, which should clearly be labelled as such. The idea behind this is that the examiner only wishes to look at the workings if errors have been made – hopefully he will not need to.

If the workings are numbered, then a reference to the working can be made in the final accounts.

Therefore in an examination the income statement and balance sheet should be shown before the workings in Step 1 and Step 5.

Conclusion

The purpose of this chapter was to illustrate the approach necessary with more complex examination-type questions where a list of account balances is given and a number of adjustments have to be made before the financial statements can be prepared. The illustration should have brought together all of the basic double entry that has been studied piecemeal in the earlier chapters of this text.

SELF-TEST QUESTIONS

Trial balance - type questions

1 Is opening inventory a debit or a credit balance in the trial balance? (1.1)

2 Where a non-current asset is part exchanged for another non-current asset how should the cost of the new non-current asset be calculated? (1.2)

3 What is the double entry necessary to ensure that the trade-in value of an old non-current asset is correctly reflected in the accounts? (1.2)

4 If the allowance for doubtful debts is increased, is this a debit or a credit to the income statement? (1.2)

5 Does a prepayment increase or decrease the expense shown in the income statement? (1.2)

6 Are discounts allowed on a debit or a credit balance? (1.2)

7 What are returns inwards? (1.2)

8 How are returns inwards presented in the financial statements? (1.2)

9 What is the correct treatment for carriage inwards in the income statement? (1.3)

10 What is carriage outwards? (1.3)

PRACTICE QUESTION

Delta

The figures below are the trial balance extracted from the books of Delta at 31 December 20X9:

You are required to draw up the income statement for the year to 31 December 20X9 and the balance sheet at that date, after taking into account the following:

(a) inventory at 31 December 20X9 $7,550

(b) interest on the loan at 5% p.a. had not been paid at 31 December

(c) rent includes $250 for premises paid in advance to 31 March next year

(d) depreciate plant and machinery by 10% p.a.; depreciate furniture and fittings by 5% p.a.

(e) adjust the allowance for doubtful debts to 5% of trade receivables

(f) show wages as part of cost of sales. **(25 marks)**

	$	$
Capital at 1 Jan 20X9		20,000
Loan account, Omega		2,000
Drawings	1,750	
Premises	8,000	
Furniture and fittings	500	
Plant and machinery	5,500	
Inventory at 1 Jan	8,000	
Cash at bank	650	
Allowance for doubtful debts		740
Purchases	86,046	
Sales revenue		124,450
Bad debts	256	
Bad debts recovered		45
Trade receivables	20,280	
Trade payables		10,056
Bank charges	120	
Rent	2,000	
Returns inwards	186	
Returns outwards		135
Salaries	3,500	
Wages	8,250	
Travelling expenses	1,040	
Carriage inwards	156	
Discounts allowed	48	
Discounts received		138
General expenses	2,056	
Gas, electricity and water	2,560	
Carriage outwards	546	
Travellers' salaries and commission	5,480	
Printing and stationery	640	
	157,564	157,564

For the answer to this question, see the 'Answers' section at the end of the book.

Chapter 9

JOURNALS AND CONTROL ACCOUNTS

CHAPTER CONTENTS

In the chapters of the text so far the double entry bookkeeping aspects of various transactions have been considered. In this chapter we will take a step back to the process of the initial recording of transactions before they are entered into the ledger accounts.

This chapter will consider the main books of prime entry and explain the system of accounts receivable and payable ledgers and control accounts. Finally the related area of dealing with cash discounts will be studied. A more detailed coverage of control accounts is in Chapter 10.

Objectives

By the time you have finished this chapter you should be able to:

- record most types of transactions in the relevant book of original entry
- understand how all the books in the bookkeeping system are related
- post the totals from the books of prime entry to the ledger accounts
- record cash discounts in the cash book
- record transactions in the petty cash book and understand the imprest system of controlling petty cash.

1 Division of ledgers

1.1 The advantages of dividing the ledger

So far we have assumed that all transactions are directly entered into the double entry books of account.

DEFINITION

The double entry books of account are called the **general ledger** or **nominal ledger**.

The double entry books of account are called the **general ledger** or **nominal ledger**. The term used in this book is 'general ledger'.

However, there are two major reasons why this is not likely to be the case in practice:

1 The result would be a vast number of entries in the general ledger making it unwieldy, and making the discovery of errors extremely difficult.

2 The general ledger is likely to be under the control of a senior accountant. He or she is not likely to have the time to enter a vast number of transactions every day. By making use of **books of original entry** and by removing certain accounts from the general ledger and replacing them with **control accounts**, much detailed work can be removed from the general ledger. Such work can then be delegated to more junior staff.

DEFINITION

Books of original entry are the books where transactions are recorded for the first time. They are also known as books of **prime** entry or **journals**.

Control accounts, most notably accounts receivable and payable control accounts, are ledger accounts that summarise a large number of transactions.

Books of original entry are the books where transactions are recorded for the first time. They are also known as books of **prime** entry or **journals**.

Control accounts, most notably accounts receivable and payable control accounts, are ledger accounts that summarise a large number of transactions.

Journals act as an initial 'store' of information before the summarising and storing of that information in ledger accounts, including control accounts.

Other advantages of dividing the ledger are:

1 Certain transactions can be kept confidential, i.e. access to the general ledger can be restricted as it only contains summary information. In some businesses, this confidentiality is reflected in an alternative title to the general ledger, the **private ledger**. In other businesses, part of the general ledger is recorded in a separate ledger which is then known as a private ledger. The term 'general ledger' is used throughout in this book.

2 The computerisation of the accounting records can be done on part of the accounting system. Computerisation of the whole accounting system can be beneficial in many instances but it may be of most benefit in those areas such as accounts receivable and payable which have most of the business transactions. The creation of a separate accounts receivable ledger can allow its computerisation.

The only disadvantage of splitting the ledger is that more control is required to ensure all data is correctly recorded. The division should result in more control if handled properly, but if it is not correctly planned, it can make matters worse.

Summary of stages of accounting

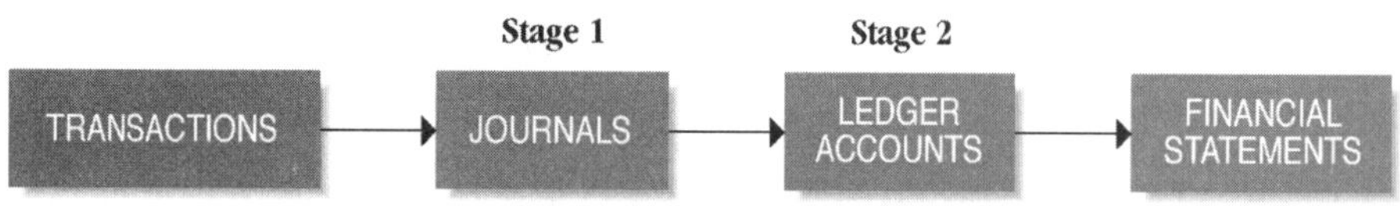

1.2 The ledgers into which double entry books are conventionally divided

To summarise, the ledgers into which double entry books are conventionally divided are as follows:

- general ledger
- accounts receivable ledger
- accounts payable ledger
- cash book.

1.3 The nature and purpose of each ledger and the meaning of the balances in each ledger

General ledger

KEY POINT

The **general ledger** contains all accounts or a summary of all the accounts.

The general ledger contains all accounts or a summary of all the accounts. In those accounts will be all the balances necessary to produce financial statements, i.e. asset, liability, income and expense accounts.

Accounts receivable ledger

The accounts receivable ledger has a ledger account for each credit customer, which shows amounts owing by each one.

Accounts payable ledger

Similarly, the accounts payable ledger has an account for each supplier. The balances show the amounts owing to each one.

Cash book

Cash and cheque transactions form a major part of the total transactions of a business. Therefore it is appropriate to have a book which records these transactions.

1.4 The main books of original entry

So, how are transactions summarised for posting into the accounts receivable ledger control account and accounts payable ledger control account? This is where consideration must be given to the books of prime entry. The main such books relevant to the syllabus are:

- purchases journal
- purchases returns journal
- sales journal
- sales returns journal
- cash book
- petty cash book
- journal.

All but the journal will be dealt with in this chapter; the journal will be studied in a later chapter.

Note particularly that in the modern business world many of these books, if not all of them in a substantial number of organisations, will take the form of computerised print-outs. Nevertheless, the same principles will apply.

2 Purchases journal

DEFINITION

The **purchases journal** is used to summarise the credit purchases made by a business, and will list the invoices received.

DEFINITION

The **accounts payable ledger** is the ledger which contains the personal accounts of the **individual** suppliers. It is also known as the **purchases ledger**.

KEY POINT

The entries are made into the purchases journal from the suppliers' invoices which the business receives.

The **purchases journal** is used to summarise the credit purchases made by a business, and will list the invoices received.

This book, which is not part of the double entry, will be summarised periodically, and the totals then posted to the relevant accounts in the general ledger (including the accounts payable ledger control account) and the **accounts payable ledger** itself (which has now been removed from the double entry system).

The accounts payable ledger is the ledger which contains the personal accounts of the **individual** suppliers. It is also known as the **purchases ledger**.

Note in the example which follows, that the purchases journal deals with all types of purchases by a business – goods for resale, raw materials to be processed into goods for sale, and expenses of running the business. It therefore deals with items which will eventually find their way into either the purchases account or the various expense accounts.

The entries are made into the purchases journal from the suppliers' invoices which the business receives. They must then be analysed, so that totals can be posted to the correct accounts.

Example of recording of transactions and posting to ledgers

During February 20X9 the purchases journal of a company appears as follows:

Date	*Supplier*	*Ledger ref*	*Total*	*Purchases*	*Lighting and heating*	*Repairs and maintenance*	*Telephone*	*Sundry expenses*
			$	$	$	$	$	$
5 Feb	Telecom	T1	160				160	
8 Feb	J Smith	S13	80	80				
11 Feb	B Orange	O17	180	180				
14 Feb	Eastern Electricity	E12	138		138			
18 Feb	Wiggins Teape	W4	20					20
21 Feb	S Green	G7	100	100				
23 Feb	D Brown	B13	140	140				
25 Feb	Mendit Ltd	M1	40			40		
			858	500	138	40	160	20

Record the transactions in the appropriate ledgers.

Solution

(a) In the general ledger

Purchases

20X9		$	*20X9*		$
Feb	Purchases journal	500			

Lighting and heating

20X9		$	*20X9*		$
Feb	Purchases journal	138			

Repairs and maintenance

20X9		$	*20X9*		$
Feb	Purchases journal	40			

Telephone

20X9		$	*20X9*		$
Feb	Purchases journal	160			

Sundry expenses

20X9		$	*20X9*		$
Feb	Purchases journal	20			

Accounts payable control account

20X9		$	*20X9*		$
			Feb	Purchases journal	858

(b) In the accounts payable ledger

Telecom (T1)

20X9		$	*20X9*		$
			Feb	Purchases journal	160

D Brown (B13)

20X9		$	*20X9*		$
			Feb	Purchases journal	140

Eastern Electricity (E12)

20X9		$	*20X9*		$
			Feb	Purchases journal	138

S Green (G7)

20X9		$	*20X9*		$
			Feb	Purchases journal	100

Mendit Ltd (M1)

20X9	$	20X9		$
		Feb	Purchases journal	40

B Orange (O17)

20X9	$	20X9		$
		Feb	Purchases journal	180

J Smith (S13)

20X9	$	20X9		$
		Feb	Purchases journal	80

Wiggins Teape (W4)

20X9	$	20X9		$
		Feb	Purchases journal	20

KEY POINT

The credits to the accounts payable ledger accounts equal the debits in the general ledger accounts.

The credits to the accounts payable ledger accounts equal the debits in the general ledger accounts.

3 Other journals

3.1 Transactions dealt with and how output dealt with

The sales journal and sales and purchases returns journals work in similar fashion, the use of all the journals being shown in summary fashion by means of the following table:

Journal	*Transaction dealt with*	*General ledger*		*Accounts payable or receivable ledger*
		Debit	*Credit*	
Purchases	Invoices for goods or services purchased from suppliers on credit	Expenditure accounts e.g. purchases, lighting and heating, telephone	Accounts payable ledger control account	Entered on supplier's personal account on individual basis
Sales	Invoices for goods to customers on credit	Accounts receivable ledger control account	Revenue accounts e.g. sales, sundry income, rental income	Entered on customer's personal account on individual basis.
Purchases returns	Credit notes for goods returned to suppliers	Accounts payable ledger control account	Purchases returns	Entered on supplier's account on 'debit' side on individual basis
Sales returns	Credit notes for goods returned by customers	Sales returns	Accounts receivable ledger control account	Entered on customer's personal account on 'credit' side on individual basis

ACTIVITY 1

Using the purchases journal as a model, draft the layout of a sales journal.

Feedback to this activity is at the end of the chapter.

3.2 Contras

One element of such a system is that on occasion there may be a set-off between accounts in the accounts receivable ledger and the accounts payable ledger. For instance, suppose a business both buys goods from and sells goods to Trollope. If at one time the accounts payable ledger shows that the business owes him $75 and the accounts receivable ledger shows that he owes $50, there are two possible methods of approach:

1. The business pays Trollope $75 and he pays it $50.
2. The business agrees with Trollope to pay him $25 and to cancel the $50 owing to it in the accounts receivable ledger with $50 of the $75 owing to him in the accounts payable ledger.

KEY POINT

The cancelling entry is called a **contra** entry.

The cancelling entry is called a **contra** entry.

If the latter course is adopted the transactions should be recorded as follows:

(a) In the accounts payable ledger

Trollope (T26)

	$		$
Accounts receivable ledger contra	50	Balance b/d	75
Balance c/d	25		
	75		75

(b) In the accounts receivable ledger

Trollope (T17)

	$		$
Balance b/d	50	Accounts payable ledger contra	50

KEY POINT

If an amount is both owed to and from the same person it can be removed by a debit to the accounts payable ledger account and a credit to the accounts receivable ledger account.

The accounts payable ledger account now correctly shows the fact that we have agreed to pay Trollope only $25 as a result of the contra agreement. Clearly Trollope himself will make equivalent adjustments in his own books.

If an amount is both owed to and from the same person it can be removed by a debit to the accounts payable ledger account and a credit to the accounts receivable ledger account.

ACTIVITY 2

Consider why there are no columns for cash discounts allowed and received in the sales journal and purchases journal respectively.

Feedback to this activity is at the end of the chapter.

4 The cash book

4.1 Introduction

The name 'cash book' is something of a misnomer, because the book is used to summarise an organisation's bank transactions; a company's transactions in cash are dealt with (in normal circumstances) through the petty cash book.

KEY POINT

Many enterprises have two distinct cash books – a **cash payments book** and a **cash receipts book**.

Many enterprises have two distinct cash books – a **cash payments book** and a **cash receipts book**, but for study and examination purposes it is convenient to think of it as a single book, the balance of which shows the cash at bank or overdraft.

4.2 The bookkeeping system summarised

The cash book is the cash account in the ledger treated as a separate record. As you have seen in earlier chapters, the cash account transactions of a business are numerous and it is really the centrepiece of the bookkeeping system, being involved in all sections of it:

- the accounts receivable ledger system when customers pay their accounts
- the accounts payable ledger system when suppliers' accounts are paid
- the general ledger system when expenses are paid or assets purchased, or when income is received or liabilities are paid off.

For this reason it is convenient to regard the cash book as a book of original entry, which in practice it is, because all cash received and paid is entered into it from the source documents.

The structure of the main elements of the bookkeeping system can now be presented thus:

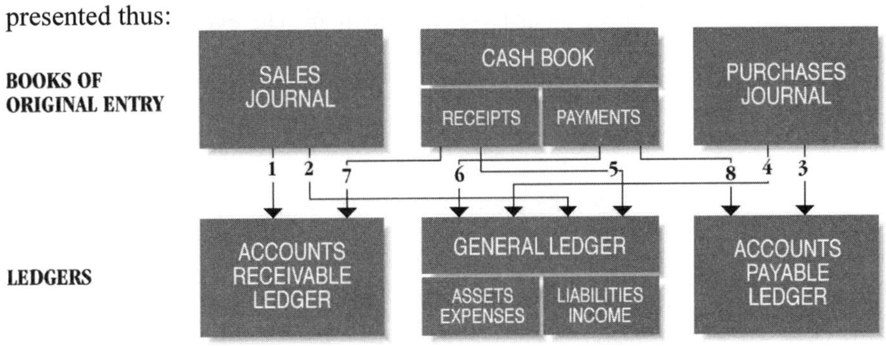

Each of the eight arrows connecting these elements of the recording system is numbered. The explanations below clarify their meaning.

(1) Sales journal → accounts receivable ledger

Individual credit sales are entered into the sales journal and into the accounts receivable ledger accounts of the credit customers. The arrow represents the entry from sales journal to the debit of the accounts receivable ledger account concerned.

(2) Sales journal → general ledger (sales revenue account)

The sales journal has two functions – to build up the total sales for a period to be credited to the sales revenue account in the general ledger and to facilitate the debiting of the individual customer accounts in the receivables ledger. The second arrow represents the transfer of the sales journal *total* to the credit of the sales revenue account. This completes the double entry – the sales journal itself is not part of the double entry system. The double entry is made up of the individual debits in the accounts receivable ledger, balanced by the single credit in the general ledger.

(3) Purchases journal → accounts payable ledger

This arrow represents the entries corresponding to arrow 1 above but for credit purchases – entered into the purchases journal and to the credit of the suppliers' accounts in the accounts payable ledger.

(4) Purchases journal → general ledger (purchases account)

Arrow 4 corresponds to arrow 2. It is the transfer of the total purchases to the debit of purchases account in the general ledger. The purchases journal, like the sales journal, is not part of the double entry system but facilitates the making of the entries. The sum of the individual credits to accounts payable ledger accounts is equal to the single debit to purchases account. You saw in the example above that items other than the purchase of goods for resale may pass through the purchases journal.

(5) Debit side of cash book → credit of general ledger accounts

The entries explained for arrow 6 below analyse the credits (payments) in the cash book. Arrow 5 indicates the corresponding process for the debits (receipts). Receipts could be sundry items of income, dividends for example, or the result of incurring a liability. When a business borrows money, the entry in the cash book records the increased cash, and the credit to the liability account in the general ledger records the obligation to repay the money in due course.

(6) Credit side of cash book → debit of general ledger accounts

Arrow 6 is the analysis of payments made. The cash book records the payment of cash and thus the reduction in the balance, and the transfer to the appropriate general ledger account analyses the payment. The expense accounts in the general ledger collect all items relating to the same expense heading. Non-current asset accounts do the same for capital expenditure on different types of non-current asset.

(7) Cash book → accounts receivable ledger

Receipts from credit customers are entered in the cash book and to the credit of the appropriate accounts receivable ledger accounts.

(8) Cash book → accounts payable ledger

Payments to suppliers are entered in the cash book and on the debit side of the appropriate accounts payable ledger account.

Example

The following transactions are recorded in the cash payments book of a company during February 20X9:

Date	*Detail*	*Cheque no*	*Ledger ref*	*Bank*	*Discount received*	*Payables ledger*	*Wages*	*Petty cash*	*Sundry expenses*
				$	$	$	$	$	$
2 Feb	Wages	124507	–	1,052			1,052		
5 Feb	J Smith	124508	S13	58	1	58			
9 Feb	B Jones	124509	–	120					120
16 Feb	Cash	124510	–	150				150	
23 Feb	S Green	124511	G7	80	6	80			
24 Feb	B Orange	124512	O17	100		100			
27 Feb	D Brown	124513	B13	119	2	119			
				1,679	9	357	1,052	150	120

Record the above transactions in the relevant ledger accounts.

KEY POINT

Every item of cash receipt or payment is then posted individually to the appropriate ledger account.

Tutorial note: the above cash book illustrates the idea of analysis columns in the cash book. In its simplest form, the cash book consists of a single column on each side with an adjacent discount column. Every item of cash receipt or payment is then posted individually to the appropriate ledger account. It is often convenient to introduce analysis columns for expense and income items to enable monthly or other totals to be posted to the accounts. Although there is only one item in each of the expense columns in this cash book, it is important to realise that the postings to the accounts are of the **column totals** ($1,052, $150 and $120) and not the individual items.

For examination purposes you will nearly always need to work with the simple 'single column' type cash book with discount columns.

4.3 Discounts

Before considering the double entry bookkeeping procedures here it is worth mentioning the **discounts received** column.

(a) It does not represent an amount paid in the period. The total of $1,679 is made up of the analysed column totals excluding discount received:

	$
Purchase ledger control	357
Wages	1,052
Petty cash	150
Sundry expenses	120
	1,679

(b) It is included in the cash payments book to show whether any cash discount has been taken for prompt payment and to facilitate its recording in both the general ledger and the accounts payable ledger.

Note that only cash (prompt payment) discounts will be included here, and not trade discounts. The distinction and different treatments are explained by the following table:

Term	*Relates to*	*Bookkeeping implications*
Cash discount	Discount for payment before a stated date	**1** Purchases are debited with the full invoice price **2** On payment of the supplier, the difference between cash paid and the full invoice price of the invoice paid represents the cash discount.
Trade discount	Favourable price for people in the same trade.	Purchases are recorded at trade price (the lower price involved). The amount of the deduction does not appear in the ledger accounts.

Solution

Returning to the example, at the end of February the transactions are recorded as follows:

(a) In the general ledger

Discount received

20X9		$	*20X9*		$
			Feb	Cash book	9

Wages

20X9		$	*20X9*		$
Feb	Cash book	1,052			

Petty cash

20X9		$	*20X9*		$
Feb	Cash book	150			

Sundry expenses

20X9		$	20X9	$
Feb	Cash book	120		

Accounts payable control account

20X9		$	20X9	$
Feb	Cash book	357		
	Cash book – discount	9		

(b) In the accounts payable ledger

D Brown (B13)

20X9		$	20X9	$
Feb	Cash book – discount	2		
	Cash	119		

S Green (G7)

20X9		$	20X9	$
Feb	Cash book – discount	6		
	Cash	80		

B Orange (O17)

20X9		$	20X9	$
Feb	Cash book	100		

J Smith (S13)

20X9		$	20X9	$
Feb	Cash book – discount	1		
	Cash	58		

Note: note once again the treatment of the discount received. It is included on the 'debit' side of the creditor's personal account, representing a reduction in the amount owing to him.

KEY POINT

All the entries in these ledger accounts are analysis of the items in the cash book.

All the entries in these ledger accounts are analysis of the items in the cash book.

Example

The following receipts are recorded in the cash book of a company during February 20X9:

Date	*Detail*	*Ledger ref*	*Bank*	*Discount allowed*	*Sales ledger*	*Cash sales*	*Rental income*	*Sundry income*
			$	$	$	$	$	$
2 Feb	Cash sales		140			140		
5 Feb	S Black	B7	75	5	75			
9 Feb	J Clark		5					5
16 Feb	Cash sales		100			100		
23 Feb	B Brown	B8	16	1	16			
24 Feb	Hire-it Ltd		80				80	
27 Feb	J Purple	P6	5		5			
			421	6	96	240	80	5

Once again the treatment of discounts merits close scrutiny. The discounts allowed column does not represent an amount received in the period, but is included in the cash receipts book to show whether any discount has been allowed and to facilitate its recording in both the general ledger and the accounts receivable ledger.

ACTIVITY 3

Record the totals from the cash receipts book in the general ledger and the individual amounts in the accounts receivable ledger.

Feedback to this activity is at the end of the chapter.

KEY POINT

The postings from the cash receipts book are to debit the bank account with the total and credit the accounts receivable ledger accounts and income accounts.

The postings from the cash receipts book are to debit the bank account with the total and credit the accounts receivable ledger accounts and income accounts.

5 Petty cash book

5.1 Purpose of petty cash system

The petty cash book is unlikely to impact on the accounts payable and receivable ledger systems, although the occasional accounts payable ledger payment might be made from petty cash.

The petty cash system is usually designed to deal with sundry small payments in cash made by a business, e.g. paying the milkman, purchasing biscuits, buying stationery or reimbursing travelling expenses.

5.2 Imprest system

KEY POINT

The best way of dealing with petty cash is by means of an **imprest** system.

The best way of dealing with petty cash is by means of an **imprest** system, which works as follows.

Step 1

To initiate the system, a round sum cheque is drawn. This will be dealt with through the cash payments book, the eventual debit being to petty cash and the credit to bank. This round sum amount will be referred to as the 'petty cash float'.

Step 2

As the petty cashier makes payments he records these in the petty cash book, which is not part of the double entry system.

Step 3

When the petty cash runs low, a cheque is drawn to return the petty cash to the exact amount of the original float. At this stage vouchers should be produced by the petty cashier to the cheque signatory which will exactly equal the cheque required.

This aspect of control is the essential feature of the petty cash system. At any stage the float should be represented in the petty cash box by the actual cash therein, plus any vouchers in support of payments made since the last reimbursement.

Example

On 1 March 20X9 a petty cash float of $100 is introduced by Dialex. During March the following payments are made out of petty cash:

		$
2 March	Biscuits	10
8 March	Stationery	20
11 March	Bus fare	3
16 March	Train fare	5
25 March	Stationery	40

On 31 March the cash is reimbursed. Write up the petty cash book for the month.

Received	*Date*	*Details*	*Voucher*	*Total*	*Stationery*	*Sundry expenses*	*Travelling expenses*
$				$	$	$	$
100	1 Mar	Cash book					
	2 Mar	Gateway biscuits	1	10		10	
	8 Mar	Basildon Bond	2	20	20		
	11 Mar	Bus fares	3	3			3
	16 Mar	Rail fares	4	5			5
	25 Mar	Office International	5	40	40		
				78	60	10	8
78	31 Mar	Cash					
		Balance c/d		100			
178				178			
100	1 Apr	Balance b/d					

5.3 Writing up the ledger accounts

No double entry bookkeeping entries are made from the receipts side of the petty cash book – in a good system the only receipt should be the reimbursement of the float, the double entry of which is dealt with in the posting of the cash book.

As regards the payments, the double entry in the general ledger is performed as follows:

Stationery

20X9		$	*20X9*		$
Mar	Petty cash book	60			

Sundry expenses

20X9		$	*20X9*		$
Mar	Petty cash book	10			

Travelling expenses

20X9		$	*20X9*		$
Mar	Petty cash book	8			

6 Accounting for sales tax

KEY POINT

Sales tax is a form of indirect taxation (e.g. VAT and GST) that can be levied on most goods and services.

6.1 Sales tax

Sales tax is a form of indirect taxation. Many countries have a sales tax, which might be called value added tax or general sales tax. Sales tax is charged on most goods and services. For example, if a business sells an item for $100 and sales tax is 15%, the customer is charged $115. If this £100 is sales revenue for the business and $15 is tax that has been collected by the business on behalf of the government. So with a sales tax, businesses act as unpaid tax collectors.

6.2 Accounting treatment

The majority of traders act as collection agents (unpaid) for the tax authorities. At no time does the tax belong to the business. At regular intervals in the year, the business either pays tax to, or has it repaid by the tax authorities.

Sales tax has to be accounted for. The important point to remember is that sales tax is excluded from the sales and purchases of a business. It is money owed to the government (sales tax collected on sales) less money recoverable from the government (sales tax paid on purchases and other expenses).

Sales tax is eventually paid by the final consumer, but it might be charged to businesses as well. Most businesses are able to set off the sales tax they pay on their purchases against the sale tax they have collected. Their payment to the government is the sales tax collected less the sales tax paid. For example, suppose that Business X sells raw materials to Business Y and charges $200 plus sales tax of 10%. Business Y pays $220, tax of $20. Now suppose that Business Y turns the raw materials into widgets that it sells to consumers for $500 plus sales tax of $50. The consumers pay $550, consisting of sales of $500 and sales tax of $50. As a result:

(a) Business X owes $20 in sales tax to the government

(b) Business Y owes tax collected minus tax paid, which is $30 ($50 - $20)

(c) The tax is actually paid by the consumer, because the tax on the widgets is $50.

The nominal ledger should include a sales tax account which acts as an account with the tax authorities. The sales tax account is debited with all tax payable on purchases and expenses and credited with all tax charged on sales. The balance on the sales tax account will, therefore, represent the net amount due to or from the tax authorities. Entries in the account will be made as follows:

- Tax on purchases/expenses on credit:

Dr	Purchases account or expense account	with cost excluding tax
Dr	Sales tax account	with sales tax
	Cr Accounts payable	with cost including tax

- Tax charged on sales:

Dr	Accounts receivable	with sales including tax
	Cr Sales account	with sales excluding tax
	Cr Sales tax account	with sales tax

- Payments to tax authorities:

  Dr Sales tax account

  Cr Cash at Bank

- Refunds of excess tax suffered from tax authorities:

  Dr Cash at Bank

  Cr Sales tax account

Example

A trader's purchase and sales analysis shows the following information for the last quarter of his financial year:

		Net	Sales Tax	Total
		$	$	$
Purchases	(all on credit)	180,000	31,500	211,500
Sales	(all on credit)	260,000	45,500	305,500

Record these transactions in the main ledger.

Solution

Sales

	$		$
		Receivables	260,000
			260,00

Purchases

	$		$
Payables	180,000		
	180,000		

Accounts receivable ledger control account

	$		$
Sales/Sales tax	305,500		
	305,000		

Accounts payable ledger control account

	$		$
		Purchases/Sales tax	31,500
			31,500

Sales tax account (a personal account with tax authorities)

	$		$
Payables	31,500	Receivables	
Balance c/d	14,000		
	45,500		45,500
			14,000

Note: As the balance on this account represents a normal trade liability it can be included in accounts payable on the balance sheet.

ACTIVITY **4**

Credit purchases are made for $9,400. This figure includes sales tax.

Half those goods are sold on credit for $6,400 **exclusive** of sales tax.

Record the above transactions in the following T accounts: purchases of stock, accounts payable, VAT, sales and accounts receivable.

Feedback to this activity is at the end of the chapter.

Conclusion

In this chapter the operation of the system of books of prime entry or journals has been studied. These are simply ways of summarising the money transactions of a business at suitable points in time and then posting these summaries to the relevant accounts in the general ledger.

SELF-TEST QUESTIONS

Division of ledgers

1 What is a book of original entry? (1.1)

2 What is the accounts receivable ledger? (1.3)

Purchases journal

3 What is the purchases journal? (2)

Other journals

4 What documents are used to write up the sales returns book? (3.1)

5 What situation might cause a contra entry to take place? (3.2)

The cash book

6 Where is the total from the discount received column in the cash payments book posted to? (4.3)

7 What is the difference between a cash discount and a trade discount? (4.3)

Petty cash

8 What is an imprest system? (5.2)

PRACTICE QUESTION

Heale

You are given the information below about the first month's trading of Heale.

You are required:

(a) to write up the sales journal, purchase journal, cash book and petty cash book **(10 marks)**

(b) from the above books of prime entry, to write up the general, accounts receivable and accounts payable ledgers **(20 marks)**

(c) to extract a trial balance at the end of the month. **(5 marks)**

(Total: 35 marks)

		$
Sales details:		
Credit sales:	Jones	94
	Smith	118
	Turnip	141
	Clog	235
	Foul	353
Purchase details:		
Credit purchases	Snell	80
	Ryan	100
	Ovett	150
	Coe	300
	Keino	100
	Telecom	50
	Gas	75
Cash Book details:		
Receipts from sales:	Jones	30
	Smith	60
	Turnip	110
	Foul	80
	Sundry income	10
Payments:	Petty cash	200
	Snell	70
	Ovett	30
	Telecom	50
	Wages	300
	Sundry expenses	80
Petty cash book details:		
Receipts:	Cash	200
Payments:	Stationery	16
	Postage	3
	Travelling	8
	Sundry expenses	12

For the answer to this question, see the 'Answers' section at the end of the book.

FEEDBACK TO ACTIVITY 1

Sales journal

Date	*Customer*	*Ledger ref*	*Total*	*Sales*	*Sundry income*

FEEDBACK TO ACTIVITY 2

The sales journal records invoices sent out to customers and the purchases journal records invoices received from suppliers. At this stage it is not known whether cash discounts will be taken or not. It is only when the money is paid or received that this information is known.

FEEDBACK TO ACTIVITY 3

(a) In the general ledger

Discount allowed

20X9		$	20X9		$
Feb	Cash book	6			

Cash sales

20X9		$	20X9		$
			Feb	Cash book	240

Rental income

20X9		$	20X9		$
			Feb	Cash book	80

Sundry income

20X9		$	20X9		$
			Feb	Cash book	5

Accounts receivable control account

20X9		$	20X9		$
			Feb	Cash book	96
				Cash book – discount	6

Again it is worth noting the treatment of the discount, being debited to discount allowed and credited to accounts receivable ledger control account (reducing the amount owed from debtors).

(b) In the accounts receivable ledger

S Black (B7)

20X9		$	20X9		$
			Feb	Cash book – discount	5
				Cash	75

B Brown (B8)

20X9		$	20X9		$
			Feb	Cash book – discount	1
				Cash	16

J Purple (P6)

20X9	$	*20X9*		$
		Feb	Cash book	5

Here the discount is included on the 'credit' side of the customer's personal account, representing a reduction owing by him.

FEEDBACK TO ACTIVITY **4**

Step 1 Work out the VAT elements

On purchases:

	$
Gross amount	9,400
Less VAT $(9{,}400 \times \frac{17.5}{117.5})$	1,400
Net amount	8,000

On sales:

	$
Net amount	6,400
Add VAT $(6{,}400 \times \frac{17.5}{100})$	1,120
Gross amount $(6{,}400 \times \frac{117.5}{100})$	7,520

Step 2 Record the transactions in the T accounts.

Purchases account

	$		$
Accounts payable (1)	8,000		

Accounts payable

	$		$
		Purchases including VAT (1)	9,400

VAT account

	$		$
Purchases (1)	1,400	Sales (2)	1,120

Sales account

	$		$
		Accounts receivable (2)	6,400

Accounts receivable

	$		$
Sales including VAT (2)	7,520		

Chapter 10
CONTROL ACCOUNT RECONCILIATIONS

CHAPTER CONTENTS

The whole process of bookkeeping revolves around the idea that the records 'balance'; every debit has a credit and the total of the debits equals the total of the credits. In other words, if there are no errors in the records, the trial balance will balance.

If the trial balance does not balance, the difference has to be found. In a system that is not computerised, it may take a lot of expensive time and effort to find the difference. However, there is a technique which simplifies the process considerably – balancing sections of the bookkeeping system separately.

You saw in the last chapter that the ledger is broken down into three parts: accounts receivable ledger, accounts payable ledger and general ledger. In most businesses, by far the greatest volume of entries passes through the accounts receivable and payable ledgers. It is fairly easy to prove the accuracy of the accounts receivable ledger and the accounts payable ledger separately. The techniques for doing so are the subject of this chapter.

Objectives

By the time you have finished this chapter you should be able to:

- prepare control accounts proving the accuracy of the accounts receivable and accounts payable ledgers.

1 Control account reconciliations

1.1 Introduction

The objective we have in this chapter is to establish a technique for proving the correctness of a section of the bookkeeping system. Let us take the accounts receivable ledger first.

1.2 Proving the accuracy of the accounts receivable ledger entries

The total of the accounts receivable ledger balances is the key to the operation. Can we establish, independently of the accounts receivable ledger, a control total with which the total of these balances can be agreed?

The entries in the accounts receivable ledger come predominantly from:

Sales journal	– credit sales
Cash book	– cash received from customers
Cash book discount column	– discounts allowed.

There will be some other minor items such as bad debts written off and, of course, the balances brought forward from the previous period.

Is it possible to obtain the totals of these items without reference to the accounts receivable ledger? Yes. All the information is available.

Item	*Source of total*
Opening balances	List of last month's balances
Credit sales	Total of sales journal
Cash from customers	Accounts receivable ledger (debtors ledger) column in cash book (you met the analysed cash book in the last chapter)
Discounts allowed	Discounts column in cash book

All these items are put together in a ledger account in the general ledger – the accounts receivable ledger control account. An example appears below:

Accounts receivable ledger control account

		$			$
1 Jan	Balance b/d	108,000	31 Jan	Cash from customers	58,400
31 Jan	Sales for month	59,000		Discount allowed	300
				Sales returns	1,200
				Balance c/d	107,100
		167,000			167,000
1 Feb	Balance b/d	107,100			

Note that the items appear on the *same side* as that on which the individual items appear in the accounts receivable ledger.

A figure for sales returns has been included – it would of course, be obtainable from the sales returns journal.

The balance of $107,100 will then be agreed with the total of the accounts receivable ledger balances.

One important point has to be cleared up. We have introduced a third entry into our double entry system. The accounts receivable ledger balances total $107,100, and the control account does also. Only one of them features in the list of account balances. Which is within the double entry system and which is the memorandum?

It is possible to regard the control account as the double entry record, and the accounts receivable ledger as the memorandum or vice versa.

1.3 Proving the accuracy of the accounts payable ledger

Exactly the same process is followed to agree the accounts payable ledger by preparing an accounts payable ledger control account which leads to a balance with which the total of the accounts payable ledger balances can be agreed.

1.4 Additional items in control accounts

As well as the items covered so far, several others can appear:

Accounts receivable ledger control account	*Accounts payable ledger control account*
Cash refunds to customers	Cash refunds from suppliers
Bad debts written off	

One other additional item appears in every examination question on control accounts – the **contra.** A contra is a transfer between two ledger accounts for the same person. It sometimes happens that a customer in the receivables ledger is also a supplier in the payables ledger. In many cases, the accounts are settled by each party paying the other in full for goods supplied. However, it is also possible to set off the balances and for the party with the greater balance to pay the difference. A contra transaction was illustrated in Chapter 9.

Example

In the ledgers of X there is an account with Y in both the accounts receivable ledger and the accounts payable ledger.

Accounts receivable ledger

Y

	$		$
Goods	4,900		

Accounts payable ledger

Y

	$		$
		Goods	5,200

Instead of paying the $5,200 due to Y, X could pay $300 and cancel the remaining debt against the accounts receivable ledger balance due from Y. The ledger accounts would become:

Accounts receivable ledger

Y

	$		$
Goods	4,900	Contra accounts payable ledger	4,900

Accounts payable ledger

Y

	$		$
Cash	300	Goods	5,200
Contra accounts receivable ledger	4,900		
	5,200		5,200

KEY POINT

The vital point to grasp about contras is that they must appear in both the accounts receivable ledger and accounts payable ledger, and therefore must necessarily be in both the accounts receivable ledger control account and accounts payable ledger control account.

Both accounts are cleared. The vital point to grasp about contras is that they must appear in both the accounts receivable ledger and accounts payable ledger, and therefore must necessarily be in both the accounts receivable ledger control account and accounts payable ledger control account.

1.5 Reconciling items

In practice (and in examination questions) the balance on the control account may not agree with the total of the ledger accounts, and in such an instance the causes of the difference must be identified and adjustments made where necessary.

Such differences may be caused by:

- errors in the accounts receivable or accounts payable ledger control accounts
- errors in the accounts receivable or accounts payable ledger
- errors in both the control accounts and the ledger accounts.

ACTIVITY 1

Suggest reasons why there might be a difference between the balance on the accounts receivable ledger control account and the total of the list of accounts receivable ledger balances.

Feedback to this activity is at the end of the chapter.

2 Agreement of the control account balance with the sum of the balances on the underlying accounts

2.1 Example

The following example illustrates the types of problem likely to arise in such a system. Full explanations of the amendments are given – such explanations would not normally be necessary in an examination question. This illustration and the entries to correct the errors are based on the accounts payable ledger control account being in the double entry system (see above).

Alston's accounts payable ledger control account is an integral part of the double entry system. Individual ledger account balances are listed and totalled on a monthly basis, and reconciled to the control account balance. Information for the month of March is as follows:

1 Individual ledger account balances at 31 March have been listed out and totalled as follows:

	$
Total of debit balances	1,012
Total of credit balances	20,778

2 The accounts payable ledger control account balance at 31 March is $21,832 (net).

3 On further examination the following errors are discovered:

- The total of discount received for the month, amounting to $1,715, has not been entered in the control account.
- On listing-out, an individual credit balance of $205 has been incorrectly treated as a debit.
- A petty cash payment to a supplier amounting to $63 has been correctly treated in the control account, but no entry has been made in the supplier's individual ledger account.
- The purchases journal total for March has been undercast (understated) by $2,000.
- Contras (set-offs) with the accounts receivable ledger, amounting in total to $2,004, have been correctly treated in the individual ledger accounts but no entry has been made in the control account.

You are required:

(a) to prepare the part of the accounts payable ledger control account reflecting the above information

(b) to prepare a statement reconciling the original total of the individual balances with the corrected balance on the control account.

2.2 Solution

The way to approach the question is to consider each of the above five points in turn and ask to what extent they affect (a) the accounts payable ledger control account and (b) the listing of accounts payable ledger balances.

Step 1

The total of discount received in the cash book is dealt with by debiting accounts payable ledger control account and crediting discount received. Thus, if the posting has not been entered in either double entry account it clearly should be.

As the individual ledger accounts in the accounts payable ledger are posted individually from the cash payments book, the total of discount received will not feature in any postings to the accounts payable ledger; hence no amendment is required.

Step 2

Individual credit balances are extracted from the accounts payable ledger. Here, this error affects the totals of the debit and credit balances of the ledger account balance. No adjustment is required to the control accounts.

Step 3

The question clearly states that the error has been made in the individual ledger accounts. Amendments should be made to the list of balances. Again, no amendment is required to the control accounts.

Step 4

The total of the purchases journal is posted by debiting purchases and crediting accounts payable ledger control account. If the total is understated, the following bookkeeping entry must be made, posting the $2,000 understatement:

Dr Purchases

Cr Accounts payable ledger control.

As the individual ledger accounts in the accounts payable ledger are posted individually from the purchases journal, the total of the journal being understated will not affect the listing of the balances in the accounts payable ledger.

Step 5

Here it is clear that the error affects the control account, not the accounts payable ledger. Correction should be made by the bookkeeping entry:

Dr Accounts payable ledger control

Cr Accounts receivable ledger control.

Accounts payable ledger control account

20X9	$	*20X9*	$
Discount received (S1)	1,715	31 Mar Balance (net)	21,832
Accounts receivable ledger control (S5)	2,004	Purchase (S4)	2,000
Balance c/d	20,113		
	23,832		23,832

Reconciliation of individual balances with control account balance

	Dr	*Cr*
	$	$
Balances as extracted	1,012	20,778
Credit balance incorrectly treated 2 × $205 (S2)		410
Petty cash payment (S3)	63	
	1,075	21,188
		1,075
Net total agreeing with control account		20,113

Conclusion

In this chapter, the reasons why control account balances should be equal to the list of individual balances in the relevant ledger were considered, as were the reasons why these two totals are very often not equal. If the totals are not equal then the reasons for the difference must be discovered and the control account and list of individual balances amended accordingly.

SELF-TEST QUESTIONS

Control account reconciliations

1 What is an alternative name for the accounts receivable ledger control account? (1.2)

2 Why should the balance on the accounts payable ledger control account equal the total of the balances in the accounts payable ledger? (1.3)

3 What three types of difference may cause control account reconciliation problems? (1.5)

Agreement of control account

4 Would the miscasting of the sales journal affect the accounts receivable ledger balances? (2.2)

5 Is the opening balance on the accounts payable ledger control account, a debit or a credit balance? (2.2)

6 What is the double entry for a discount received that has not been entered in the accounts? (2.2)

7 If a credit balance on a supplier's account had been included in the list of balances as a debit balance, what amendment would be required? (2.2)

8 Is the entry in a supplier's individual account for a payment to him out of petty cash, a debit or a credit entry? (2.2)

9 If the purchases journal is under-cast, what would be the double entry to amend this? (2.2)

10 What is the double entry for a contra? (2.2)

MULTIPLE-CHOICE QUESTION

In an accounts receivable ledger control account, which of the following lists is composed only of items which would appear on the credit side of the account?

A Cash received from customers, sales returns, bad debts written off, contras against amounts due to suppliers in the accounts payable ledger

B Sales, cash refunds to customers, bad debts written off, discounts allowed

C Cash received from customers, discounts allowed, interest charged on overdue accounts, bad debts written off

D Sales, cash refunds to customers, interest charged on overdue accounts, contras against amounts due to suppliers in the accounts payable ledger.

For the answer to this question, see the 'Answers' section at the end of the book.

EXAM-TYPE QUESTIONS

Question 1: Excel Stores

The book-keeper of Excel Stores prepared a schedule of balances of individual suppliers' accounts from the accounts payable ledger at 30 June 20X4 and arrived at a total of $86,538.28.

He passed the schedule over to the accountant who compared this total with the closing balance on the accounts payable ledger control account reproduced below.

During his investigation into the discrepancy between the two figures, the accountant discovered a number of errors in the control account and the individual ledger accounts and schedule. You may assume that the total of each item posted to the control account is correct except to the extent that they are dealt with in the list below:

1 One supplier had been paid $10.22 out of petty cash. This had been correctly posted to his personal account but had been omitted from the control account.

2 The credit side of one supplier's personal account had been under-added by $30.00.

3 A credit balance on a supplier's account had been transposed from $548.14 to $584.41 when extracted on to the schedule.

4 The balance on one supplier's account of $674.32 had been completely omitted from the schedule.

5 Discounts received of $12.56 and $8.13 had been posted to the wrong side of two individual creditors' accounts.

6 Goods costing $39.60 had been returned to the supplier but this transaction had been completely omitted from the returns journal.

You are required:

(a) to prepare a statement starting with the original closing balance on the accounts payable ledger control account then identifying and correcting the errors in that account and concluding with an amended closing balance **(9 marks)**

(b) to prepare a statement starting with the original total of the schedule of individual accounts payable then identifying and correcting errors in that schedule and concluding with an amended total. **(7 marks)**

(Total: 16 marks)

Accounts payable ledger control

20X4			20X4		
June		$	*June*		$
30	Purchase returns	560.18	1	Balance b/d	89,271.13
30	Bank	96,312.70	30	Purchases	100,483.49
30	Balance c/d	84,688.31	30	Discount received	2,656.82
			30	Accounts receivable ledger control (contras)	3,049.75
		192,561.19			195,261.19
			July		
			1	Balance b/d	84,688.31

Question 2: DEF – Accounts receivable ledger

DEF has a computerised accounts receivable ledger which is not integrated with the remainder of its accounting records which are kept manually.

A summary report (produced by totalling the individual customer accounts) from the computer system at 30 September 20X8 is as below.

The computerised customer records were inspected and two customers were found to have credit balances. These were:

B Green	$434.00
J Jones	$158.00

The balances on the manually prepared accounts receivable ledger control account in the general ledger at the same date were:

Debit	$12,814.00
Credit	$592.00

The accounts were reviewed and the following errors were found:

1 One of the pages in the sales journal had been over-added by $850.00.

2 The total on one page of the sales returns journal had been carried forward as $1,239 instead of $1,329.

3 XT had settled its account of $474 by accounts payable ledger contra. This had not been entered on a computer journal.

4 A sales return valued at $354 was entered in J Smith's account as a sale.

5 A repayment of $217 made to B Green was entered in his account as a payment received from him.

6 The balance on AS's account of $793 had been written off as a bad debt but was not entered on a computer journal.

7 A sale to CG for $919 was entered in EG's account.

8 Discount allowed to XYZ of $57 had not been entered in its account.

9 The total of the discount received column in the cash book was under-added by $100.

Accounts receivable ledger control report 30 September 20X8

	$
Balance brought forward	15,438.00
Add: Sales	74,691.00
Repayments made	1,249.00
Adjustments	23.00
Less: Sales returns	2,347.00
Payments received	71,203.00
Bad debts written off	646.00
Accounts payable ledger contra	139.00
Discounts allowed	4,128.00
Adjustments	58.00
Balance carried forward	12,880.00

You are required:

(a) to restate the manual control account commencing with the balances given

(b) to show a corrected computerised control account using the format given

(c) to explain the effect of each of items 1 to 9 above. **(14 marks)**

Question 3: Explain open item accounts receivable ledger system

What is an open item accounts receivable ledger system? How does such a system assist a company to control the amount of credit its customers obtain?

(6 marks)

For the answers to these questions, see the 'Answers' section at the end of the book.

FEEDBACK TO ACTIVITY 1

- The sales journal, sales returns journal or cash receipts book have been incorrectly totalled.
- A total from a book of prime entry has been transferred to the control account as a different figure.
- An individual entry from a book of prime entry has been transferred to the individual customer's account as a different figure.
- An entry in the control account or the individual customer's account has been omitted or posted to the wrong side of the account.
- The double entry for a journal total has been incorrectly made.
- An individual customer's account has been incorrectly balanced.
- The list of accounts receivable ledger balances has been incorrectly totalled.
- An entry has been made in either the control account or the individual customer's account but not in both.
- An individual customer's balance has been omitted from the list of balances.

Chapter 11
BANK RECONCILIATIONS

CHAPTER CONTENTS

In this chapter the relationship between the balance in the cash book (or cash account), and the balance on the bank statement will be considered. The likely reasons for any differences will be investigated and a statement reconciling the two balances prepared.

Objectives

By the time you have finished this chapter you should be able to:

- amend the cash book for any errors or omissions
- prepare a statement reconciling the amended cash book balance with the bank statement balance.

1 The nature and purpose of a bank reconciliation statement

1.1 Bank statement and cash book

DEFINITION

The **cash book** records all transactions with the bank.

The **bank statement** records all the bank's transactions with the business.

The **cash book** records all transactions with the bank. The **bank statement** records all the bank's transactions with the business.

A moment's thought will suggest that the contents of the cash book are exactly the same as the record provided by the bank in the form of a bank statement, and therefore our records should correspond with the bank statement.

This is in fact so, but with two important provisos:

1 The ledger account maintained by the bank is the opposite way round to the cash book. This is because the bank records the balance in favour of an individual as a credit balance, i.e. a liability of the bank to the individual. From the individual's point of view it is, of course, an asset, i.e. a debit balance in his cash book (or bank control account in the general ledger).

KEY POINT

Timing differences must inevitably occur.

2 **Timing differences** must inevitably occur. A cheque payment is recorded in the cash book when the cheque is despatched. The bank only records such a cheque when it is paid by the bank, which may be several days later.

The existence of the bank statement provides an important check on the most vulnerable of a company's assets – cash. However, the timing differences referred to above make it essential to reconcile the balance on the ledger account with that of the bank statement.

KEY POINT

Reconciliation takes the form of a **bank reconciliation statement**

This reconciliation takes the form of a bank reconciliation statement.

1.2 Why the bank statement and cash book balances may not agree

The reconciliation is carried out at frequent intervals , e.g. monthly (some businesses may carry out the reconciliation weekly or even daily!).

How is the reconciliation carried out? Two types of items must be identified:

1 those which appear in the bank statement but which have not yet been entered in the cash book

2 those which have been entered in the cash book but which have not yet appeared on the bank statement.

1.3 Items not yet entered in the cash book

These may include:

- bank charges
- bank interest (on overdrafts)
- standing orders and direct debits
- credit transfers – where a receipt has been paid direct into the firm's bank account.

All of these items must eventually be entered in the cash book because they relate to cash transactions of the business. This will then bring the cash book in line with the bank statement.

1.4 Items not yet on the bank statement

These will be timing differences that include:

Outstanding or unpresented cheques

Suppose a cheque relating to a payment to a supplier of Poorboy is written, signed and posted on 29 March. It is also entered in the cash book on the same day. By the time the supplier has received the cheque and paid it into his bank account, and by the time his bank has gone through the clearing system, the cheque does not appear on Poorboy's statement until, say, 6 April. Poorboy would regard the payment as being made on 29 March (and the payables balance reduced) and its cash book balance as reflecting the true position at that date.

Outstanding deposits

In a similar way, a trader may receive cheques by post on 31 March, enter them in the cash book and pay them into the bank on the same day. Nevertheless, the cheques may not appear on the bank statement until 2 April. Again the cash book would be regarded as showing the true position.

ACTIVITY 1

The balance in a business's cash book is $1,600 debit. That includes $200 of cheques that have been drawn but not yet presented to the bank and $350 of deposits which have not yet appeared on the bank statement. Once these timing differences have been dealt with the cash book and bank statement balances agree.

What is the bank statement balance?

Feedback to this activity is at the end of the chapter.

1.5 Errors

KEY POINT

Error sources:

- **bookkeeper errors**
- **bank errors.**

There might be errors by the bookkeeper. In this case the appropriate correcting entries should be put through the cash book.

There might also be errors by the bank. In this (hopefully rare) case, it is the bank statement which is wrong and where the correction must be made.

1.6 Cheques not paid

Consider an example. Suppose that for the past two months Patterdale's ledger balance has shown an amount owing to you of $28. He sends you a cheque for $28 on 3 June which you promptly enter in the cash book and pay into the bank. This increases cash and reduces receivables by $28. A week later the bank returns the cheque marked R/D (refer to drawer), i.e. it has not been met. Since Patterdale's bank account is heavily overdrawn, his own bank has refused to honour the cheque. What effect does this have? There are two points to consider:

1 The overall effect on your bank statement is nil. The receipt of $28 shown earlier on the bank statement will be cancelled out by the subsequent reversing entry by the bank (shown on the payments side of the bank statement).

2 Patterdale still owes $28 – his earlier cheque was a worthless piece of paper. The receipt of the cheque will have been recorded in the cash receipts book in the usual way, and it will be included in the total posted by debiting bank and crediting accounts receivable ledger control account at the end of the month. This must now be corrected by debiting accounts receivable ledger control account and crediting bank.

Patterdale's account in the accounts receivable ledger will appear as follows:

Patterdale

	$		$
Balance b/d	28	Bank	28
Unpaid cheque	28	Balance c/d	28
	56		56

Example

On 31 July 20X7 Blyth's cash book showed a balance in hand of $52 compared with a balance of $134 shown by his bank statement. He discovered the following:

(a) Cheques drawn by Blyth during July, amounting to $356, $1,732 and $196, had been entered in the cash book but had not been presented at the bank by the end of the month.

(b) Blyth had forgotten to enter in the cash book a standing order of $50 relating to a trade subscription.

(c) The bank had incorrectly credited Blyth's account with a dividend receipt of $25 relating to another customer.

(d) Bank charges of $105 shown on the bank statement had not yet been entered in the cash book.

(e) Cheques received from customers amounting to $1,211 were entered in the cash book on 31 July but were not credited on the bank statement until 3 August.

(f) Direct credits from customers of $180 and $31 had been paid direct into the bank, but no entry had been made in the cash book.

(g) The payments side of the cash book for July had been undercast by $1,000 (this means that the total of the payments side is understated by $1,000).

(h) The statement shows an item 'return cheque $72'. This has not yet been accounted for in the cash book.

You are required to show adjustments to the cash book and to prepare the bank reconciliation statement at 31 July 20X7.

Solution

Step 1

Identify those items which have yet to be entered in the cash book. These include (b), (d), (f) and (h). The error by the bookkeeper (g) must be corrected through the cash book since the unadjusted balance of $52 has been affected by the addition error.

Step 2

Identify those items which appear in the cash book but not in the statement: these include (a) and (e). These will appear on the bank reconciliation statement.

Step 3

The error by the bank (c) will be adjusted on the face of the bank reconciliation statement.

Cash book

20X7		$	*20X7*		$
31 Jul	Balance b/d	52		(b) Subscriptions	50
	(f) Direct credit	180		(d) Bank charges	105
	(f) Direct credit	31		(g) Cash book	1,000
				(h) Unpaid cheque	72
		263			
	Corrected balance c/d	964			
		1,227			1,227
				Corrected balance b/d (overdrawn)	964

Bank reconciliation statement at 31 July 20X7

	$	$	
Balance per statement		134	
Correction of error by bank – amount wrongly credited (c)		25	
		109	
Unpresented cheques:			
(a)	356		
(a)	1,732		
(a)	196		
		2,284	
		2,175	O/D
Outstanding deposits (e)		1,211	
Balance per cash book (overdrawn)		964	O/D

Notes: the bank reconciliation statement is rather complicated because it starts with a balance in hand and ends up with an overdraft balance (O/D). The logic is as follows:

(a) If the $25 had been credited to the correct customer, Blyth's balance would have been only $109 (in hand).

(b) The three unpresented cheques are regarded as payments for July. Had they appeared in the bank statement in July, they would have had the effect of turning a $109 balance in hand into an overdraft of $2,175 (be careful with the arithmetic!).

(c) Operating in the opposite direction, if the deposits of $1,211 had been included in the bank statement in the same month as the cash book, the overdraft would have been reduced from $2,175 to $964.

(d) This illustration shows how important it is to understand the processes rather than to memorise a layout.

KEY POINT

The cash book and the bank statement balance have now been reconciled.

The cash book and the bank statement balance have now been reconciled. A balance sheet at 31 July 20X7 would show a bank overdraft of $964 under the heading of current liabilities.

ACTIVITY 2

The cash book of a business shows an opening balance of $270, cash receipts of $4,600 and cash payments of $4,800. There is also a standing order payment of $40 that has been omitted from the cash book.

The cash book includes $60 of cheques written but not appearing on the bank statement, and $490 of deposits not yet appearing on the bank statement. The balance on the bank statement was $400 in debit.

Prepare the bank reconciliation statement.

Feedback to this activity is at the end of the chapter.

Conclusion

There are a number of reasons why the balance on an organisation's bank statement may not agree with the balance in its cash book. These differences will include errors or omissions in the cash book or by the bank, and timing differences such as unpresented cheques and outstanding deposits. As part of the system of control over the cash of the business, it is important that a reconciliation is prepared on a regular basis between the cash book and bank statement balances.

An examination question will typically require you to produce an adjusted cash book and then a reconciliation of the bank statement figure to that adjusted balance. It is quite wrong to include adjustments which need to be made in the cash book in the bank reconciliation statement.

SELF-TEST QUESTIONS

Nature and purpose of a bank reconciliation statement

1 Why does the bank statement appear to be the opposite way round to a ledger account? (1.1)

2 What types of items might appear on the bank statement but not be in the cash book? (1.1)

3 What are the two types of timing difference that might cause there to be a difference between the cash book and the bank statement? (1.4)

4 What is the double entry for a cheque not met on presentation? (1.6)

5 What is the net effect on the bank statement if a cheque is not met on presentation? (1.6)

6 What would be the treatment of bank charges omitted from the cash book? (1.6)

7 What is the treatment of direct credits, paid into the bank from customers, in the cash book? (1.6)

8 Is an opening overdraft a debit or a credit balance in the cash book? (1.6)

MULTIPLE-CHOICE QUESTIONS

Question 1

The attempt below at a bank reconciliation statement has been prepared by Q Limited. Assuming the bank statement balance of $38,600 to be correct, what *should* the cash book balance be?

A $76,500 overdrawn, as stated

B $5,900 overdrawn

C $700 overdrawn

D $5,900 cash at bank

	$
Overdraft per bank statement	38,600
Add: deposits not credited	41,200
	79,800
Less: outstanding cheques	3,300
Overdraft per cash book	76,500

Question 2

After checking a business cash book against the bank statement, which of the following items could require an entry in the cash book?

1 Bank charges

2 A cheque from a customer which was dishonoured

3 Cheque not presented

4 Deposits not credited

5 Credit transfer entered in bank statement

6 Standing order entered in bank statement.

A 1, 2, 5 and 6

B 3 and 4

C 1, 3, 4 and 6

D 3, 4, 5 and 6

For the answers to these questions, see the 'Answers' section at the end of the book.

EXAM-TYPE QUESTION

Spanners

The following is a summary from the cash book of Spanners for the month of October:

Cash book

	$		$
Balance b/d	1,407	Payments	15,520
Receipts		Balance c/d	960
	16,480		16,480

On investigation you discover that:

(1) Bank charges of $35 shown on the bank statement have not been entered in the cash book.

(2) A cheque drawn for $47 has been entered in error as a receipt.

(3) A cheque for $18 has been returned by the bank because it was not met on presentation, but it has not been written back in the cash book.

(4) The balance brought forward should have been $1,470.

(5) Three cheques paid to suppliers for $214, $370 and $30 have not yet been presented to the bank.

(6) Takings of $1,542 were placed in a night safe deposit on 31 October but were not credited by the bank until 3 November.

(7) The bank charged a cheque for $72 in error to the company's account.

(8) The bank statement shows an overdraft of $124.

You are required:

(a) to show what adjustments you would make in the cash book

(b) to prepare a bank reconciliation statement as at 31 October.

(14 marks)

For the answer to this question see the 'Answers' section at the end of this book.

FEEDBACK TO ACTIVITY **1**

Your answer should be as follows:

	$
Balance per bank statement	1,450
Less: Unpresented cheques	(200)
Add: Outstanding deposits	350
Balance per cash book	1,600

FEEDBACK TO ACTIVITY **2**

Your answer should be as follows:

Cash book

	$		$
Balance b/d	270	Cash payments	4,800
Cash receipts	4,600	Standing order	40
		Balance c/d	30
	4,870		4,870
Balance b/d	30		

FOULKS LYNCH PUBLICATIONS

Bank reconciliation statement

	$	
Balance per bank statement	400	O/D
Outstanding cheques	60	
	460	O/D
Outstanding deposits	490	
Balance per cash book	30	

Chapter 12
JOURNAL ENTRIES AND THE SUSPENSE ACCOUNT

CHAPTER CONTENTS

In order for many adjustments to ledger accounts to be made, such as annual depreciation charges, bad debt allowances and accruals and prepayments, instructions must be given to the bookkeeper to put through these entries.

Adjustments of these kinds must require an amount to be transferred from one ledger account to another. Sometimes several accounts are involved, as when a number of bad debts are written off on the same date.

It is essential to keep an orderly record of such transfers for several reasons:

(a) the accounts receivable and payable ledger control accounts will not agree with the underlying ledgers if the totals of transfers to or from these ledgers are not available

(b) transfers between ledger accounts are by definition non-routine items. They must all be properly authorised and capable of being checked – a record obviously facilitates this.

The record is in the form of a **journal** – an additional book in the system designed to give details of all transfers between ledger accounts. Each entry in the journal consists of the names of the accounts involved and the debit and credit entries required, set out as explained below.

You have already met some specialised journals – the sales journal for example – designed to facilitate the entry of routine transactions. The journal we are now about to study is for non-routine transactions which cannot be accommodated in these specialised journals. We refer to it as 'the journal' or 'the general journal'.

Journal entries are also used in the correction of errors. If the error causes the trial balance not to balance, a **suspense account** is opened for the amount of the difference. The balance on the suspense account is cleared as the difference is found.

Objectives

By the time you have finished this chapter you should be able to:

- draft journal entries
- correct errors in the ledger accounts
- clear the balance on a suspense account by the correction of errors and the application of double entry principles.

1 Journal

1.1 The nature and purposes of a journal

DEFINITION

The **journal** is a book or other record containing details of non-routine ledger transfers.

The **journal** is a book or other record containing details of non-routine ledger transfers.

The use of the journal varies widely in practice, but it is critical to appreciate that the journal is not part of the double entry – it is a record of double entries made in ledger accounts.

1.2 Presentation

A journal should be laid out in the following way:

Date/No	*Details*	*Ledger folio*	*Dr* $	*Cr* $
20X9				
6 Feb	Van account	V1	2,000	
	Motor expenses account	M3		2,000
	Purchase of van incorrectly debited to motor expenses			

Notice particularly:

- The names of the accounts to be debited and credited should be entered in the details column.
- The debit entries should be entered before the credit entries.
- The names of the accounts to be credited are often inset slightly from the names of the accounts to be debited.
- The **narrative** explaining the journal should give a brief explanation of the entry – unless a question specifically states that no narrative is required. In practice, the narrative is included to aid comprehension if the journal is reconsidered at a later date.
- For reasons of clarity it can be helpful to rule lines between each journal entry.

Example

Journal entries for the following are required:

(a) closing inventory $3,500

(b) motor expenses of $200 incorrectly debited to heat and light

(c) telephone accrual $58

(d) rent prepayment $78.

Solution

Date/No	*Details*	*Dr* $	*Cr* $
1	Inventory (balance sheet)	3,500	
	Inventory (income statement)		3,500
	Inclusion of closing inventory in accounts.		
2	Motor expenses	200	
	Heat and light		200
	Invoice for motor expenses incorrectly charged to heat and light.		
3	Telephone expense	58	
	Accruals		58
	Accrual for telephone bills.		
4	Prepayments	78	
	Rent expense		78
	Prepayment of rent.		

KEY POINT

A **journal entry** is simply a clear and comprehensible way of setting out a bookkeeping double entry that is to be made.

Note that, as above, in examination questions the ledger folio column is not needed.

A **journal entry** is simply a clear and comprehensible way of setting out a bookkeeping double entry that is to be made.

ACTIVITY 1

Draft the following journal entries.

(a) increase in allowance for doubtful debts from $200 to $300

(b) receipt of $1,000 for sale of non-current asset which originally cost $6,000 and has a net book value of $1,500.

Feedback to this activity is at the end of the chapter.

2 Suspense accounts

2.1 Introduction

DEFINITION

A **suspense account** is an account in which debits or credits are held temporarily until sufficient information is available for them to be posted to the correct accounts.

A **suspense account** is an account in which debits or credits are held temporarily until sufficient information is available for them to be posted to the correct accounts.

Suspense accounts are often encountered, both in practice and examinations, and must be dealt with according to the usual rules of double entry bookkeeping; this applies however they were originally set up.

2.2 Creation of suspense accounts

There are two main reasons why suspense accounts may be created:

1 On the extraction of a trial balance the debits are not equal to the credits and the difference is put to a suspense account.

2 When a bookkeeper performing double entry is not sure where to post one side of an entry he may debit or credit a suspense account.

2.3 Differences on a trial balance

Before opening a suspense account, the accountant will try to ascertain the reason the trial balance does not balance. This may be the result of either:

- errors in the double entry bookkeeping
- an error in the extraction of the trial balance.

If no error is discovered he or she may set up a suspense account, with either a debit or credit balance on it, so as to balance the trial balance. The entry in the suspense account is made to balance the trial balance. For example, if the credit side of the trial balance is greater than the debit side, the opening suspense account entry for the difference will be a debit.

This is the only occasion when an entry is made in a bookkeeping system without a corresponding entry!

2.4 Uncertainties in bookkeeping

In this case the suspense account arises because of uncertainties as to where to put one side of a double entry, and thus is a product of the double entry bookkeeping system.

2.5 Clearing suspense accounts

In whatever circumstances a suspense account is set up, it clearly should not remain permanently in the books of account, but as it forms a 'T' account it should be cleared by means of normal bookkeeping procedures.

Example

On extracting a trial balance, the accountant of ETT discovered a suspense account with a debit balance of $1,075 included therein; she also found that the debits exceeded the credits by $957. She posted this difference to the suspense account and then investigated the situation. She discovered:

(a) A debit balance of $75 on the postages account had been incorrectly extracted on the list of balances as $750 debit.

(b) A payment of $500 to a creditor, X, had been correctly entered in the cash book, but no entry had been made in the creditor's account.

(c) When a motor vehicle had been purchased during the year the bookkeeper did not know what to do with the debit entry so he made the entry Dr Suspense, Cr Bank $1,575.

(d) A credit balance of $81 in the sundry income account had been incorrectly extracted on the list of balances as a debit balance.

(e) A receipt of $5 from a debtor, Y, had been correctly posted to his account but had been entered in the cash book as $625.

(f) The bookkeeper was not able to deal with the receipt of $500 from the owner's own bank account, and he made the entry Dr Bank and Cr Suspense.

(g) No entry has been made for a cheque of $120 received from a debtor M.

(h) A receipt of $50 from a debtor, N, had been entered into his account as $5 and into the cash book as $5.

Solution

Step 1

The $1,075 debit balance is already included in the books, whilst the $957 is entered on the credit side of the suspense account because the list of account balances, as extracted, shows debits exceeding credits by $957. Although the two amounts arose in different ways they are both removed from suspense by the application of double entry.

Step 2

The incorrect extraction is corrected by amending the balance in the trial balance and debiting the suspense account with $675. In this case the 'credit' entry is only on the trial balance, as the postages account itself shows the correct balance, the error coming in putting that balance on the trial balance.

Step 3

The non-entry of the $500 to the debit of X's account causes the account to be incorrectly stated and the trial balance to be unbalanced. To correct matters Dr X, Cr Suspense, amending both X's ledger account and the trial balance.

Step 4

The suspense entry here arose from adherence to double entry procedures, rather than a numerical error. In this case the bookkeeper should have Dr Non-current asset – cost, Cr Bank instead of Dr Suspense, Cr Bank. To correct matters, the entry Dr Non-current asset – cost, Cr Suspense is made.

Step 5

Step 5 is similar to Step 2, but note that the incorrect extraction of a credit balance as a debit balance means that twice the amount involved has to be amended on the list of account balances and debited to suspense account.

Step 6

Step 6 is similar to Step 3. On this occasion Dr Suspense, Cr Cash, and amend the cash book balance on the list of balances.

Step 7

Step 7 is similar to Step 4. The bookkeeper should have Dr Bank, Cr Capital – ETT, but has instead Dr Bank, Cr Suspense. To correct matters, Dr Suspense, Cr Capital.

Step 8

Item (g) does not appear in the suspense account as the error does not affect the imbalance of the trial balance. As **no** entry has been made for the cheque, the correcting entry is:

	$	$
Dr Cash	120	
Cr Accounts receivable – M		120

Step 9

Item (h) also does not appear in the suspense account. Although an entry has been made in the books which was wrong, the entry was incorrect for both the debit and credit entry. The correcting entry is:

	$	$
Dr Cash	45	
Cr Accounts receivable – N		45

Suspense account

	$		$
Balance b/d (S1)	1,075	Trial balance – difference (S1)	957
Postages (trial balance only) (S2)	675	X (S3)	500
Sundry income (trial balance only) (S5)	162	Non-current asset – cost (S4)	1,575
Cash (S6)	620		
Capital account – ETT (S7)	500		
	3,032		3,032

KEY POINT

Once a suspense account has been created it should be cleared by the application of double entry principles.

Once a suspense account has been created, it should be cleared by the application of double entry principles. Not all errors affect the suspense account. If no entry at all has been made for a transaction, then the trial balance still balances.

2.6 Transposition errors

Though not encountered in the example above, a common cause of bookkeeping error is through the transposition of digits, e.g. $527 is recorded at $725, (the 5 and 7 have been transposed). The difference the error creates is always divisible by 9.

Conclusion

In order to put through many items of double entry bookkeeping and to correct errors, journal entries must often be drafted. Errors or omissions in the double entry bookkeeping system will often lead to the temporary creation of a suspense account.

The reasons for the creation of this suspense account must be investigated and the balance cleared by correcting the error by applying double entry principles.

SELF-TEST QUESTIONS

Journal

1 What is a journal? (1.1)

2 How should a journal entry be set out? (1.2)

3 Why is a narrative required for a journal entry? (1.2)

4 What is the journal entry required for an accrual? (1.2)

Suspense accounts

5 What is a suspense account? (2.1)

6 What are the two ways in which a suspense account may be created? (2.2)

7 If the debits in a trial balance exceed the credits will the suspense account balance be a debit or a credit? (2.3)

8 If an entry is omitted from the ledger entirely will a suspense account be created? (2.5)

9 If a credit balance is extracted on the trial balance as a debit balance what will be the amending entry in the suspense account? (2.5)

10 What is a transposition error? (2.6)

MULTIPLE-CHOICE QUESTIONS

Question 1

Y purchased some plant on 1 January 2000 for $38,000. The payment for the plant was correctly entered in the cash book but was entered on the debit side of plant repairs account.

Y charges depreciation on the straight line basis at 20% per year, with a proportionate charge in the year of acquisition and assuming no scrap value at the end of the life of the asset.

How will Y's profit for the year ended 31 March 2000 be affected by the error?

A Understated by $30,400

B Understated by $36,100

C Understated by $38,000

D Overstated by $1,900

Question 2

The trial balance of Z failed to agree, the totals being:

Debit	$836,200
Credit	$819,700

A suspense account was opened for the amount of the difference and the following errors were found and corrected:

1 The totals of the cash discount columns in the cash book had not been posted to the discount accounts. The figures were Discount Allowed $3,900 and Discount Received $5,100.

2 A cheque for $19,000 received from a customer was correctly entered in the cash book but was posted to the customer's account as $9,100.

What will the remaining balance on the suspense account be after the correction of these errors?

A $25,300 credit

B $7,700 credit

C $27,700 credit

D $5,400 credit

Question 3

The trial balance of C did not agree, and a suspense account was opened for the difference. Checking in the bookkeeping system revealed a number of errors.

1 $4,600 paid for motor van repairs was correctly treated in the cash book but was credited to motor vehicles asset account.

2 $360 received from B, a customer, was credited in error to the account of BB.

3 $9,500 paid for rent was debited to the rent account as $5,900.

4 The total of the discount allowed column in the cash book had been debited in error to the discounts received account.

5 No entries had been made to record a cash sale of $100.

Which of the errors above would require an entry to the suspense account as part of the process of correcting them?

A 3 and 4

B 1 and 3

C 2 and 5

D 2 and 3

For the answers to these questions, see the 'Answers' section at the end of the book.

EXAM-TYPE QUESTIONS

Question 1: Journal entries

Draft the journal entries with narratives for the following transactions:

(a) A repair bill of $150 on a motor car had been incorrectly posted to cost of motor vehicles account, and an adjustment is required.

(b) Pimple agrees to offset $1,500 due on his accounts receivable ledger account against the amount owing on his accounts payable ledger account.

(c) A customer, Black, owes $270 and is adjudicated bankrupt with no assets to his name. An allowance for doubtful debts of $300 is also to be created. The business uses a bad debts account.

The business does not have control accounts for the accounts receivable and payable ledgers.

(9 marks)

Question 2: February

February, having been unable to balance his trial balance at 31 December, opened up a suspense account and entered in it the amount he was out of balance. The debits had exceeded the credits by $736.

The following errors were subsequently discovered:

(a) A discount of $265 to a debtor, January, was entered in his account as $256.

(b) The total of the discount received column in the cash book for the month of December $237 had not been posted.

(c) $500, representing the sale proceeds of a machine scrapped, had been passed through the sales revenue account.

(d) A balance of $268, owing by a customer, March, had been omitted from the list of account balances at 31 December.

(e) The bank overdraft of $313 had been entered in the list of account balances as $331.

(f) Sale of goods for $1,000 to April on credit had been completely missed from the books.

(g) Discounts received balance of $379 had been entered in the list of account balances as $397 (debit balance).

You are required to show the suspense account after the rectification of all errors and to state the entries to be made to correct the errors which do not pass through the suspense account.

(13 marks)

For the answers to these questions, see the 'Answers' section at the end of the book.

FEEDBACK TO ACTIVITY 1

Your solution should be as follows:

Date/No	*Details*	*Dr* $	*Cr* $
(a)	Bad debts expense	100	
	Allowance for doubtful debts		100
	Increase in allowance for doubtful debts.		
(b)	Cash	1,000	
	Non-current asset – accumulated depreciation (6,000 – 1,500)	4,500	
	Income statement (loss on disposal)	500	
	Non-current asset at cost		6,000
	Disposal of non-current asset for $1,000.		

Chapter 13

APPLICATIONS OF INFORMATION TECHNOLOGY

CHAPTER CONTENTS

This chapter is designed to provide a review of the uses of computers in financial accounting. It describes the use of computers for:

- accounting records
- word processing
- spreadsheets
- databases.

Practical experience of using computers for accounting and related tasks will obviously help you to appreciate the issues involved. Try to obtain this experience.

Objectives

By the time you have finished this chapter you should be able to:

- discuss the advantages and disadvantages of computerisation in a business
- discuss various practical applications of computer technology in business situations
- discuss the application of computers in areas of accounting in particular.

1 The form of accounting records

1.1 A typical manual accounting system

A typical manual system consists of:

- separate books of original entry, which are the original accounting records of a business and are not part of the double entry
- the general ledger, which is a book within which there is a page for each ledger account in the double entry system
- further ledgers, the main ones being the accounts receivable ledger, the accounts payable ledger and the cash book.

Often these records are in the form of books but they are equally likely to be in some other form. For example, an accounts receivable ledger may be a collection of individual cards with one or more cards for each customer. The advantage of cards lies in the ability to insert additional cards for customers who have a lot of transactions or cards for new customers and still retain the alphabetical order of customers.

Often the subsidiary ledgers may not be laid out as ledger accounts but as running totals of amounts owing. See the example below:

Sales ledger

Customer: J Bloggs

Date		*Dr*	*Cr*	*Balance*
		$	$	$
1 Mar	Brought forward			3,978.45
19 Mar	Invoice 2354	1,549.00		5,527.45
23 Mar	Cash Receipt Book		3,978.45	1,549.00

Whatever the format, the reasons for the types of records and the double entry principles remain the same.

1.2 A typical computerised accounting system

A 'typical' computerised system is a bit of a misnomer as computerised systems can vary in the form they take. All of the accounts may be computerised but in many businesses only some are. For example, a business may have just the accounts receivable ledger on computer.

KEY POINT

A fully computerised system will operate under the same principles as a manual system except that all the records will be stored in one place, i.e. the hard disk of the computer.

A fully computerised system will operate under the same principles as a manual system except that all the records will be stored in one place, i.e. the hard disk of the computer. This does not necessarily mean that all accounting personnel have access to all records. The system will be broken down into sections in very much the same way as the manual system.

Another difference in a computerised system may be that when the data is printed out, the form of that information may look very different from a manual system, particularly with regard to the general ledger. Whereas in a manual system the general ledger is a collection of 'T' accounts, the general ledger on a computer system will probably appear as an arithmetic listing of debits and credits. This does not mean, however, that the system is not performing double entry; it is.

Later in the chapter we will take a closer look at the various accounting systems available.

2 Manual vs computerised accounting systems

2.1 Introduction

The comparison between manual and computerised accounting systems will be considered from the viewpoint of the advantages and disadvantages of computers as, most often, a business is considering whether to move from a manual to a computerised system rather than vice versa.

2.2 Advantages of computers

1 **Speed**. The computer is very fast – much faster than a clerk or any other type of office machine. This speed can be of value to the business in two ways:

   - high volumes of work can be handled by a computer
   - rapid turn-round and response can be achieved.

   Thus, one company might value a computer primarily for its ability to cope with large numbers of orders; another might be more interested in speeding up its order processing.

2 **Stored program**. Once the programs have been written and tested, the computer can perform large amounts of work with the minimum of labour costs. Only small teams of operators are needed for the largest machines. This is possible because the computer runs under the control of its stored program, and operator activity is limited to loading and unloading peripherals and indicating what work is to be done.

3 **Decision-making**. The computer can be programmed to undertake complicated decision making processes. It can handle work to a much higher degree of complexity than other office machines – and often more than the manager.

4 **File storage and processing**. Large files of data can be stored on magnetic media which require very little space. More important, files thus stored can be reviewed

and updated at high speeds, and information can be retrieved from them very quickly.

5 **Accuracy and reliability**. The computer is very accurate (provided always that its programs are free from faults). It is also very reliable.

2.3 Disadvantages of computers

1 **Lack of intelligence**. The computer is a machine. It cannot recognise errors made in its program, nor notice that data is incomplete or incorrect. Errors that would be detected by clerks in a manual system may go unnoticed in a computer-based system. It is therefore necessary to devote the utmost care to the development of computer-based systems, to foresee every contingency and to test every instruction. Thus, system development is often both prolonged and costly.

2 **Quantifiable decisions**. The program can only take decisions that can be quantified, e.g. that can be expressed as two numbers or amounts that can be compared with each other. It cannot make value judgements of the type involved, in, for example, selecting personnel, or deciding whether to take legal action if debts are overdue. The solution indicated by the program may have to be modified because of intangible factors known to the manager but incapable of being expressed in the program.

3 **Initial costs**. Initial costs, e.g. hardware, software, site preparation and training, tend to be high. Note that today software costs often exceed hardware costs.

4 **Inflexibility**. Because of the care and attention to detail needed in systems and program development and maintenance, computer systems tend to be inflexible. They take longer and cost more to alter than manual systems.

5 **Vulnerability**. The more work an organisation transfers to a computer, the greater is its dependence on a single resource. If the machine breaks down or is damaged, or if computer staff take industrial action, many systems may be brought to a halt.

2.4 Examples of the benefits of computer systems

1 **Reduced data processing costs**. The computer may provide a cheaper way of performing a given task.

2 **Other cost savings**. Money may be saved even though the cost of processing data remains constant or even increases. For example, fewer errors may be made by management once they have better information.

3 **Increased throughput**. The computer can cope with increasing volumes of work better than manual systems.

4 **Faster processing**. Transactions can be dealt with more rapidly.

5 **Greater accuracy**. Less errors occur than in manual systems.

6 **Staff shortage**. The computer can reduce the problems caused by shortage of office staff.

7 **Improved control**. Constant high-speed monitoring of files often improves control.

8 **Communication**. The use of terminals and data transmission facilities greatly improves communications.

9 **Quantitative techniques**. A wide range of quantitative techniques becomes available to aid management decision-making.

10 **Computer facilities**. The work of staff who require calculations to be made can be greatly facilitated (e.g. design staff, research staff, engineers, statisticians).

3 Applications of information technology in processing financial and related information

3.1 Introduction

The main applications of information technology are:

- financial accounting systems
- word processing
- spreadsheets
- database systems.

Each of these will be examined in turn.

4 Financial accounting systems

4.1 Introduction

The usual pattern for financial accounting has been for computerisation on a piecemeal basis, tackling the aspects involving most work first, e.g.:

- accounts receivable ledger
- accounts payable ledger
- payroll.

4.2 Integrated accounting packages

However, now a number of integrated accounting packages exist which handle all parts of the process and ultimately produce the financial statements. Each package varies, but the broad groups are:

Cash book systems

This group merely emulates a manual cash book. Such a system might be suitable for a small business which does not sell on credit and which either (i) provides a service or (ii) buys its inventory for cash or on credit from a small number of suppliers.

Basic bookkeeping systems

These might be suitable for the smaller business selling mainly on a cash basis, requiring basic bookkeeping. Such a system will normally offer basic facilities for maintaining an accounts receivable ledger (the accounts of credit customers), an accounts payable ledger (the accounts of credit suppliers) and a general ledger (all other accounts including the bank account, cash account, sales and purchases, etc.). There should be facilities for automatically producing a full print out of transactions and perhaps bank reconciliation statements. The package will also generate trial balances, income statements and balance sheets.

Bookkeeping and accountancy systems

In addition to offering the basic facilities described above, these packages can cope with greater number of customer and supplier accounts and offer more sophisticated credit control facilities. They can generate invoices, print out customers' statements and produce ageing schedules of receivables. They may be able to produce standard letters automatically to send to customers whose accounts are overdue or who have exceeded their agreed credit limit.

Within this group the more advanced packages may incorporate inventory control facilities. Separate records are maintained for each inventory item recording units purchased and sold and the balance of inventory in hand.

4.3 Micro-computer accounting packages

Most micro-computer accounting packages are used by people who are not computer programmers or systems analysts. The users of such systems are normally accountants and their accounting staff. To run an accounting package, the user will normally have the program on a hard disk. Data may be on separate disks. The program will probably operate on a 'menu system', i.e. the user will select the required options from a list of choices (the menu).

A typical initial menu would include the following options:

1 create new accounts

2 edit account data

3 post transactions

4 create report layouts

5 print reports

6 quit.

To select an option, the user will key in the appropriate number. For example, to create new accounts, number one would be keyed in.

Each of these options would involve another sub-menu, e.g. having selected *Create new accounts*, the sub-menu would probably display the following options:

- new customer accounts
- new supplier accounts
- new income accounts
- new expense accounts
- new balance sheet accounts
- return to main menu.

Thus, the initial set-up of a computerised accounting system is similar to a manual system, i.e. accounts receivable and payable ledgers and general ledger are set up and account codes allocated for each individual account. In the majority of cases, the bank account is contained within the general ledger.

The computer program will have been set up to 'recognise' different transaction types, such as:

- sales invoices
- credit notes (re sales)
- purchase invoices
- credit notes (re purchases)
- receipts
- payments
- journals.

To post to the ledger, the user would batch up the appropriate source documents – for example, sales invoices, and compute the batch total. The user would select the *Post to ledger* option from the appropriate sub-menu and key-in the following data for each sales invoice:

- customer account code
- date
- invoice number
- description
- total value of goods sold.

Provided valid code numbers are used and the totals agree, the posting will be accepted; similarly, the batch total will need to be verified before the program will actually post the transactions to the ledgers. An additional security measure is that of passwords, e.g. the user would have to know the appropriate password to load the system in the first place and possibly different passwords for each ledger.

5 Word processing

5.1 Introduction

Word processing is the name given to the production of typescript using computer facilities. The facilities are the ability to store text and to manipulate it on a VDU screen.

The minimum hardware requirements are:

- visual display unit and keyboard
- processor
- disk drive
- printer.

5.2 Evolution of word processing

Word processing developed to overcome some of the problems of using a typewriter for the production of typescript:

Repetition

If several drafts of a document have to be produced the whole document will have to be retyped each time.

Corrections

Even with the advent of correcting fluid, correcting typing errors is a time consuming business and quite messy. A typed letter with several corrections on it does not create a good impression.

Checking

Every time a document is retyped it must be checked in its entirety.

Memory typewriters evolved which allowed a line of text to be stored in memory before being typed. It would be shown on a 'window screen' for visual checking by the typist.

Typewriters which simultaneously produced a roll of paper tape which would then control the typewriter the next time the text was required were also developed.

Neither of these methods proved entirely satisfactory as they both had their limitations. But as the costs of computer hardware, especially main storage decreased it became possible to obtain at a reasonable price the processing power required to manipulate text on VDU screens.

5.3 Types of word processors

Word processors may be of two types:

1 dedicated – only used as a word processor

2 a word processing software package on a micro-computer.

In practice, the latter has proved more popular.

5.4 Features of word processing

Entering the text

Text is typed into the word processor using a keyboard, with the text visible on a visual display unit. Each 'document' is assigned a reference so that it can be stored and subsequently retrieved. As the text is typed in, it appears on the VDU screen to enable the 'typist' to check visually that there are no typing errors. Any errors can be corrected by moving the cursor to the error and over typing.

The way the text appears on the screen is not necessarily how the final document will appear.

Storing the text

After the text has been typed in, it is stored on disk under its unique reference number. Once the text has been stored, a hard copy of the text can be printed to be reviewed by the author for errors or subsequent amendments.

Retrieving the text

If for any reason amendments need to be made to any stored text, it is retrieved from store into the main memory of the word processor and displayed on the VDU screen. Retrieval is by means of the unique reference assigned to the text when it was first entered.

Editing the text

This is the stage where the text is made ready for printing. There are two aspects. First, any errors are corrected and any amendments made. Amendments may include changing the order of paragraphs, adding and deleting whole or parts of paragraphs. This is known as editing.

The second aspect is text formatting. This means arranging the text to exactly how the author wishes it to appear. What size of paper (e.g. A4, A5, foolscap) or special form (like a polling card) is to be used? How wide should the margins be, what line spacing, etc.?

All the instructions for editing and formatting are keyed in using the VDU. All word processors enable 'on screen' editing – i.e. you can see the results of the amendments on the VDU screen; many enable 'on screen' formatting (WYSIWYG – 'what you see is what you get').

Printing the text

After all amendments have been made, the text is put back into store in its final form. A copy is printed to enable the author to ensure that his instructions have been carried out. Provided that the author is satisfied with the finished product it can then be sent to its intended recipient.

6 Spreadsheets

6.1 Introduction

A spreadsheet displays on the screen a series of rows and columns. The number of rows and columns depends upon the package used. The original spreadsheets (e.g. 'Multiplan 1') had 255 rows and 63 columns. Current spreadsheets (e.g. 'Lotus 1-2-3' and 'Excel') have in the order of 65,000 rows and 256 columns. The intersection of rows and columns form 'cells' into which the user can type information using the computer keyboard. Three types of information are entered:

1 text, e.g. January, February, March, April

2 numbers, e.g. 200, 300, 400, 500

3 formulae, e.g. Sales – Costs = Profit.

When the content of any cell is altered the effects of the alteration are reflected, using the formula, on all other cells.

Once a model has been entered into the computer using the spreadsheet, it can be stored on disk. It can then be recalled, altered and used with new data. The output can be printed in tabular form. Some spreadsheets allow data to be displayed and printed graphically.

The model on the spreadsheet is often too large to be displayed on the screen in its entirety and so the VDU can then be thought of as a 'window' which can be moved to the various parts of the spreadsheet.

ACTIVITY 1

From the description of a spreadsheet given above, draw what you would imagine would appear on the computer screen if you were using a spreadsheet.

Feedback to this activity is at the end of the chapter.

6.2 Features of a spreadsheet

'What if' analysis

A major feature of a spreadsheet is its ability to calculate the effect of changes in the data or formula used in the model. This is sometimes described as the 'what if' facility, e.g. what would be the profit if sales increased by 20%?

Conditional statements

Calculations may be made dependent upon values in other cells, e.g. if sales are greater than $500,000 then costs are 10% of sales; otherwise fixed costs are $50,000.

Look-up tables

The value to be inserted in a specific cell can be selected from a range of values held in a table, e.g. tax rates at different levels of income.

Selective printing

The user may specify a portion of the model to be printed rather than the whole of it.

Graphics

Some spreadsheets can produce bar charts, pie-charts with shading and sometimes in colour.

Goal-seeking facility

Some spreadsheets can provide all possible input value combinations which produce a specified bottom line output value.

Statistical function

Most spreadsheets provide statistical analysis so that they are able to calculate values such as an average, sum, standard deviation, etc.

Flexibility

Spreadsheets should allow considerable flexibility to the user in designing the model, e.g. inserting blank rows and columns, deleting rows and columns and moving blocks of rows and columns to another part of the spreadsheet.

Databases

Spreadsheets can be used as simple databases (see below).

ACTIVITY **2**

Make a list of the ways in which you might think that spreadsheets could be used in business.

Feedback to this activity is at the end of the chapter.

KEY POINT

A **spreadsheet** is a computer package that can be used for numerous 'modelling' type business applications.

A spreadsheet is a computer package that can be used for numerous 'modelling' type business applications.

7 Database systems

7.1 Introduction

DEFINITION

A **database** is a collection of information that can be used for many different purposes.

A **database** is a collection of information that can be used for many different purposes.

A database is analogous to an electronic card index. Each card contains some information, e.g. about a client – it is a record. The items of information held (e.g. name, address, fees) are fields.

The advantages of a database over a card index are the following:

- expandability
- amount of information held in each record/field can be much larger than a card index
- calculations can be performed automatically, e.g. return on capital employed
- records may be sorted, or those matching a certain criterion selected, automatically, and in a variety of orders
- reports based on the information may be prepared and printed.

7.2 Database design

KEY POINT

Database types:

- **flat file**
- **relational**
- **programmable.**

There are various ways of designing database systems so as to link the data together:

- A flat file database is a single file database. All records in this type of database are of a standard format. Data can be stored, accessed, sorted and updated.
- A relational database is one where files can be linked together and data can be accessed from any file.
- A programmable database is one which has its own programming language which enables the database to be tailored to individual needs.

Database systems will continue to be a major area of expansion of computer applications in the future.

7.3 Database management system

The software that runs the database is known as the database management system. The database management system organises the data input into the database and allows various application programs to use the database.

KEY POINT

Database: a collection of data files, which provides access to the common data to different users.

A database is a collection of information or data files which provides access to the common data to a number of different users with different needs.

Conclusion

After studying this chapter you should be able to discuss applications of computers in business in general and in accounting in particular. Spreadsheets, databases and micro-computer accounting packages should now be familiar terms.

SELF-TEST QUESTIONS

The form of accounting records

1 What are the three main parts of a typical manual accounting system? (1.1)

Advantages and disadvantages of computerised accounts

2 What are the five advantages of computers in business? (2.2)

Financial accounting systems

3 Which parts of an accounting system are normally computerised first? (4.1)

4 What are computerised accounting systems called that handle all parts of the accounting system? (4.2)

Spreadsheets

5 What is a 'cell' of a spreadsheet? (6.1)

6 What are the distinguishing features and uses of a spreadsheet? (6.2)

Databases

7 What is a database? (7.1)

EXAM-TYPE QUESTIONS

Question 1: Saavik

The company accountant of Saavik is interested in purchasing a spreadsheet type of financial modelling package. As his assistant with experience in using a spreadsheet during your recent examination training, he has asked you to explain the principal features of a spreadsheet.

You are required to draft a memorandum to the company accountant to:

(a) explain the principal features of a spreadsheet

(b) list the main criteria that the company accountant should use to evaluate a spreadsheet package. **(8 marks)**

Question 2: Database

(a) Explain the term 'database' and how the operation of a data processing system using a database differs from one using conventional file structures.

(b) What advantages are to be gained from using a database system? **(8 marks)**

For the answers to these questions, see the 'Answers' section at the end of the book.

FEEDBACK TO ACTIVITY 1

A blank spreadsheet would show empty columns probably called A, B, C, etc, and blank rows usually numbered 1, 2, 3, etc.

	A	B	C	D
1				
2				
3				
4				
5				
6				

FEEDBACK TO ACTIVITY 2

Possible uses of spreadsheet packages in practice in business might include the following:

- cash flow forecasting
- budgeting and control
- income statements
- profit projections
- inventory count records
- marketing analysis
- sales forecasting
- tax budgeting.

Chapter 14
ACCOUNTING CONVENTIONS AND POLICIES

CHAPTER CONTENTS

This chapter collects together the accounting conventions and concepts which underlie the preparation of financial statements. Many of these concepts have already been explained as we progressed through the double entry system and the preparation of accounts.

The contents of this chapter will often form a part of a question in the examination.

Objectives

By the time you have finished this chapter you should be able to:

- explain a number of accounting conventions
- explain accounting bases and policies
- explain the purpose of each element of a conceptual *Framework*
- understand the principles of revenue recognition.

1 Introduction

1.1 Sources of accounting concepts and conventions

This is an important chapter to prepare you for the non-computational content of the Preparing Financial Statements examination.

For the International syllabus, the sources of the concepts and conventions underlying accounting practice are:

1 IAS 1 *Presentation of Financial Statements*

IAS 1 deals with two main matters: the overall considerations underlying financial statements, and the structure and content of financial statements. The overall considerations are to be found in this chapter, and the structure and contents in Chapter 20.

2 The IASB's *Framework for the Preparation and Presentation of Financial Statements*

The *Framework* is an important attempt to establish the underlying concepts of accounting. Some of the concepts in the *Framework* are repeated in IAS 1.

3 Generally accepted accounting principles (GAAP)

There are a number of principles underlying accounting practice which do not appear in either IAS 1 or the *Framework*. These too are summarised in this chapter.

1.2 The nature and purpose of accounting conventions

Accounting conventions are principles or accepted practice which apply generally to transactions. Some of the conventions are of more relevance to some transactions than to others but all have an influence in determining:

- which assets and liabilities are recorded on a balance sheet
- how assets and liabilities are valued
- what income and expenditure is recorded in the income statement

- at what amount income and expenditure is recorded.

It is useful to state and clarify the meaning of accounting conventions so that unusual transactions or situations can be dealt with.

2 IAS 1: *Presentation of Financial Statements*

2.1 Introduction

IAS 1 *Presentation of Financial Statements* contains a number of accounting principles and conventions that must be followed when preparing financial statements.

The fundamental accounting concepts that must be followed are:

- fair presentation
- going concern
- accruals
- consistency.

2.2 Fair presentation

Financial statements should be 'fairly presented'. Compliance with IASs goes a long way towards achieving this. IAS 1 states that additional disclosures, beyond those required by IASs, should be made when necessary to achieve a fair presentation.

In areas where no IAS exists, the financial statements should be presented in accordance with the stated accounting policies of the enterprise, in a manner which provides relevant, reliable, comparable and understandable information.

2.3 Going concern

DEFINITION

The **going concern** assumption is that an enterprise will continue in operational existence for the foreseeable future.

The **going concern** assumption is that an enterprise will continue in operational existence for the foreseeable future.

Management are required to review the going concern status of the enterprise to confirm that it is appropriate for the financial statements. In doing so they should consider all available information for the foreseeable future covering, but not limited to, twelve months from the reporting date.

2.4 Accruals

DEFINITION

The **accruals basis of accounting** means that assets, liabilities, equity, income and expenses are recognised when they occur and not when cash or its equivalent is received or paid.

The **accruals basis of accounting** means that assets, liabilities, equity, income and expenses are recognised when they occur and not when cash or its equivalent is received or paid.

The accruals basis is defined so as to include matching.

In brief, the accruals basis means that income and expenses are recognised as they occur, and the related matching concept means that costs should be set off against the revenues they have contributed to.

2.5 Consistency

DEFINITION

Consistency: the presentation and classification of items in the financial statements should be retained from one period to the next.

The presentation and classification of items in the financial statements should be retained from one period to the next unless a significant change in the nature of the operations of the enterprise or a review of its financial statement presentation demonstrates that more relevant information is provided by presenting items in a different way, or a change is required by a new IAS.

2.6 Other matters dealt with in IAS 1

Selection and disclosure of accounting policies

The accounting policies of an enterprise should be selected and applied so that the financial statements comply with International Accounting Standards.

In areas where there are no IASs, the policies should be selected and applied so that the financial statements are:

1 relevant to the decision-making needs of users

2 reliable. To be reliable they need to:
   - represent faithfully the results and financial position
   - reflect the substance rather than the form of transactions
   - be neutral
   - exercise prudence without impairing neutrality
   - be complete.

The accounting policies must be disclosed by note to the financial statements.

Materiality and aggregation

IAS 1 requires similar items to be aggregated together, but information that is material should not be aggregated with other items.

DEFINITION

Information is **material** if its non-disclosure could influence the economic decisions of users.

Information is material if its non-disclosure could influence the economic decisions of users. Materiality depends on the size of the item judged in the particular circumstances of its omission.

Offsetting

Assets and liabilities should not be offset unless this is allowed or required by an IAS.

Income and expense items should not be offset unless allowed or required by an IAS, or unless the amounts involved are not material.

2.7 Some other fundamental accounting concepts

The concepts dealt with here are not in IAS 1 or in the IASC's *Framework for the Preparation and Presentation of Financial Statements*, but they are generally recognised principles which underlie accounting and financial statements.

Historical cost

The historical cost accounting system is a system of accounting in which all values are based on the historical costs incurred.

The advantages and disadvantages of historical cost accounting are discussed in Chapter 24 below.

Stable monetary unit

Business activity involves the undertaking of all types of transactions. These diverse transactions are expressed in terms of a common unit of measurement, namely the monetary unit. Financial statements prepared on a historical cost basis make the assumption that the currency unit is stable. This means, therefore, that 20X1 $s can be added to 20X9 $s and a meaningful result obtained – not always a justifiable assumption!

Example

A company balance sheet states its plant and machinery at *cost less aggregate depreciation,* made up as follows:

Cost	*Aggregate*	*Net book depreciation*	*Value*
	$	$	$
Assets acquired 20X1	80,000	24,000	56,000
Assets acquired 20X2	100,000	20,000	80,000
Assets acquired 20X3	60,000	6,000	54,000
	240,000	50,000	190,000

If the dollar is a stable currency unit, the above aggregation is meaningful. The problem arises, however, that even in periods of gradual inflation, the currency is not a stable unit of measurement. The purchasing power of a 20X2 $ is quite different from that of a 20X1 or 20X3 $. This is a severe criticism of accounts prepared on a conventional or historical cost basis.

Money measurement

DEFINITION

Accounts only record items to which a **monetary value** can be attributed.

Accounts only record items to which a monetary value can be attributed.

All items, in theory, can have a monetary value attributed to them but not all items can be measured due to the practical difficulties of valuation. Can values be attributed to the worth of employees for example?

Some would argue that it is desirable to value employees and record them as an asset on the balance sheet, but it is very difficult to arrive at a value.

Realisation

DEFINITION

Realisation concept: a transaction should be recognised when the event from which it stems has taken place and the receipt of cash from the transaction is reasonably certain.

The realisation concept states that a transaction should be recognised when the event from which the transaction stems has taken place and the receipt of cash from the transaction is reasonably certain.

Therefore a sale on credit is recognised when the sale is made and the invoice sent out, rather than waiting until the cash from the sale is received.

Business entity

DEFINITION

The **business entity** concept states that financial accounting information relates only to the activities of the business entity and not to the activities of its owner or any other entity.

The business entity concept states that financial accounting information relates only to the activities of the business entity and not to the activities of its owner or any other entity.

Under this concept, accounting is seen as relating to an independent unit, the entity. The entity is seen as being separate from its owners, whatever its legal status. Thus, a company is both legally and for accounting purposes a separate entity distinct from its owners, the shareholders. On the other hand, the business of a sole trader is not necessarily a legal entity distinct from its proprietor; however, for accounting purposes, the business is regarded as being a separate entity and accounts are drawn up for the business separately from the trader's own personal financial dealings.

The entity concept is essential in order to be able to account for the business as a separate economic unit. Thus, flows of money between the business and the proprietors may be separately identified from other money flows.

Duality

DEFINITION

Duality: every transaction has two effects.

Every transaction has two effects.

The duality concept underpins double entry and the balance sheet, which is why we have examined this principle in detail in earlier chapters.

Accounting period convention

For accounting purposes, the lifetime of the business is divided into arbitrary periods of a fixed length, usually one year. At the end of each arbitrary period, usually referred to as the accounting period, two financial statements are prepared:

KEY POINT

Two financial statements:

- the balance sheet
- the income statement.

1 the **balance sheet**, showing the position of the business as at the end of the accounting period
2 the **income statement** for the accounting period. Profit or loss is arrived at on the basis of the **matching** concept.

Some accountants argue that profit can only be meaningfully measured over the lifetime of a business, i.e. the period starting with the date the business is formed and ending with the date the business goes into liquidation. This is because, by avoiding the use of arbitrary accounting periods, the problem of matching does not arise. There is also certainty of income and expenditure.

In spite of the arbitrary nature of the accounting period convention, it is necessary to strike a compromise between theoretical accuracy and the needs of the financial community. These needs require periodic financial statements which will form the basis of subsequent financial decisions.

ACTIVITY 1

Which accounting conventions or concepts would be likely to be used in the following situations?

(a) Determining which accounting period an item of expenditure relates to.

(b) Valuing an asset of the business that is to appear in the balance sheet.

Feedback to this activity is at the end of the chapter.

2.8 The usefulness of these conventions

These conventions have the following uses:

- They are of some help in dealing with unusual transactions or situations as they provide some principles which can be applied to a specific transaction.
- They can help a user of accounting information to understand detailed accounting entries.
- However it can be argued that they are of limited use for the following reasons.
- Some are statements of the obvious.
- Some are too general to be of practical help.
- They would be much more helpful if integrated. As presented above, they are mainly a listing of conventions which by and large are not related to each other. The IASC has published a more comprehensive *Framework for the Preparation and Presentation of Financial Statements* and this is considered below.

3 The IASB's *Framework for the Preparation and Presentation of Financial Statements*

3.1 Introduction

The IASB has published an important document, the *Framework for the Preparation and Presentation of Financial Statements* (the *Framework*). The *Framework* sets out the concepts that underlie financial statements for external users. It is designed to:

- assist the Board of the IASB in developing new standards and reviewing existing ones

- assist in harmonising accounting standards and procedures
- assist national standard-setting bodies in developing national standards
- assist preparers of financial statements in applying IASs and in dealing with topics not yet covered by IASs
- assist auditors in forming an opinion as to whether financial statements conform with IASs
- assist users of financial statements in interpreting financial statements
- provide those interested in the work of the IASB with information about its approach to the formulation of IASs.

3.2 The scope of the *Framework*

The *Framework* deals with:

- the objective of financial statements
- the qualitative characteristics that determine the usefulness of information in financial statements
- the definition, recognition and measurement of the elements from which financial statements are constructed
- concepts of capital and capital maintenance.

3.3 Users and their financial needs

The users of financial statements are:

- investors
- employees
- lenders
- suppliers and other trade creditors
- customers
- governments and other agencies
- the public.

These users and their financial needs were considered in Chapter 1. Take a look back to revise these points.

3.4 The objective of financial statements

The objective of financial statements is to provide information about the financial position, performance and changes in financial position of an enterprise that is useful to a wide range of users (see above) in making economic decisions.

3.5 Underlying assumptions of the *Framework*

The *Framework* identifies two underlying assumptions:

1 the accrual basis of accounting

2 the going concern basis.

These appear also in IAS 1.

A moment's thought should convince you of the fundamental nature of the accruals basis. No other basis gives a more reliable measure of profit in the income statement, or a more accurate measure of assets and liabilities in the balance sheet. But the accruals basis cannot stand alone. It needs help first from the other fundamental assumption – going concern. Financial statements are virtually always prepared on a going concern basis, but if the enterprise is in fact about to liquidate, then clearly another basis has to be used.

The accruals basis also needs the support of a range of other attributes – the qualitative characteristics in the *Framework*.

3.6 Qualitative characteristics of financial statements

The qualitative characteristics are a set of attributes which together make the information in financial statements useful to users. The following diagram showing these characteristics may help by providing a summary of them. It is not from the IASB's *Framework*, but based on a very similar UK statement issued by the Accounting Standards Board, the UK equivalent of the IASB.

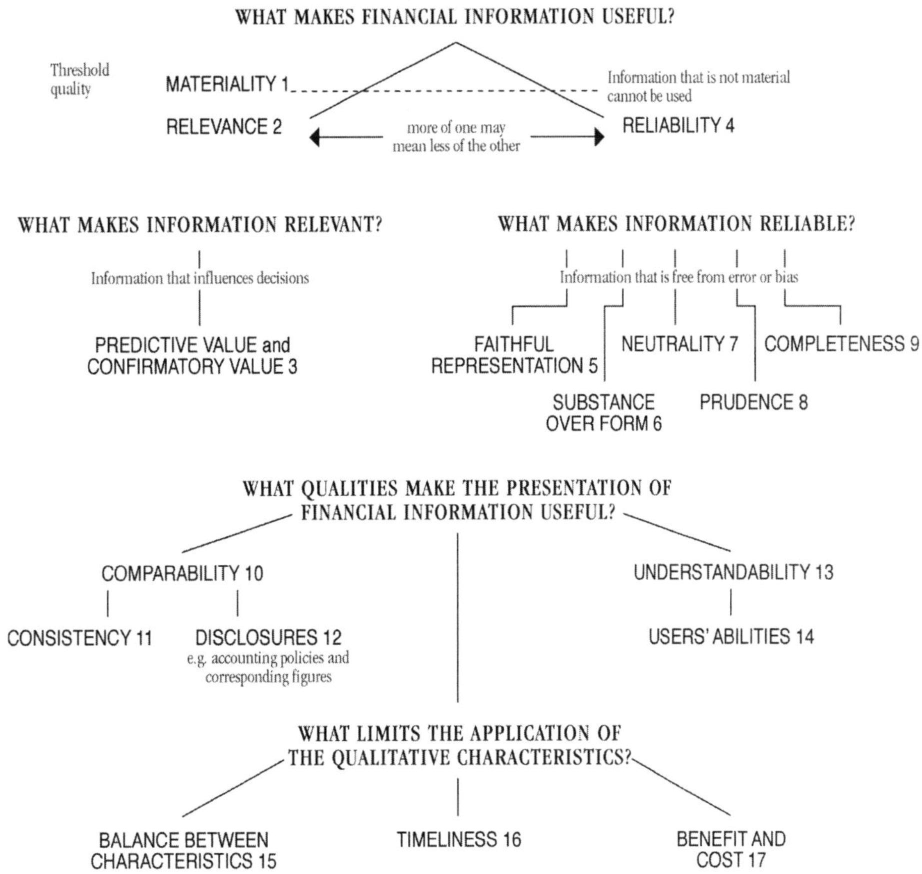

Each of the items is numbered and they are briefly considered below:

Materiality (1)

As you can see in the diagram, this is described as a 'threshold' quality. If information could influence users' decisions taken on the basis of financial statements, it is material. In the income statement an item is normally regarded as material, and therefore disclosable, if it is more than 5% of the normal level of pre-tax profit, though materiality cannot be measured in percentage terms alone.

Relevance (2)

Relevance is one of the two basic requirements that financial information must have. (The other is reliability). Financial information is relevant if it can assist users' decision-making by helping them to evaluate past, present or future events or by confirming, or correcting, their existing evaluations.

Relevant information may have predictive value or confirmatory value (3). That is, it helps users in assessing the future of the business or confirming past predictions.

Reliability (4)

Information is obviously of limited use if it is unreliable. To be reliable, it must be free from bias and error. Some contingent items may by their nature be bound to be unreliable. IAS 37 gives guidance as to the extent to which such items should be recognised or disclosed.

The subsidiary qualities that make information reliable are:

- **Faithful representation (5)**

  Information must faithfully represent the effects of transactions and other events.

- **Substance over form (6)**

  Some transactions have a real nature (substance) that differs from their legal form. An example is a hire purchase transaction. Ownership in an asset being acquired on hire purchase does not pass until the last instalment is paid, but it could be misleading to present a balance sheet in which such assets did not appear until the end of the contract.

  Whenever it is legally possible then, the real substance prevails over the legal form.

- **Neutrality (7)**

  Judgement is necessary in arriving at many items in the financial statements. Judgement is involved in fixing depreciation rates, valuing inventory, determining the level of doubtful debt allowances and many others. Neutrality means that these judgements are made without bias.

- **Prudence (8)**

  Caution must be exercised in preparing financial statements and in estimating the outcome of uncertain events. This does not mean, however, that the approach should be over-cautious. The aim should be to report the most likely outcome, with a slight element of caution, not to prepare financial statements on the most pessimistic basis. That could be seriously misleading.

- **Completeness (9)**

  Information presented in financial statements should be complete, subject to the constraints of materiality and cost.

Presentation in financial statements

The *Framework* identifies further qualities in the presentation of information that makes it useful:

- **Comparability (10)**

  Comparability means that the financial statements should be comparable with the financial statements of other companies and with the financial statements of the same company for earlier periods.

  To achieve comparability we need consistency and disclosure of accounting policies (11 and 12). Accounting standards contribute to comparability by reducing the options available to enterprises in their treatment of transactions. IAS 1's requirement that companies disclose their accounting policies helps with adjustments to allow for differences between companies. Also, if a company changes its accounting policies there must be full disclosure of the effect of the change.

- **Understandability (13)**

  Companies differ greatly in the extent of the efforts they make to enable users to understand their financial statements. Understandability is dependent upon users' abilities (14), and the *Framework* suggests that a reasonable knowledge of business and accounting has to be assumed here.

Limiting factors

You can see that some of the characteristics discussed above conflict to some extent with others. Information that is more reliable can be less relevant and vice versa. In other words a balance between characteristics (15) needs to be achieved. Timeliness (16) is another limiting factor. Financial statements may have to be prepared before all aspects of a transaction are known. A balance has to be struck between timeliness and reliability to achieve the best compromise to satisfy the economic decision-making needs of users.

Finally, benefit and cost (17) have to be considered. As far as possible, the benefits from presenting the information should exceed the cost of providing it.

3.7 The elements of financial statements

For the *Preparing Financial Statements* syllabus you do not need to be concerned with the detail of this section of the IASB's *Framework*. However, it does contain three important definitions that you should know – definitions of assets, liabilities and equity.

DEFINITION

An **asset** is a resource controlled by an enterprise as a result of past events and from which future economic benefits are expected to flow to the enterprise.

A **liability** is a present obligation of the enterprise arising from past events, the settlement of which is expected to result in an outflow from the enterprise of resources embodying economic benefits.

Equity is the residual interest in the assets of the enterprise after deducting all its liabilities.

An **asset** is a resource controlled by an enterprise as a result of past events and from which future economic benefits are expected to flow to the enterprise.

This very general definition requires some explanation. The first point to note is that ownership is not required. As long as the item is **controlled** by the enterprise it can be recognised as an asset, provided its cost or value can be measured with reliability.

Second, there is the reference to future economic benefits. If an item does not yield benefits of some kind in the future (profit, for example) it has no value as an asset.

Finally, the definition refers to past events. The commonest past event giving rise to an asset is the purchase of that asset.

A **liability** is a present obligation of the enterprise arising from past events, the settlement of which is expected to result in an outflow from the enterprise of resources embodying economic benefits.

Equity is the residual interest in the assets of the enterprise after deducting all its liabilities. In the terms used in earlier chapters, it is the proprietor's capital. When we come to study company accounting in later chapters, it will be the shareholders' interest in a company.

4 Revenue recognition

4.1 Introduction

IAS 18 *Revenue* defines when revenue from various sources may be recognised.

It deals with revenue arising from three types of transaction or event:

- sale of goods
- rendering of services
- interest, royalties and dividends from the assets of the enterprise.

4.2 Sale of goods

KEY POINT

Revenue from the sale of goods should be recognised when five conditions have been satisfied.

Revenue from the sale of goods should be recognised when all the following conditions have been satisfied:

(a) All the significant risks and rewards of ownership have been transferred to the buyer.

(b) The seller retains no effective control over the goods sold.

(c) The amount of revenue can be reliably measured.

(d) The benefits to be derived from the transaction are likely to flow to the enterprise.

(e) The costs incurred or to be incurred for the transaction can be reliably measured.

Conditions (a) and (b) are usually met at the time when legal ownership passes to the buyer, but there may be cases where the seller retains significant risks. IAS 18 gives four examples of these cases:

- when the seller has an obligation for unsatisfactory performance beyond normal warranty provisions
- when the receipt of the cash for the sale is contingent upon the buyer selling the goods on and receiving cash
- when the goods are to be installed at the buyer's site and this has not yet been completed
- when the buyer has the right to cancel the contract.

Revenue and associated costs are recognised simultaneously in accordance with the matching concept.

4.3 Rendering of services

The essential difference between a sale of goods and the rendering of a service is that the sale usually takes place at a point of time whereas the provision of the service is likely to be spread over a period of time.

IAS 18 states that revenue from services may be recognised according to the stage of completion of the transaction at the balance sheet date.

KEY POINT

Revenue from the services should be recognised when four conditions have been satisfied.

As with the sale of goods, conditions must be satisfied:

(a) The amount of the revenue can be measured reliably.

(b) The benefits from the transaction are likely to flow to the enterprise.

(c) The stage of completion of the work can be measured reliably.

(d) The costs incurred or to be incurred for the transaction can be reliably measured.

When a partly completed service is in its early stages, or the outcome of the transaction cannot be reliably estimated, revenue should be recognised only up to the amount of the costs incurred to date, and then only if it is probable that the enterprise will recover in revenue at least as much as the costs.

If it is probable that the costs of the transaction will not be recovered, no revenue is to be recognised.

4.4 Interest, royalties and dividends

Provided the amount of revenue can be reliably measured and the receipt of the income is reasonably assured, these items should be recognised as follows:

Interest

Interest should be recognised on a time proportion basis taking account of the yield on the asset.

Royalties

Royalties should be recognised on an accruals basis in accordance with the relevant agreement.

Dividends

Dividends should be recognised when the shareholder's right to receive payment has been established.

4.5 Disclosure requirements of IAS 18

The financial statements should disclose:

- the accounting policies for revenue recognition, including the methods used to determine the stage of completion of transactions involving services
- the amount of revenue recognised for each of the five categories (sale of goods, rendering of services, interest, royalties and dividends), where material
- the amount, if material, in each category arising from exchanges of goods or services.

Conclusion

This chapter provides the main coverage of accounting assumptions, concepts and conventions, plus a detailed review of the relevant parts of the IASC's *Framework*. It is easy to underestimate these areas and to concentrate on the computational aspects of accounting. Remember that about 40% of your paper will deal with non-computational topics. About half of that 40% is likely to come from this chapter. Work at it!

SELF-TEST QUESTIONS

IAS 1

1 What is the going concern concept? (2.3)

2 With what should a business be consistent in its accounting policies? (2.5)

3 What is the accruals concept? (2.4)

4 Does IAS 1 require disclosure of accounting concepts? (2.6)

5 What is the business entity convention? (2.7)

6 What is the accounting period convention? (2.7)

IASB's *Framework*

7 Name seven users of financial statements. (3.3)

8 List the factors in financial statements which make information relevant. (3.6)

9 List the factors in financial statements which make information reliable. (3.6)

10 What qualities assist comparability of financial statements? (3.6)

11 How does the *Framework* define:

(a) assets

(b) liabilities

(c) equity? (3.7)

Revenue recognition

12 What conditions must be satisfied before revenue from the sale of goods may be recognised? (4.2)

13 What conditions must be satisfied before revenue from the rendering of services may be recognised? (4.3)

MULTIPLE-CHOICE QUESTION

The IASB's *Framework for the Preparation and Presentation of Financial Statements* gives five qualitative characteristics that make financial information reliable.

These five characteristics are:

A Prudence, consistency, understandability, faithful representation, substance over form

B Accruals basis, going concern concept, consistency, prudence, true and fair view

C Faithful representation, neutrality, substance over form, completeness, consistency

D Substance over form, prudence, faithful representation, neutrality, completeness.

For the answer to this question, see the 'Answers' section at the end of the book.

EXAM-TYPE QUESTIONS

Question 1: Fundamental accounting assumptions

In producing financial statements, it is essential that they should be comparable with those of the same company for previous years to identify trends. In order to try and ensure this, the IASB has identified three fundamental accounting assumptions and included them in an International Accounting Standard.
These are:

(a) going concern

(b) accruals

(c) consistency.

You are required to briefly define these three assumptions with an example to illustrate each answer. **(9 marks)**

Question 2: Advertising campaign

On 20 December 20X7 your client paid $10,000 for an advertising campaign. The advertisements will be heard on local radio stations between 1 January and 31 January 20X8. Your client believes that as a result, sales will increase by 60% in 20X8 (over 20X7 levels) and by 40% in 20X9 (over 20X7 levels). There will be no further benefits.

You are required to write a memorandum to your client explaining your views on how this item should be treated in the accounts for the three years 20X7 to 20X9. Your answer should include explicit reference to at least three relevant traditional accounting conventions, and to the requirements of two classes of user of published financial statements. **(12 marks)**

Question 3: Cost concepts

'The historical cost convention looks backwards but the going concern convention looks forwards.'

You are required:

(a) to explain clearly what is meant by

(i) the historical cost convention

(ii) the going concern convention. **(6 marks)**

(b) Does traditional financial accounting, using the historical cost convention, make the going concern convention unnecessary? Explain your answer fully. **(6 marks)**

(Total: 12 marks)

Question 4: Accounting concepts

If the information in financial statements is to be useful, regard must be had to the following accounting concept, among others:

(a) materiality **(4 marks)**

(b) substance over form **(3 marks)**

(c) money measurement **(3 marks)**

Explain the meaning of each of these concepts, including in your explanations one example of the application of each of them. **(Total: 10 marks)**

For the answers to these questions, see the 'Answers' section at the end of the book.

FEEDBACK TO ACTIVITY 1

(a)
- accruals concept
- accounting period convention

(b)
- historical cost accounting convention
- prudence concept
- objectivity convention
- going concern concept

Chapter 15
INTANGIBLE ASSETS: GOODWILL AND RESEARCH AND DEVELOPMENT

CHAPTER CONTENTS

This chapter considers two important types of intangible assets which are in the syllabus. Intangible assets are assets which do not have a physical substance but have value to the business. In accounting terms they most commonly arise when the business has paid money to acquire them or has incurred expenditure which has created an intangible asset.

Objectives

By the time you have finished this chapter you should be able to:

- explain the nature and permissible accounting treatments of goodwill
- explain the methods of accounting for research and development costs laid down in IAS 38.

1 Goodwill

1.1 Introduction

DEFINITION

Goodwill is the excess of the cost of the acquisition over the acquirer's interest in the fair value of the identifiable assets and liabilities acquired as at the date of the exchange transaction.

When a business changes hands, the price paid will commonly exceed the net value of the tangible assets owned by the business (even when these are valued at market prices). The difference is an intangible asset referred to as 'goodwill'. **Goodwill** has been defined as 'the advantage, whatever it may be, which a person gets by continuing to carry on, and being entitled to represent to the outside world that he is carrying on, a business which has been carried on for some time previously'.

Thus goodwill may be seen as an intangible asset – the value of the going concern element of the business.

Goodwill is the excess of the cost of the acquisition over the acquirer's interest in the fair value of the identifiable assets and liabilities acquired as at the date of the exchange transaction.

ACTIVITY 1

Consider why goodwill may exist.

Feedback to this activity is at the end of the chapter.

1.2 Purchased and non-purchased goodwill

KEY POINT

Purchased goodwill arises as a result of a purchase transaction.

KEY POINT

Non-purchased goodwill is not generally recognised in the accounts because no event has occurred to identify the value of the business as a whole.

Purchased goodwill arises as a result of a purchase transaction (e.g. when one business acquires another as a going concern).

Purchased goodwill will be recognised within the accounts because at a specific point in time the fact of purchase has established a figure of value for the business as a whole which can be compared with the fair value of the individual assets acquired, and this figure will be incorporated in the accounts of the acquiring business as the cost of the acquisition.

Non-purchased, or inherent, **goodwill** is not generally recognised in the accounts because no event has occurred to identify the value of the business as a whole.

1.3 Accounting treatment of goodwill

IAS 22 requires goodwill arising on an acquisition to be recognised as an asset and amortised over its useful life. The useful life taken should not normally exceed twenty years, but a longer life may be taken if it can be justified by the circumstances.

KEY POINT

Amortisation: the depreciation of intangible assets like goodwill or development costs.

Amortisation is the term used for depreciation of intangible assets like goodwill or development costs.

A knowledge of IAS 22 is not required for this examination.

2 Research and development costs

2.1 Introduction

IAS 38 *Intangible Assets* governs the accounting treatment of these costs and contains the following definitions:

DEFINITION

Research is original and planned investigation undertaken with the prospect of gaining new knowledge and understanding.

Development is the application of research findings.

Research is original and planned investigation undertaken with the prospect of gaining new scientific or technical knowledge and understanding.

Development is the application of research findings or other knowledge to a plan or design for the production of new or substantially improved materials, devices, products, processes, systems or services prior to the commencement of commercial production or use.

2.2 Recognition of research and development expenditure

The requirements are:

Research expenditure

KEY POINT

No intangible asset arising from research should be recognised.

No intangible asset arising from research should be recognised. (This does not, of course, prohibit the recognition of tangible assets used in research.)

Development expenditure

An intangible asset arising from development (or from the development phase of an internal project) should be recognised if, and only if, an enterprise can demonstrate all of the following:

- the technical feasibility of completing the intangible asset so that it will be available for use or sale
- its intention to complete the intangible asset and use or sell it
- its ability to use or sell the intangible asset
- how the intangible asset will generate probable future economic benefits. Among other things, the enterprise should demonstrate the existence of a market for the output of the intangible asset or the intangible asset itself or, if it is to be used internally, the usefulness of the intangible asset.
- the availability of adequate technical, financial and other resources to complete the development and to use or sell the intangible asset
- its ability to measure reliably the expenditure attributable to the intangible asset during its development.

KEY POINT

Expenditure once treated as an expense cannot be reinstated as an asset.

The amount to be included is the cost of the development. Note that expenditure once treated as an expense cannot be reinstated as an asset.

Amortisation

Capitalised development costs must be amortised.

KEY POINT

Capitalised development costs must be amortised.

The amortisation method used should reflect the pattern in which the asset's economic benefits are consumed by the enterprise. If that pattern cannot be determined reliably, the straight-line method should be used.

Disclosure

The financial statements should disclose the following for capitalised development costs:

- the amortisation method used and the expected period of amortisation
- a reconciliation of the carrying amounts at the beginning and end of the period, showing new expenditure incurred, amortisation and amounts written off because a project no longer qualifies for capitalisation
- amortisation during the period.

In addition, the financial statements should also disclose the total amount of research and development expenditure recognised as an expense during the period.

The position of each development project must be reviewed annually, and any projects no longer meeting the IAS 38 criteria must be written off. For projects whose expenditure is being amortised, the amortisation period and method must also be reviewed annually and revised if necessary.

Example

ABC is developing a new product, the widget. This is expected to be sold over a three-year period starting in 20X2. The data is as follows:

	20X1	*20X2*	*20X3*	*20X4*
	$'000	$'000	$'000	$'000
Net revenue from other activities	400	500	450	400
Net revenue from widgets	-	450	600	400
Development costs of widgets	(900)			

Show how the development costs should be treated if:

(a) the costs *do not* qualify for capitalisation

(b) the costs *do* qualify for capitalisation.

Solution

(a) Profit treating development costs as expenses when incurred

	20X1	*20X2*	*20X3*	*20X4*
	$'000	$'000	$'000	$'000
Other activities – Net revenue	400	500	450	400
Widgets – Net revenue	-	450	600	400
Development costs	(900)	-	-	-
Net profit/(loss)	(500)	950	1,050	800

(b) Net profit amortising development costs over life of widgets

	20X1	*20X2*	*20X3*	*20X4*
	$'000	$'000	$'000	$'000
Other activities - Net revenue	400	500	450	400
Widgets - Net revenue	-	450	600	400
Development costs of widgets $\frac{\$900,000}{3}$	-	(300)	(300)	(300)
Net profit	400	650	750	500

Conclusion

This chapter has dealt with two types of intangible assets which may be recorded on a balance sheet. The crucial point about goodwill is its residuary nature – it cannot exist by itself. In the area of research and development expenditure, it is only development expenditure which is carried forward and only then if certain conditions are satisfied.

SELF-TEST QUESTIONS

Goodwill

1 What is goodwill? (1.1)

2 How should purchased goodwill be accounted for? (1.3)

Research and development costs

3 Distinguish between research expenditure and development expenditure. (2.1)

4 What conditions need to be satisfied in order to carry forward development expenditure? (2.2)

MULTIPLE-CHOICE QUESTION

Which of the following statements concerning the accounting treatment of research and development expenditure are true, according to IAS 38 *Intangible Assets*?

1 If certain criteria are met, research expenditure may be recognised as an asset.

2 Research expenditure, other than capital expenditure on research facilities, should be recognised as an expense as incurred.

3 In deciding whether development expenditure qualifies to be recognised as an asset, it is necessary to consider whether there will be adequate finance available to complete the project.

4 Development expenditure recognised as an asset must be amortised over a period not exceeding five years.

5 The financial statements should disclose the total amount of research and development expenditure recognised as an expense during the period.

A 1, 4 and 5

B 2, 4 and 5

C 2, 3 and 4

D 2, 3 and 5

For the answer to this question, see the 'Answers' section at the end of the book.

EXAM-TYPE QUESTION

Research and development expenditure

You are required:

(a) to explain the two classifications of research and development expenditure **(6 marks)**

(b) to discuss the treatment of research and development expenditure with special reference to the fundamental concepts of accounting. **(8 marks)**

(Total: 14 marks)

For the answer to this question, see the 'Answers' section at the end of the book.

FEEDBACK TO ACTIVITY 1

Goodwill may exist because of any combination of a number of possible factors, for example:

- reputation for quality and/or service
- a good location
- technical 'know-how' and experience
- possession of favourable contracts
- good management and/or technical personnel.

Chapter 16
CONTINGENT LIABILITIES, CONTINGENT ASSETS AND EVENTS AFTER THE BALANCE SHEET DATE

The accounting standards covered in this chapter relate to the problems of whether to include or not to include certain items in the financial statements. It is important to learn the definitions contained in this chapter.

Objectives

By the time you have finished this chapter you should be able to:

- define and distinguish between different types of contingency
- account for each type of contingency in line with IAS 37
- define and distinguish between different categories of events after the balance sheet date in accordance with IAS 10
- account for each category of event after the balance sheet date in line with IAS 10.

1 Accounting for contingencies

1.1 Introduction

The rules relating to contingencies and events after the balance sheet date were changed in 1998 and 1999. IAS 37, *Provisions, Contingent Liabilities and Contingent Assets* was introduced in September 1998 and updates the rules relating to contingencies. Only the sections of IAS 37 relating to contingencies are relevant for your studies.

IAS 10, *Events After the Balance Sheet Date* was issued in May 1999 and modifies the rules relating to such events.

1.2 Definitions

DEFINITION

A **contingent liability** is:

1 a possible obligation that arises from past events or

2 a present obligation that arises from past events but is not recognised.

Contingent liability

A contingent liability is:

1 a possible obligation that arises from past events and whose existence will be confirmed only by the occurrence or non-occurrence of one or more uncertain future events not wholly within the control of the enterprise; or

2 a present obligation that arises from past events but is not recognised because:

- it is not probable that an outflow of resources embodying economic benefits will be required to settle the obligation; or
- the amount of the obligation cannot be measured with sufficient reliability.

DEFINITION

A **contingent asset** is a possible asset that arises from past events.

Contingent asset

A contingent asset is a possible asset that arises from past events and whose existence will be confirmed only by the occurrence or non-occurrence of one or more uncertain future events not wholly within the control of the enterprise.

1.3 Accounting for contingent liabilities and contingent assets

The requirements of IAS 37 as regards contingent liabilities and assets are summarised in the following table:

	Contingent liabilities	*Contingent assets*
Virtually certain (therefore not contingent)	Provide	Recognise
Probable	Provide	Disclose by note
Possible	Disclose by note	No disclosure
Remote	No disclosure	No disclosure

Note that when there is the possibility of recovery from a third party of all or part of a contingent liability, this must be treated as a separate matter, and a contingent asset only recognised if its receipt is virtually certain, as shown in the table.

1.4 Degrees of probability

KEY POINT

Four degrees of probability for contingencies – virtually certain, probable, possible and remote.

IAS 37 recognises four degrees of probability for contingencies – virtually certain, probable, possible and remote. It gives no guidance as to the meaning of these terms. One possible interpretation could be:

Virtually certain	Probability above 95%
Probable	Probability above 50% and up to 95%
Possible	Probability 5% to 50%
Remote	Probability below 5%

The table shows that the accounting treatment depends on the degree of probability and on whether the contingency is a potential asset or a potential liability.

KEY POINT

Disclosure by note should state:

- nature of the contingency
- the uncertain factors
- an estimate of the financial effect, or why estimate cannot be made.

When disclosure is made by note (possible liabilities and probable assets) the note should state:

- the nature of the contingency
- the uncertain factors that may affect the future outcome
- an estimate of the financial effect, or a statement that such an estimate cannot be made.

In the case of a contingent asset, care should be taken not to give a misleading impression as to the likelihood of realisation.

2 Events after the balance sheet date

2.1 Definition and categories

DEFINITION

Events after the balance sheet date are those events, both favourable and unfavourable, that occur between the balance sheet date and the date on which the financial statements are authorised for issue.

Suppose the year end of a company is 31 December 20X7 and the directors authorise the issue of the financial statements at a board meeting held on 22 March 20X8. Certain events occurring during the intervening period will provide information which will help in preparing the financial statements.

Events after the balance sheet date are those events, both favourable and unfavourable, that occur between the balance sheet date and the date on which the financial statements are authorised for issue.

Events occurring after the balance sheet date are of two kinds:

(a) those which provide additional evidence to assist with the estimation of amounts relating to conditions at the balance sheet date (adjusting events)

(b) those which do not affect the condition of assets or liabilities at the balance sheet date but are of such importance that their non-disclosure would affect users' decision-making (non-adjusting events).

IAS 10 requires the financial statements to be *adjusted* for type (a) events and to contain a *note* giving details of type (b) events.

2.2 Events requiring adjustment in the financial statements

These events provide additional evidence of conditions existing at the balance sheet date. For example, bad debts arising one or two months after the balance sheet date may help to quantify the bad debt allowance as at the balance sheet date. Adjusting events may, therefore, affect the amount at which items are stated in the balance sheet.

Examples include:

- sales of inventory at less than cost, necessitating a reduction in the valuation of closing inventory
- bankruptcy of a trade customer, requiring the debt to be written off in whole or part
- amounts received or receivable in respect of insurance claims which were being negotiated at the balance sheet date.

2.3 Events requiring disclosure by note

These are events arising after the balance sheet date but which, unlike those events above, do *not* concern conditions existing at the balance sheet date. Such events will not, therefore, have any effect on items in the balance sheet or income statement. However, in order to prevent the financial statements from presenting a misleading position, some form of additional disclosure is required if the events are material, by way of a note to the financial statements giving details of the event.

Examples of non-adjusting events include:

- the issue of new share or loan capital
- major changes in the composition of the company (for example, acquisitions of new businesses)
- financial consequences of losses of non-current assets or inventory as a result of fires or floods.

2.4 Proposed dividends

Different countries have different practices as regards accounting for proposed dividends. Some require them to be included as liabilities, others require disclosure by note.

IAS 10 as revised in 1999 has changed the requirements of the original IAS 10 in this area. It is now *not acceptable* to include dividends proposed or declared on equity after the balance sheet date in that balance sheet as liabilities.

Proposed equity dividends must be shown either in the notes to the financial statements or on the face of the balance sheet as an appropriation within equity. In this study text, proposed dividends have consistently been shown by note.

2.5 Further requirements of IAS 10

Going concern status in doubt

If, after the balance sheet date, the management of an enterprise determines either that it intends to liquidate the enterprise or cease trading, or that it has no realistic alternative but to do so, the financial statements should not be prepared on a going concern basis.

Date of issue of financial statements

The financial statements should disclose the date they were authorised for issue and who gave that authorisation.

Disclosure of power to amend

If the owners or others have the power to amend the financial statements after issue, that fact should be disclosed.

Updating of disclosures

An enterprise should update disclosures in the financial statements that relate to conditions existing at the balance sheet date in the light of information received after the balance sheet date.

ACTIVITY 1

How would the following be dealt with?

1 When drafting the final accounts, a company's accountant includes a figure of $2,000 as the net realisable value of damaged items of inventory.

2 The cost of these items was $3,000, and the normal selling price would be $4,000. Between the balance sheet date and the approval of the accounts the items are sold for $3,100.

Feedback to this activity is at the end of the chapter.

ACTIVITY 2

A company is engaged in the construction of its own factory. The estimated value on completion is $200,000, costs to date are $80,000 and at the balance sheet date expected further costs to completion were $90,000.

After the balance sheet date, serious defects – which must have existed unnoticed for some time – are discovered in the foundations of the building, necessitating partial demolition and rebuilding at an estimated cost of $70,000 (in addition to the estimated further costs to completion of $90,000).

How would this be dealt with in the accounts?

Feedback to this activity is at the end of the chapter.

Examples

In the following examples X and Y are limited liability companies with a year end of 31 December and the directors of X approve the financial statements on 11 March.

1 X has guaranteed a loan of $10,000 granted to Y. At the time when the financial statements of X are being finalised, it is clear that Y is in financial difficulties and it is probable that X will have to meet the guarantee.

Accounting treatment

Since it is probable that the liability will arise, an accrual is necessary in X's financial statements:

		$	$
Dr	Income statement	10,000	
Cr	Provision for liability		10,000

2 X has guaranteed a loan of $5,000 granted to Y. At the date when the directors approve the financial statements of Y there is no reason to believe that the guarantee will be invoked.

Accounting treatment

Assuming that the amount of $5,000 is a material amount for X, the contingent liability should be disclosed by way of note to the financial statements.

3 X has guaranteed a loan of $20,000 granted to Y. After the balance sheet date of X, but before the financial statements are approved by the directors, X receives notice that Y is in liquidation and that the guarantee will be invoked by the creditor of Y.

Accounting treatment

This is an event after the balance sheet date requiring adjustment under IAS 10. The amount should therefore be accrued as a liability in the financial statements of X.

ACTIVITY **3**

The company is suing another company for $50,000 damages. At the date on which the financial statements are approved, counsel's opinion is that the company is likely to win its case.

How should this matter be treated in the financial statements?

Feedback to this activity is at the end of the chapter.

ACTIVITY **4**

The company is being sued for $100,000 damages. Counsel assesses the chances of losing the case as 50–50.

How should this matter be treated in the financial statements?

Feedback to this activity is at the end of the chapter.

Conclusion

The accounting standards covered in this chapter relate to the problems of whether to include or not to include certain items in the accounts. It is important to learn the definitions contained in this chapter and the accounting entries which result.

SELF-TEST QUESTIONS

Accounting for contingencies

1 What is a contingent liability? (1.2)

2 What are the four classifications of contingent liabilities and contingent assets? (1.3)

3 When should contingent liabilities and contingent assets be accrued in the financial statements? (1.3, 1.4)

Events after the balance sheet date

4 What is the definition in IAS 10 of an event after the balance sheet date? (2.1)

5 Can you give two examples of events after the balance sheet date which require adjustment? (2.2)

6 Can you give two examples of events after the balance sheet date requiring disclosure by note? (2.3)

MULTIPLE-CHOICE QUESTION

IAS10 *Events after the Balance Sheet Date* regulates the extent to which events after the balance sheet date should be reflected in financial statements.

Which of the following lists of such events consists only of items that, according to IAS10 should normally be classified as non-adjusting?

A Insolvency of a debtor whose account receivable was outstanding at the balance sheet date, issue of shares or loan notes, a major merger with another company.

B Issue of shares or loan notes, changes in foreign exchange rates, major purchases of non-current assets.

C A major merger with another company, destruction of a major non-current asset by fire, discovery of fraud or error which shows that the financial statements were incorrect.

D Sale of inventory, giving evidence about its value at the balance sheet date, issue of shares or loan notes, destruction of a major non-current asset by fire.

For the answer to this question, see the 'Answers' section at the end of the book.

EXAM-TYPE QUESTIONS

Question 1: Events

In relation to IAS 10 *Events after the balance sheet date,* **you are required:**

(a) to explain the two different types of event occurring after the balance sheet date

(b) to give two examples of each. **(12 marks)**

Question 2: Jurien

The directors of Jurien are considering the draft financial statements for the year ended 31 March 20X1.

Matters under discussion are:

(a) After a party in February 20X0, 18 people died as a result of food poisoning from eating food manufactured by Jurien. At 31 March 20X0 the company was advised that there was probably no liability and the matter was disclosed as a contingent liability at that date. As the result of developments in the case, which is still not settled, the company has been advised that it is now probable, as at 31 March 20X1, that the company will be found liable. Some directors consider that the matter should remain a contingent liability until the court case decides the matter, while others consider that provision should be made for it in the financial statements for the year ended 31 March 20X1.

(3 marks)

(b) No allowance has yet been made for an account receivable of $560,000 outstanding at 31 March 20X1. In June 20X1 the directors of Jurien became aware that the debtor was in financial difficulties. Directors are divided as to whether an allowance should be made or not. **(3 marks)**

(c) The company's closing inventory of finished goods is valued by taking the cost of labour and materials plus an allocation of overheads. One director has queried the basis on which overheads are added and has asked for clarification of the relevant rules, with two examples of overheads which must not be excluded. **(4 marks)**

Required:

Write a memorandum to the directors advising them on the three points raised, explaining the authority for your advice in each case. **(Total: 10 marks)**

For the answers to these questions, see the 'Answers' section at the end of the book.

FEEDBACK TO ACTIVITY 1

The valuation in the financial statements should be adjusted to $3,000, i.e. cost, since net realisable value has, in the event, turned out to be greater than cost. This is an event after the balance sheet date requiring adjustment.

FEEDBACK TO ACTIVITY 2

This is an event requiring adjustment. There is an anticipated loss on the factory of $40,000 (value $200,000 less costs to date $80,000 less estimated further costs $160,000). The asset should, therefore, be valued at $40,000 (costs to date $80,000 less attributable loss $40,000).

FEEDBACK TO ACTIVITY 3

This is a material contingent asset, which should be disclosed by way of note.

FEEDBACK TO ACTIVITY 4

Since the chances are 50–50, the loss is not 'probable'; the contingent liability should, therefore, be disclosed by way of note. This is clearly a borderline case and prudence might dictate that a provision should be made.

Chapter 17
INCOMPLETE RECORDS

CHAPTER CONTENTS

So far in this text, the ledger accounting that has been encountered has been complete, even if errors have been made. Many enterprises, however, do not maintain a complete set of double entry books. The term 'incomplete records' refers to the varying situations that fall short of full double entry. In most cases this will tend to be the situation with a sole trader rather than other forms of enterprise. This chapter will, therefore, concentrate on the approach and techniques required to prepare an income statement and balance sheet for a sole trader who does not keep a full set of double entry records.

Objectives

By the time you have finished this chapter you should be able to:

- calculate the profit of an enterprise from information about its balance sheet only
- reconstruct the ledger accounts for an enterprise from details of its transactions and prepare a set of financial statements
- understand gross profit margins and mark-ups and be able to use them in an incomplete records situation
- understand some basic liquidity and working capital ratios and be able to use these to reconstruct the financial statements of a business.

1 Incomplete and limited accounting records

1.1 Distinction between incomplete and limited accounting records

DEFINITION

Limited accounting records are records kept by a trader of certain transactions but additional information is required to prepare financial statements.

Incomplete accounting records are records which the trader has not fully completed or where no records at all have been kept of transactions.

Limited accounting records are records kept by a trader of certain transactions but additional information is required to prepare financial statements.

Incomplete accounting records are records which the trader has not fully completed or where no records at all have been kept of transactions.

Many businesses fall into each of the above categories. Many businesses keep limited accounting information, such as daily records of cash received, invoices paid (i.e. some form of purchases journal) and wages paid. They leave it to the accountant who prepares the annual financial statements to make sense of the information and to ask for other information at that time.

With limited accounting records, the accountant thus has (generally) sufficient information to prepare the accounts but no ledger accounts have been prepared. We will look at the procedures used to prepare financial statements in this situation later in the chapter.

A trader who has kept very little information on his daily transactions is providing the accountant with the task of preparing financial statements from incomplete data. In this section we will see how limited the data can be and yet it is still possible to prepare financial statements. However, these financial statements are more prone to error because of the incomplete records.

In practice, the term incomplete records is used to cover both situations.

1.2 Incomplete accounting records for a sole trader

The most basic incomplete records situation of all is where one is required to calculate net profit, given details only of a sole trader's capital at the beginning and end of the year and of amounts he has withdrawn (drawings).

Example

A sole trader's capital position is as follows:

	31 December	
	20X6	*20X7*
	$	$
Motor vehicle:		
Cost	2,000	2,000
Depreciation	(800)	(1,200)
	1,200	800
Inventory	2,040	2,960
Receivables	865	1,072
Bank	1,017	1,964
Cash	351	86
	5,473	6,882
Payables	1,706	1,905
Net assets	3,767	4,977

He has estimated his drawings for the year at $3,000. An estimate of his net profit for the year is required.

Solution

From the basic balance sheet equation: capital equals assets less liabilities. Hence, his opening and closing capital account balances are $3,767 and $4,977 respectively. His net profit may be calculated by completing his capital account.

Capital account

20X7		$	*20X7*		$
	Drawings	3,000	1 Jan	Balance b/d	3,767
31 Dec	Balance c/d	4,977		Net profit (bal fig)	4,210
		7,977			7,977
			20X8		
			1 Jan	Balance b/d	4,977

Note that the net profit figure is very much an estimate and depends on the reliability of the drawings and the opening and closing net asset positions.

It also assumes that no new capital has been introduced by the owner during the year.

Alternative method

An alternative method of calculation is:

	$
Net assets this year end	4,977
Net assets last year end	3,767
Increase in net assets	1,210
Less: Capital introduced by owner	–
Add: Drawings	3,000
Profit for the year	4,210

KEY POINT

Profit = Increase in net assets – Capital introduced + Drawings.

The alternative method emphasises that profit represents an increase in the net assets of the business unless it is withdrawn by the owner.

Profit for the year = Increase in net assets – Capital introduced + Drawings.

ACTIVITY 1

On 1 January 20X5 B Freen commenced business. At that date he purchased a shop premises for $14,000 and paid $2,000 for interior fittings. He also paid $4,000 into the business bank account. On 31 December 20X6 he realised the need for a profit figure for the two years he had been in business, but his records were completely inadequate. At this date the assets he possessed in addition to the premises and fittings were:

	$
Inventory	6,000
Receivables	1,040
Motor lorry purchased 30 June 20X6 for	8,000
Cash at bank	2,500

He owed $1,400 to trade suppliers and had borrowed $10,000 from a friend. Interest accrued but unpaid on the loan amounted to $200. Freen estimated that he was withdrawing $300 a month from the business.

Compute the net profit for the two years valuing the non-current assets at cost less depreciation (on a straight line basis): on premises at 2% p.a., on fittings at 5% p.a. and on the motor lorry at 20% p.a.

Feedback to this activity is at the end of the chapter.

2 Financial statements from limited accounting records

2.1 Cash and bank transactions

In the first example above, no details were given of transactions taking place during the year. If basic information regarding receipts and payments is provided, it is possible to build up to a balance sheet and income statement, although some important assumptions may well need to be made.

2.2 Basic procedure for limited records

The procedure suggested below is a full procedure suitable for a wide range of limited records questions and may be set out in basic steps. We will see later how some of these steps can be cut back on for examination purposes.

Step 1

Set aside one sheet of paper for the income statement and one sheet for the balance sheet. Some information can be inserted straight into them.

Step 2

Prepare the opening balance sheet from information on assets and liabilities.

KEY POINT

The opening capital account balance can be calculated as a balancing figure (capital = assets less liabilities).

The opening capital account balance can be calculated as a balancing figure (capital = assets less liabilities).

Step 3

Insert the opening balances in 'T' accounts. For example:

Balance	*Account*
Cash at bank	Cash at bank (bank)
Cash in hand	Cash in hand (cash)
Receivables	Accounts receivable control account
Payables	Accounts payable control account
Accrued expenses	Separate account for each expense category
Prepayments	Separate account for each expense category

The accounts payable control account and accounts receivable control account have a similar layout to control accounts in a double entry system. The difference is that their key objective in incomplete records is often to calculate purchases and sales made in the accounting period which will be transferred to the income statement.

Step 4

Information is almost certain to be given as regards cash and bank transactions. Accordingly the cash and bank accounts can be prepared, making use of double entry principles and completing the entries by debiting and crediting whichever accounts are appropriate.

Notes:

1 Cash withdrawn is cash taken out of the bank (Cr Bank) and into cash in hand (Dr Cash).

2 Cash banked operates in the opposite direction – it is a reduction of cash (Cr Cash) and an increase in money at bank (Dr Bank).

Depending on the degree of incompleteness, cash is likely to contain one or two missing items of information. This aspect of the problem will receive more attention later.

Step 5

Insert into the accounts the closing balances provided in the question in respect of receivables, payables, accrued expenses and prepayments. In simple questions, the respective transfers to the income statement may be calculated as balancing items.

Accounts receivable control account

	$		$
Opening receivables b/d	X	Cash	X
Sales revenue (bal fig)	X	Closing receivables c/d	X
	X		X

Accounts payable control account

	$		$
Cash	X	Opening trade payables b/d	X
Bank	X	Purchases (bal fig)	X
Closing trade payables c/d	X		
	X		X

Rent account (assuming paid in advance)

	$		$
Opening prepayment b/d	X	Income statement (bal fig)	X
Bank	X	Closing prepayment c/d	X
	X		X

Step 6

Carry out any further adjustments as required, such as dealing with doubtful debts and depreciation.

ACTIVITY 2

A business has a cash float of $50 and the following expenses are paid out of the till before cash is banked:

	$
Purchases	20
Wages	100
Expenses	80

The bank statement shows that the takings banked in the period were $4,000.

Write up the cash account.

Feedback to this activity is at the end of the chapter.

ACTIVITY 3

The following information relates to a business's transactions for a month.

	$
Opening cash	100
Closing cash	50
Opening receivables	460
Closing receivables	420
Cash expenses	750
Bankings	4,220
Cash drawings by proprietor	1,200
Cash sales	2,500
Credit sales	3,700

Bad debts written off	50
Discounts allowed	70

Write up the cash account and accounts receivable control account.

Feedback to this activity is at the end of the chapter.

Example

Yatton does not keep proper accounting records. You ascertain that his bank payments and receipts during the year to 31 December 20X8 were as follows:

Bank account

	$		$
Balance 1 Jan 20X8	800	Cash withdrawn	200
Cheques for sales	2,500	Purchases	2,500
Cash banked	3,000	Expenses	800
		Drawings	1,300
		Delivery van (bought 1 Oct 20X8)	1,000
		Balance 31 Dec 20X8	500
	6,300		6,300

From a cash notebook you ascertain that:

	$
Cash in hand 1 January 20X8	70
Cash takings	5,200
Purchases paid in cash	400
Expenses paid in cash	500
Cash in hand 31 December 20X8	30
Drawings by proprietor in cash	Unknown

You discover that assets and liabilities were as follows:

	1 Jan 20X8	*31 Dec 20X8*
	$	$
Trade receivables	300	450
Trade payables	800	900
Expense payables	100	150
Inventory in hand	1,400	1,700

Yatton says that he has no hope of receiving an amount of $100 due from one customer and that an allowance of 10% of trade receivables would be prudent. Depreciation on the van is to be provided at the rate of 20% per annum.

You are required to prepare an income statement for the year to 31 December 20X8 and a balance sheet at that date.

Solution

Step 1

The sheets set aside for the financial statements can be started with the main headings and certain information, such as opening and closing inventory, can be inserted.

Step 2

The preparation of the opening balance sheet is usually achieved by drawing up a statement of opening capital using information given in the question about the opening balances. A careful scrutiny of the question reveals:

(W1) **Calculation of opening capital**

	Dr	Cr
	$	$
Bank	800	
Cash	70	
Receivables	300	
Payables		800
Expense payables		100
Inventory	1,400	
	2,570	900
	900	
	1,670	

Thus debits (assets) exceed credits (liabilities) by $1,670. Accordingly, Yatton's business has net assets of $1,670, represented on the balance sheet by his opening capital account.

Step 3

Insert the opening balances into T accounts if construction of the accounts is required. Leave plenty of space between the ledger accounts.

Thus a ledger account for Bank is not required as the question has already provided this. Accounts for inventory and capital are not required as the information can be inserted immediately into the financial statements.

(W2) **Cash**

	$		$
Balance b/d	70		

(W3) **Accounts receivable control account**

	$		$
Balance b/d	300		

(W4) **Accounts payable control account**

	$		$
		Balance b/d	800

(W5) **Payables – expenses**

	$		$
		Balance b/d	100

Step 4

Prepare the cash account, and post the cash and bank entries to the other accounts.

(W2) **Cash**

	$		$
Balance b/d	70	Bank	3,000
Bank	200	Accounts payable control account	400
Accounts receivable control account	5,200	Expenses	500
		Drawings (bal fig)	1,540
		Balance c/d	30
	5,470		5,470

(W3) **Accounts receivable control account**

	$		$
Balance b/d	300	Bank	2,500
		Cash	5,200

(W4) **Accounts payable control account**

	$		$
Bank	2,500	Balance b/d	800
Cash	400		

(W5) **Expenses**

	$		$
Bank	800	Balance b/d	100
Cash	500		

(W6) **Drawings**

	$		$
Bank	1,300		
Cash	1,540		

(W7) **Van cost**

	$		$
Bank	1,000		

Two points are worth noting at this stage:

- The commentary above is designed to show what happens after each step; there is no question of writing out each account on more than one occasion.
- If a question gives full details of the bank account (as this one does), there is no need to write it out again as part of your workings.

Step 5

Insert the closing balances and calculate the transfers to the income statement.

(W4) **Accounts payable control account**

	$		$
Bank	2,500	Balance b/d	800
Cash	400	Income statement	
Balance c/d	900	(bal fig)	
	3,800		3,800

(W5) **Expenses**

	$		$
Bank	800	Balance b/d	100
Cash	500	Income statement	
Balance c/d	150	(bal fig)	
	1,450		1,450

The accounts receivable control account has not yet been closed, as there is an adjustment for bad debts still to be made.

Step 6

Carry out any further adjustments. These will be familiar, and the principles behind them are unchanged.

Bad debts

(W3) **Accounts receivable control account**

	$		$
Balance b/d	300	Bank	2,500
Income statement		Cash	5,200
(bal fig)		Bad debts	100
		Balance c/d ($450 – $100)	350
	8,150		8,150

(W8) **Bad debts**

	$		$
Accounts receivable control account	100	Income statement	135
Allowance for doubtful debts	35		
	135		135

(W9) **Allowance for doubtful debts**

	$		$
Balance c/d (10% × $350)	35	Balance b/d	Nil
		Bad debts	35
	35		35

Depreciation

(W7) **Van cost**

	$		$
Bank	1,000	Balance c/d	1,000

(W10) **Van accumulated depreciation**

	$		$
Balance c/d	50	Income statement	50

Charge 20% × 3 months × \$1,000 = \$50

Drawings

(W6) **Drawings**

	$		$
Bank	1,300	Capital	2,840
Cash	1,540		
	2,840		2,840

The remaining figures can be inserted into the final accounts.

Yatton
Income statement for year ended 31 December 20X8

	$	$
Sales revenue (W3)		7,850
Cost of sales:		
Opening inventory	1,400	
Purchases (W4)	3,000	
	4,400	
Less: Closing inventory	1,700	
		2,700
Gross profit		5,150
Expenses (W5)	1,350	
Bad debts (W8)	135	
Depreciation of van (W10)	50	
		1,535
Net profit		3,615

Yatton
Balance sheet as at 31 December 20X8

	$	$	$
Non-current assets:			
Van at cost		1,000	
Depreciation to date (W10)		50	
			950
Current assets:			
Inventory		1,700	
Receivables (W3)	350		
Less: Allowance for doubtful debts	35		
		315	
Cash at bank		500	
Cash in hand		30	
			2,545
			3,495
Capital account:			
Capital at 1 January 20X8 (W1)		1,670	
Add: Profit for year		3,615	
		5,285	
Less: Drawings in year (W6)		2,840	
			2,445
Current liabilities:			
Trade payables		900	
Accrued expenses		150	
			1,050
			3,495

3 Using ratios and percentages

3.1 Introduction

In the example above, drawings was the only unknown in the cash account. What happens if there are *two* unknowns in the cash account – for example, drawings and takings? We can still construct the financial statements provided we are given some additional information.

3.2 Gross profit percentages

DEFINITION

Gross profit percentage = $\frac{\text{Gross profit}}{\text{Sales revenue}} \times 100$

$$\text{Gross profit percentage} = \frac{\text{Gross profit}}{\text{Sales revenue}} \times 100$$

For instance, if we know that sales revenue totals $8,000 and the gross profit percentage is 25%, the following can be deduced:

	$	%
Sales revenue	8,000 (given)	100
Less: Cost of sales	6,000	75
Gross profit	2,000	25 (given)

ACTIVITY 4

Assume that we are told that the gross profit percentage is 30% and gross profit $6,000. What are sales revenue and cost of sales?

Feedback to this activity is at the end of the chapter.

3.3 Margins and mark-ups

The gross profit percentage in the previous examples is also known as the **profit margin**. The percentage of profit is given by reference to sales revenue.

Alternatively information on the **mark-up** may be given.

DEFINITION

Mark-up percentage = $\frac{\text{Gross profit}}{\text{Cost of sales}} \times 100$

$$\text{Mark-up percentage} = \frac{\text{Gross profit}}{\text{Cost of sales}} \times 100$$

Thus if we know that cost of sales is $6,000 and the mark-up is one third, we can set out the following:

	$	*Ratio*
Sales revenue		
Cost of sales (given)	6,000	3
Gross profit		1

The 'ratio' is an alternative to using percentages. One third is awkward to work with in percentage terms.

In ratio terms gross profit is one part to three parts costs. Sales are therefore four parts (1 + 3), so total sales = $\frac{4}{3}$ × $6,000 = $8,000.

	$	*Ratio*
Sales revenue	8,000	4
Cost of sales	6,000	3
Gross profit	2,000	1

ACTIVITY 5

The sales of a business are $280,000 and there is a mark up on cost of 40%. What are the figures for cost of sales and gross profit?

Feedback to this activity is at the end of the chapter.

3.4 Converting margins to mark-ups and vice versa

Suppose we have been told that sales are $60,000 and the mark-up is 25%. The information given can be set out:

	$	%
Sales revenue	60,000	
Cost of sales		100
Gross profit		25

Laying out the information as above should show that gross profit and cost of sales can still be worked out. In percentage terms, sales are 125% (100 + 25). Profit is therefore $\frac{25}{125}$ × $60,000 = $12,000.

	$	%
Sales revenue	60,000	125
Cost of sales	48,000	100
Gross profit	12,000	25

KEY POINT

$$\text{Margin} = \frac{\text{Mark - up}}{\text{Mark - up} + 100}$$

$$\text{Mark-up} = \frac{\text{Margin}}{100 - \text{Margin}}$$

To convert mark-up to margin (where figures are percentages):

$$\text{Margin} = \frac{\text{Mark - up}}{\text{Mark - up} + 100}$$

To convert margin to mark-up:

$$\text{Mark-up} = \frac{\text{Margin}}{100 - \text{Margin}}$$

Example

Kendal, a sole trader, has provided you with the following information relating to the year ended 31 December 20X5:

1 He has not made a note of drawings or of cash received. The following items were paid from takings prior to banking:

Purchases	$760
Sundry expenses	$400

2 Kendal has estimated that his gross profit percentage is 20%.

3 His summarised bank account was as follows:

Bank account

20X5		$	*20X5*		$
1 Jan	Balance b/d	1,700		Rent	1,000
	Bankings	16,940		Electricity	235
				Purchases	16,140
				Drawings	265
			31 Dec	Balance c/d	1,000
		18,640			18,640

4 Assets and liabilities were as follows:

	31 Dec 20X5	*31 Dec 20X4*
		$
Inventory	4,800	5,600
Receivables	1,650	2,100
Payables:		
Goods	1,940	1,640
Electricity	65	–
Cash float	2,400	170

5 He started paying rent in 20X5. A year's rent was paid in advance on 1 April 20X5.

You are required to prepare:

(a) an income statement for the year ended 31 December 20X5

(b) a balance sheet at that date.

Solution

Step 1

Sheets of paper are reserved for the income statement and balance sheet. In particular the gross profit calculation becomes a key working in situations where a margin or mark-up is given. Insert the opening and closing inventory figures (if given) and also the margin percentages.

Step 2

Up till now the opening balance sheet has been completed in order to derive the opening capital balance. This working will now be done after the accounts receivable and payable control accounts have been completed as it only helps in finding one figure to go into the final accounts.

We need to recognise that there may be time pressure in the examination and therefore we should spend our time first on the control accounts.

Step 3

Insert the opening balances in 'T' accounts.

Step 4

Deal with the information given as regards cash and bank transactions. Note that the bank account is not included in the workings, full details being given in the question.

In addition, no ledger accounts have been shown for the various expenses. Instead workings have been shown on the face of the income statement, e.g. Rent.

There is a rent prepayment of $250 (three months' rent). The expense is therefore $750. The derivation of the $750 (1,000 – 250) has been shown in brackets by the narrative on the income statement.

Where *simple* adjustments are to be made, this method allows the speedier preparation of the solution.

Step 5

Insert the closing balances into the accounts. At this point the figure for purchases can be calculated.

Having reached this far, a little more thought is now required.

The position as regards unknowns can be summarised as follows:

Receivables The figures for sales and receipts from customers are unknown.

Cash The figures for drawings and receipts from customers are unknown.

This is where the gross profit percentage is utilised as follows:

	$		$	%
Sales revenue			22,500	100
Less: Cost of goods sold:				
Opening inventory	5,600	(given)		
Purchases	17,200	(calculation)		
	22,800			
Less: Closing inventory	4,800	(given)		
			18,000	80
Gross profit			4,500	20 (given)

The sales figure has now been derived, leaving only one unknown in the receivables account – receipts from customers, which is calculated as a balancing figure.

The resulting double entry (Dr Cash $22,950, Cr Receivables $22,950) means that there is now only one unknown in the cash account, the drawings figure.

Workings

(W1) **Cash**

	$		$
Balance b/d	170	Bank	16,940
Accounts receivable	22,950	Payables – goods	760
		Payables – expenses	400
		Drawings (bal fig)	2,620
		Balance c/d	2,400
	23,120		23,120

(W2) **Accounts receivable control**

	$		$
Balance b/d	2,100	Cash (bal fig)	22,950
Income statement	22,500	Balance c/d	1,650
	24,600		24,600

(W3) **Accounts payable control**

	$		$
Bank	16,140	Balance b/d	1,640
Cash	760	Income statement	
Balance c/d	1,940	(bal fig)	
	18,840		18,840

(W4) **Drawings**

	$		$
Bank	265	Capital	2,885
Cash	2,620		
	2,885		2,885

(W5) **Statement of opening capital**

	Dr $	*Cr* $
Bank	1,700	
Inventory	5,600	
Receivables	2,100	
Payables – goods		1,640
Cash	170	
	9,570	1,640
	1,640	
	7,930	

(a) **Income statement for the year ended 31 December 20X5**

	$	$	%
Sales revenue		22,500	100
Opening inventory	5,600		
Purchases	17,200		
	22,800		
Closing inventory	4,800		
Cost of sales		18,000	80
Gross profit		4,500	20
Rent (1,000 – 250)	750		
Electricity (235 + 65)	300		
Sundry	400		
		1,450	
Net profit		3,050	

(b) **Balance sheet as at 31 December 20X5**

	$	$
Current assets:		
Inventory	4,800	
Receivables	1,650	
Prepayment	250	
Bank	1,000	
Cash	2,400	
		10,100
		10,100
Capital account:		
Opening capital	7,930	
Add: Net profit	3,050	
	10,980	
Less: Drawings	2,885	
		8,095
Current liabilities		
Payables (1,940 + 65)		2,005
		10,100

3.5 Variations on the theme

No two incomplete records questions are quite the same, although the differences between them are often fairly small. Two examples of possible variations are:

1 Suppose that inventory was destroyed in a fire and that there was enough information to calculate sales, purchases and opening inventory. The gross profit percentage would enable sales to be converted to cost of sales. Closing inventory could then be calculated as a balancing figure.

2 Suppose that a trader always received a rebate from his suppliers amounting to 1% of purchases, and that in the current year the rebate amounted to $172. Clearly this tells us that purchases were $17,200. If cash paid to suppliers was unknown, it could be calculated as a balancing figure.

KEY POINT

The fact that all incomplete records questions are different means that there is no universally correct way of attempting them.

The fact that all incomplete records questions are different means that there is no universally correct way of attempting them. The key feature is to treat each question on its merits, remembering the overall criterion that double entry bookkeeping should be used to prepare the required financial statements, namely converting the incomplete records into suitable accounting form.

Conclusion

No two incomplete records situations are exactly the same whether this is in practice or in examination questions. For examination questions, what is required is a knowledge of the techniques covered in this chapter for reconstructing financial statements from a variety of types of incomplete information, together with a thorough grasp and application of double entry bookkeeping.

The six step approach set out in the chapter is a good starting point in most questions although all six steps may not always be required. You should then be aware of the use of the cash and bank accounts, accounts receivable and payable control accounts and any margins, mark-ups or other ratios that are given in the question. A good tip is that if a margin or mark-up is given in the question then it is highly likely that the only way to calculate either sales or purchases will be by applying this percentage to the information in the question.

SELF-TEST QUESTIONS

Incomplete and limited accounting records

1 How can the profit of a business be measured if opening and closing net assets and drawings are known? (1.2)

Financial statements for Limited accounting needs

2 What is the accounts receivable control account? (2.2)

3 What are the six basic steps for the approach to an incomplete records question? (2.2)

Using ratios and percentages

4 How is the gross profit percentage calculated? (3.2)

5 How is a mark-up percentage calculated? (3.2)

6 How is a cost mark-up converted to a profit margin? (3.3)

7 If inventory was destroyed in a fire but sales, purchases and opening inventory could be calculated, how would the figure for inventory destroyed be estimated? (3.4)

MULTIPLE-CHOICE QUESTIONS

Question 1

The following information is relevant to the calculation of the sales figure for Alpha, a sole trader who does not keep proper accounting records:

	$
Opening accounts receivable	29,100
Cash received from credit customers and paid into the bank	381,600
Expenses paid out of cash received from credit customers before banking	6,800
Bad debts written off	7,200
Refunds to credit customers	2,100
Discounts allowed to credit customers	9,400
Cash sales	112,900
Closing accounts receivable	38,600

The figure which should appear in Alpha's income statement for sales is:

A $525,300

B $511,700

C $529,500

D $510,900

Question 2

A sole trader who does not keep full accounting records wishes to calculate her sales revenue for the year.

The information available is:

1	Opening inventory	$17,000
2	Closing inventory	$24,000
3	Purchases	$91,000
4	Standard gross profit percentage on sales revenue	40%

Which of the following is the sales revenue figure for the year calculated from these figures?

A $117,600

B $108,000

C $210,000

D $140,000

Question 3

A business compiling its accounts for the year to 31 January each year pays rent quarterly in advance on 1 January, 1 April, 1 July and 1 October each year. After remaining unchanged for some years, the rent was increased from $24,000 per year to $30,000 per year as from 1 July 2000.

Which of the following figures is the rent expense which should appear in the income statement for the year ended 31 January 2001?

A $27,500

B $29,500

C $28,000

D $29,000

Question 4

On 31 December 2000 the inventory of V was completely destroyed by fire. The following information is available:

1 Inventory at 1 December 2000 at cost $28,400

2 Purchases for December 2000 $49,600

3 Sales for December 2000 $64,800

4 Standard gross profit percentage on sales revenue 30%

Based on this information, which of the following is the amount of inventory destroyed?

A $45,360

B $32,640

C $40,971

D $19,440

For the answers to these questions, see the 'Answers' section at the end of the book.

PRACTICE QUESTION

B Letitslide

B Letitslide is in business but does not keep proper accounting records. In order to prepare his income statement for the year ended 31 December 20X5, you are given the following information:

	20X5 *1 Jan* $	*20X5* *31 Dec* $
Inventory on hand	1,310	1,623
Receivables	268	412
Payables: goods	712	914
Payables: expenses	116	103

In addition, you are able to prepare the following summary of his cash and bank transactions for the year:

Cash account

	$		$
Balance 1 Jan	62	Payments into bank	3,050
Shop takings (cash sales)	4,317	Purchases	316
Cheques cashed	200	Expenses	584
		Drawings	600
		Balance 31 Dec	29
	4,579		4,579

Bank account

	$		$
Balance 1 Jan	840	Cash withdrawn	200
Cheques from customers	1,416	Purchases	2,715
Cash paid in	3,050	Expenses	519
		Drawings	400
		Delivery van (purchased 1 Sep)	900
		Balance 31 Dec	572
	5,306		5,306

In addition, Mr Letitslide says that he had taken goods for personal consumption and estimates those goods cost $100.

In considering the receivables, Mr Letitslide suggests that there is no hope of receiving an amount of $30 from one customer. There are other doubtful debts and an allowance is to be made of 5% of trade receivables after writing off the bad debt of $30.

Allowing depreciation on the delivery van of 20% per annum, prepare the income statement for the year ended 31 December 20X5 and a balance sheet as at that date. **(25 marks)**

For the answer to this question, see the 'Answers' section at the end of the book.

EXAM-TYPE QUESTION

Ben White

Ben White, a retailer, adds 25% to the cost of goods purchased for resale to arrive at his selling prices.

His financial position at 30 June 20X5 was:

	$
Assets:	
Plant and machinery (NBV)	5,000
Inventory	3,825
Receivables	7,175
Cash at bank	2,200
Liabilities:	
Payables	3,000
Loan from Z (interest-free)	2,000

During the year ended 30 June 20X6 he:

1 paid $11,675 for goods for resale (cheque)

2 repaid $500 of the loan from Z (cheque)

3 purchased a van for $700 (cheque) on the last day of the year

4 withdrew from the bank $80 per month personal expenses

5 paid into the bank a legacy of $300

6 paid income tax $600 (treat as drawings) (cheque)

7 withdrew an unspecified amount of cash from takings prior to banking.

At 30 June 20X6 inventory at cost was $4,000, receivables totalled $7,000 and payables were $3,500; the balance at bank amounted to $1,950. Depreciation of plant was 10% on reducing balance. No depreciation is to be provided on the van.

You are required to prepare:

(a) an income statement for the year ended 30 June 20X6

(b) the balance sheet as at 30 June 20X6. **(18 marks)**

For the answer to this question, see the 'Answers' section at the end of the book.

FEEDBACK TO ACTIVITY 1

Your solution should be as follows:

Calculation of capital at:	*1 Jan 20X5*	*31 Dec 20X6*	
	Assets	*Liabilities*	*Assets*
	$	$	$
Shop premises	14,000		14,000
Shop depreciation 2% × $14,000 × 2 years			(560)
Fittings	2,000		2,000
Fittings depreciation 5% × $2,000 × 2 years			(200)
Cash	4,000		2,500
Inventory			6,000
Receivables			1,040
Motor lorry			8,000
Motor lorry depreciation 20% × $8,000 × 6 months			(800)
Payables		1,400	
Loan		10,000	
Accrued interest		200	
		11,600	31,980
			(11,600)
Capital	20,000		20,380

Capital account

	$		$
Drawings 24 × $300	7,200	Opening capital	20,000
Closing capital	20,380	Net profit (bal fig)	7,580
	27,580		27,580

FEEDBACK TO ACTIVITY 2

Your solution should be as follows:

Cash

	$		$
Balance b/d	50	Purchases	20
Cash takings (sales) (bal fig)	4,200	Wages	100
		Expenses	80
		Bankings	4,000
		Balance c/d	50
	4,250		4,250

FEEDBACK TO ACTIVITY 3

Your solution should be as follows:

Cash

	$		$
Balance b/d	100	Expenses	750
Sales revenue	2,500	Bank (bankings)	4,220
Cash from customers – accounts receivable control (bal fig)	3,620	Drawings	1,200
		Balance c/d	50
	6,220		6,220

Accounts receivable control

	$		$
Balance b/d	460	Bad debt	50
Sales revenue	3,700	Discounts allowed	70
		Cash received	3,620
		Balance c/d	420
	4,160		4,160

FEEDBACK TO ACTIVITY 4

Your solution should be as follows:

	$	%
Sales revenue	20,000	100
Less: Cost of sales	14,000	70
Gross profit	6,000 (given)	30 (given)

The percentages provided may have been calculated by reference to a similar business or from the previous years' results of this business.

FEEDBACK TO ACTIVITY 5

Your solution should be as follows:

	$	%
Sales revenue	280,000	140
Cost of sales (280,000 × 100/140)	200,000	100
Gross profit (280,000 × 40/140)	80,000	40

Chapter 18
PARTNERSHIP ACCOUNTS

CHAPTER CONTENTS

Partnerships are a popular form of exam question. There is some new terminology to learn but more importantly there are a number of special accounting entries that have to be dealt with.

The emphasis of exam questions is on dealing with the computational aspects of partnerships but there are occasional questions, or parts of questions, requiring an explanation of terms or accounting entries.

Objectives

By the time you have finished this chapter you should be able to:

- divide profit between partners
- prepare partnership financial statements

Note that partnership questions in the examination no longer deal with changes requiring goodwill alignments, or dissolutions.

1 Partnerships – basic principles

1.1 Identification of partnership

DEFINITION

A **partnership** involves the sole proprietor taking in one or more partners in common with a view to profit.

A partnership is a natural progression from a sole trader, the sole proprietor taking in one or more partners (co-proprietors) in common with a view to profit. In many countries a partnership is not a corporate entity, but a collection of individuals jointly carrying on business.

1.2 Advantages and disadvantages of partnerships

Comparing a partnership to sole trading, the advantages of operating as a partnership are as follows:

Business risks are spread among more than one person.

- Individual partners can develop special skills upon which the other partners can rely, whereas in a sole business one person has responsibility for everything.
- Certain partners may be able to draw upon larger capital resources to set up the partnership or expand the partnership.

The disadvantages are:

- There may be disputes between partners on such matters as the direction the business is taking or how much money individual partners are taking out of the business. Some partners may feel they are contributing more time and effort to the partnership than others and not being sufficiently financially rewarded as a result.
- In many countries a partner is 'jointly and severally liable' for his partners. This means that if one partner is being sued in relation to the business of the partnership, the other partners share in the responsibility.

A partnership has some advantages over a company as the arrangement is less formal than setting up a company, which requires the issue of shares and the appointment of directors. If the partners wish to dissolve the business, that is easier to achieve by a partnership than by a company.

The advantage of a company is that the owners of the business – the shareholders –may be protected from the creditors of the company as regards the payment of outstanding debts. This point is looked at more closely when we examine company financial statements in a later chapter.

1.3 Dividing profit and maintaining equity

A partnership agreement, which need not necessarily be in written form, will govern the relationships between the partners. Important matters to be covered include:

- name of firm, the type of business, and duration
- capital to be introduced by partners
- distribution of profits between partners
- drawings by partners
- arrangements for dissolution, or on the death or retirement of partners
- settling of disputes
- preparation and audit of accounts.

The division of profit stated in the partnership agreement may be quite complex in order to reflect the expected differing efforts and contributions of the partners. For example, some or all of the partners may be entitled to a salary to reflect the differing management involvement in the business. Interest on capital may be provided to reflect the differing amounts of capital contributed. The profit shares may differ to reflect seniority or greater skills.

KEY POINT

A **partnership salary** is merely a device for calculating the division of profit; it is not a salary in the normal meaning of the term.

It is important to appreciate, however, that all of the above examples are *means of dividing* the profits of the partnership and are not expenses of the business. A partnership salary is merely a device for calculating the division of profit; it is not a salary in the normal meaning of the term.

1.4 Accounting distinctions between partnerships and sole traders

The accounting techniques developed for sole traders are generally applicable to partnerships, but there are certain important differences:

Item	*Sole trader's books*	*Partnership's books*
Capital introduced	Capital account	Partners' fixed capital accounts
Drawings and share of the profit	Capital account	Partners' current accounts
Division of profits	Inapplicable – one proprietor only	Income statement (see below)

2 Preparing partnership financial statements

2.1 Capital accounts

KEY POINT

Whatever the form of assets introduced and debited to asset accounts, it is normal to make the credit entry to fixed capital accounts.

At the commencement of the partnership, an agreement will have to be reached as to the amount of capital to be introduced. This could be in the form of cash or other assets. Whatever the form of assets introduced and debited to asset accounts, it is normal to make the credit entry to fixed capital accounts. These are so called because they are not then used to record drawings or shares of profits but only major changes in the relations between partners. In particular, fixed capital accounts are used to deal with:

- capital introduced or withdrawn by new or retiring partners
- revaluation adjustments.

KEY POINT

Fixed capital accounts are used to deal with:

- capital introduced or withdrawn by new or retiring partners
- revaluation adjustments.

KEY POINT

Current accounts **are used to deal with the regular transactions between the partners and the firm.**

The balances on fixed capital accounts do not necessarily bear any relation to the division of profits. However, to compensate partners who provide a larger share of the capital, it is common for notional interest on capital accounts to be paid to partners. This is dealt with in the calculations for the profit shares transferred from the income statement.

2.2 Current accounts

Current accounts are used to deal with the regular transactions between the partners and the firm, i.e. matters other than those sufficiently fundamental to be dealt with through the capital accounts. Most commonly these are:

- share of profits, interest on capital and partners' salaries, usually computed annually
- monthly drawings against the annual share of profit.

2.3 Ledger accounts and balance sheet presentation

Example 1

Nab and Crag commenced business in partnership on 1 January 20X6, contributing as fixed capital $5,000 and $10,000 cash respectively. All profits and losses are shared equally. The profit for the year ended 31 December 20X6 amounted to $10,000. Drawings for Nab and Crag amounted to $3,000 and $4,000 respectively.

You are required to prepare the capital and current accounts and balance sheet extracts.

Partners' capital accounts

	Nab	Crag		Nab	Crag
	$	$		$	$
			20X6		
			1 Jan Cash	5,000	10,000

Partners' current accounts

	Nab	Crag		Nab	Crag
	$	$		$	$
20X6			20X6		
31 Dec Drawings	3,000	4,000	31 Dec Income statement		
Balance c/d	2,000	1,000	– profit share	5,000	5,000
	5,000	5,000		5,000	5,000
			20X7		
			1 Jan Balance b/d	2,000	1,000

The above accounts are presented in a columnar format. This is convenient for examination purposes and is quite common in a partnership set of books as each partner will have similar transactions during the year. A columnar format allows two (or more) separate accounts to be shown using the same narrative. It is important to remember though that each partner's account is separate from the other partner(s).

Balance sheet at 31 December 20X6 (extract)

	Capital accounts	*Current accounts*	
	$	$	$
Partners' accounts:			
Nab	5,000	2,000	7,000
Crag	10,000	1,000	11,000
	15,000	3,000	18,000

Note that the current account balances of $2,000 and $1,000 will be credited in the following year with profit shares and debited with drawings.

One of the main differences between the capital section of the balance sheet of a sole trader and a partnership is that the partnership balance sheet will often only give the closing balances whereas the sole trader's movements in capital are shown. The main reason for the difference is simply one of space. Movements in the capital and current accounts for a few partners cannot be easily accommodated on the face of the balance sheet. In answering examination questions, the partners' capital and current accounts are often required as well as a balance sheet. It is a waste of time to repeat in the balance sheet detail already given in the partners' accounts.

Example 2

The information is the same as in Example 1, except that Nab's drawings are $5,300. The current accounts now become:

Partners' current accounts

		Nab	*Crag*			*Nab*	*Crag*
		$	$			$	$
20X6				20X6	Income statement		
	Drawings	5,300	4,000		– profit share	5,000	5,000
31 Dec	Balance c/d		1,000	31 Dec	Balance c/d	300	
		5,300	5,000			5,300	5,000
20X7				20X7			
1 Jan	Balance b/d	300		1 Jan	Balance b/d		1,000

Note that Nab's current account is overdrawn. How do we present this in the balance sheet?

It is convenient to show it thus:

Balance sheet at 31 December 20X6 (extract)

	Capital accounts	*Current accounts*	
	$	$	$
Partners' accounts:			
Nab	5,000	(300)	4,700
Crag	10,000	1,000	11,000
	15,000	700	15,700

2.4 Division of profit

The division of the profit among the partners is shown in an addition to the income statement.

It is important to realise that all allocations to partners are part of the process of dividing the profit, not expenses of the business.

Example 3

Pike and Scar are in partnership and have the following profit-sharing arrangements:

1. interest on capital is to be provided at a rate of 8% p.a.
2. Pike and Scar are to receive salaries of $6,000 and $8,000 p.a. respectively
3. the balance of profit or loss is to be divided between Pike and Scar in the ratio 3 : 2.

Net profit for the year amounts to $20,000 and capital account balances are Pike $12,000 and Scar $9,000.

You are required to prepare:

(a) a statement showing the division of profit between the partners

(b) relevant entries in the income statement.

Solution

(a) Division of net profit of $20,000

	Pike	*Scar*	*Total*
	$	$	$
Interest on capital	960	720	1,680
Salaries	6,000	8,000	14,000
Balance of profits ($20,000 – $15,680) in ratio 3 : 2	2,592	1,728	4,320
	(3/5)	(2/5)	
Totals	9,552	10,448	20,000

Note that this is only a calculation of the allocation of profit and not part of the double entry bookkeeping system, merely providing the figures for the closure of the income statement.

(b) Extract from income statement for the year ended …

	$	$
Sales revenue		X
Cost of sales		X
Gross profit		X
Expenses		X
Net profit		20,000
Allocated to:		
Pike	9,552	
Scar	10,448	
		20,000

The allocations are dealt with by transferring them to the credit of the partners' current accounts. The double entry is therefore:

Debit	*Credit*	*With*
Income statement	Pike's current account	$9,552
Income statement	Scar's current account	$10,448

For the purposes of examinations (and in practice), parts (a) and (b) above can be amalgamated as follows:

Extract from income statement for the year ended ...

	$
Sales revenue	x
Cost of sales	x
Gross profit	x
Expenses	x
Net profit for year	20,000

Division of profit

	Pike		*Scar*		*Total*
	$		*$*		*$*
Interest on capital	960		720		1,680
Salaries	6,000		8,000		14,000
Balance of profits ($20,000 – $15,680) in ratio 3 : 2	2,592	(3/5)	1,728	(2/5)	4,320
Totals	9,552		10,448		20,000

The debits actually being made are as before ($9,552 and $10,448).

Example 4

The facts are the same as for Example 3, except that net profit is now only $3,680.

You are required to show the division of profit between the partners.

Division of net profit of $3,680

	Pike	*Scar*	*Total*
	$	$	$
Interest on capital	960	720	1,680
Salaries	6,000	8,000	14,000
Balance of loss $3,680 – $15,680 = ($12,000) to be shared in ratio 3 : 2	(7,200)	(4,800)	(12,000)
Totals	(240)	3,920	3,680

The double entry in this case is:

Debit	*Credit*	*With*
Income statement	Scar's current account	$3,920
Pike's current account	Income statement	$240

The relevant part of the income statement would show:

	$	$
Net profit		3,680
Allocated to:		
	3,920	
	(240)	
		3,680

KEY POINT

A partner's salary is part of the division of profit, whereas a salary paid to an employee is an expense.

One point which regularly causes difficulties is the partners' salaries. The key is to remember at the outset that a partner's salary is part of the division of profit, whereas a salary paid to an employee is an expense.

Accordingly a salary to which a partner is entitled is included as part of the credit to his or her current account as part of the division of profit. Questions sometimes state that a partner has withdrawn his salary. In this case:

1 Include the salary in the division of profit as usual.

2 Quite separately treat the withdrawal of the salary as drawings.

Debit	*Credit*	*With*
Partners' current account	Bank	Amount withdrawn

2.5 Guaranteed minimum profit share

In certain partnership agreements, a partner may be guaranteed a minimum share of profits. The division of profit would proceed in the normal way. If the result is that the partner has less than this minimum, the deficit will be made good by the other partners in profit-sharing ratio or in any other way they have agreed.

Example 5

Tessa, Laura and Jane are in partnership and have the following profit-sharing arrangements:

1 Tessa and Laura are to receive salaries of $20,000 and $30,000 respectively.

2 The balance of profit or loss is to be divided Tessa 1, Laura 2, Jane 3.

3 Tessa is guaranteed a minimum profit share of $25,000.

The net profit for the year is $68,000.

You are required to show the division of profit for the year.

Division of profit

	Tessa $	*Laura* $	*Jane* $	*Total* $
Net profit				68,000
Salaries	20,000	30,000	–	(50,000)
				18,000
Balance of profits in ratio 1 : 2 : 3	3,000	6,000	9,000	(18,000)
	23,000	36,000	9,000	
Adjustment	2,000			
Laura 2/5 × 2,000		(800)		
Jane 3/5 × 2,000			(1,200)	
Totals	25,000	35,200	7,800	68,000

2.6 Interest on drawings

Occasionally there is a provision in a partnership agreement for a notional interest charge on the drawings by each partner. The interest charges are merely a negative profit share – they are a means by which total profits are allocated between the partners.

The reason for an interest on drawings provision is that those partners who draw out more cash than their colleagues in the early part of an accounting period should suffer a cost.

Example 6

Dick and Dastardly are in partnership. The capital and current accounts as at 1 January 20X7 show:

	Capital	*Current*
	$	$
Dick	50,000	2,500
Dastardly	20,000	3,000

The partnership agreement provides for the following:

1 Profits and losses are shared between Dick and Dastardly in percentages 60 and 40.

2 Interest on capital at 10% per annum is allowed.

3 Interest on drawings is charged at 12% per annum.

Drawings for the year to 31 December 20X7 are:

	Dick	*Dastardly*
	$	$
1 February 20X7	5,000	2,000
30 September 20X7	2,000	5,000

The profit for the year is $20,000.

You are required to prepare a statement showing the division of profits and the current accounts for the year ended 31 December 20X7.

Solution

Division of profits for the year ended 31 December 20X7

	Dick	*Dastardly*	
	$	$	$
Profit for the year			20,000
Add: Interest on drawings (see working)	(610)	(370)	980
			20,980
Less: Interest on capital:			
50,000 × 10%	5,000		
20,000 × 10%		2,000	(7,000)
			13,980
Balance in profit-sharing ratio:			
13,980 × 60%	8,388		
13,980 × 40%		5,592	(13,980)
Total allocation	12,778	7,222	20,000

Current accounts

		Dick	*Dastardly*			*Dick*	*Dastardly*
		$	$			$	$
20X7:				20X7:			
1 Feb	Drawings	5,000	2,000		Balance b/d	2,500	3,000
30 Sep	Drawings	2,000	5,000	31 Dec	Share of profits	12,778	7,222
	Balance c/d	8,278	3,222				
		15,278	10,222			15,278	10,222

Working

		Dick	Dastardly
		$	$
Interest on drawings:			
1 February 20X7	5,000 × 12% × 11/12	550	
	2,000 × 12% × 11/12		220
30 September 20X7	2,000 × 12% × 3/12	60	
	5,000 × 12% × 3/12		150
		610	370

2.7 Pulling the topics together

You should now be in a position to follow through from the list of account balances stage a full example of partnership accounts.

You are provided with the following information regarding the partnership of Dacre, Hutton and Tod:

1 Trial balance at 31 December 20X6 is as follows:

	Dr	Cr
	$	$
Sales revenue		50,000
Inventory at 1 January 20X6	6,000	
Purchases	29,250	
Carriage inwards	250	
Carriage outwards	400	
Payables		4,000
Cash at bank	3,900	
Current accounts:		
Dacre		900
Hutton		750
Tod		1,350
Capital accounts:		
Dacre		4,000
Hutton		5,000
Tod		6,000
Drawings:		
Dacre	2,000	
Hutton	3,000	
Tod	5,000	
Sundry expenses	2,800	
Receivables	13,000	
Shop fittings:		
Cost	8,000	
Accumulated depreciation		1,600
	73,600	73,600

2 Closing inventory is valued for accounts purposes at $5,500.

3 Depreciation of $800 is to be provided on the shop fittings.

4 The profit-sharing arrangements are as follows:

- interest on capital to be provided at a rate of 10% per annum
- Dacre and Tod to receive salaries of $3,000 and $4,000 per annum respectively
- the balance of profit or loss to be divided between Dacre, Hutton and Tod in the ratio of 3 : 8 : 4.

You are required to prepare the partnership financial statements for 20X6 and the current accounts of the partners.

Solution

Dacre, Hutton and Tod
Income statement for the year ended 31 December 20X6

	$	$
Sales revenue		50,000
Opening inventory	6,000	
Purchases	29,250	
Carriage inwards	250	
	35,500	
Less: Closing inventory	5,500	
		30,000
Gross profit		20,000
Sundry expenses	2,800	
Carriage outwards	400	
Depreciation	800	
		4,000
Net profit		16,000
Allocated to:		
Dacre	4,900	
Hutton	4,500	
Tod	6,600	
		16,000

Balance sheet as at 31 December 20X6

	Cost $	*Acc dep'n* $	$
Non-current assets:			
Shop fittings	8,000	2,400	5,600
Current assets:			
Inventory		5,500	
Receivables		13,000	
Cash		3,900	
			22,400
			28,000

Partners' accounts

	Capital accounts $	*Current accounts* $	$
Dacre	4,000	3,800	7,800
Hutton	5,000	2,250	7,250
Tod	6,000	2,950	8,950
	15,000	9,000	24,000
Current liabilities			
Payables			4,000
			28,000

Partners' current accounts

	Dacre	*Hutton*	*Tod*		*Dacre*	*Hutton*	*Tod*
	$	$	$		$	$	$
20X6:				20X6:			
Drawings	2,000	3,000	5,000	1 Jan Balance b/d	900	750	1,350
31 Dec Balance c/d	3,800	2,250	2,950	Income stmt	4,900	4,500	6,600
	5,800	5,250	7,950		5,800	5,250	7,950
				20X7:			
				1 Jan Balance b/d	3,800	2,250	2,950

Workings and commentary

The adjustments for inventory and depreciation should by now be familiar.

The new development is that, having calculated the profit for the period, it has to be divided between Dacre, Hutton and Tod. To calculate their respective shares a statement of the form shown below is convenient:

	Dacre	*Hutton*	*Tod*	*Total*
	$	$	$	$
Interest on capital	400	500	600	1,500
Salaries	3,000	–	4,000	7,000
Balance of profit ($16,000 – $8,500) in ratio 3 : 8 : 4	1,500	4,000	2,000	7,500
	4,900	4,500	6,600	16,000

This gives us the figures for the double entry:

Dr Income statement

Cr Partners' current accounts

In the case of a sole trader, the net profit is transferred to the credit of his or her capital account. The procedure is exactly the same for a partnership, except that each partner's share must first be calculated as shown.

A final point

The majority of examination questions specify separate capital and current accounts. Occasionally you may be faced with a question specifying only one account for each partner. Such an account acts as a capital and current account combined.

Conclusion

Accounting for partnerships is similar to accounting for sole traders in many respects, except that profit needs to be allocated between the partners, and the capital section of the balance sheet is more complex.

SELF TEST QUESTION

Partnerships – basic principles

1 What is a partnership? (1.1)

2 What are the advantages and disadvantages of partnership? (1.2)

Preparing partnership financial statements

3 What are the differences between partners' capital and current accounts? (2.1, 2.2)

4 What elements may form part of the process of dividing partnership profits among the partners? (2.4)

3 Is interest on drawings an expense of the partnership? (2.6)

MULTIPLE-CHOICE QUESTION

D, E and F are in partnership, sharing profits in the ratio 5:3:2 respectively, after charging salaries for E and F of $24,000 each per year.

On 1 July 2000 they agreed to change the profit-sharing ratio to 3:1:1 and increase E's salary to $36,000 per year, F's salary continuing unchanged.

For the year ended 31 December 2000 the partnership profit amounted to $480,000.

Which of the following correctly states the partners' total profit shares for the year?

	D	*E*	*F*
A	$234,000	$136,800	$109,200
B	$213,000	$157,800	$109,200
C	$186,000	$171,600	$122,400
D	$237,600	$132,000	$110,400

For the answer to this question, see the 'Answers' section at the end of the book.

PRACTICE QUESTION

Oliver and Twist

Oliver and Twist are in partnership, sharing profits equally after Oliver has been allowed a salary of $5,000 per year. No interest is charged on drawings or allowed on current accounts, but interest of 10% p.a. is allowed on the opening capital account balances for each year. Their bookkeeper has been having trouble balancing the books and has eventually produced the following balances as at 31 December.

	$
Capital account:	
Oliver	9,000
Twist	10,000
10% loan account:	
Twist	5,000
Williams	6,000
Current account balance on 1 January:	
Oliver	1,000
Twist	2,000
Drawings:	
Oliver	6,500
Twist	5,500
Sales revenue	113,100
Sales returns	3,000

Closing inventory	17,000
Cost of goods sold	70,000
Accounts receivable ledger control account	30,000
Accounts payable ledger control account	25,000
Operating expenses (including current year's depreciation)	26,100
Non-current assets at cost	37,000
Accumulated depreciation	18,000
Bank overdraft	3,000
Suspense account	?

You ascertain the following information:

(a) The accounts receivable ledger control account does not agree with the list of balances from the ledger. The following errors when corrected will remove the difference:

- The sales returns journal has been undercast by $100.
- A contra entry with the accounts payable ledger for $200 has been omitted frc
- An invoice for $2,000 was incorrectly entered in the sales journal as $200.

(b) A fully depreciated non-current asset, original cost $5,000, was sold during the year. The proceeds of $1,000 were entered in the bank account only, and no other entries in connection with the disposal were made.

(c) It is agreed that hotel bills for $500 paid by Twist from his personal bank account are proper business expenses. Oliver has taken goods out of the business for his own use, costing $1,000. No entry has been made for either of these items.

(d) No interest of any kind has yet been paid or recorded.

(e) Any remaining balance on the suspense account cannot be traced, and is to be treated in the most suitable manner.

You are required:

(a) to prepare a trial balance to establish the balance on the suspense account. **(4 marks)**

(b) to incorporate the necessary adjustments, showing your workings clearly in any way you feel appropriate **(8 marks)**

(c) to prepare final accounts for presentation to the partners. **(13 marks)**

(Total: 25 marks)

For the answer to this question, see the 'Answers' section at the end of the book.

Chapter 19
ACCOUNTING FOR LIMITED COMPANIES I

CHAPTER CONTENTS

In this chapter attention will be turned to the special problems of accounting for limited companies.

Double entry bookkeeping and the recording of transactions in books of prime entry are exactly the same for a sole trader or a limited company. Even the financial statements of the two types of organisation are fairly similar.

However, there are some differences in the way that companies are financed and the way in which their profits are dealt with from that of a sole trader. It is these areas that will be covered in detail in this chapter.

Objectives

By the time you have finished this chapter you should be able to:

- understand the advantages and disadvantages of operating as a limited company
- recognise different forms of company finance
- prepare financial statements for a company in a form that is suitable for internal usage within the company
- account for different types of share issues
- understand the uses of different reserves and be able to account for transfers to reserves.

1 Introduction to limited companies

1.1 Regulation

Most countries have developed some form of limited liability company. Legislation governing them varies greatly from country to country; for the purpose of this examination we are not adopting any one country's company legislation but considering the rules set up by International Accounting Standards.

1.2 Key factors distinguishing companies

KEY POINT

Factors of companies:

- separate legal entity
- separation of the ownership from the management
- limited liability
- formalities required.

There are four key factors which normally distinguish companies from other forms of business enterprise:

1 The fundamental concept of the **separate legal entity** of the company: the company is a separate entity in law. From this flow 2 and 3 below.

2 The **separation of the ownership** (shareholders) **from the management** (directors) of the company. It is most important to understand this.

3 The **limited liability** of shareholders for the debts of a company. Generally speaking, their liability will be limited to any portion of the nominal value of shares which is unpaid. Today it is unusual for shares to be issued other than fully paid.

4 The formalities required. These vary from country to country but frequently require public availability of financial statements and an annual audit by qualified auditors.

1.3 Sole traders and companies compared

These factors lead to differences between companies and sole traders in the following respects:

1 the form of the capital accounts

2 the form of loans to the company

3 the way in which profits are withdrawn by the proprietors

4 the form in which retained funds are presented.

The differences may be summarised as follows:

Item		*Sole trader*	*Company*
1	Capital introduced by proprietors	Capital account	Issued share capital
2	Loans from third parties	Loan account	Loan notes and bonds
3	Profits withdrawn by proprietors	Drawings	Dividends
4	Profits retained in the business	Capital account	Reserves

1.4 Advantages and disadvantages of operating as a limited company

The advantages of operation as a limited company rather than as a sole trader can be as follows:

- The liability of the shareholders is limited to the capital already introduced by them.
- There is a formal separation of the business from the owners of the business, which may be helpful to the running of the business. For example, if several members of a family are the shareholders in a company but only two of the family are directors, it is clear to all concerned who is running the company.
- Ownership of the business can be shared between people more easily than other forms of business organisation, e.g. a partnership.
- Shares in the business can be transferred relatively easily.
- There may be tax advantages.

The disadvantages of operation as a limited company rather than as a sole trader can be as follows:

- The costs of formation of the company.
- Costs of complying with companies legislation, including the audit requirement, if any.
- Directors of a company are subject to greater legislative duties than others running an unincorporated business.
- It is difficult/expensive to return capital surplus to the business's requirements back to the shareholders.
- There may be tax disadvantages.

2 Company finance

2.1 Introduction

The way in which the assets of a company (non-current assets, inventory, receivables and cash) are financed will vary from one company to another. Part of the finance may be provided by the owners or proprietors of the company (referred to as shareholders), while part may be provided by outsiders, including trade suppliers, banks and other lenders of funds.

The principal sources of company finance may be summarised as follows:

(a)	Ordinary shares (equity capital)	Share capital
(b)	Preference shares	
(c)	Deferred shares	
(d)	Loan notes and bonds	Liabilities
(e)	Bank overdraft	
(f)	Trade payables	

2.2 The nature and purpose of share capital and reserves

KEY POINT

Share capital represents part of the capital invested in the company by its shareholders but may also represent past reserves of the company which have been 'capitalised' by an issue of shares.

Reserves represent the balance of net assets accruing to the shareholders.

Share capital represents part of the capital invested in the company by its shareholders but may also represent past reserves of the company which have been 'capitalised' by an issue of shares (dealt with later).

Reserves represent the balance of net assets accruing to the shareholders and may include part of past issues of share capital (known as share premium), accumulated profits and revaluation gains on the revaluation of non-current assets.

The total of share capital and reserves represents the book value of the net assets of the company.

2.3 Nominal value and market value of share capital

KEY POINT

Each share usually has a stated nominal (or par) value.

Each share usually has a stated nominal (or par) value. This has little practical significance except as a base line price below which further shares may not generally be issued. The nominal value is also used as a means of calculating dividends to shareholders.

The market value of a share is not fixed at any particular date. The market value is related to the market value of the business of the company. For example, if a business is worth $100,000 and there are 1,000 $1 shares in issue in the company, the market value of each share is $100.

KEY POINT

If the company is listed on a stock exchange then a price will be quoted for the shares based upon recent transactions between purchasers and sellers of shares.

If the company is listed on a stock exchange then a price will be quoted for the shares based upon recent transactions between purchasers and sellers of shares. This is also referred to as the market value of a share, but this may not be the same value that would apply if the entire business was sold and thus all the shares were sold as one transaction.

2.4 Why companies are concerned with the value of their shares

Companies are concerned with the value the stock market places on their shares for two main reasons:

1 Shareholders will look at a steadily rising price of the shares as evidence of sound management of the company by the directors. It would indicate additional profits being made every year.

2 If the company wishes to raise further finance through the issue of shares, the current market price will be used as a basis for issuing more shares. The higher the price, the fewer shares will need to be issued and the less dilution there will be of the existing shareholders' effective interest in the company.

It is important to appreciate that the market value of a share quoted on the Stock Exchange has no direct relationship to the nominal value.

2.5 Types of share capital

KEY POINT

The company's internal regulations define the respective rights attached to the various shares.

The share capital of a company may be divided into various classes. The company's internal regulations define the respective rights attached to the various shares, e.g. as regards dividend entitlement or voting at company meetings. The various classes of share capital are dealt with below. In practice it is usually only larger companies which have different classes of share capital.

Ordinary shares

DEFINITION

Ordinary shares are the normal shares issued by a company.

Ordinary shares are the normal shares issued by a company. The normal rights of ordinary shareholders are to vote at company meetings and to receive dividends from profits.

Ordinary shares are often referred to as equity shares. The ordinary shareholders are the real owners of the business.

KEY POINT

Ordinary shareholders may receive **dividends**.

Ordinary shareholders may receive dividends from their company out of its profits. These dividends are often paid twice each year, an *interim* dividend during an accounting year and a *final* dividend after the balance sheet date when the company's profit for the year is known. Dividends will vary according to the company's level of profits and its dividend policy. Ordinary dividends are often expressed in terms of cents (or dollars) per share. Sometimes in examination questions they are given as a percentage on the issued share capital.

KEY POINT

No dividend may be paid on the ordinary shares until the dividend on the preference shares has been paid in full.

No dividend may be paid on the ordinary shares until the dividend on the preference shares has been paid in full.

Dividends are not expenses of the company to be deducted in computing profit, but a share of the final profit paid to the owners of the company.

Preference shares

DEFINITION

Preference shares are shares carrying a fixed rate of dividend.

Preference shares are shares carrying a fixed rate of dividend, the holders of which have a prior claim to any company profits available for distribution. They may also be called *preferred* shares.

Special categories of preference shares include:

- **participating preference shares** – where shareholders are entitled to participate together to a specified extent in distributable profits and surpluses on liquidation
- **redeemable preference shares** – the terms of issue specify that they are repayable by the company.

Deferred shares

These are sometimes referred to as founders' shares. Their right to a dividend is deferred until the preference shareholders have received their fixed amounts, and the ordinary shareholders have received a stated minimum dividend.

The following table summarises the key points about ordinary and preference shares:

Aspect	*Ordinary shares*	*Preference shares*
Voting power	Carry a vote.	May not carry a vote.
Distribution of profits (dividends)	A dividend which may vary from one year to the next after the preference shareholders have received their dividend.	A fixed dividend (fixed percentage of nominal value) in priority to ordinary dividend.
Liquidation of the company	Entitled to surplus assets on liquidation after liabilities and preference shares have been repaid.	Priority of repayment over ordinary shares but not usually entitled to surplus assets on liquidation.

2.6 Loan notes and bonds

KEY POINT

Long-term company borrowings usually take the form of **notes** or **bonds**.

Long-term company borrowings usually take the form of **notes** or **bonds**. A note represents debt issued to a single investor, while bonds are issued in units to a number of investors. Holders of notes or bonds are in no way owners of the business. They receive *interest* which is an expense of the company.

Notes or bonds may be **secured** on one or more assets of the company. If the company defaults on its payment obligations, those assets can be sold to raise the required money for the holders of the notes or bonds.

2.7 Trade payables

These are unsecured liabilities of the company for goods and services supplied to them.

3 Financial statements

3.1 Purpose of financial statements

A distinction must be made between:

- financial statements which are prepared for internal purposes, e.g. for management – these statements need not comply with legal and accountancy requirements
- financial statements which are presented to shareholders and available to other users – these must comply with the requirements of International Accounting Standards.

For the remainder of this chapter we are concerned with company financial statements for internal purposes. Those for shareholders and others are considered in the next chapter.

3.2 Balance sheet

A vertical form balance sheet of a company might appear as follows:

	$	$
Non-current assets:		
Land and buildings		124,700
Plant and machinery		29,750
		154,450
Goodwill		50,000
Investments		20,000
		224,450
Current assets:		
Inventory	59,670	
Receivables	49,350	
Cash at bank and in hand	4,645	
		113,665
		338,115
Capital and reserves:		
Equity capital, shares of 50c	75,000	
Accumulated profits	74,690	
		149,690
Non-current liabilities:		
8% Loan notes		100,000
Current liabilities:		
Trade payables	31,690	
Taxation	56,735	
		88,425
		338,115

The accumulated profits balance represents the retained profits of the company, that is, those profits of the company which have not yet been paid out by way of dividend to the shareholders.

A term you have not met fully yet is 'reserves'. In a sole trader's accounts, the proprietor's capital consists of the original capital introduced to set up the business plus, each year, the profit that has been made minus drawings taken out.

In the case of a company, the initial capital is the share capital, and this is held in the balance sheet at the same figure year after year unless new shares are issued. The company's profit for the year minus dividends paid to the members is shown under the heading 'accumulated profit' in the balance sheet.

It is important to realise that the shareholders' interest in the company consists of the share capital plus reserves ($149,690 in the above example) and not merely the share capital figure.

KEY POINT

The accumulated profit is an example of a **reserve.**

The accumulated profit is an example of a **reserve.** Any balances in a company balance sheet representing profits or surpluses, whether they are realised or not, are collectively referred to as **reserves.** There is more about reserves later in this chapter.

It is helpful if you can produce company balance sheets in the form shown above when practising questions.

ACTIVITY 1

List the ways in which the balance sheet shown above differs from that of a sole trader.

Feedback to this activity is at the end of the chapter.

3.3 The nature and purpose of a dividend

KEY POINT

A dividend is a return of part of the profits made by the company to the shareholders.

A dividend is a return of part of the profits made by the company to the shareholders.

Dividends can be stated as a percentage based on the nominal value of the share or alternatively as an amount per share. For example, an 8c dividend on a $1 share can be expressed either as 8% or 8c per share.

Modern practice tends to state dividends on a cents per share basis and not as a percentage.

KEY POINT

Dividends are **declared** by the company in general meeting.

Dividends are **declared** by the company in general meeting. The directors on their own responsibility can declare an interim dividend during the accounting period on account of the total dividend for the year.

3.4 The recording of dividends in the ledger accounts

The bookkeeping for payment of a dividend is:

Debit	*Credit*	*With*
Accumulated profit	Bank	Dividend

KEY POINT

Only dividends *paid* in the period are accounted for in that period.

IAS 10 *Events after the Balance Sheet Date* prohibits a company from including dividends which are proposed or declared after the balance sheet date as liabilities in the balance sheet. Such dividends are disclosed by note to the financial statements only. In other words, only dividends paid in the period are accounted for in that period.

ACTIVITY 2

How would an 8 cent dividend on a 50 cent share be expressed?

Feedback to this activity is at the end of the chapter.

3.5 Simple company income statement

The format of the income statement for the year can vary. Costs can be analysed in different ways, but all that is required is the application of common sense as to a reasonable layout.

3.6 Company taxation

KEY POINT

It is customary to include a company's liability for tax on its profits in the income statement and in the balance sheet.

It is customary to include a company's liability for tax on its profits in the income statement and in the balance sheet. Subtotals in the income statement show the profit before and after tax. The name given to company tax varies from country to country. In International Accounting Standards such taxes are referred to as 'taxes on income' or 'income tax'.

XY
Income statement for the year ended ...

		$
Sales revenue		X
Costs – various analyses can be made		(X)
Net profit before tax	say	150,000
Income tax		(48,000)
Net profit after tax		102,000

The income statement is followed by a statement or note showing the changes in equity for the year. This statement includes dividends paid and reserve movements also.

Accumulated profit (from statement of changes in equity)

	$
Balance at beginning of period	46,690
Net profit for year	102,000
Dividends paid in the year:	
Ordinary	(54,000)
Preference	(20,000)
Balance at end of period	74,690

The statement of changes in equity is best presented in columnar form, with a column for each class of share capital and each reserve, followed by a total column:

	Ordinary share capital	*Share premium*	*Revaluation reserve*	*Accumulated profit*	*Total*
	$'000	$'000	$'000	$'000	$'000
Opening balance	X	X	X	X	X
Surplus on revaluation			X		X
Net profit for period				X	X
Dividends paid				(X)	(X)
Issue of share capital	X	X			X
Closing balance	X	X	X	X	X

3.7 The recording of taxation in the ledger accounts

Company tax is normally payable after the end of the accounting period. The entry to record the liability in the financial statements is:

Debit	*Credit*	*With*
Income statement	Tax payable (shown as current liability on balance sheet)	Estimate of tax charge

ACTIVITY **3**

The trial balance (below) at 31 December 20X3 has been extracted from the books of Tefex:

Additional information:

(1) Inventory at 31 December 20X3 was $5,200.

(2) Machinery costing $1,200 on which $700 depreciation had been charged was sold for $400 in the year.

There were no non-current asset purchases in the year.

(3) Depreciation on machinery is provided on the reducing balance basis on the net book value at the end of the year at the rate of 10%.

No depreciation is provided on land.

(4) The doubtful debt allowance is to be $600.

You are required:

(a) to prepare an income statement for the year ended 31 December 20X3

(b) to prepare a balance sheet at that date.

	Dr	*Cr*
	$	$
Payables		3,600
Receivables	8,300	
Land at cost	2,000	
Machinery at cost	12,000	
Proceeds of sale of machinery		400
Doubtful debt allowance at 31 Dec 20X2		500
Accumulated depreciation at 31 Dec 20X2		4,500
Cash in hand	500	
Wages	2,400	
Insurance	600	
Interest paid	800	
Bank balance		4,300
Inventory at 31 Dec 20X2	4,800	
Sales revenue		24,200
Purchases	22,000	
Share capital		10,000
Accumulated profit at 31 Dec 20X2		5,900
	53,400	53,400

Feedback to this activity is at the end of the chapter.

4 Issue of shares

4.1 Distinction between authorised and issued share capital

DEFINITION

The **authorised** share capital is the maximum number of shares a company may issue.

The **issued** share capital is the actual number of shares in issue at any point in time.

The **authorised** share capital is the maximum number of shares a company may issue.

The **issued** share capital is the actual number of shares in issue at any point in time.

It is the issued share capital which appears on a company's balance sheet.

4.2 Issues of shares at nominal value

A company issues 200,000 50c ordinary shares at their nominal value.

Cash book

	$		$
Ordinary share capital	100,000		

Ordinary share capital account

	$		$
		Cash	100,000

4.3 Issues at a value in excess of nominal value

In this case the amount by which the issue price exceeds the nominal value must normally by law be transferred to a share premium account.

A company issues 200,000 50c ordinary shares at an issue price of 75c.

Cash book

	$		$
Ordinary share capital	100,000		
Share premium	50,000		

Ordinary share capital account

	$		$
		Cash	100,000

Share premium account

	$		$
		Cash	50,000

Balance sheet extract

	$
Capital and reserves:	
Share capital – 50c ordinary shares	100,000
Share premium account	50,000
Accumulated profit	X

4.4 Definition of bonus issue

DEFINITION

Bonus shares: the issue of shares to existing shareholders in proportion to their holdings, using company reserves.

The issue of bonus shares (a bonus, scrip or capitalisation issue) represents the issue of shares to existing shareholders in proportion to their existing holdings, using the reserves of the company.

It is effectively the conversion of part of the reserves of the company into share capital.

No cash or other consideration is passed from shareholders to the company.

Recording a bonus issue in ledger accounts

The bonus issue is financed internally by a capitalisation of reserves.

Debit	*Credit*	*With*
Reserves	Share capital	Amount of bonus issue

KEY POINT

Any reserve may be used to finance the bonus issue.

Any reserve may be used to finance the bonus issue. Clearly a reserve which, by statute, cannot be distributed, like share premium, would be used in preference to reserves which can be distributed.

The advantages and disadvantages of this method

The effects of a bonus issue are threefold:

- issued share capital is brought more into line with the assets employed in the company
- issued share capital is divided into a larger number of shares
- market price per share falls, roughly pro rata to the bonus issue.

The third effect is the main reason why bonus issues are made in practice. It is felt that if the market price per share becomes very high, investors are more reluctant to purchase the shares. Of course, nothing has changed to the real worth of the company – the effect is purely psychological.

4.5 Definition of rights issues

DEFINITION

A **rights issue** represents the offer of shares to existing shareholders in proportion to their existing holding at a stated price.

A rights issue represents the offer of shares to existing shareholders in proportion to their existing holding at a stated price. Unlike the bonus issue the shareholders do not have to take up their offer and have the alternative of selling their rights on the stock market.

Recording a rights issue in ledger accounts

Debit	*Credit*	*With*
Cash book		Proceeds
	Share capital	Nominal value
	Share premium	Premium (if any)

The advantages and disadvantages of raising finance by this method

The advantages are:

- A rights issue is the cheapest way a company can raise further finance by the issue of shares.
- A rights issue to existing shareholders has a greater chance of success, i.e. actually finding buyers compared to a share issue to the public

- It may be more appropriate compared to issuing loan notes or bonds if further profits will take a long time to arise from additional investment (i.e. interest does not have to be paid).

Disadvantages include the following:

- A rights issue is more expensive than issuing debt (loan notes or bonds).
- It may not be successful in raising the finance required.

ACTIVITY 4

(a) A has 200,000 50 cent ordinary shares in issue and makes a bonus issue of 50,000 50 cent ordinary shares. Its only available reserve is the accumulated profit balance of $230,000.

(b) B has 200,000 50 cent ordinary shares in issue and makes a rights issue of 50,000 50 cent shares at a price of 80 cents each and the issue is fully taken up.

Write up the ledger accounts for each transaction.

Feedback to this activity is at the end of the chapter.

5 Reserves

5.1 Introduction

KEY POINT

All reserves are added to the share capital to build up the total shareholders' interest in the company.

Prominently displayed on the balance sheet is the heading 'Capital and reserves'. We have already considered capital and this section will consider reserves. All reserves are added to the share capital to build up the total shareholders' interest in the company.

5.2 Types of reserve

Share premium

Share premium is the excess of the issue price of a share over its nominal value. It is normally against the law to distribute the share premium as dividend.

Revaluation reserve

Revaluation reserve arises when an increase in the value of a non-current asset is recognised. It is the excess of the new value over the previous book value (carrying value).

Accumulated profit

As we have seen, this is the total profit made by the company since it was formed, minus dividends paid or payable. It is often referred to as a **revenue** reserve, whereas (a) and (b) above are **capital** reserves.

In most countries, only (c) is distributable as dividend, though all may be converted into share capital by means of a bonus (capitalisation) issue.

ACTIVITY 5

A company owns a building that was originally bought for $100,000. Since that date the accumulated depreciation on the building has totalled $30,000. The building has recently been revalued at $150,000.

How would this be reflected in the ledger accounts? (Refer back to the chapter on depreciation if you are unsure).

Feedback to this activity is at the end of the chapter.

5.3 Creating other revenue reserves

The profit for the year (after allowing for expenses and taxation) may be dealt with as follows:

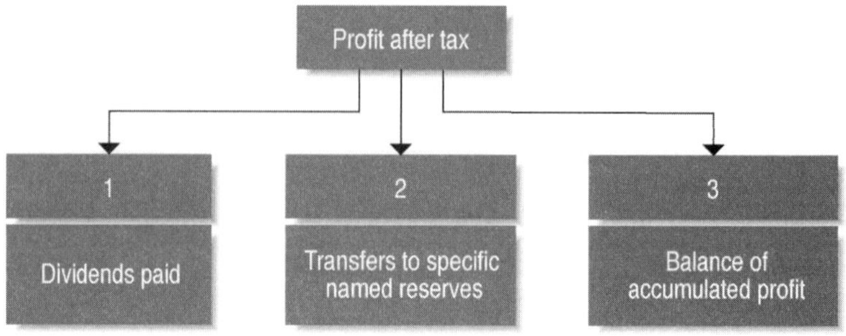

Where profit is transferred to a named reserve, the directors are indicating that these amounts are not available to support a dividend payment (although there is nothing in law to prevent their distribution).

Examples of reserves given special names or titles include:

Plant replacement reserve

KEY POINT

A **plant replacement reserve** helps to cover the increased cost of replacing plant.

During a period of rising prices the replacement cost of new plant will be far greater than its original cost, and consequently the assets representing the historical cost depreciation will fall short of the required amount. Setting up a plant replacement reserve will help to solve this problem. Each year profit is reduced by a further amount (over and above historical cost depreciation). The double entry each year is:

Debit	*Credit*	*With*
Accumulated profit	Plant replacement reserve	Additional depreciation

Inventory replacement reserve

A similar problem arises with inventory: during a period of increasing prices, each successive unit of inventory costs more. By reducing distributable profits, amounts which might otherwise have been distributed as dividends are retained within the business. The double entry is:

Debit	*Credit*	*With*
Accumulated profit	Inventory replacement reserve	Additional deduction relating to cost of sales

General reserve

Questions often state, for example, that 'the directors wish to transfer $3,000 to a general reserve' without indicating a specific purpose for the reserve. Although legally the reserve can be distributed as a dividend, the directors are indicating that it is not available for distribution. The double entry is:

Debit	*Credit*	*With*
Accumulated profit	General reserve	Transfer to general reserve

5.4 Statement of changes in equity

In order to cope with the double entry involved in and disclosure of the transfers between various reserves, it is helpful to present the movement in the various reserves in columnar format. This statement can be put immediately below the income statement for the year.

Example

ZZ's summarised balance sheet at 31 December 20X7 showed:

	$
Total assets	280,000
Capital and reserves:	
Share capital:	
50c ordinary shares	75,000
$1 8% preference shares	60,000
Share premium account	25,000
Plant replacement reserve	30,000
Accumulated profit	90,000
	280,000

The net profit before tax for the year to 31 December 20X8 has been computed as $180,000.

The following additional information is available for 20X8:

1 The tax charge for the year is estimated at $70,000.

2 An interim dividend of 2c has been paid on the ordinary shares, and one half of the dividend on the preference shares. Earlier in the year a final dividend of 4c per ordinary share had been paid for the year ended 31 December 20X7, together with the second dividend on the preference shares for that year.

3 It is proposed to pay the remaining dividend on the preference shares and a final dividend of 5c on the ordinary shares.

4 $20,000 is to be transferred to the plant replacement reserve.

You are required:

(a) to construct the income statement for the year and the statement of changes in equity

(b) to show the balance sheet at the end of the year to the extent that information is available.

Solution

Income statement for the year ended 31 December 20X8

	$
Profit before tax	180,000
Tax	70,000
Profit after tax	110,000

Balance sheet (extracts) as at 31 December 20X8

	$
Capital and reserves:	
Share capital:	
50c ordinary shares	75,000
$1 8% preference shares	60,000
Share premium	25,000
Plant replacement reserve	50,000
Accumulated profit	166,200
	376,200
Current liabilities:	
Tax	70,000

Note: the total amount of capital and reserves (and thus the net assets) has increased by the amount of *retained* profits of the company, proved below.

	$
Net assets last year	280,000
Retained profit	96,200
Net assets this year	376,200

Statement of changes in equity

	Ordinary share capital $	*Preference share capital* $	*Share premium* $	*Accumulated profit* $	*Plant replacement* $	*Total* $
Balance at 1 January 20X8	75,000	60,000	25,000	90,000	30,000	280,000
Profit for the year				110,000		110,000
Dividends paid:						
Preference				(4,800)		(4,800)
Ordinary				(9,000)		(9,000)
Transfer				(20,000)	20,000	–
Balance at 31 December 20X8	75,000	60,000	25,000	166,200	50,000	376,200

Note: At 31 December 20X8 the company proposes to pay the second dividend on the preference shares ($2,400) and a final dividend of 5c per share on the ordinary shares ($7,500).

6 Drafting financial statements of companies for internal use

6.1 Introduction

KEY POINT

The term **financial statements** includes the balance sheet and the income statement.

The term **financial statements** includes the balance sheet and the income statement. A detailed example is shown in this section.

One of the questions we must ask is 'How much information should the financial statements include?' We know that the answer to this depends on for whom the statements are required. For the sake of clarity, the users may be divided into two groups:

KEY POINT

Types of user:

- internal
- external.

1 **Internal users** – directors and management require a detailed income statement and balance sheet. For the purpose of simplicity, it will be assumed that these are required on an annual basis.

2 **External users** – the requirements for published financial statements are fixed in most countries by legislation. For the purposes of this international syllabus, we take the requirements of International Accounting Standards as the basis. We deal with these in more detail in the next chapter.

Example

You are provided with the following trial balance of Aysgarth, a limited liability company, at 31 December 20X6:

	Dr	*Cr*
	$	$
Ordinary share capital (50c shares)		60,000
5% Preference share capital ($1 shares)		20,000
Sales revenue		80,000
Discount allowed	400	
Discount received		200
Carriage inwards	1,000	
Carriage outwards	800	
Receivables and payables	10,000	2,000
Inventory at 1 January 20X6	10,000	
10% Loan notes 20X9		50,000
Loan interest paid	5,000	
Non-current assets, at cost	230,000	
Non-current assets, aggregate depreciation		100,000
Purchases	49,000	
Administrative expenses	4,000	
Salaries (excluding directors)	4,000	
Preference dividend paid	1,000	
Ordinary dividend for year ended 31 December 20X6, paid during year	3,000	
Accumulated profit 1 January 20X6		11,000
Cash at bank	5,000	
	323,200	323,200

Adjustments are required for:

- inventory at 31 December 20X6, at cost $15,000
- directors' salaries not yet paid $5,000
- tax for the year $5,000
- depreciation charge for the year $4,600
- accrued audit fee $1,000
- creation of a plant replacement reserve of $1,000.

You are required to prepare a balance sheet and income statement in vertical form, suitable for presentation to the directors.

Solution

Aysgarth
Income statement for year ended 31 December 20X6

	$	$
Sales revenue		80,000
Opening inventory	10,000	
Purchases	49,000	
Carriage inwards	1,000	
	60,000	
Less: Closing inventory	15,000	
Cost of sales		45,000
Gross profit		35,000
Discount received		200
		35,200
Discount allowed	400	
Carriage outwards	800	
Administrative expenses	4,000	
Staff salaries	4,000	
Directors' salaries (W1)	5,000	
Audit fee (W4)	1,000	
Depreciation (W3)	4,600	
Loan interest	5,000	
		24,800
Net profit before tax		10,400
Tax (W2)		5,000
Net profit for year		5,400

Aysgarth
Balance sheet as at 31 December 20X6

	$	$
Non-current assets:		
Land and buildings		
($230,000 – 104,600 (W3))		125,400
Current assets:		
Inventory	15,000	
Receivables	10,000	
Cash at bank	5,000	
		30,000
		155,400
Capital and reserves:		
Share capital:		
Ordinary 50c shares	60,000	
5% $1 preference shares	20,000	
Plant replacement reserve (W5)	1,000	
Accumulated profit	11,400	
		92,400
Non-current liabilities:		
10% Loan notes		50,000
Current liabilities:		
Trade payables	2,000	
Tax (W2)	5,000	
Accruals [$5,000 (W1) + $1,000 (W4)]	6,000	
		13,000
		155,400

Statement of changes in equity (reserve movements only)

	Accumulated profit	*Plant replacement reserve*
	$	$
Balance at 1 January 20X6	11,000	
Profit for year	5,400	
Dividends paid:		
Preference	(1,000)	
Ordinary	(3,000)	
Transfer	(1,000)	1,000
	11,400	1,000

Workings

Tutorial note: The format for the income statement follows the format of the sole trader until the net profit before taxation figure. At this point the taxation for the period is shown, giving the net profit after taxation. This profit figure is entered into the statement of changes in equity, where the movements during the year are shown.

Many of the workings which follow are not necessary as the adjustments are straightforward. The ledger accounts have been shown to emphasise the double entry involved in the adjustments.

(W1) **Directors' salaries**

	$		$
Balance c/d	5,000	Income statement	5,000

(W2) **Current taxation**

	$		$
Balance c/d	5,000	Income statement	5,000

(W3) **Non-current assets – Accumulated depreciation**

	$		$
Balance c/d	104,600	Balance b/d	100,000
		Income statement	4,600
	104,600		104,600

(W4) **Audit fee**

	$		$
Balance c/d	1,000	Income statement	1,000

Creation of plant replacement reserve

The creation of the reserve is shown as a movement in the statement of changes in equity.

(W5) **Plant replacement reserve**

	$		$
Balance c/d	1,000	Accumulated profit	1,000

Conclusion

This chapter has concentrated on the areas of accounting and producing financial statements that differ from accounting for a sole trader, in particular the way in which limited companies are financed by a mixture of share capital and third party liabilities and how these are issued and accounted for. Also, we saw the way in which profits are distributed to the owners of the business in the form of dividends, to the government in the form of taxes and retained within the business by means of various reserves.

The preparation of financial statements for a company in a form that is suitable for internal use within the company is an important examination topic. The key to success with this topic is to have a clear picture of the required format for the balance sheet and income statement, together with plenty of question practice.

SELF-TEST QUESTIONS

Limited companies

1 What are the four key factors that distinguish a company from a sole trader? (1.2)

2 Who are the owners of a company? (1.2, 1.4)

3 Who are the managers of a company? (1.2)

Company finance

4 What is the relationship between the nominal value and the market value of a company's shares? (2.3)

5 What are preference shares? (2.5)

6 What are loan notes and bonds? (2.6)

Financial statements

7 What is the double entry for the payment of a dividend? (3.4)

Issue of shares

8 How is an issue of shares at a price in excess of their nominal value accounted for? (4.3)

Reserves

9 What are the names of two reserves? (5.2)

MULTIPLE-CHOICE QUESTION

At 1 January 2000 the capital structure of Q, a limited liability company, was as follows:

	$
Issued share capital 1,000,000 ordinary shares of 50c each	500,000
Share premium account	300,000

On 1 April 2000 the company made an issue of 200,000 50c shares at $1.30 each, and on 1 July the company made a bonus (capitalisation) issue of one share for every four in issue at the time, using the share premium account for the purpose.

Which of the following correctly states the company's share capital and share premium account at 31 December 2000?

	Share capital	Share premium account
A	$750,000	$230,000
B	$875,000	$285,000
C	$750,000	$310,000
D	$750,000	$610,000

For the answer to this question, see the 'Answers' section at the end of the book.

EXAM-TYPE QUESTION

Floyd

You are presented with the following summarised trial balance of Floyd, a limited liability company, in respect of the year ended 31 March 20X5:

	$	$
Ordinary share capital (25c shares)		100,000
Plant and machinery:		
Cost	307,400	
Depreciation (1 Apr 20X4)		84,600
Receivables	52,030	
Payables		38,274
Inventory	61,070	
Accumulated profit 1 April 20X4		57,910
Cash at bank	41,118	
Cash in hand	126	
Share premium		20,000
Sales revenue		998,600
Final dividend for previous year paid	12,000	
Interim dividend for current year paid	2,500	
Allowance for doubtful debts		1,860
9% loan notes 20X9		75,000
Cost of sales	800,000	
Administrative costs	100,000	
	1,376,244	1,376,244

The following final adjustments are required:

1. The allowance for doubtful debts is to be adjusted to 5% of the receivables figure. The charge is to be included in administrative costs.
2. Tax on the current year profits is estimated at $31,200.
3. Depreciation of plant and machinery at 10% of cost is to be provided. The charge is to be included in cost of sales.
4. Interest for the year ended 31 March 20X5 was paid on 1 April 20X5. No accrual has been made.

You are required to prepare an income statement for the year ended 31 March 20X5, and a balance sheet as at that date, insofar as information permits.

(18 marks)

PRACTICE QUESTION

Nimrod

The following balances have been extracted from the books of Nimrod, a limited company, as at 30 September 20X7

			$
Payables			18,900
Sales revenue			240,000
Land at cost			54,000
Buildings at cost			114,000
Furniture and fittings at cost			66,000
Bank (credit balance)			18,000
Accumulated depreciation:	Buildings		18,000
	Furniture and fittings		30,000
Discounts received			5,292
Accumulated profit at 1 Oct 20X6			10,800
Allowance for doubtful debts			2,448
Goodwill			49,200
Cash in hand			696
Inventory at 1 Oct 20X6			42,744
Rent			6,372
Wages and salaries			24,000
Insurance			5,688
Returns inwards			1,116
General expenses			1,308
Receivables			37,920
Purchases			131,568
Loan interest			1,200
Bad debts			2,028
5% bonds			48,000
6% $1 preference shares			60,000
$1 ordinary shares			60,000
General reserve			30,000
Share premium			3,000
Dividends paid:	preference:	half year to 30 September 20X6	1,800
		half year to 31 March 20X7	1,800
	ordinary:	year to 30 September 20X6	3,000

Additional information:

1 inventory on hand at 30 September 20X7: $46,638

2 insurance paid in advance: $300

3 wages owing: $840

4 depreciation is to be provided at 10% on cost of buildings, and at 20% on the written down value of furniture and fittings

5 allowance for doubtful debts is to be reduced to 5% of receivables;

6 loan interest outstanding is $1,200

7 the directors propose to pay a 6% ordinary dividend and the final preference dividend

8 a transfer of $24,000 from accumulated profits to general reserve is to be made

9 the tax charge for the year is $20,000.

You are required to prepare the income statement for the year ended 30 September 20X7 and a balance sheet as at that date. **(25 marks)**

For the answers to these questions, see the 'Answers' section at the end of the book.

FEEDBACK TO ACTIVITY 1

- A current liability appears for taxation payable.
- The capital and reserves section brings together the share capital and accumulated profit to show the total shareholders' interest in the company.
- Loan notes appear as a long-term liability.

FEEDBACK TO ACTIVITY 2

16%, ($\frac{8}{50} \times 100\%$) or 8 cents per share.

FEEDBACK TO ACTIVITY 3

Your solution should be as follows:

(a) **Tefex**

Income statement for the year ended 31 December 20X3

	$	$
Sales revenue		24,200
Opening inventory	4,800	
Purchases	22,000	
	26,800	
Closing inventory	5,200	
Cost of goods sold		21,600
Gross profit		2,600
Expenses:		
Wages	2,400	
Insurance	600	
Interest	800	
Depreciation (Working (1))	700	
Loss on sale of machinery (Working (2))	100	
Bad debts (600 – 500)	100	
		4,700
Loss for year		(2,100)

Workings

(W1) **Depreciation**

	Cost $	*Dep'n* $
Opening balances	12,000	4,500
Sale	(1,200)	(700)
	10,800	3,800
	(3,800)	
NBV	7,000	
Depreciation charge 10% × $7,000 = $700		
Balance after sale	10,800	3,800
Depreciation charge for year		700
	10,800	4,500

(W2) **Loss on sale of machinery**

	$
Cost	1,200
Depreciation	700
	500
Sold for	400
Loss	100

(b) **Balance sheet as at 31 December 20X3**

	Cost	Dep'n	
	$	$	$
Non-current assets:			
Tangible assets:			
Land	2,000	–	2,000
Machinery (working 1)	10,800	4,500	6,300
	12,800	4,500	8,300
Current assets:			
Inventory		5,200	
Receivables ($8,300 – 600)		7,700	
Cash		500	
			13,400
			21,700
Capital and reserves:			
Share capital			10,000
Accumulated profit ($5,900 – 2,100)			3,800
			13,800
Current liabilities:			
Bank overdraft		4,300	
Trade payables		3,600	
			7,900
			21,700

FEEDBACK TO ACTIVITY **4**

Your solution should be as follows:

(a)

Share capital

	$		$
Balance c/d	125,000	Balance b/d (200,000 × 50c)	100,000
		Accumulated profit (50,000 × 50c)	25,000
	125,000		125,000

Accumulated profit

	$		$
Share capital	25,000	Balance b/d	230,000
Balance c/d	205,000		
	230,000		230,000

(b)

Bank

	$		$
Share capital	25,000		
Share premium	15,000		

Share capital

	$		$
Balance c/d	125,000	Balance b/d	100,000
		Bank	25,000
	125,000		125,000

Share premium

	$		$
		Bank	15,000

FEEDBACK TO ACTIVITY 5

Your solution should be as follows:

Building – cost

	$		$
Balance b/d	100,000	Building – valuation	100,000

Building – accumulated depreciation

	$		$
Building – valuation	30,000	Balance b/d	30,000

Building – valuation

	$		$
Building – cost	100,000	Building – acc dep'n	30,000
		Balance c/d	70,000
	100,000		100,000
Balance b/d	70,000		
Revaluation reserve	80,000	Balance c/d	150,000
	150,000		150,000

Revaluation reserve

	$		$
		Building – valuation	80,000

Chapter 20

ACCOUNTING FOR LIMITED COMPANIES II

CHAPTER CONTENTS

Most countries have legislation governing the publication of company financial statements and the minimum information to be disclosed in them.

This legislation obviously varies considerably from country to country. We are therefore looking at the rules set by International Accounting Standards for company financial statements. In particular we look at:

how financial statements should be presented (IAS 1)

- extraordinary items, disclosures, etc. (IAS 8)
- discontinuing operations (IAS 35).

Objectives

By the time you have finished this chapter you should be able to:

- prepare financial statements for companies in accordance with the requirements of international accounting standards
- be familiar with the disclosure requirements of international accounting standards.

1 The need for regulation

1.1 Introduction

Regulation of company accounts is seen as necessary for three main reasons:

Separation of ownership from control

Except for very small companies, most companies are managed by directors who do not own all of the shares. This means that those who own shares, but are not directors, have a moral right to receive a periodic account of the stewardship of the directors.

Limited liability status

Shareholders cannot normally be required to contribute additional funds to meet unsatisfied creditors' claims against an insolvent company. Potential creditors need certain assurances about a company's future before they will be prepared to lend money or to provide goods or services on credit. To some extent they can obtain these assurances from accounting information provided by the company.

Economic power

Certain large companies wield extensive economic power and influence, which affects society generally, as well as affecting those normally seen as having a direct stake in those companies. For example, a large manufacturing company could employ a significant proportion of the 'breadwinners' in a particular locality. If the company were to go out of business, the effect on those living in the locality, even though not employed by the company, could be greatly affected by the closedown. House prices might fall, retailers might be forced to close down and a general economic malaise could pervade the area. Many people would argue that the general economic power of certain companies requires that there is a relatively high degree of accountability by companies to society generally.

Clearly not all of these points apply to companies of all sizes. In particular, they do not all tend to apply to smaller companies.

Though regulation may be seen by companies as irksome, in fact a vigorous private sector cannot really exist without it. Unless companies provide accounting information they will find it very difficult to attract investors, lenders and suppliers who will provide goods and services on credit. They may also find it more difficult to attract employees and, in some cases, customers. They may also find resistance by society to accept certain companies operating at all. It is interesting to note that the USA, which is widely seen as a bastion of private enterprise, has one of the strictest and most far-reaching accounting regulatory frameworks. Regulation should not be seen as the enemy of the private sector, rather the opposite.

2 The provisions of IAS 1 *Presentation of Financial Statements*

2.1 Introduction

KEY POINT

IAS 1 *Presentation of Financial Statements* covers:

- accounting concepts and policies
- balance sheet
- income statement.

In August 1997 the IASC (now IASB) published an important new statement – IAS 1 *Presentation of Financial Statements*. IAS 1 deals with accounting concepts and policies and with the structure and content of the balance sheet and income statement. It includes recommended formats for the published balance sheet, income statement and two other statements to accompany the balance sheet and income statement (see below). Although these formats are not obligatory, they obviously have great importance for examination purposes and must be thoroughly learnt.

2.2 The objective of general purpose financial statements

KEY POINT

Financial statements provide information about:

- the financial position
- performance
- cash flows.

The objective of general purpose financial statements, as stated in IAS 1, is to provide information about the financial position, performance and cash flows of an enterprise that is useful to a wide range of users in making economic decisions. Financial statements also show the results of management's stewardship of the resources entrusted to it.

2.3 Components of financial statements

Financial statements consist of:

- balance sheet
- income statement
- a statement showing either:
  - all changes in equity
  - changes in equity other than those arising from capital transactions with owners and distributions to owners
- cash flow statement with supporting notes (dealt with in a later chapter)
- accounting policies and explanatory notes.

2.4 Supplementary information

KEY POINT

Supplementary information:

- factors re performance
- sources of funding
- equity and loan funding
- strengths and resources of the enterprise
- environment: changes in and response to.

The complexity of many modern business operations means that supplementary information is often desirable. IAS 1 suggests, but does not require, a financial review by management which could include:

- the main factors determining performance for the period
- sources of funding and the policy on the balance between equity and loan funding
- strengths and resources of the enterprise whose value is not fully reflected in the balance sheet
- changes in the environment and the enterprise's responses to them.

You would not be required to produce such a review in the examination, but you need to know that the IASB regards it as desirable and the four possible contents listed.

2.5 Structure and content of financial statements

First you should note some basic requirements for the financial statements:

- Financial statements should be clearly identified and separated from other information in the same document.
- The financial statements should show prominently:
  - the name of the enterprise
  - the reporting date (balance sheet) or period covered (income statement).
- The currency in which the financial statements are prepared should be stated.
- The degree of accuracy of the figures should be stated (this is often done by heading the figures $'000, $million or the like).
- Financial statements should be presented annually. If, exceptionally, the period is longer or shorter than this, the reason should be stated and the fact that comparative figures for the previous year are not comparable should also be stated.

2.6 The suggested format for the balance sheet

The suggested format for the balance sheet is (slightly simplified for the syllabus for *Preparing Financial Statements*):

	$m	$m
Assets		
Non-current assets		
Property, plant and equipment*	X	
Goodwill	X	
Investments	X	
		X
Current assets		
Inventories	X	
Trade and other receivables	X	
Prepayments	X	
Cash	X	
		X
Total assets		X
Equity and liabilities		
Capital and reserves		
Issued capital*	X	
Reserves*	X	
Accumulated profits*	X	
		X
Non-current liabilities		
Loans		X
Current liabilities		
Trade and other payables	X	
Overdrafts	X	
Tax	X	
		X
Total equity and liabilities		X

The four items marked with an asterisk (*) will require disclosure notes giving details of them, including movements during the period. Many other notes will appear in a full set of financial statements, but these four are singled out as being the ones required in the syllabus for Preparing Financial Statements.

2.7 Notes and supporting statements to the balance sheet

Here are the disclosure requirements for the four notes:

Property, plant and equipment

IAS 16 *Property, Plant and Equipment* requires a reconciliation of movements in each class of asset. A typical form for the note could be:

	Land and buildings	*Plant, equipment and vehicles*	*Total*
	$m	$m	$m
Cost:			
Beginning of year	2,499.3	817.5	3,316.8
Additions	312.9	110.6	423.5
Disposals	(16.9)	(48.2)	(65.1)
End of year	2,795.3	879.9	3,675.2
Depreciation:			
Beginning of year	177.6	432.2	609.8
Charged during year	50.3	88.5	138.8
Disposals	(7.6)	(46.6)	(54.2)
End of year	220.3	474.1	694.4
Net book value:			
Beginning of year	2,321.7	385.3	2,707.0
End of year	2,575.0	405.8	2,980.8

There is a column for each type of non-current asset. The movement in the cost is shown first. The opening figures plus additions and minus disposals lead to the closing figure.

Then comes the depreciation. The opening figures are adjusted for the charge for the year and the amount eliminated for disposals.

Finally, the net book value (cost less depreciation) is shown.

Intangible assets

A similar note to that above for property, plant and equipment will be provided.

One asset which might appear here is development costs. These are governed by IAS 38. Details of IAS 38's requirements, including disclosures, were in Chapter 15.

Issued capital

The note has to disclose, for each class of share capital:

- number of shares authorised
- number of shares issued and fully paid, or issued and not fully paid
- par value of each share
- a reconciliation of the number of shares outstanding at the beginning and end of the year.

Statement of changes in equity

A note has to give details of all movements of capital, reserves and accumulated profit during the year.

Here is a typical format for this note:

Statement of changes in equity

	Share capital	*Share premium*	*Revaluation reserve*	*Accumulated profits*	*Total*
	$m	$m	$m	$m	$m
Balance at 1 January	100	50	40	30	220
Equity shares issued	50	40			90
Revaluation surplus recognised in year			20		20
Net profit				80	80
Dividends				(50)	(50)
	150	90	60	60	360

More details of the Statement of changes in equity appear later in this chapter.

2.8 The income statement

The income statement must be presented with an analysis of the income and expenses.

There are two illustrative types of format. The first is very similar to the format usually adopted for company financial statements for internal use, but with the operating expenses collected under three headings – cost of sales, distribution costs and administrative expenses. This method is called the **function of expenditure** or **cost of sales** method.

The second format, intended for manufacturing businesses, analyses the expenses in a different way according to their nature. This is called the **nature of expenditure** method.

Here are the two formats, slightly simplified.

(a) Function of expenditure method

	$m
Sales revenue	X
Cost of sales	(X)
Gross profit	X
Other operating income	X
Distribution costs	(X)
Administrative expenses	(X)
Profit from operations	X
Net interest cost (interest paid less interest received)	(X)
Profit before tax	X
Income tax expense	(X)
Net profit for the period	X

(b) Nature of expenditure method

	$m	$m
Sales revenue		X
Other operating income		X
Changes in inventories of finished goods and work in progress	(X)	
Raw materials and consumables used	(X)	
Staff costs	(X)	
Depreciation and amortisation expense	(X)	
Other operating expenses	(X)	
		(X)
Profit from operations		X
Net interest cost (interest paid less interest received)		(X)
Profit before tax		X
Income tax expense		(X)
Net profit for the period		X

The second format will probably seem more difficult than the first. Two items in it perhaps need further explanation:

Changes in inventories of finished goods and work in progress

This is simply the difference between the opening and closing amounts and could thus be a debit or a credit in the statement – if inventories have risen it will be a credit and if they have fallen a debit. Note that raw materials inventories are included below rather than here.

Raw materials and consumables used

This is purchases of raw materials adjusted for opening and closing inventories.

In an examination question, the nature of the items in the trial balance should give a clear idea of the format required. The first one is more likely to appear.

ACTIVITY 1

The extract below is from the trial balance of Unity, a limited liability company, at 31 March 20X4, after the necessary year-end adjustments had been made.

Show the first part of the published income statement of the company using the function of expenditure method.

	Dr	*Cr*
	$'000	$'000
Cost of sales	1,823	
Distribution costs	547	
Sales revenue		4,487
Loan interest	647	
Administrative expenses	974	

Feedback to this activity is at the end of the chapter.

ACTIVITY 2

The directors of Unity (see previous Activity) are interested to see how the company's income statement would look if it were prepared following the nature of expenditure method. You discover that the sum of cost of sales, distribution and administrative expenses which appears in the original income statement as 3,344 (1,823 + 547 + 974) can be alternatively analysed as:

	$'000
Decrease in inventories of finished goods and work in progress	52
Raw materials and consumables	875
Depreciation	943
Staff costs	1,065
Other operating expenses	409
	3,344

Show the income statement for Unity as it would appear if it were to be produced following the nature of expenditure format.

Feedback to this activity is at the end of the chapter.

3 Preparing company financial statements for publication

3.1 Introduction

The procedures for preparing company financial statements for publication are much the same as those applied in the previous chapter for financial statements for internal use. Some of the headings required for the formats in this chapter were deliberately introduced there.

Only one different technique is required – this is for use when the income statement is to be drawn up following the function of expenditure method – format (a) above. With this format, all the operating expenses have to appear under one of three headings, so set up a three-column working:

Cost of sales	*Distribution costs*	*Administrative expenses*
$'000	$'000	$'000

All expense items in the trial balance are then entered into the appropriate column to build up the three totals needed.

An examination question will often tell you how to analyse some of the expenses. For example, depreciation of vehicles could be partly for distribution and partly administrative.

Bad debts and allowance for doubtful debts could be regarded as a distribution cost or an administrative expense. Some books say one and some the other. Put them under distribution costs and do not waste time worrying about them.

Practise with the questions at the end of this chapter to develop fluency and familiarity with the formats.

4 The current/non-current distinction

4.1 Introduction

The suggested balance sheet format makes a distinction between current and non-current assets and liabilities. IAS 1 sets down the rules to be applied in making this distinction.

4.2 Current assets

KEY POINT

Current asset if:

- part of operating cycle
- expected to be realised within 12 months
- cash or an equivalent.

An asset should be classified as a current asset if it is:

(a) part of the enterprise's operating cycle; or

(b) held for trading purposes, or for the short-term, and expected to be realised within twelve months of the balance sheet date; or

(c) cash or a cash equivalent.

All other assets should be classified as non-current assets.

Note that this definition allows inventory or receivables to qualify as current assets under (a) above, even if they may not be realised into cash within twelve months.

4.3 Current liabilities

KEY POINT

Current liability if:

- settled as part of operating cycle
- due to be settled within 12 months of balance sheet date.

The rules for current liabilities are similar to those for current assets.

A liability should be classified as a current liability if:

- it is expected to be settled in the normal course of the enterprise's operating cycle
- it is due to be settled within twelve months of the balance sheet date.

All other liabilities should be classified as non-current liabilities.

The operating cycle or working capital cycle is explained in greater detail in Chapter 23.

Liabilities which were originally non-current should continue to be classified as such even when they are due to be settled within twelve months of the balance sheet date if all three of the following conditions are met:

- the original term was for a period of more than twelve months
- the liability is to be refinanced on a long-term basis
- the intention to refinance is supported by an agreement completed before the financial statements are approved.

5 The statement of changes in equity

This statement presents, in columnar form, all the changes which have affected the various headings of share capital and reserves.

The statement opens with the balances of the various items as at the beginning of the period. Any adjustment to these figures to reflect a change in accounting policy or the correction of a fundamental error comes next. (See later in this chapter.)

Other items which may appear in the statement are:

- issues of shares
- surpluses or deficits on revaluation of assets
- net profit for the period
- dividends paid.

A typical statement could look like this:

Statement of changes in equity for the year ended 31 December 20X8

	Share capital	*Share premium*	*Revaluation reserve*	*Accumulated profit*	*Total*
	$m	$m	$m	$m	$m
Balance at 31 December 20X7	100	40	20	30	190
Correction of fundamental error				(2)	(2)
	100	40	20	28	188
Surplus on revaluation of properties			35		35
Deficit on revaluation of investments			(10)		(10)
Net gains and losses not recognised in the income statement			25		25
Net profit for the period				42	42
Dividends				(20)	(20)
Issue of share capital	50	25			75
Balance at 31 December 20X8	150	65	45	50	310

6 The statement of recognised gains and losses

KEY POINT

The statement may be confined to gains and losses arising during the year, distinguishing those not in the income statement from the net profit for the period which is in the income statement.

As an alternative, the statement may be confined to gains and losses arising during the year, distinguishing those not in the income statement from the net profit for the period which is in the income statement. Dividends do not appear. A statement in this form is referred to as a 'statement of recognised gains and losses'.

Here is a specimen statement, using the same figures as the statement of changes in equity:

Statement of recognised gains and losses for the year ended 31 December 20X8

	$m
Surplus on revaluation of properties	35
Deficit on revaluation of investments	(10)
Net gains not recognised in the income statement	25
Net profit for the period	42
Total recognised gains and losses	67

This second form of statement is in some ways more useful to users than the statement of changes in equity, because it focuses on the performance of the period. If the statement of recognised gains and losses is presented as above, it is still necessary to disclose by note a reconciliation of opening and closing balances of share capital, reserves and accumulated profit, as shown in the statement of changes in equity.

7 IAS 8 *Net Profit or Loss for the Period, Fundamental Errors and Changes in Accounting Policies* and IAS 35 *Discontinuing Operations*

7.1 Introduction

IAS 8 is mainly relevant for company financial statements for publication, so it is logical to deal with it in this chapter.

It deals with five main issues:

- extraordinary items
- disclosure of unusual items, knowledge of which is relevant to an understanding of the performance of the enterprise
- changes in accounting estimates
- fundamental errors
- changes in accounting policies.

One or two minor disclosure details previously in IAS 8 are now in IAS 35 *Discontinuing Operations*. These are indicated below.

7.2 Extraordinary items

Extraordinary items are income or expenses that arise from events or transactions that are clearly distinct from the ordinary activities of the enterprise and are not expected to recur frequently or regularly.

Examples of extraordinary items given in IAS 8 are:

- the expropriation of assets (e.g. nationalisation)
- an earthquake or other natural disaster.

Extraordinary items should be shown separately at the end of the income statement. If there is an extraordinary item, the income statement (see above) will conclude:

	$m
Net profit from ordinary activities	X
Extraordinary items	(X)
Net profit for the period	X

A note should give details of the nature of the extraordinary items.

7.3 Disclosure of unusual items

These items are sometimes described as 'exceptional' items.

They are items which users of financial statements should be aware of because, although not qualifying as extraordinary, they are of such size, nature or incidence that their disclosure is relevant to users.

Examples of such items are:

- writing down of non-current assets or inventories to their recoverable amount (or the reversal of such write-downs)
- costs of restructuring
- profits or losses on disposals of property, plant and equipment
- profits or losses on discontinuance of part of the enterprise (now in IAS 35 – see below)
- litigation settlements.

These items are normally included in the appropriate expense heading in the income statement, with disclosure given by note.

7.4 IAS 35 *Discontinuing Operations* (issued June 1998)

The only parts of IAS 35 that are examinable are the disclosure requirements for discontinuing operations previously in IAS 8 and now transferred to IAS 35. (Note that all other provisions of IAS 8 remain in force and in your syllabus.)

The wording has changed somewhat but the effect is much the same.

The disclosure requirements are:

- a description of the discontinuing operation
- the date and nature of the discontinuance (e.g. by sale)
- the carrying amounts, at the balance sheet date, of the total assets and total liabilities to be disposed of
- the amounts of revenue, expenses, and pre-tax profit or loss from the discontinuing operation in the current period, and the income tax expense relating to it
- the gain or loss on the sale, and the income tax expense related to it, shown separately from operating profit.

KEY POINT

Disclosure required when discontinuance occurred:

- during the financial year
- between balance sheet date and approval of financial statements.

The disclosures listed above are required if the discontinuance occurred during the financial year or *in the period after the balance sheet date up to the date the financial statements are approved by the directors.*

7.5 Changes in accounting estimates

The uncertainties inherent in business activities mean that estimates made when preparing the financial statements for the year may have to be changed in the next year's financial statements.

Any necessary change should be included in the current income statement under the same heading as the previous estimate, with a note giving details of the change if it has a material effect. Income statements of future years may, of course, also be affected by a change to an estimate.

7.6 Fundamental errors

If a fundamental error in the financial statements for prior periods is discovered, it obviously has to be corrected. IAS 8 allows two treatments:

1. **Benchmark treatment** – correct the error by adjusting the opening balance of retained earnings. Comparative information for previous years should be restated unless it is impracticable to do so.
2. **Allowed alternative treatment** – include the correction of the error in the current year's income statement. If this treatment is adopted, additional information according to the benchmark treatment should also be presented in a note.

In either case a note should disclose the nature and amount of the error and the manner in which it has been corrected.

7.7 Changes in accounting policies

The consistency concept normally means that a company's accounting policies remain the same from year to year. However, they do occasionally have to be changed and IAS 8 gives guidance on this point.

When may accounting policies be changed?

IAS 8 recognises three valid reasons for a policy change:

- a new accounting standard
- a statutory requirement
- the change will result in a more appropriate presentation of events or transactions in the financial statements.

How should the change of policy be reflected in the financial statements?

If the change is the result of the issue of a new IAS, it should be accounted for in accordance with the requirements of that standard.

If the change is for any other reason, IAS 8 has a benchmark treatment and an allowed alternative.

1 Benchmark treatment

- The change will be applied retrospectively by adjusting the opening balance of accumulated profit (retained earnings). This would be shown in the statement of changes in equity. Comparative information should be restated unless this is impracticable.
- In other words, the financial statements should be presented as if the new policy had always been in use.
- The only exception to this treatment is if the effect on prior periods is not reasonably determinable.

2 Allowed alternative treatment

- The allowed alternative is to include the adjustment for prior periods in the current year's income statement, with no change in the comparative information.

If this treatment is adopted, it is still necessary to present additional information by note according to the benchmark treatment.

Whichever treatment is adopted, a note must show whenever the effect of the change is material, the reasons for the change of policy, the amount of the adjustment in the current period, and the amount of the adjustment for prior periods.

Conclusion

For examination purposes this is probably the most important chapter in the book. Building on the introductory material on company accounting in the previous chapter, it covers the preparation of financial statements for publication, including not only the income statement and balance sheet but also the supporting statements – the statement of changes in equity and the statement of recognised gains and losses. Note too the coverage of IASs 1, 8 and 35.

SELF-TEST QUESTIONS

IAS 1 *Preparation of Financial Statements*

1 What is the objective of general purpose financial statements? (2.2)

2 What supplementary information could be desirable in addition to financial statements? (2.4)

3 Draw up an illustrative format for a company balance sheet. (2.6)

4 Draw up the formats for the notes to the balance sheet giving details of non-current asset movements and movements in equity capital and reserves. (2.7)

5 Draw up the two formats for the income statement. (2.8)

The Statement of changes in equity

6 Draw up a format for a statement of changes in equity. (5)

The Statement of recognised gains and losses

7 Draw up a format for a statement of recognised gains and losses. (6)

IAS 8 and IAS 35

8 What is an extraordinary item according to IAS 8? (7.2)

9 Give three examples of items which should be disclosed by note to the income statement even though they do not qualify as extraordinary. (7.3)

10 How should the correction of fundamental errors and the effects of a change in accounting policy be dealt with in financial statements? (7.6, 7.7)

PRACTICE QUESTION

General Warehouses

The trial balance of General Warehouses, a limited liability company, shows the following balances at 31 December 20X3:

	Dr $m	*Cr* $m
Ordinary share capital		150
Share premium		10
Contingency reserve		10
Accumulated profit 1 January 20X3		25
Inventory of goods for resale at 1 January 20X3	30	
Sales revenue		500
Purchases	270	
Purchase returns		13
Sales returns	14	
Carriage outwards	14	
Warehouse wages	40	
Salespersons' salaries	30	
Administrative wages	20	
Warehouse plant and machinery	63	
Delivery vehicle hire	10	
Accumulated depreciation – plant and machinery, 1 January 20X3		25
Goodwill	50	
Distribution expenses	5	
Administrative expenses	15	
Directors' salaries (charge to administrative expenses)	15	
Rents receivable		8
Trade receivables	165	
Cash at bank	30	
Trade payables		30
	771	771

Notes*:* The following final adjustments need to be made:

1 Inventory of goods for resale at 31 December 20X3, $50m.

2 Annual depreciation of $16m on warehouse plant and machinery.

3 Provide for tax, due 30 September 20X4, $25m.

4 Amortisation of goodwill, $5m.

Prepare the published income statement and balance sheet for the 20X3 financial year, using the function of expenditure method for the income statement.

(20 marks)

EXAM-TYPE QUESTIONS

Question 1: Board of Directors

After the directors of General Warehouses had seen the draft income statement and balance sheet for the 20X3 financial year they concluded that the income statement showed too much analysis of their expenses.

Prepare a further income statement using the nature of expenditure method, for comparison by the Board of Directors of General Warehouses. **(10 marks)**

Question 2: Ople

The following income statement for the year to 31 March 20X2 has been prepared for the management of Ople:

	$'000		$'000
Opening inventory	500	Sales revenue	8,500
Purchases	4,400	Closing inventory	700
Gross profit c/d	4,300		
	9,200		9,200
Auditors' remuneration	50	Gross profit b/d	4,300
Depreciation:		Dividends received	240
Delivery vans	40		
Office furniture	20		
Plant and machinery	85		
Directors' salaries	95		
Distribution expenses	425		
Factory expenses	970		
Hire of plant and machinery	15		
Office expenses	190		
Legal expenses	35		
Rent (warehouse)	65		
Wages and salaries	1,200		
Net profit c/d	1,350		
	4,540		4,540
Provision for tax	380	Net profit b/d	1,350
		Over-provision of previous	
Net profit after tax c/d	1,000	year's tax	30
	1,380		1,380

Additional information

Wages and salaries (other than those for directors) are to be apportioned as follows:

Distribution	80%
Office expenses	20%

You are required, insofar as the information permits, to prepare Ople's income statement for the year to 31 March 20X2 in accordance with the requirements of International Accounting Standards, using the function of expenditure method. **(15 marks)**

Question 3: Small

Small is a quoted company with an authorised share capital of $250,000, consisting of ordinary shares of $1 each. The company prepares its accounts as on 31 March in each year and the list of account balances, before final adjustments, extracted on 31 March 20X5 showed:

	$	$
Ordinary share capital, issued and fully paid		200,000
Accumulated profits as on 1 April 20X4		61,000
6% Loan notes (secured on factory)		60,000
Factory:		
Cost at beginning of year	200,000	
Accumulated depreciation at beginning of year		76,000
Plant and machinery:		
Cost at beginning of year	80,000	
Accumulated depreciation		30,000
Additions in year	10,000	
Payables and accrued expenses		170,000
Inventory as on 31 March 20X5	160,000	
Receivables	100,000	
Prepayments	80,000	
Balance at bank	90,000	
Profit for the year (subject to any items in the following notes)		111,000
Proceeds of sale of plant		12,000
	$720,000	$720,000

You ascertain that:

1 The loan notes are repayable at par by six equal annual drawings starting on 31 December 20X5.

2 Annual depreciation is calculated as to:

Factory	2% on cost
Plant and machinery	20% reducing balance on NBV as at 31 March 20X4 plus additions less disposals in the year.

3 Plant disposed of originally cost $16,000. Accumulated depreciation is $3,200.

4 Inventory has been valued consistently at the lower of cost and net realisable value.

You are required to prepare in a form suitable for publication and in conformity with the requirements of International Accounting Standards, the balance sheet as on 31 March 20X5.

(15 marks)

Question 4: Pride

The following extracts have been taken from the trial balance of Pride, a limited liability company, at 31 March 20X1:

		$000	$000
Issued share capital			
500,000 ordinary shares of 50c each			250
Share premium account 1 April 20X0			180
Accumulated profits 31 March 20X1			34
Land at cost		210	
Building:	Cost 1 April 20X0	200	
	Accumulated depreciation at 1 April 20X0		120
Plant and equipment:	Cost	318	
	Accumulated depreciation at 1 April 20X0		88
Receivables		146	
Cash at bank		50	
Payables			94
10% loan notes issued 19X5			100
Allowance for doubtful debts			10
Suspense account			166

Notes:

The accumulated profits balance of $34,000 shown above is the final balance of retained profit for the year and may be incorporated into your answer as such.

The balance on the suspense account is made up as follows:

	$000
Receipt of cash on 8 January 20X1 on the issue of 200,000 ordinary shares of 50c each at a premium of 30c per share	160
Proceeds of sale of plant*	6
	166

*This plant had originally cost $18,000 and had been written down to $6,000 at 31 March 20X0.

The company's policy is to provide depreciation for a full year in the year of acquisition of assets and none in the year of sale.

Depreciation is to be provided on the straight line basis at the following annual rates:

Land	Nil
Buildings	2 per cent
Plant and Equipment	20 per cent

The allowance for doubtful debts is to be increased to $12,000.

Payments and accruals at 31 March 20X1 were:

	$000
Prepayments	8,000
Accruals	4,000

The closing inventory was $180,000.

Required:

Prepare the balance sheet of Pride as at 31 March 20X1 for publication complying as far as possible with the provisions of IAS 1 *Presentation of Financial Statements.* **(10 marks)**

For the answers to these questions, see the 'Answers' section at the end of the book.

FEEDBACK TO ACTIVITY 1

The income statement of Unity for the year ended 31 March 20X4, using the function of expenditure method is as follows:

Unity
Income statement for the year ended 31 March 20X4

	$'000	$'000
Sales revenue		4,487
Cost of sales		1,823
Gross profit		2,664
Distribution costs	547	
Administrative expenses	974	1,521
Profit from operations		1,143
Interest payable		647
Profit before tax		496

FEEDBACK TO ACTIVITY 2

The income statement of Unity for the year ended 31 March 20X4, using the nature of expenditure format would be as follows:

Unity
Income statement for the year ended 31 March 20X4

	$'000	$'000
Sales revenue		4,487
Decrease in inventories of finished goods and work in progress		52
		4,435
Raw materials and consumables	875	
Staff costs	1,065	
Depreciation	943	
Other operating expenses	409	
		3,292
Profit from operations		1,143
Interest payable		647
Profit before tax		496

Chapter 21
BASIC CONSOLIDATED ACCOUNTS

CHAPTER CONTENTS

So far we have been looking at the financial statements of individual companies. In practice, most large businesses operate as groups of companies. In its simplest form, a group consists of one company which owns a controlling interest in another. The controlling company is referred to as the **parent company** or **holding company** and the controlled company as its **subsidiary**. The balance sheet combining the two companies is referred to as a **consolidated balance sheet.**

Objectives

By the time you have finished this chapter you should be able to:

- prepare a consolidated balance sheet for a company with one subsidiary
- make appropriate adjustments for goodwill, minority interests and pre-acquisition profit.

1 Consolidated accounts

1.1 What are consolidated accounts?

When one company invests in another, the investment appears as an asset in the investor's balance sheet, and dividends received are credited to the income statement. As long as the investment remains a small percentage of the total share capital of the company in which the shares are held, no one would want to quarrel with this treatment.

Suppose, however, that the holding represents all or most of the total share capital. Now the investing company is in a position to **control** the other company, and for all practical purposes is entitled to the whole or most of its profit, whether or not these profits are actually paid out in the form of dividends. Also, the increase in value of its assets over the years, reflecting retained profits, accrues ultimately to the investing company.

KEY POINT

Consolidated accounts is the name given to the accounting techniques which seek to reflect the true position, as regards both profits and assets, when one company controls another.

In these circumstances, the accounting treatment described above does not reflect the true nature of the relationship between the parent company and the subsidiary. In reality, the two companies can be regarded as a single entity because the subsidiary is controlled by the parent. **Consolidated accounts** is the name given to the accounting techniques which seek to reflect the true position, as regards both profits and assets, when one company controls another. The parent company prepares consolidated accounts incorporating the results of the whole group.

DEFINITION

Parent company: owns a controlling interest in another company.

Subsidiary company: a company controlled by a parent company.

Group of companies: parent company and its subsidiaries.

Consolidated accounts: the aggregated balance sheet and income statement of a group.

Minority interest: a part owner of a subsidiary.

1.2 Definitions

- **Parent company**. A company owning a controlling interest (e.g. more than 50% of equity) in another.
- **Subsidiary company**. A company which is controlled by a parent company.
- **Group of companies**. A parent company plus its subsidiaries.
- **Consolidated accounts**. Consolidated accounts consist of a **consolidated balance sheet**, in which all assets and liabilities of group undertakings are aggregated, and a **consolidated income statement** aggregating the profits and losses of all group undertakings. (For Paper 1.1 we are concerned only with the consolidated balance sheet.)

- **Minority interest**. If the subsidiary is not wholly owned by the parent, the 'outside' interest is referred to as the 'minority interest'.

2 The basic balance sheet consolidation procedure

2.1 A basic example

P was incorporated on 1 January 20X1. On 1 January 20X3 it acquired 100% of the ordinary shares in S which was incorporated on that day. Five years later, on 31 December 20X7, the balance sheets of the two companies were as follows.

	P	*S*
	$	$
Non-current assets	10,000	5,000
Investment in S: 5,000 $1 shares	5,000	
Net current assets	5,000	3,000
	20,000	8,000
Share capital: ordinary shares of $1 each	10,000	5,000
Accumulated profits	10,000	3,000
	20,000	8,000

Prepare a consolidated balance sheet at 31 December 20X7 for P and its subsidiary.

Discussion

KEY POINT

Preparing a consolidated balance sheet really means 'adding together' the two balance sheets.

Preparing a consolidated balance sheet really means 'adding together' the two balance sheets. In doing so the $5,000 investment in S appearing in the P balance sheet is cancelled by the $5,000 share capital in the balance sheet of S.

Try to produce your own answer using common sense, then check with the solution below.

P and its subsidiary
Consolidated balance sheet as at 31 December 20X7

	$
Non-current assets	15,000
Net current assets	8,000
	23,000
Share capital	10,000
Accumulated profits	13,000
	23,000

The effect of the consolidation has really been to extend the balance sheet of the parent company. The investment in the subsidiary has been replaced by the underlying net assets of the subsidiary. The $3,000 increase in value of the assets since acquisition is represented by the $3,000 post-acquisition reserves of S, which are combined with those of P in the consolidated balance sheet.

KEY POINT

Note that the share capital of the subsidiary company *never* appears as part of the figure of the share capital in the consolidated balance sheet.

Note that the share capital of the subsidiary company *never* appears as part of the figure of the share capital in the consolidated balance sheet.

It was possible to answer that simple question without proper workings. For more complex questions we need a systematic approach to workings. We begin by looking at the working for goodwill on consolidation.

KEY POINT

If the parent pays more for the investment in the subsidiary than the value of the subsidiary's net assets, the difference represents the amount paid for the unrecorded goodwill in the subsidiary.

2.2 Goodwill on consolidation

If the parent pays more for the investment in the subsidiary than the value of the subsidiary's net assets, the difference represents the amount paid for the unrecorded goodwill in the subsidiary.

In the example above, the amount paid for 100% of the shares in S, $5,000, exactly equalled the net assets of S, and no goodwill arose.

Let us modify the example to illustrate what happens when the amount paid for the shares exceeds the value of the net assets acquired. Our approach is to calculate the net value of the subsidiary's assets on the date it was acquired, which of course is equal to its share capital and accumulated reserves as on that date. We compare this with the amount paid by the parent company, and the difference represents goodwill.

Facts as above, except that P paid $6,000 for the shares. The balance sheets of the two companies are now as follows:

Balance sheets at 31 December 20X7

	P	*S*
	$	$
Tangible non-current assets	10,000	5,000
Investment in S: 5,000 $1 shares	6,000	
Net current assets	4,000	3,000
	20,000	8,000
Share capital: ordinary shares of $1 each	10,000	5,000
Accumulated profits	10,000	3,000
	20,000	8,000

The net current assets of P have been reduced by $1,000 to reflect the higher price paid for the shares.

When we set the cost of the investment off against the net assets of the subsidiary, a goodwill balance of $1,000 emerges. (Remember that we calculate the net assets by adding the share capital and reserves. By the balance sheet equation, this total always equals the net assets, and it is usually a simpler calculation than adding all the net assets separately.)

Setting off investment against subsidiary's net assets

	$	$
Cost of investment in S		6,000
Share of net assets acquired		
Share capital	5,000	
Accumulated profits (at acquisition)	nil	
	5,000	
P's interest	100%	5,000
Goodwill on acquisition		$1,000

This is the standard working for goodwill.

DEFINITION

Goodwill: the difference between the cost of an entity and the fair values of that entity's net assets.

The calculation shows that P paid $1,000 more than their value for the assets of S. The difference is **goodwill**, defined as the difference between the cost of an entity and the fair values of that entity's net assets.

The calculation above depends on the fact that share capital plus reserves equals net assets. In our example, the reserves of S are nil because P acquired the shares on the day S was incorporated. S had not had any time to build up reserves.

ACTIVITY 1

Calculate the goodwill arising on acquisition in each of the following cases:

1 P acquired 100% of the shares of T for $126,000, when the net assets of T were valued at $94,000.

2 Q acquired 100% of the shares of V for $250,000. At the time of the acquisition, the share capital and reserves of V were as follows:

	$
Ordinary shares of $1 each	80,000
Share premium	45,000
Accumulated profit	92,000
	217,000

The balance sheet value of the assets of T reflects their fair value.

3 R acquired 75% of the shares of X for $300,000, when the value of the net assets of X was $364,000.

Feedback to this activity is at the end of chapter.

2.3 Amortisation of goodwill

Goodwill can be described as the additional value obtained from an acquisition over and above the value of the net assets acquired. For example, if C pays $100,000 to acquire 100% of D, whose net assets are worth $40,000, goodwill is $60,000. This $60,000 represents the additional value placed by C on the business of D.

This additional value does not last for ever. In other words goodwill does not retain its value. Like other non-current assets, its value erodes over time. It is therefore appropriate to depreciate or amortise goodwill over a number of years after a subsidiary has been acquired. When goodwill is amortised:

- The charge for amortisation each year is treated as an expense in the consolidated income statement.
- The value of goodwill in the consolidated balance sheet is its original value minus accumulated amortisation.

KEY POINT

Goodwill arising at acquisition must be amortised (depreciated) over its estimated economic life, through the income statement.

In the example above, the goodwill on acquisition amounted to $1,000. Look back at the original example and you will see that we are preparing a consolidated balance sheet five years after the acquisition. The goodwill arising at acquisition must be amortised (depreciated) over its estimated economic life, through the income statement. If we assume a life of ten years for this goodwill, the consolidated balance sheet at 31 December 20X7 will be as follows.

P and its subsidiary
Consolidated balance sheet as at 31 December 20X7

	$	$
Non-current assets:		
Goodwill	1,000	
Less: amortisation	500	500
Tangible non-current assets		15,000
		15,500
Net current assets		7,000
		22,500
Share capital – ordinary shares of $1 each		10,000
Accumulated profits (10,000 + 3,000 – 500)		12,500
		22,500

The amortisation through the income statement at $100 per year has reduced the accumulated profit balance.

ACTIVITY 2

Peter has prepared a consolidated balance sheet for the AVP Group as at 31 December 20X4 as follows:

	$
Tangible non-current assets	600,000
Goodwill	120,000
Net current assets	80,000
	800,000
Ordinary shares of $1	200,000
Share premium	140,000
Accumulated profits	460,000
	800,000

AVP acquired 100% of ZZ on 1 January 20X4 for $260,000, when the fair value of the net assets of ZZ was $140,000. Peter's boss sees that Peter has forgotten to provide for amortisation of the goodwill. Goodwill should be amortised straight line over 10 years.

Required:

Adjust the balance sheet to provide for the amortisation of goodwill.

Feedback to this activity is at the end of chapter.

2.4 Minority interests

KEY POINT

A company is a subsidiary if more than 50% of its shares is owned by its parent company.

Minority interest: balance of shares in a subsidiary company.

What if a parent company does not buy 100% of the shares in the subsidiary? As long as it owns more than 50%, the company is a subsidiary. If the parent company owns, say, 80% of the ordinary share capital, the holders of the remaining 20% are referred to as the 'minority', or 'minority interest'. Total assets and liabilities are shown exactly as before, but a new item representing the 'minority interest' must be introduced into the bottom half of the consolidated balance sheet. The minority interest can be calculated by taking the appropriate percentage of the net assets at the balance sheet date, but net assets will again equal share capital plus reserves and it is convenient to calculate the minority interest by dividing up the share capital and reserves. The example below shows the technique.

Facts as before, but P paid $4,800 for 80% of the share capital of S.

Balance sheets at 31 December 20X7

	P	*S*
	$	$
Non – current assets	10,000	5,000
Investment in S: 4,000 $1 shares	4,800	
Net current assets	5,200	3,000
	20,000	8,000
Share capital: ordinary shares of $1 each	10,000	5,000
Accumulated profits	10,000	3,000
	20,000	8,000

Before calculating the minority interest, let us calculate the goodwill in this example.

	$	$
Cost of investment in S		4,800
Share of net assets acquired:		
Share capital	5,000	
Accumulated profits(as before)	nil	
	5,000	
P's interest	80%	4,000
Goodwill on acquisition		$800

The minority interest

The minority interest is calculated as at the current balance sheet date and not as at acquisition like the goodwill. The calculation is as follows:

	$	$
Net assets of S at the balance sheet date		
Share capital	5,000	
Accumulated profits	3,000	
	8,000	
Minority interest 20%		1,600

This is the standard working for minority interest.

The consolidated balance sheet is now as follows:

P and its subsidiary
Consolidated balance sheet as at 31 December 20X7

	$	$
Non-current assets		
Goodwill at cost	800	
Amortisation	400	400
Tangible non-current assets		15,000
		15,400
Net current assets		8,200
		23,600
Share capital – ordinary shares of $1 each		10,000
Accumulated profits		
10,000 + (80% × 3,000) – 400		12,000
		22,000
Minority interest		1,600
		23,600

Study all the work so far and work through the examples several times until you understand everything completely.

2.5 Pre-acquisition profit

There is one final adjustment to consider. In the examples so far, the subsidiary was acquired at its formation. It had had no chance to trade and earn profits before the acquisition.

KEY POINT

If a subsidiary is acquired after its formation and has accumulated some retained profit, only the **post-acquisition** profit may be combined with the parent's accumulated profits.

If a subsidiary is acquired after its formation and has accumulated some retained profit, only the **post-acquisition** profit may be combined with the parent's accumulated profits. The pre-acquisition portion represents assets at the date of acquisition, and so must form part of the calculation of goodwill.

Here is an example to illustrate the adjustment for pre-acquisition profit.

Example

Q acquired 80% of the share capital of T on 1 January 20X1 for $10,000, when the accumulated profits of T amounted to $4,000. At 31 December 20X3, three years later, the companies' balance sheets were as follows:

Balance sheets at 31 December 20X3

	Q	*T*
	$	$
Non-current assets	8,000	11,000
Investment in T at cost	10,000	
Net current assets	4,000	3,000
	22,000	14,000
Ordinary share capital (shares of $1 each)	10,000	5,000
Accumulated profits	12,000	9,000
	22,000	14,000

Goodwill is to be amortised on the straight line basis over five years.

1 Calculation of goodwill

	$	$
Cost of investment in T		10,000
Share of net assets acquired:		
Share capital	5,000	
Accumulated profits	4,000	
	9,000	
Q's interest	80%	7,200
Goodwill on acquisition		2,800
Amortisation 3 × 20% = 60% × $2,800		1,680
Balance at 31 December 20X3		1,120

2 Calculation of minority interest

	$	$
Net assets of T at the balance sheet date		
Share capital	5,000	
Accumulated profits	9,000	
	14,000	
Minority interest 20%		2,800

3 Calculation of post-acquisition profit

	$
Q: all	12,000
T: 80% × (9,000 – 4,000)	4,000
	16,000
Amortisation of goodwill per working 1	(1,680)
	$14,320

Q and its subsidiary
Consolidated balance sheet as at 31 December 20X3

	$
Non-current assets (8,000 + 11,000)	19,000
Goodwill (Working 1)	1,120
Net current assets	7,000
	27,120
Share capital	10,000
Accumulated profits (Working 3)	14,320
	24,320
Minority interest (Working 2)	2,800
	27,120

ACTIVITY 3

The balance sheet of A and B as at 1 May 20X4 were as follows:

	A	B
	$	$
Net non-current assets	100,000	60,000
Net current assets, including cash	180,000	5,000
	280,000	65,000
Ordinary shares of £1	100,000	20,000
Share premium	40,000	15,000
Accumulated reserve	140,000	30,000
	280,000	65,000

On 1 May 20X4, A acquired all the shares in B for $80,000 paying for them in cash.

Required:

Prepare a consolidated balance sheet for the A Group immediately after the acquisition has taken place.

Feedback to this activity is at the end of chapter.

Conclusion

The process of preparing a simple consolidated balance sheet will usually require the three calculations we have seen:

- goodwill on consolidation
  minority interest
- division of subsidiary's accumulated profits into pre-acquisition and post-acquisition.

That is as far as it is necessary to go with consolidation procedures for Paper 1.1.

SELF-TEST QUESTIONS

Balance sheet consolidation

1 What is represented by the procedure excess of the price paid for an entity over the value of the net assets acquired? (2.2)

2 What is the required accounting treatment for purchased goodwill? (2.2)

3 Why must a distinction be drawn between a subsidiary's pre-acquisition and post-acquisition reserves? (2.5)

MULTIPLE-CHOICE QUESTIONS

Question 1

On 1 January 1998 H acquired 80% of the share capital of S for $160,000. At that date the share capital of S consisted of 100,000 ordinary shares of $1 each and its reserves totalled $40,000. Goodwill of acquisition of subsidiaries is amortised on the straight line basis over five years.

In the consolidated balance sheet of H and its subsidiary S at 31 December 2000 the amount appearing for goodwill should be:

A $16,000

B $19,200

C $28,800

D $4,000

Question 2

On 1 January 1998 H acquired 60% of the share capital of S for $180,000. At that date the share capital of S consisted of 200,000 shares of 50c each. The reserves of H and S are stated below:

	At 1 January 1998	*At 31 December 2000*
	$	$
H	280,000	340,000
S	50,000	180,000

In the consolidated balance sheet of H and its subsidiary S, at 31 December 2000, what amount should appear for the minority interest in S?

A $92,000

B $280,000

C $152,000

D $112,000

Question 3

H acquired 75% of the share capital of S for $280,000 on 1 January 1994. Goodwill arising on consolidation has been fully amortised.

Details of the share capital and reserves of S are as follows:

	At 1 January 1994	*At 31 December 2000*
	$	$
Share capital	200,000	200,000
Accumulated profits	120,000	180,000

At 31 December 2000 the accumulated profits of H amounted to $480,000.

What figure should appear in the consolidated balance sheet of H and S at 31 December 2000 for the group accumulated profits?

A $530,000

B $525,000

C $485,000

D $575,000

For the answers to these questions, see the 'Answers' section at the end of the book.

EXAM-TYPE QUESTIONS

Question 1: Park and Gate

The following balances relate to Park and Gate at 31 December 20X4.

	Park	*Gate*
	$	$
Freehold property, net of depreciation	–	99,000
Other non-current assets, net of depreciation	182,300	35,000
48,000 shares in Gate at cost	72,000	–
Current assets	62,100	68,000
	316,400	202,000
Issued share capital ($1 ordinary shares)	200,000	80,000
Accumulated profits at 31 December 20X3	45,100	37,500
Profit for 20X4	17,600	28,500
Unsecured loan repayable 20X8	–	30,000
Current liabilities	53,700	26,000
	316,400	202,000

Park acquired its shares in Gate on 31 December 20X3.

Prepare the consolidated balance sheet of the group at 31 December 20X4 presented in good style so far as the information permits. Goodwill should be amortised over five years on the straight line basis. **(13 marks)**

Question 2: Rich and Poor

On 1 July 20X4, Rich acquired 70% of the ordinary share capital of Poor for $140,000. At that date Poor had accumulated profits of $50,000.

The following balance sheets have been prepared at 30 June 20X8.

	Rich	Poor
	$	$
Non-current assets:		
Tangible assets	190,000	170,000
Investments: shares in Poor	140,000	
	330,000	
Current assets	270,000	186,000
	600,000	356,000
Capital and reserves:		
Issued share capital:		
Ordinary shares of $1 each	200,000	130,000
Accumulated profits	175,000	89,000
	375,000	219,000
Current liabilities	225,000	137,000
	600,000	356,000

You are required to prepare the consolidated balance sheet of Rich and its subsidiary as at 30 June 20X8. Goodwill is amortised over five years on the straight line basis.

(10 marks)

For the answers to these questions, see the 'Answers' section at the end of the book.

FEEDBACK TO ACTIVITY 1

1 $32,000 ($126,000 - $94,000)

2 $33,000 ($250,000 - £217,000)

3 Value of net assets acquired

= 75% of $364,000 = $273,000

So, goodwill = $300,000 - $273,000

= $27,000

FEEDBACK TO ACTIVITY 2

Amortisation of goodwill for the year should be $120,000/10 = $12,000

Corrected consolidated balance sheet:

	$
Tangible non-current assets	600,000
Goodwill	108,000
Net current assets	80,000
	788,000
Ordinary shares of $1	200,000
Share premium	140,000
Accumulated reserve	448,000
(460,000 – 12,000)	788,000

FEEDBACK TO ACTIVITY **3**

Goodwill = $80,000 - $65,000 = $15,000

A Group
Consolidated balance sheet

	$
Net fixed assets (10,000 + 60,000)	160,000
Goodwill	15,000
Net current assets (180,000 – 80,000 + 5,000)	105,000
	280,000
Ordinary shares of $1 (A only)	100,000
Share premium (A only)	40,000
Accumulated reserve	140,000
(exclude pre-acquisition income of B)	280,000

Chapter 22
CASH FLOW STATEMENTS

CHAPTER CONTENTS

Financial accounting is primarily concerned with external financial reporting. Companies are required by IAS 7 *Cash Flow Statements* to include a cash flow statement in their financial statements. The best way to acquire knowledge of IAS 7 is to work through the examples in the chapter.

Objectives

By the time you have finished this chapter you should be able to:

- classify cash flows into appropriate headings
- prepare a cash flow statement from various data sources
- understand the link between profits and cash
- comment on the advantages of a cash flow statement to the user of accounts.

1 Introduction

1.1 Profit versus liquidity

In the preparation of financial statements we have covered so far, we have stressed the importance of accounting concepts of accruals and matching in order to compute a profit figure which shows the additional wealth created for the owners of the business during an accounting period. However, it is important for a business to generate cash as well as make profits. The two do not necessarily go hand in hand.

We explained in the chapter dealing with incomplete records that profit represents the increase in net assets in a business during an accounting period.

KEY POINT

Profit represents an increase in net assets, which can be in cash or may be 'tied up' in other assets.

This increase can be in cash or it may be 'tied up' in other assets, for example:

- non-current assets may have been purchased
- there may be an increased amount of receivables
- there may be increased investment in inventory
- the liabilities of the business may have decreased, i.e. more cash has been spent this year in paying off suppliers more quickly than was the case last year.

We can reconcile profit to cash in an accounting period by taking into account these and other factors. This reconciliation is examined in detail later in the chapter.

KEY POINT

Purposes of **cash flow statement**:

- additional information
- assess current liquidity
- show major cash flows
- estimate future cash flows
- distinguish transaction and other cash flows.

1.2 The need for a cash flow statement

A cash flow statement is needed as a consequence of the above differences between profits and cash. In particular, there is a need for a further statement to be presented as part of the financial statements which will help to achieve the following:

- provide additional information on business activities
- help to assess the current liquidity of the business
- allow the user to see the major types of cash flows into and out of the business
- help the user to estimate future cash flows
- determine cash flows generated from trading transactions rather than other cash flows.

2 The requirements of IAS 7 *Cash Flow Statements*

2.1 Introduction

The IASC (now IASB) issued IAS 7 in 1977 and revised it in 1992. It requires enterprises to present a cash flow statement as part of their financial statements.

A cash flow statement can be presented in a number of ways. It is simply a summary of the cash receipts and payments of an enterprise. Thus a summarised cash book would be a cash flow statement. A cash flow statement is often prepared from the balance sheet and income statement of an enterprise, opening with a reconciliation between reported profit and operating cash flow.

KEY POINT

Cash flow statement **standard headings**:

- operating activities
- investing activities
- financing activities.

IAS 7 requires the cash flow statement to be presented using standard headings. The objective of the standard headings is to ensure that cash flows are reported in a form that highlights the significant components of cash flow and facilitates comparison of the cash flow performance of different businesses.

The standard headings shown in the statement are:

- operating activities
- investing activities
- financing activities.

2.2 Specimen format for cash flow statement

Here is the specimen format for a cash flow statement from IAS 7, eliminating items not relevant for Paper 1.1. Explanatory notes follow it.

Cash flow statement for the period ended ...

	$'000	$'000
Cash flows from operating activities		
Net profit before taxation	2,850	
Adjustments for:		
Depreciation	490	
Interest expense	400	
Operating profit before working capital changes	3,740	
Increase in trade receivables	(500)	
Decrease in inventories	1,050	
Decrease in trade payables	(1,740)	
Cash generated from operations	2,550	
Interest paid	(270)	
Dividends paid	(300)	
Income taxes paid	(420)	
Net cash from operating activities		1,560
Cash flows from investing activities		
Purchase of property, plant and equipment	(900)	
Proceeds of sale of equipment	20	
Interest received	200	
Dividends received	200	
Net cash used in investing activities		(480)

Cash flows from financing activities		
Proceeds of issue of shares	1,210	
Repayment of loans	(2,000)	
Net cash used in financing activities		(790)
Net increase in cash and cash equivalents		290
Cash and cash equivalents at the beginning of the period		120
Cash and cash equivalents at the end of the period		410

Explanatory notes

Cash flows from operating activities

This section of the statement begins with the profit before tax as shown in the income statement. The remaining figures are the adjustments necessary to convert the profit figure to the cash flow for the period.

Depreciation	Added back to profit because it is a non-cash expense
Interest expense	Added back because it is not part of cash generated from operations (the interest *actually paid* is deducted later)
Increase in trade receivables	Deducted because this is part of the profit not yet realised into cash but tied up in receivables
Decrease in inventories	Added on because the decrease in inventories liberates extra cash
Decrease in trade payables	Deducted because the reduction in payables must reduce cash
Interest paid Dividends paid Income taxes paid	These are the amounts *actually paid* in the year

Cash flows from investing activities

The items here are cash spent on non-current assets, *proceeds of sale* of non-current assets and income from investments.

Cash flows from financing activities

Under this heading go the proceeds of issue of shares and long-term borrowings made or repaid.

Net increase in cash and cash equivalents

This is the overall increase (or decrease) in cash and cash equivalents during the year. After adding the cash and cash equivalents at the beginning of the year, the final balance of cash and cash equivalents at the end of the year emerges.

Meaning of 'cash and cash equivalents'

KEY POINT

Cash: cash on hand and available on demand.

Cash equivalents: short-term highly liquid investments.

'Cash' means cash on hand and deposits available on demand.

'Cash equivalents' means short-term highly liquid investments that are readily convertible to known amounts of cash and which are subject to an insignificant risk of changes in value. (Investments are thus *not* cash equivalents unless they have these two attributes of being readily convertible and with little or no risk of change in value).

IAS 7 requires a note to the cash flow statement giving details of the make-up of cash and cash equivalents:

Cash and cash equivalents

	At end of year	*At beginning of year*
	$'000	$'000
Cash on hand and balance at banks	40	25
Short-term investments	370	95
	410	120

3 Preparation of a cash flow statement

3.1 Direct and indirect methods

Figures for the cash flow statement will be derived either from the accounting records or from the other financial accounting statements – the balance sheets for the current year end and the previous period, and the income statement for the period.

The item requiring most work will often be the top of the statement – to determine the net cash flow from operating activities. The two alternative methods of calculation are shown below (figures invented) in a simplified example:

Direct method	$'000	*Indirect method*	$'000
Cash received from customers	15,424	Profit before tax	6,022
Cash payments to suppliers	(5,824)	Depreciation charges	899
Cash paid to and on behalf of employees	(2,200)		
Other cash payments	(511)	Increase in inventories	(194)
		Increase in receivables	(72)
		Increase in payables	234
Net cash inflow from operating activities	6,889		6,889

KEY POINT

Direct method: records the gross trading cash flows.

Indirect method: starts with profit, not cash, and adjusts profit for the non-cash expense of depreciation and for the movements in working capital.

The direct method is so called because it records the gross trading cash flows; the indirect method starts with profit, not cash, and adjusts profit for the non-cash expense of depreciation (added to profit) and for the movements in working capital items as shown.

The information for the direct method could be found in the accounting records or derived from the other financial statements. The information for the indirect method is found in the other financial statements. For example, we shall need to calculate the operating cash flow from the profit, as shown in the example below.

Example of calculations using the indirect method

The summarised balance sheets of Grasmere, a limited company, at 31 December 20X4 and 20X5 were as follows:

	20X4	20X5
	$	$
Non-current assets		
Plant and machinery, at cost	15,000	16,500
Less: Depreciation	8,000	10,000
	7,000	6,500
Current assets		
Inventory	20,000	23,500
Receivables	10,000	15,000
Cash	5,000	2,000
	42,000	47,000
Share capital	20,000	20,000
Reserves	17,000	21,000
Payables	5,000	6,000
	42,000	47,000

No non-current assets have been sold during the period under review. Depreciation provided for the year amounted to $2,000. There is no interest paid, dividends paid or taxation paid.

You are required to prepare a cash flow statement for the year ended 31 December 20X5.

Discussion

Examination questions often present two balance sheets like this from which you are to prepare a cash flow statement. At first sight there may seem to be no connection between the balance sheets and the company's cash flows, but there is. Take the first item in these balance sheets – the plant and machinery. The cost has risen from $15,000 to $16,500. This must mean that $1,500 has been spent on new plant during the year, a cash outflow of $1,500 under investing activities. All the other differences between the opening and closing balances are various types of cash flow, or otherwise required to produce the cash flow statement.

KEY POINT

Using the indirect method, we need to calculate the operating cash flow by adjusting the profit figure for non-cash expenses like depreciation and for the movements in the working capital items inventory, receivables and payables.

Using the indirect method we need to calculate the operating cash flow by adjusting the profit figure for non-cash expenses like depreciation and for the movements in the working capital items inventory, receivables and payables.

If a question gives you an income statement you obviously have the profit before tax figure. If you only have the balance sheets it is still possible to calculate the profit. How? By using the increase in the retained profit (in the case of Grasmere ($21,000 minus $17,000 or $4,000) and adding back the period's dividends and tax charge to arrive at profit before tax. In the simplified Grasmere situation there are no dividends or tax, so the profit before tax must be $4,000.

A possible way of preparing a cash flow statement from examination-style information is to set up a format consisting of the three headings in the specimen layout above, leaving plenty of space between them, then go through the given balance sheets from the top entering the differences in the correct positions in the format.

With this explanation you may like to try to produce Grasmere's cash flow statement before looking at the answer below.

Grasmere
Cash flow statement for the year ended 31 December 20X5

	$	$
Cash flows from operating activities		
Profit before tax (21,000 – 17,000)	4,000	
Depreciation (10,000 – 8,000)	2,000	
Increase in inventories	(3,500)	
Increase in receivables	(5,000)	
Increase in payables	1,000	
Net cash outflow from operating activities		(1,500)
Cash flows from investing activities		
Payments to acquire non-current assets		(1,500)
Decrease in cash and cash equivalents		(3,000)
Cash and cash equivalents at beginning of year		5,000
Cash and cash equivalents at end of year		2,000

Tutorial note: as there is no tax or dividends, the movement in reserves per the balance sheets represents the profit before tax for the year.

The example shows the important information that can be directly given by a cash flow statement. Despite making a profit of $4,000 in the period, the business has suffered a $3,000 reduction in cash. This is largely due to the amount of profit tied up in increased working capital (inventory, receivables less payables).

A further example

The balance sheets of Fox, a limited company, as at 31 December were as follows:

	20X8		*20X7*	
	$'000	$'000	$'000	$'000
Non-current assets				
Property (as revalued)		22,000		12,000
Plant and machinery				
Cost	10,000		5,000	
Aggregate depreciation	2,250	7,750	2,000	3,000
		29,750		15,000
Trade investment at cost		–		7,000
		29,750		22,000
Current assets				
Inventory	16,000		11,000	
Receivables	9,950		2,700	
Cash	–		1,300	
		25,950		15,000
		55,700		37,000
Capital and reserves				
Issued share capital		16,000		14,000
Revaluation reserve		4,000		–
Accumulated profit		10,000		2,000
		30,000		16,000
Non-current liabilities				
10% loan notes		6,000		10,000
Current liabilities				
Trade payables	8,000		11,000	
Bank overdraft	11,700		–	
		19,700		11,000
		55,700		37,000

Notes

1 At the beginning of the year machinery which had cost $1,000,000 and which had a book value of $250,000, was sold for $350,000.

2 In addition to the interest on the loan notes, interest paid on the overdraft amounted to $800,000.

3 $4,000,000 of loan notes were redeemed on 31 December 20X8.

4 The trade investment was sold for $10,000,000 during the year. No dividends were received from it.

You are required to prepare a cash flow statement for the company for the year ended 31 December 20X8 complying with the requirements of IAS 7.

Discussion

With this question we meet a new problem – sales of non-current assets. It is now not possible to calculate all the figures needed from the balance sheets without some further workings. The clue to this is that further information is given below the balance sheet. As soon as you see this you know that you will have to have some extra workings. In the case of non-current asset sales, three working ledger accounts will be needed:

- non-current asset – cost
- non-current asset – accumulated depreciation
- non-current asset – disposal.

The technique is to enter the opening and closing balances from the balance sheets, then record the additional information given in the notes below the balance sheet. Note that a *double entry* is required for all additional information – either an entry between two working accounts or an entry between one working and the cash flow statement (i.e. cash). In using these three working accounts you are simply reconstructing the non-current asset accounts as they would be in the underlying records.

Solution

Fox

Cash flow statement for the year ended 31 December 20X8

	$'000	$'000
Cash flows from operating activities		
Net profit before taxation (10,000 – 2,000)	8,000	
Depreciation (W2)	1,000	
Profit on sale of plant (W3)	(100)	
Profit on sale of investment	(3,000)	
Interest expense	1,800	
Operating profit before working capital changes	7,700	
Increase in inventory	(5,000)	
Increase in receivables	(7,250)	
Decrease in payables	(3,000)	
Cash generated from operations	(7,550)	
Interest paid	(1,800)	
Net cash outflow from operating activities		(9,350)

Cash flows from investing activities		
Purchase of:		
Plant and machinery (W1)	(6,000)	
Property (10,000 – 4,000)	(6,000)	
Proceeds of sale of investments	10,000	
Proceeds of sale of plant	350	
Net cash outflow from investing activities		(1,650)
Cash flows from financing activities		
Issue of ordinary shares	2,000	
Redemption of loan notes	(4,000)	
Net cash used in financing activities		(2,000)
Net decrease in cash and cash equivalents		(13,000)
Cash and cash equivalents at 1 January 20X8		1,300
Cash and cash equivalents at 31 December 20X8		(11,700)

IAS 7 requires the inclusion of a note disclosing the components of cash and cash equivalents and reconciling them with the amounts in the balance sheet. In a case like this, where the only items are cash at bank and overdraft, the last lines of the statement itself provide the information.

The note takes the form:

Cash and cash equivalents

	31 December	
	20X7	*20X8*
	$'000	$'000
Cash on hand and balances with banks	1,300	(11,700)

Workings

(W1) **Plant and machinery – cost**

	$'000		$'000
Balance b/d	5,000	Transfer – disposal	1,000
Additions during year (balancing figure)	6,000	Balance c/d	10,000
	11,000		11,000

(W2) **Plant and machinery – accumulated depreciation**

	$'000		$'000
Depreciation: disposals during year $(1,000 – 250)	750	Balance b/d	2,000
Balance c/d	2,250	Depreciation for year (bal fig)	1,000
	3,000		3,000

(W3) **Plant and machinery – disposal**

	$'000		$'000
Cost of disposals	1,000	Depreciation on disposals	750
Profit on sale	100	Sale proceeds	350
	1,100		1,100

That was quite a difficult example. Points to note are:

1 The calculation of the cash from operations. The retained profit has increased by $8,000,000. To calculate operating profit it is necessary to deduct the profit on sale of the plant and the trade investment.

2 The workings necessary to calculate the movement on the non-current assets.

The opening and closing balances for cost and accumulated depreciation were first entered, then from Note 1 to the question we may insert the transfers from those accounts for the disposal. The balancing figure on the cost account is then the additions during the year, and the balance on the depreciation account is the depreciation charge for the year. Finally, in the disposal account, the inclusion of the sale proceeds allows us to calculate the profit on the sale which has to be eliminated from the profit as part of the calculation of the operating cash flow.

3 The fact that some loan notes were repaid at the end of the year means that loan interest at 10% must have been paid on the whole $10,000,000.

3.2 Example of calculations using direct method

KEY POINT

Gross cash flows can be derived:

- by totalling the cash receipts and payments directly or
- from the opening and closing balance sheets and income statement.

As previously stated, gross cash flows from operating activities can be used to compute net cash flow from operating activities. The gross cash flows can be derived:

1 from the accounting records of the entity by totalling the cash receipts and payments directly, or

2 from the opening and closing balance sheets and income statement for the year by constructing summary control accounts for:

- sales (to derive cash received from customers)
- purchases (to derive cash payments to suppliers)
- wages (to derive cash paid to and on behalf of employees).

3.3 Example using control accounts

The balance sheets of a business are:

	Last year	*This year*
	$	$
Non-current assets	153,364	149,364
Inventories	–	–
Receivables	265,840	346,000
Cash	–	165,166
	419,204	660,530
Share capital	200,000	200,000
Reserves	–	141,640
	200,000	341,640
Current liabilities	219,204	318,890
	419,204	660,530

Extracts from the income statement for the year are:

	$	$
Sales revenue		1,589,447
Cost of sales		
Purchases (no inventory)	1,021,830	
Wages and salaries	145,900	
Depreciation	84,000	
		(1,251,730)
Administration		
Purchases	96,077	
Salaries	100,000	
		(196,077)
Operating profit and retained profit for the year		141,640

Additional information

1 Payables consist of:

	Last year $	*This year* $
Payables ledger		
Re non-current assets		46,000
Other	210,564	258,240
Wages accrued	8,640	14,650

2 Purchase invoices relating to the acquisition of non-current assets totalling $80,000 have been posted to the payables ledger during the year.

Prepare the cash flow statement using the direct method.

Solution

Cash flow statement

	$
Operating activities	
Cash received from customers (W1)	1,509,287
Cash payments to suppliers (W2)	(1,070,231)
Cash paid to and on behalf of employees (W3)	(239,890)
Net cash inflow from operating activities	199,166
Investing activities	
Purchase of non-current assets (W4)	(34,000)
Increase in cash and cash equivalents	165,166
Cash and cash equivalents at start of period	–
Cash and cash equivalents at end of period	165,166

Workings

(W1) **Receivables ledger control**

	$		$
Balance b/d	265,840	Cash receipts	1,509,287
Sales revenue	1,589,447	Balance c/d	346,000
	1,855,287		1,855,287

(W2) **Payables ledger control (excluding non-current asset purchases)**

	$		$
Cash paid (bal fig)	1,070,231	Balance b/d	210,564
Balance c/d	258,240	Purchases	
		– Cost of sales	1,021,830
		– Administration	96,077
	1,328,471		1,328,471

Tutorial note: information relating to non-current assets is not included in the payables ledger control account above in order to compute cash paid to suppliers of operating costs.

(W3) **Wages control**

	$		$
Net wages paid (bal fig)	239,890	Balance b/d	8,640
Balance c/d	14,650	Cost of sales	145,900
		Administration	100,000
	254,540		254,540

Non-current asset expenditure

Cash paid for non-current assets is 80,000 – 46,000 = $34,000. The $80,000 invoices agrees with the movement in non-current assets per the balance sheets.

(W4) **Non-current assets (NBV)**

	$		$
Balance b/d	153,364	Depreciation charge	84,000
Addition (bal fig)	80,000	Balance c/d	149,364
	233,364		233,364

Tutorial note: Net cash inflow from operating activities could have been derived from operating profit as follows:

Reconciliation of operating profit to net cash inflow from operating activities

	$
Operating profit	141,640
Depreciation charges	84,000
Increase in inventory	–
Increase in receivables	(80,160)
Increase in payables (excluding those for non-current assets)	53,686
	199,166

3.4 Non-cash transactions

Non-cash transactions, such as a revaluation of non-current assets, cannot appear in the cash flow statement. They may, however, need to be included in workings calculating other figures needed for the statement.

3.5 Approach to examination question

The summarised financial statements of Charlton, a limited company, are as follows:

(a) **Balance sheets at 31 December**

	20X5	*20X6*
	$	$
Non-current assets (net book value)	40,406	47,759
Inventory	27,200	30,918
Receivables	15,132	18,363
Bank	4,016	2,124
	86,754	99,164
Share capital	40,000	50,000
Share premium	8,000	10,000
Accumulated profit	19,933	22,748
Loan notes	10,000	–
Payables	3,621	10,416
Taxation	5,200	6,000
	86,754	99,164

(b) **Income statement for the year ended 31 December 20X6**

	$
Profit (after charging depreciation of $2,363 and interest of $900)	17,215
Taxation	6,000
Profit after tax	11,215

An interim dividend of $2,000 was paid during the year, as well as a final dividend for the year ended 31 December 20X5 of $6,400.

An item of machinery with a net book value of $1,195 was sold for $1,614. The depreciation charge of $2,363 does not include the profit/loss on the sale of the non-current asset.

You are required to prepare a cash flow statement for the year ended 31 December 20X6.

Solution

Step 1

Allocate a page to the cash flow statement so that easily identifiable cash flows can be inserted. Use a separate page if the main statement is likely to be long. Allocate a further page to workings.

Step 2

Go through the balance sheets and take the balance sheet movements to the cash flow statement or to workings as appropriate. Tick off the information in the balance sheets once it has been used.

Step 3

Go through the additional information provided and deal with as per Step 2.

Step 4

The amounts transferred to workings can now be reconciled so that the remaining cash flows can be inserted on the statement.

Step 5

Complete the cash flow statement.

Charlton
Cash flow statement for the year ended 31 December 20X6

	$	$
Cash flows from operating activities		
Net profit before taxation	17,215	
Adjustment for:		
Depreciation	2,363	
Profit on sale of non-current asset (W1)	(419)	
Interest expense	900	
Operating profit before working capital changes	20,059	
Increase in inventory	(3,718)	
Increase in receivables	(3,231)	
Increase in payables (10,416 – 3,621)	6,795	
Cash generated from operations	19,905	
Interest paid	(900)	
Dividends paid	(8,400)	
Tax paid (W2)	(5,200)	
Net cash from operating activities		5,405
Cash flows from investing activities		
Purchase of non-current assets (W1)	(10,911)	
Proceeds of sale of non-current assets	1,614	
Net cash used in investing activities		(9,297)
Cash flows from financing activities		
Proceeds of issue of shares (10,000 + 2,000)	12,000	
Repayment of loan	(10,000)	
Net cash from financing activities		2,000
Net decrease in cash and cash equivalents		(1,892)
Cash and cash equivalents at 1 January 20X6		4,016
Cash and cash equivalents at 31 December 20X6		2,124

Cash and cash equivalents

	31 December 20X5	*31 December 20X6*
	$	$
Cash at bank	4,016	2,124

Workings

(W1) **Non-current assets – NBV**

	$		$
Balance b/d	40,406	Non-current assets disposal	1,195
Bank (bal fig)	10,911	Depreciation (income statement)	2,363
		Balance c/d	47,759
	51,317		51,317

Tutorial note: the above account summarises the balances and transactions relating to non-current assets during the year. It was necessary to combine non-current asset cost and non-current asset depreciation in one account because only the net book values were given.

The account is required in order to derive the expenditure on non-current assets for the year.

Non-current assets disposal

	$		$
Non-current assets – NBV	1,195	Bank	1,614
Profit on sale (income statement)	419		
	1,614		1,614

(W2) **Taxation**

	$		$
Bank (bal fig)	5,200	Balance b/d	5,200
Balance c/d	6,000	Income statement	6,000
	11,200		11,200

Tutorial note: the taxation paid in the year has been last year's charge. Often there will be a change from last year's estimate and thus a ledger account will derive the correct figure paid.

This question is probably as hard as any you will get in the examination. All of the problems in it could arise, but it is unlikely that they will all arise in one question.

4 Interpretation using the cash flow statement

4.1 Introduction

The next chapter deals with the interpretation of financial statements, using ratios largely based on the income statement and balance sheet. To conclude this chapter on cash flow statements we shall review the information users may derive from the cash flow statement.

4.2 Objective of IAS 7

The objective of IAS 7 is to require the provision of information about the historical changes in cash and cash equivalents in a cash flow statement in which cash flows are classified under the three headings – operating, investing and financing activities.

KEY POINT

Cash flow statement shows:

- whether overall activities reveal a positive cash flow
- whether operating activities yield positive cash flow
- how capital expenditure has been financed.

4.3 Information revealed by the cash flow statement

- Whether the overall activities reveal a positive cash flow.
- Whether the operating activities yield a positive cash flow.
- The manner in which the capital expenditure has been financed (for example, whether it has come from internally-generated resources, borrowings, issues of shares or from cash balances).

4.4 An appraisal of the requirements of IAS 7

Formats

The formats in IAS 7 are illustrative only and not obligatory. However, it makes sense to follow them in examination work and they have been followed throughout this chapter.

Benefits of cash flow statements to users

Cash flow statements provide:

- information as to how the enterprise generates and uses cash and cash equivalents
- information to allow an evaluation of changes in net assets, financial structure (including liquidity and solvency) and the ability of the enterprise to adapt to changing circumstances
- information to assess the ability of the enterprise to generate cash
- information which is comparable between different enterprises because the effects of using different accounting treatments are eliminated
- the means by which forecasts of future cash flows may be made
- the means by which the accuracy of past assessments of future cash flows may be checked.

Conclusion

This chapter has concentrated on the computational techniques involved in the preparation of a cash flow statement. If such a question comes up in the examination you should find that most of the marks are fairly easy to obtain. Practice on the examples in the chapter will result in the IAS 7 format becoming second nature.

Do not ignore, however, the possibility of a written question. The information in the chapter will be useful in this regard.

SELF-TEST QUESTIONS

Cash flow statements

1 What are the standard headings in a cash flow statement? (2.1, 2.2)

The requirements of IAS 7 *Cash Flow Statements*

2 What are the main categories of items to adjust profit for in order to arrive at net cash flow from operating activities? (2.2)

3 Is an increase in inventory a deduction or addition to operating profit in the cash flow statement? (2.2)

4 Is a decrease in payables a deduction or addition to operating profit in the cash flow statement? (2.2)

5 Is a decrease in receivables a deduction or addition to operating profit in the cash flow statement? (2.2)

6 Are receipts from the sale of non-current assets an investing activity or a financing activity? (2.2)

Preparation of cash flow statement

7 Is a surplus on the revaluation of property included in the cash flow statement? (3.4)

MULTIPLE-CHOICE QUESTION

IAS 7 *Cash Flow Statements* requires the cash flow statement prepared using the indirect method to include the calculation of net cash from operating activities.

Which of the following lists consists only of items which could appear in such a calculation?

A Depreciation, increase in receivables, decrease in payables, proceeds of sale of plant.

B Increase in payables, decrease in inventories, profit on sale of plant, depreciation.

C Increase in payables, depreciation, decrease in receivables, proceeds of sale of plant.

D Depreciation, interest paid, equity dividends paid, purchase of plant.

For the answer to this question, see the 'Answers' section at the end of the book.

PRACTICE QUESTIONS

Question 1: Bogdanovitch

The summarised financial statements of Bogdanovitch, a limited company, are as follows.

(a) **Balance sheet as at 31 December**

	20X8		*20X9*	
	$	$	$	$
Non-current assets:				
Plant and machinery		2,086		2,103
Fixtures and fittings		1,381		1,296
		3,467		3,399
Current assets:				
Inventory	1,292		1,952	
Receivables	1,763		2,086	
Cash	197		512	
		3,252		4,550

		6,719		7,949
Capital and reserves:				
Equity capital	4,200		4,500	
Share premium	800		900	
Accumulated profit	563		1,334	
		5,563		6,734
Current liabilities:				
Trade payables	899		903	
Taxation	257		312	
		1,156		1,215
		6,719		7,949

(b) **Income statement for year ended 31 December 20X9**

	$
Profit before tax	1,381
Tax	310
Profit for year	1,071

Dividends paid in the year

	$
Final for year ended 31 December 20X8	132
Interim for year ended 31 December 20X9	168

You are informed that:

(a) plant and machinery with a net book value of $184 was disposed of for $203, whilst a new item of plant was purchased for $312

(b) fixtures and fittings with a net book value of $100 were disposed of for $95. Depreciation provided on fixtures and fittings amounted to $351.

You are required to prepare a cash flow statement for the year ended 31 December 20X9. **(20 marks)**

Question 2: Algernon

You are given below, in summarised form, the accounts of Algernon, a limited company, for 20X6 and 20X7.

	20X6 Balance sheet			*20X7 Balance sheet*		
	Cost	*Dep'n*	*Net*	*Cost*	*Dep'n*	*Net*
	$	$	$	$	$	$
Plant	10,000	4,000	6,000	11,000	5,000	6,000
Buildings	50,000	10,000	40,000	90,000	11,000	79,000
			46,000			85,000
Investments at cost			50,000			80,000
Land			43,000			63,000
Inventory			55,000			65,000
Receivables			40,000			50,000
Bank			3,000			
			237,000			343,000

Ordinary shares of $1 each	40,000	50,000
Share premium	12,000	14,000
Revaluation reserve (land)	–	20,000
Accumulated profit	45,000	45,000
10% Loan notes	100,000	150,000
Payables	40,000	60,000
Bank	–	4,000
	237,000	343,000

Income statements

	20X6	*20X7*
	$	$
Sales revenue	200,000	200,000
Cost of sales	(100,000)	(120,000)
	100,000	80,000
Expenses	(50,000)	(47,000)
	50,000	33,000
Interest	(10,000)	(13,000)
Net profit for year	40,000	20,000
Dividends for year (paid after the balance sheet dates)	20,000	20,000

You are required:

(a) To prepare a cash flow statement for Algernon for 20X7, to explain as far as possible the movement in the bank balance. The cash flow statement should be prepared using the *direct* method. **(10 marks)**

(b) Using the summarised accounts given, and the statement you have just prepared, comment on the position, progress and direction of Algernon. **(8 marks)**

(Total: 18 marks)

EXAM-TYPE QUESTION

Crash

The balance sheets of Crash, a limited liability company, at 31 March 2000 and 31 March 2001 were as follows:

	31 March 2000		*31 March 2001*	
	$000	$000	$000	$000
Non-current assets				
Cost or valuation	9,000		10,950	
Accumulated depreciation	(3,300)	5,700	(3,600)	7,350
Current assets				
Inventory	1,215		1,350	
Receivables	1,350		1,290	
Cash	60	2,625	105	2,745
		8,325		10,095
Issued share capital		2,250		3,000
Share premium account		750		1,200
Revaluation reserve		–		750
Accumulated profits		2,640		3,045
		5,640		7,995
Non-current liabilities: 10% loan notes		1,500		750
Current liabilities				

Trade payables	990		1,080	
Bank overdraft	195	1,185	270	1,350
		8,325		10,095

Notes

Non-current assets

- During the year non-current assets, which had cost $1,500,000 and which had a book value of $300,000 at 31 March 2000, were sold for $375,000.
- Land acquired in 1997 was revalued upwards by $750,000 in preparing the balance sheet at 31 March 2001.

Loan notes

- Interest is due half-yearly on 30 September and 31 March and was paid on the due dates.
- The company repaid $750,000 loan notes on 31 March 2001.
- Profit before interest for the year to 31 March 2001 was $555,000. No dividends were paid during the year.

Ignore taxation.

Required:

Prepare a cash flow statement for Crash for the year ended 31 March 2001 using the indirect method, complying as far as possible with the requirements of IAS 7 *Cash Flow Statements*. **(10 marks)**

For the answers to these questions, see the 'Answers' section at the end of the book.

Chapter 23

RATIOS: INTERPRETATION AND USEFULNESS

CHAPTER CONTENTS

Financial statements are prepared not as an end in themselves but in order that users can make decisions. The financial statements therefore need to be interpreted. The calculation of ratios, with which most of this chapter is concerned, allows the relationships between different parts of the financial statements to be more clearly seen.

Objectives

By the time you have finished this chapter you should be able to:

- calculate the ratios specified in the syllabus
- interpret the ratios
- suggest possible reasons for the results obtained.

1 Analysis of accounting statements and use of ratios

1.1 Users of accounting information

Users of accounting information have been stated in an earlier chapter. The main users we will normally be concerned with are management, lenders and shareholders (including potential shareholders).

1.2 Information relevant to each user group

The various users of financial statements require information for quite different purposes. There are a large number of ratios, not all of which will be relevant to a particular situation. It is therefore important to determine the precise information needs of the user, and the decisions he has to take after analysing the relevant information.

The needs of the three particular users may be summarised:

User	*Needs information for*
Management	Control of costs, improved profitability
Lenders	Borrowing and credit purposes
Shareholders and investment analysts	Investment decisions – buying and selling shares

Ask yourself the questions 'What decision is being made?' and 'What information is relevant to that decision?'

1.3 The shortcomings of interpretation

The main function for many users is to estimate the future. However, an estimation can only be made by interpretation of the past. There is thus a significant shortcoming in any interpretation as to its effectiveness in estimating the future.

Even if the needs of the user are more concerned with historical stewardship of the enterprise, there are limitations of interpretation as the information presented to the user is of necessity summarised in some form. The summarisation process may have the effect of distorting the nature of some of the information. For example, liabilities may be classified into those payable within one year and those payable beyond one year. Two loans which have two days difference in their payment date may well, as a consequence, be classified under separate headings. The user, unless he is provided with further information, will tend to take the two resultant totals at face value.

Finally, it should be noted that the emphasis on information produced by an enterprise is financial. In many cases, non-financial data would be useful in order to see a complete picture of the state of the organisation. Non-financial data includes for example, the number of employees in the organisation and the type of skills they possess or indicators of efficiency with which the organisation addresses complaints from customers.

1.4 Why understandability is an important characteristic of financial statements

A user needs to understand information in order to draw valid conclusions from it. He needs to understand the basis upon which it is prepared and this is an area where the accountant can advise the user.

Understanding the information presented will allow the user to determine when more information is required, i.e. what information is missing. Also, the user may need to re-analyse the data so that it is relevant to his particular needs. Financial information is presented in a certain way in order to satisfy a range of user needs and therefore it follows that it may need to be adapted for certain specific needs.

1.5 The major techniques of interpretation

The syllabus at this level of accounting emphasises the use of ratios to interpret information but this is only one stage in the interpretation process. A most important first step is to understand the environment in which the business operates.

Factors that need to be considered include:

Markets in which the enterprise operates

Consideration needs to be given to the growth opportunities in the market. Is it a new and expanding market or is there an expectation that the market is contracting? It is far easier to make profits in a market which is expanding than in one that is contracting.

General economic conditions

The state of the economy in which the enterprise operates will affect its ability to make sales. If the economy is in recession, then it will be harder for an enterprise which sells goods to the public to make profits.

Size of business in relation to competitors

The success or failure of an enterprise can be related to its size relative to its competitors in the market. In some markets it is necessary to be large in order to benefit from economies of scale, such as advertising branded products.

Other markets may suit small units of operation which can be more flexible to the needs of customers.

In the context of examination questions much of this information is not available and thus we start at the calculation of ratios stage.

KEY POINT

When **calculating ratios**:

- calculate only those ratios relevant to the user
- state the definitions used.

When calculating ratios, the two main points to bear in mind are as follows:

- Calculate only those ratios which are relevant to the needs of the user.
- State the definitions used.

Some ratios can be calculated in alternative ways and therefore it is important to define the terms used.

Having calculated the ratios, the results must be analysed. Consideration needs to be given to such matters as these:

- If a ratio has been computed over a number of time periods, does it show a worsening or an improving situation?
- Can the ratio be compared to an objective standard? That is, can it be compared with an 'ideal' ratio?
- Do all the ratios when taken together support the conclusions drawn from each individual ratio?

The final stage of interpretation is the critical review.

The limitations of the data used to calculate the ratios need to be considered so that a prudent overall conclusion can be reached.

1.6 The technique of ratio analysis and its potential shortcomings

KEY POINT

Ratios allow us to compare:

- with previous years
- with the same year (budgeted or planned)
- with other businesses.

The information gathered by calculating ratios will allow comparisons with:

- the performance of the business in previous years
- the budgeted or planned performance in the current year
- the performance of similar businesses.

The ratios themselves do not tell one what to do, but they do help to point one in the right direction. Ratios should, therefore, make it easier to make better decisions.

It must be emphasised that accounting ratios are only a means to an end; they are not an end in themselves. By comparing the relationship between figures, they merely highlight significant features or trends in the accounts. Indeed, they may well create more problems than they solve. The real art of interpreting accounts lies in defining the reasons for the features and fluctuations disclosed. To do this effectively, you may need more information and a deeper insight into the affairs of the business. You also need to bear in mind the following points.

- The date at which the accounts are drawn up. Accurate information can only be obtained with any degree of certainty from up-to-date figures. Furthermore, seasonal variations in the particular trade should be taken into account. Final accounts tend to be drawn up at the end of seasonal trade when the picture they present is of the business at its strongest point financially.
- The accuracy of the position shown in the balance sheet. The arrangement of certain matters can be misleading and present a more favourable picture, e.g. such 'window-dressing' operations as:
  - making a special effort to collect debts just before the year-end in order to show a larger cash balance and lower receivables than is normal
  - ordering goods to be delivered just after the year-end so that stocks and creditors can be kept as low as possible.
- Interim accounts. Whenever possible, interested parties should examine accounts prepared on a monthly basis, as a clearer picture of the trends and fluctuations will emerge from these than from the annual financial statements.

- Accounting ratios are based on accounting information and are, therefore, only as accurate as the underlying accounting information. At a time, as at present, when traditional accounting procedures are coming in for heavy criticism, students should remember that ratios based on those procedures can be easily criticised.
- The accounting ratios of one company must be compared with those of another similar company in order to draw meaningful conclusions. These conclusions will only be valid if that other company's trade is similar.

2 Using ratios

2.1 Types of ratios

KEY POINT

Ratio groupings:

- operating
- short-term liquidity
- working capital efficiency
- medium and long-term solvency
- investor.

Ratios fall into several groups, the relevance of particular ratios depending on the purpose for which they are required. The groups to be considered here are as follows:

- operating ratios
- short-term liquidity ratios
- working capital efficiency
- medium and long-term solvency ratios
- investor ratios.

Illustration

The above ratios will be illustrated by reference to the following:

Summarised balance sheets at 30 June

	20X7		*20X6*	
	$'000	$'000	$'000	$'000
Non-current assets (net book value)		130		139
Current assets:				
Inventory	42		37	
Receivables	29		23	
Bank	3		5	
		74		65
		204		204
Ordinary share capital (50c shares)		35		35
8% Preference shares ($1 shares)		25		25
Share premium		17		17
Revaluation reserve		10		-
Accumulated profits		31		22
		118		99
Long-term liabilities:				
5% secured loan notes		40		40
Current liabilities:				
Trade payables	36		55	
Tax	10		10	
		46		65
		204		204

Summarised income statement for the year ended 30 June

	20X7		20X6	
	$'000	$'000	$'000	$'000
Sales revenue		209		196
Opening inventory	37		29	
Purchases	162		159	
	199		188	
Closing inventory	42		37	
		157		151
Gross profit		52		45
Interest	2		2	
Depreciation	9		9	
Sundry expenses	14		11	
		25		22
Net profit		27		23
Tax		10		10
Net profit after tax		17		13
Dividends paid were:				
Ordinary		6		5
Preference		2		2
		8		7

2.2 The ratios which primarily measure profitability

There are several ratios which attempt to assess the profitability of a business. These are more conveniently expressed in percentage form and include:

The gross profit percentage

DEFINITION

The **gross profit percentage:** Gross profit is expressed as a percentage of sales.

Gross profit is expressed as a percentage of sales, i.e.:

$$\text{Gross profit percentage} = \frac{\text{Profit}}{\text{Sales}} \times 100$$

This is a very popular ratio and is used by even the smallest of businesses. In the illustration, the ratios for the two years are as follows:

Example	*20X7*	*20X6*
Gross profit percentage	$\frac{52}{209} \times 100 = 24.9\%$	$\frac{45}{196} \times 100 = 23.0\%$

What can be learned from these figures? Clearly, the gross profit percentage has improved but it is not known why. Nor is it obvious whether these figures are better or worse than those which would be expected in a similar type of business. Before coming to definite conclusions one would need further information. For example, most enterprises sell a wide range of products, usually with different gross profit percentages (or profit margins). It may be that in 20X7 the **sales mix** changed and that a larger proportion of items with a high profit percentage were sold, thus increasing the overall gross profit percentage of the enterprise.

Percentage change in sales

DEFINITION

The **percentage change in sales:** Change in sales as a percentage of sales.

It is relevant to consider the change in sales at this point. This is measured by:

$$\text{Percentage growth in sales} = \frac{\text{Sales this year} - \text{Sales last year}}{\text{Sales last year}} \times 100$$

Example

$$\text{Percentage change in sales} = \frac{209 - 196}{196} \times 100 = 6.6\%$$

This is perhaps not a significant increase. A larger increase might have given some evidence of the type of changes in trading conditions that may have occurred.

Net profit as a percentage of sales

DEFINITION

Net profit as a percentage of sales.

This ratio is defined as:

$$\frac{\text{Net profit}}{\text{Sales}} \times 100$$

Example	*20X7*	*20X6*
Net profit as % sales	$\frac{27}{209} \times 100 = 12.9\%$	$\frac{23}{196} \times 100 = 11.7\%$

As an alternative the net profit before interest could be taken for this ratio (29 in 20X7 and 25 in 20X6).

What conclusions can be drawn from this apparent improvement? Very few! Since net profit equals gross profit less expenses, it would be useful to tabulate, for each of the two years, the various expenses and express them as a percentage of sales. A suitable tabulation might be:

Expenses as a percentage of sales

		20X7		*20X6*
	$'000	%	$'000	%
Sales	209	100.0	196	100.0
Cost of sales	157	75.1	151	77.0
Gross profit	52	24.9	45	23.0
Interest	(2)	(1.0)	(2)	(1.1)
Depreciation	(9)	(4.3)	(9)	(4.6)
Sundry expenses	(14)	(6.7)	(11)	(5.6)
Net profit	27	12.9	23	11.7

Given a detailed income statement, the above type of summary could be very useful. Care must be taken in interpreting the results, particularly since sales ($) are used as the denominator. An increase in sales ($) could be due to a combination of price and quantity effects.

Return on capital employed (ROCE)

This is an important ratio as it relates profit to the capital invested in a business. Finance for an enterprise is only available at a cost – loan finance requires interest payments and further finance from shareholders requires either the immediate payment of dividends or the expectation of higher dividends in the future. Therefore an enterprise needs to maximise the profits per $ of capital employed.

Due to its importance the ROCE is sometimes referred to as the **primary ratio**.

There are several ways of measuring ROCE, but the essential point is to relate the profit figure used to its capital base, e.g.

DEFINITION

Total capital employed in the business.

Total capital employed in the business

$$\text{ROCE (1)} = \frac{\text{Profit before interest and tax}}{\text{Share capital} + \text{Reserves} + \text{Long term liabilities}} \times 100$$

The denominator in this version of the ratio could alternatively be calculated as total assets less current liabilities.

DEFINITION

Equity shareholders' capital employed.

Equity shareholders' capital employed

$$\text{ROCE (2)} = \frac{\text{Profit after interest and preference dividend but before tax}}{\text{Ordinary share capital} + \text{Reserves}} \times 100$$

Points to note

- The interest referred to is the interest payable on the long-term liabilities. Any interest on short-term liabilities, such as a bank overdraft, is deducted from the profit, i.e. the numerator and the denominator must be computed on a consistent basis.
- The denominator in this second version of the ratio could alternatively be calculated as net assets less preference shares.
- Although it is better to base the calculation on average capital employed during the year, the calculation is often based on year-end capital employed (because there is insufficient data for all years to compute an average).

ACTIVITY 1

Calculate ROCE for 20X6 and 20X7 using each of these alternatives.

Feedback to this activity is at the end of the chapter.

2.3 Structure of operating ratios

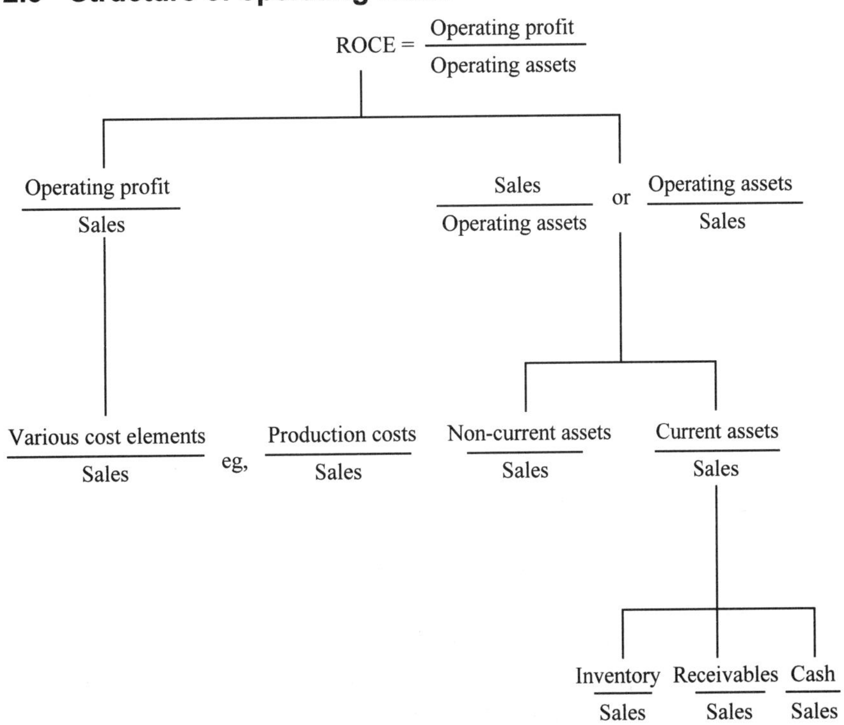

2.4 Factors affecting return on capital employed

There are two factors relevant here:

- profitability of sales
- rate of asset utilisation.

The product of these two gives the return on capital employed:

$$\frac{\text{Operating profit}}{\text{Sales}} \times \frac{\text{Sales}}{\text{Operating assets}} = \frac{\text{Operating profit}}{\text{Operating assets}} = \text{ROCE}$$

In the example for 20X7:

$$\frac{\text{Operating profit}}{\text{Sales}}$$

$$\frac{\text{Sales}}{\text{Operating assets}} = \frac{\$209{,}000}{\$158{,}000} = 1.32$$

Note

13.9% × 1.32 × 100 = 18.3%, i.e. ROCE subject to a rounding difference.

One may, in turn, subdivide these into their component elements.

2.5 Factors affecting operating profit/sales

This ratio may be subdivided as far as detail in our profit and loss account permits, since:

$$\frac{\text{Operating profit}}{\text{Sales}} + \frac{\text{Cost elements}}{\text{Sales}} = 1$$

Cost elements may include production, marketing, distribution, administration and so on.

2.6 Factors affecting operating assets/sales

In the first place, operating assets may be subdivided into non-current and current assets, since:

$$\frac{\text{Operating assets}}{\text{Sales}} = \frac{\text{Non - current assets}}{\text{Sales}} + \frac{\text{Current assets}}{\text{Sales}}$$

Each of these may be appropriately subdivided, e.g.:

Non-current assets = plant and machinery + land + etc.

Current assets = inventory + receivables + cash + etc.

Thus, two of the ratios give the months' inventory and receivables carried by the company.

From the analysis it becomes clear that the subdivision of the key ratio, return on capital employed, is limited only by the detail in the data available. The important point to remember is that in each case the ultimate result is directly related to each individual ratio by the pyramid, i.e. there is an arithmetical relationship between all the pyramid ratios, so it is possible to determine the effect that a change in one of the ratios will have on the key ratio – return on capital employed.

3 Liquidity and funds management

3.1 Short term liquidity ratios

The two main ratios are:

DEFINITION

Total current ratio is assets/liabilities.

The **current ratio** is the ratio of current assets to current liabilities, i.e.:

$$\text{Current ratio} = \frac{\text{Current assets}}{\text{Current liabilities}}$$

In the case of our example, the ratios for the two years are:

The current ratio is sometimes referred to as the working capital ratio.

Example	*20X7*	*20X6*
Current ratio	$\frac{74}{46} = 1.61:1$	$\frac{65}{65} = 1.0:1$

DEFINITION

The liquidity (or quick) ratio is assets (less inventory)/ liabilities.

The **liquidity (or quick) ratio** is the ratio of current assets excluding inventory to current liabilities, i.e.:

$$\text{Quick ratio} = \frac{\text{Current assets (less inventory)}}{\text{Current liabilities}}$$

In the case of our example, the ratios for the two years are:

Both of these ratios show a strengthening.

Example	*20X7*	*20X6*
Liquidity (quick) ratio	$\frac{32}{46} = 0.7:1$	$\frac{28}{65} = 0.43:1$

Both of these ratios show a strengthening.

The extent of the change between the two years seems surprising and would require further investigation.

It would also be useful to know how these ratios compare with those of a similar enterprise, since typical ratios for supermarkets are quite different from those for heavy engineering firms.

What can be said is that in 20X7 the current liabilities were well covered by current assets. Liabilities payable in the near future, however, are only half covered by cash and receivables.

Conventional wisdom has it that an ideal current ratio is 2:1 and an ideal quick ratio is 1:1. It is very tempting to draw definite conclusions from limited information or to say that the current ratio *should* be 2, or that the liquid ratio *should* be 1. However, this is not very meaningful without taking into account the type of ratio expected in a similar business. Many enterprises manage on much lower ratios than this.

It should also be noted that a high current or liquid ratio is not necessarily a good thing. It may indicate that working capital is not being used efficiently. The next group of ratios can help to identify whether or not this is the case.

3.2 Elements of working capital

It is necessary to consider three ratios concerned with current assets and current liabilities:

(a) **Inventory turnover ratio**

Companies have to strike a balance between being able to satisfy customers' requirements out of inventory and the cost of having too much capital tied up in inventory.

DEFINITION

The **inventory turnover ratio** is the cost of sales divided by the average level of inventory during the year.

The inventory turnover ratio is the cost of sales divided by the average level of inventory during the year, i.e.:

$$\text{Inventory turnover ratio} = \frac{\text{Cost of sales}}{\text{Average inventory level}}$$

For our example, the figures are as follows.

Example	*20X7*	*20X6*
Inventory turnover ratio	$\frac{157}{1/2(37+42)} = 4.0$ times p.a.	$\frac{151}{1/2(29+37)} = 4.6$ times p.a.

The inventory turnover ratio has fallen.

Note: the average of opening and closing inventory is used here, but examination questions frequently do not provide the opening inventory figure and the **closing** inventory has to be taken instead of the average inventory. In any case, the average of opening and closing inventory will not necessarily give the true average level of inventory during the year if the inventory fluctuates a lot from month to month.

Unless the nature of the business is known, it is not possible to say whether either 4.6 or 4.0 is satisfactory or unsatisfactory. A jeweller will have a low inventory turnover ratio, but it is hoped that a fishmonger selling fresh fish has a very high turnover ratio.

DEFINITION

An alternative definition of inventory turnover ratio is the ratio of average inventory to cost of sales.

An alternative calculation of the inventory turnover ratio is to show the result in days. The calculation is as follows.

$$\text{Inventory turnover ratio} = \frac{\text{Average inventory during the accounting period}}{\text{Cost of sales}} \times 365$$

Where 365 days is the length of accounting period.

So, for our example, the periods are:

Example	*20X7*	*20X6*
Inventory turnover ratio	$\frac{(37+42)/2}{157} \times 365 = 92$ days	$\frac{(29+37)/2}{151} \times 365 = 80$ days

(b) **Receivables collection period (or average period of credit allowed to customers)**

Businesses which sell goods on credit terms specify a credit period. Failure to send out invoices on time or to follow up late payers will have an adverse effect on the cash flow of the business.

DEFINITION

The **receivables collection period** is the ratio of closing trade receivables to the average daily credit sales.

The receivables collection period relates closing trade debts to the average daily credit sales. It is calculated by:

$$\text{Receivables collection period} = \frac{\text{Closing trade receivables}}{\text{Average daily credit sales}}$$

Example	*20X7*	*20X6*
Credit sales per day	$\frac{\$209{,}000}{365} = \$573$	$\frac{\$196{,}000}{365} = \$537$
Closing trade receivables	\$29,000	\$23,000
Receivables collection period	$\frac{\$29{,}000}{\$573} = 50.6 \text{ days}$	$\frac{\$23{,}000}{\$537} = 42.8 \text{ days}$

Compared with 20X6 the receivables collection period has worsened in 20X7 but is still low in current conditions.

If the average credit allowed to customers was, say, thirty days, then something is clearly wrong. Further investigation might reveal delays in sending out invoices or failure to 'screen' new customers.

The quickest way to compute the receivables collection period is to use the formula:

$$\frac{\text{Closing trade receivables}}{\text{Credit sales for year}} \times 365$$

Example	*20X7*	*20X6*
Receivables collection period	$\frac{29{,}000}{209{,}000} \times 365 = 50.6 \text{ days}$	$\frac{23{,}000}{196{,}000} \times 365 = 42.8 \text{ days}$

Average period of credit allowed by suppliers

DEFINITION

The average period of credit allowed to suppliers relates closing creditors to average daily credit purchases.

This relates closing creditors to average daily credit purchases, i.e.:

$$\text{Average period of credit} = \frac{\text{Closing trade payables}}{\text{Credit purchases per day}}$$

Example	*20X7*	*20X6*
Credit purchases per day	$\frac{\$162{,}000}{365} = \$444$	$\frac{\$159{,}000}{365} = \$436$
Closing trade payables	\$36,000	\$55,000
Average period of credit allowed by suppliers	81.1 days	126.3 days

The average period of credit allowed has fallen substantially from last year. It is however, in absolute terms still a high figure.

Often, suppliers request payment within 30 days. The company is taking nearly three months. Trade payables are thus financing much of the working capital requirements of the enterprise which is beneficial to the company in some ways.

However, there are three potential disadvantages of extending the credit period:

- Future supplies may be endangered.
- Possibility of cash discounts is lost.
- Suppliers may quote a higher price for the goods knowing the extended credit taken by the company.

The quick calculation is:

$$\frac{\text{Closing trade payables}}{\text{Credit purchases for year}} \times 365$$

This gives us:

Example	*20X7*	*20X6*
Credit purchases per day	$\frac{36,000}{162,000} \times 365 = 81.1$ days	$\frac{55,000}{159,000} \times 365 = 126.3$ days

3.3 The working capital cycle

The investment made in working capital is largely a function of sales and, therefore, it is useful to consider the problem in terms of a firm's working capital (or **cash operating**) cycle.

The cash operating cycle

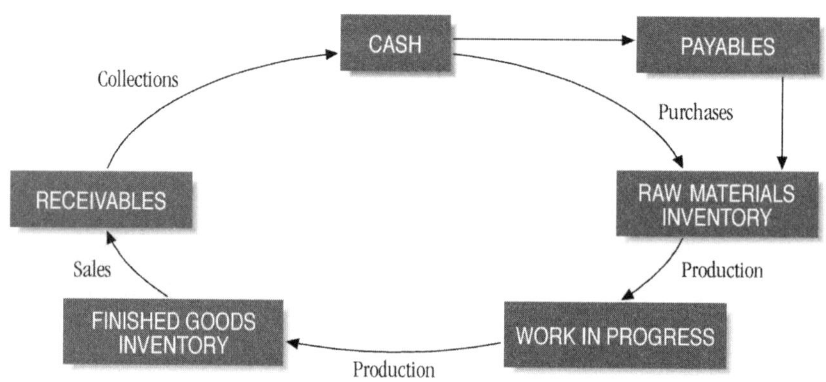

The cycle reflects a firm's investment in working capital as it moves through the production process towards sales. The investment in working capital gradually increases, firstly being only in raw materials, but then in labour and overheads as production progresses. This investment must be maintained throughout the production process, the finished goods holding period and up to the final collection of cash from trade receivables. Note that the net investment can be reduced by taking trade credit from suppliers.

The faster a firm can 'push' items around the operating cycle the lower its investment in working capital will be. However, too little investment in working capital can lose sales, since customers will generally prefer to buy from suppliers who are prepared to extend trade credit, and if items are not held in inventory when required by customers, sales may be lost.

With some fairly basic financial information, it is possible to measure the length of the working capital cycle for a given firm.

Example

Extracts from the income statement for the year and the balance sheet as at the end of the year for a company show:

Profit and loss and balance sheet extracts

	$
Sales revenue	250,000
Cost of goods sold	210,000
Purchases	140,000
Trade receivables	31,250
Trade payables	21,000
Inventory	92,500

Note: assume all sales and purchases are on credit terms.

Calculate the working capital cycle.

Solution

Payables

$$\text{Average payment collection period} = \left(365 \times \frac{\text{Payables}}{\text{Purchases}}\right) \qquad = 55 \text{ days}$$

$$= 365 \times \frac{21}{140}$$

Receivables

$$\text{Average collection period} = \left(365 \times \frac{\text{Receivables}}{\text{Sales}}\right) \qquad = 46 \text{ days}$$

$$= 365 \times \frac{31.25}{250}$$

Inventory turnover

$$= 365 \times \frac{\text{Inventory}}{\text{Cost of goods sold}} \qquad = 161 \text{ days}$$

$$= 365 \times \frac{92.5}{210}$$

Length of working capital cycle = 152 days

3.4 Overtrading

An expanding business may find itself short of working capital. If increased sales on credit are made, receivables rise and the business is likely to have difficulty in finding the cash to pay suppliers, wages and other expenses as it has to wait for customers to pay. The term 'overtrading' may be used to describe the condition of such a business. Several steps are available to remedy the situation:

- obtain a bank overdraft to smooth out cash flows
- issue extra shares to increase cash resources or, for a sole trader or partnership, have the owners introduce more capital
- make longer term borrowings, again to increase cash resources
- negotiate longer credit terms from major suppliers
- sell non-trading assets such as investments

- offer customers discounts for prompt payment
- try to make cash sales as well as credit sales

Movements in accounting ratios or figures in the balance sheet can indicate overtrading. Points to look for include:

- deterioration in quick ratio or current ratio
- overdraft at or near its limit
- increase in trade payables as payments to suppliers are delayed
- increase in sales revenue and trade receivables.

3.5 Equity to assets ratio

The manner in which a company is financed is crucial to an assessment of its stability and the risk of its collapse.

A company with high loans compared with equity capital is at greater risk than one with few or no loans, because the interest on the loans has to be paid regardless of whether a company makes a profit or not.

We may measure the extent to which the company is exposed to this risk by calculating the **equity to assets ratio**.

The calculation is:

$$\frac{\text{Equity capital plus reserves}}{\text{Total assets minus current liabilities}} \times 100$$

Example	*20X7*	*20X6*
Equity to assets ratio	$\frac{35+17+10+31}{204-46} \times 100 = 58.9\%$	$\frac{35+17+22}{204-65} \times 100 = 53.2\%$

These are both fairly low values – the company has significant borrowings and preference share capital, and is thus fairly vulnerable if there should be a downturn in profits.

3.6 Gearing ratio

KEY POINT

Gearing is the proportion of a company's total capital provided by loan capital as opposed to equity.

The equity to assets ratio measures the mix of equity funding and debt funding that a company has chosen in its balance sheet. Low equity to assets means high debt and therefore potential risk. Another way of calculating this mix is to look at the gearing ration (also called leverage).

$$\text{Gearing ratio} = \frac{\text{Loans + Preference share capital}}{\text{Total assets} - \text{Current liabilities}}$$

A high gearing ration means a low equity to assets ratio, and vice versa. High gearing therefore means that the company is exposed to the risk of collapse if profit levels fall.

3.7 The advantages and disadvantages of raising finance by issuing loan notes or bonds

The equity to assets ratio may have an important effect on the distribution of profits. For example, consider two companies with different capital structures. The return of the ordinary shareholders can vary considerably.

	A Ltd	*B Ltd*
	$	$
Capital structure:		
10% Loan notes	20,000	-
Ordinary share capital and reserves	10,000	30,000
	30,000	30,000

If profits before interest are (a) $4,000, (b) $8,000, what is the effect on profits available to the shareholders in each company?

Solution

	A Ltd	*B Ltd*
	$	$
(a) Profits $4,000 before interest		
∴ Returns:		
10% Interest	2,000	-
Ordinary shares – balance	2,000	4,000
	4,000	4,000
(b) Profits double to $8,000 before interest		
∴ Returns:		
10% Interest	2,000	-
Ordinary shares – balance	6,000	8,000
	8,000	8,000
Therefore, increase in return to ordinary shareholders	3 times	2 times

Thus, the doubling of the profits in year 2 has the effect of tripling the return to the equity shareholders in A. The effect would be even more dramatic if the profits fell below $2,000 because then there would be no return at all to the ordinary shareholders in A. Thus an investment in ordinary shares in a company with large loans is a far more speculative investment than a purchase of ordinary shares in a company with low loans.

3.8 Interest cover

Interest on loan notes must be paid whether or not the company makes a profit. This ratio emphasises the cover (or security) for the interest by relating profit before interest and tax to interest paid.

Example	*20X7*	*20X6*
Interest cover	$\frac{52-9-14}{2} = \frac{29}{2}$	$\frac{45-9-11}{2} = \frac{25}{2}$
	= 14.5 times	= 12.5 times

From the point of view of medium and long term solvency, the company is in a strong position as regards the payment of interest. Profit would have to drop considerably before any problem of paying interest arose.

The impact of the preference dividend should also be calculated in considering the safety of the ordinary dividend – see next section.

4 Ratios for investment appraisal

4.1 Information required by investors

An investor is interested in the income earned by the company for him and the return on his investment (the income earned related to the market price of the investment).

An investor in ordinary shares can look to the earnings of the company available to pay the ordinary dividend or to the actual ordinary dividend paid as a measure of the income earned by the company for him. The ratios he would compute in each case would be:

Dividends	*Earnings*
Dividends per share	Earnings per share
Times covered	Price earnings ratio
Dividend yield	

Suppose that the company in the illustration is quoted on a Stock Exchange and that the market value of each ordinary share is 204 cents.

4.2 Dividend per share

This relates to ordinary shares and is calculated as follows:

$$\text{Dividend per share} = \frac{\text{Dividend paid}}{\text{Number of shares}}$$

Example	*20X7*	*20X6*
Dividend per share	$\frac{\$6{,}000}{70{,}000} = 8.6\text{c per share}$	$\frac{\$5{,}000}{70{,}000} = 7.1\text{c per share}$

4.3 Dividend cover

This is calculated by dividing profit available for ordinary shareholders by the dividend for the year (i.e. interim plus final) as follows:

$$\text{Dividend cover} = \frac{\text{Profit} - \text{Payment to preference shareholders}}{\text{Dividend paid}}$$

Example	*20X7*	*20X6*
Dividend cover	$\frac{\$17{,}000 - \$2{,}000}{\$6{,}000}$	$\frac{\$13{,}000 - \$2{,}000}{\$5{,}000}$
	= 2.5 times	= 2.2 times

Note that the profits available for ordinary shareholders are after the deduction of the preference dividend. The cover represents the 'security' for the ordinary dividend – in this company the cover is reasonable.

4.4 Dividend yield

This expresses dividend per share as a percentage of the current share price.
The dividend yield at today's date is:

$$\frac{8.6\text{c}}{204\text{c}} \times 100 = 4.2\%$$

4.5 Earnings per share

When a company pays a dividend, the directors take many factors into account, including the need to retain profits for future expansion. Earnings per share looks at the profits which could in theory be paid to each ordinary shareholder.

Earnings are profits after tax and preference dividends, but before ordinary dividends.

The denominator is:

The number of equity shares in issue.

Example	*20X7*	*20X6*
Earnings per share (EPS)	$\frac{\$17,000 - \$2,000}{70,000}$	$\frac{\$13,000 - \$2,000}{70,000}$
	= 21.4c per share	= 15.7c per share

4.6 Price earnings ratio (P/E ratio)

This is regarded as a most important ratio. It expresses the current share price (market value) as a multiple of the earnings per share. For 20X7, the price earnings ratio is:

$$\frac{204\text{c}}{21.4\text{c}} = 9.5$$

The ratio of 9.5 implies that if the current rate of EPS is maintained it will take nine and a half years to repay the cost of investing. The higher the PE ratio the longer the payback period. Thus we could conclude that the lower the PE ratio, the better investment it is. However, this is not generally the case. *High* PE ratios are generally viewed as better than low ones.

The apparent paradox is resolved if the forward looking nature of Stock Exchange investments is considered. The PE ratio is based on **current** EPS but the stock market is pricing the share on expectations of **future** EPS. If the market considers that a company has significant growth prospects, the market price of the share will rise.

4.7 Earnings yield

This term is not often referred to these days. It expresses the earnings per share as a percentage of the current share price, i.e.:

$$\text{Earnings yield} = \frac{21.4\text{c}}{204\text{c}} \times 100 = 10.5\%$$

It is merely the reciprocal of the PE ratio:

$$\frac{1}{\text{PE ratio}} = \text{Earnings yield}$$

$$\frac{1}{95} = 0.105, \text{ i.e. } 10.5\%$$

4.8 Determination of the value of a share

We saw in the above example that a value of 204c was given for each ordinary share. How did this value arise?

A number of factors give rise to a share price on the Stock Exchange, but the actual determination of the price is simple: it is the price at which recent transfers of shares between buyers and sellers have been made. A share price will rise if there are more buyers than sellers in order to attract further selling. There may be an increase in demand for buying the shares as the potential shareholders expect the company to grow and to make increasing profits which will lead to increased dividends.

For companies which are not quoted on a Stock Exchange, the value of a share is derived from first principles, i.e. how much the business as a whole is worth.

The main method used to arrive at a value is to capitalise (i.e. multiply) current annual earnings by a number which is based on the PE ratio of a comparable company on the stock exchange.

You are not required to make such computations at this level of accounting.

4.9 The calculation of the return on a shareholding

In simple terms, the return on a shareholding can be defined as the dividend yield as computed above, i.e. the annual dividend is the return.

However, the full return on a shareholding is more complicated than this as a shareholder also expects a gain from the growth in value of the share between the purchase and sale dates. The growth in value arises because some of the profits made by the company are not paid out as dividends but retained in the company to finance the future growth of the business. The enterprise will thus grow in value; such growth is known as capital growth.

How capital growth is measured so that it can be expressed as an annual amount which can be added to the dividend yield is examinable later in your studies.

5 Appraising the position and prospects of a business

5.1 Introduction

The examiner lays great emphasis on the ability of students to make use of accounting data, not merely to prepare the data. Unfortunately it is a difficult area for which to prepare, as a wide variety of situations can be encountered. The key points to remember are:

1. If a ratio is computed, define what items have been included in the numerator and denominator, as for some ratios definitions vary.
2. A question is usually in two parts, each carrying about the same marks. The first part is the calculation of the ratios and the second is the interpretation. Both must be provided.
3. Show the ratio in the 'normal' form, e.g. a ratio based on a profit figure is normally expressed as a percentage.
4. Do not be frightened of making what may be regarded as an obvious comment. Thus, a statement that 'the gross profit to sales ratio has increased from last year' is stating something important – that the enterprise is more profitable. It is only an obvious comment because the computation of a ratio made it so obvious. That is the main point of ratios – to highlight trends.
5. Always show your workings for all ratios.

5.2 Example

A has been trading steadily for many years as ski shoe manufacturers. In 20X4 a surge in skiing increased the level of the company's sales significantly. The summarised balance sheets of the last two years are given below:

	20X4		*20X3*	
	$'000	*$'000*	*$'000*	*$'000*
Non-current assets:				
Property		640		216
Plant		174		142
Goodwill		30		40
		844		398
Current assets:				
Inventory	540		140	
Receivables	440		170	
Investments	–		120	
Cash at bank	4		150	
		984		580
		1,828		978
Capital and reserves:				
Equity share capital:				
Ordinary 50c shares		300		250
Revaluation reserve		270		–
Accumulated profit		548		398
		1,118		648
Long-term liabilities:				
10% loan notes		120		–
Current liabilities:				
Trade payables	520		250	
Tax	70		80	
		590		330
		1,828		978

Sales for 20X4 and 20X3 respectively were $1,600,000 and $1,150,000. Cost of goods sold for 20X4 and 20X3 respectively were $1,196,000 and $880,000.

Given that this is the only information available, you are required to comment as fully as you can on the company's financial position.

5.3 Solution comments on A – financial position

Profitability and growth

Profit and loss accounts have not been given, but laying these out as far as they are available:

Profit and loss

	20X4	20X3
	$	$
Sales revenue	1,600,000	1,150,000
Cost of sales	1,196,000	880,000
Gross profit	404,000	270,000

Profit margin

$\frac{\text{Gross profit}}{\text{Sales}}$	25.25%	23.48%

Sales have grown considerably:

20X4 Sales	$1,600,000
20X3 Sales	$1,150,000
Percentage increase	39.13%

Solvency: long term – equity to assets ratio

There was no debt in 20X3. The 10% loan notes issued in 20X4 were to enable the investment to be made to finance growth.

The year-end equity to assets ratio is:

$$\frac{\text{Share capital plus reserves}}{\text{Net assets}} \times 100 = \frac{1{,}118{,}000}{1{,}238{,}000} \times 100 = 90.31\%$$

In absolute terms this is a high figure.

Solvency: short-term

Current ratio	*20X4*	*20X3*
$\frac{\text{Current assets}}{\text{Current liabilites}}$	$\frac{984{,}000}{590{,}000} = 1.7$	$\frac{580{,}000}{330{,}000} = 1.8$
Quick ratio		
$\frac{\text{Current assets - Inventory}}{\text{Current liabilites}}$	$\frac{444{,}000}{590{,}000} = 0.8$	$\frac{440{,}000}{330{,}000} = 1.3$

Both ratios have shown a decline – particularly the quick ratio. Conventional opinion states that for many businesses an ideal current ratio is 2 and an ideal quick ratio is 1. However, the ideal ratio will depend on the type of business of a company. More important is the constancy of the ratio over time (assuming that the ratios reflect the efficient use of working capital).

The decline should not be viewed with alarm, particularly as the 20X3 figures include current assets which were surplus to the working capital requirements of the business at that time, i.e. the investments and cash. Both these items have been spent in purchasing new non-current assets. The quick ratio is, however, now low and should be watched carefully.

Short-term solvency: working capital efficiency

Example	*20X4*	*20X3*
Inventory turnover = $\frac{\text{Cost of sales}}{\text{Year end inventory}}$	$\frac{1{,}196{,}000}{540{,}000}$ = 2.2 times p.a.	$\frac{880{,}000}{140{,}000}$ = 6.3 times p.a.

Year-end stock has been taken so that the 20X3 figure can be computed.

This is a very significant fall in inventory turnover. It may indicate that:

- the growth in sales has been made by offering many more types of shoes, some of which are not selling quickly; or
- further growth in sales is expected so that the company has stepped up production to anticipate this.

A closer look at this area is required.

Receivables collection period

Example	*20X4*	*20X3*
Receivables collection period = $\frac{\text{Year end trade recevables}}{\text{Sales}}$	$\frac{440{,}000}{1{,}600{,}000} \times 365$	$\frac{170{,}000}{1{,}150{,}000} \times 365$
	= 100.4 days	= 54.0 days

54 days to collect debts is quite good – 100 days is poor. Immediate action is required to ensure prompter payment, although the situation may not be as bad as it appears if it is the case that the growth in sales took place shortly before the year end rather than throughout the year. Receivables at the year end would then not be typical of the sales throughout the whole year.

6 Appraising information for users

6.1 The nature and purpose of financial accounting

The nature of financial accounting is the reporting of transactions which can be expressed in monetary terms.

The purpose of such an exercise is to inform users of such information and to satisfy their needs.

6.2 The validity of the information

There are limitations in achieving the purpose of financial accounting, such as:

- Non-financial information may be just as important and helps in obtaining a complete picture of the state of the organisation. It includes, for example, the number of employees in the organisation and the types of skills they possess or indicators of efficiency with which the organisation addresses complaints from customers.
- The information is backward looking. Most users are concerned with the future.
- There is a tendency in financial accounting for increased complexity. This results from the continuing need to satisfy user needs for information but the end result may be that users do not understand the more detailed information presented.
- The changing purchasing power of money is not dealt with.

Conclusion

The number of ratios that can be calculated may easily lead to confusion. Try to organise your thoughts in this area by mentally using the categories into which this chapter is broken down: operating ratios; liquidity, working capital and solvency; and Stock Exchange ratios, if required by the question.

Remember above all that the ratios are not an end in themselves. The examiner is also interested in your ability to draw conclusions from accounts. Calculating a ratio is not the same as drawing a conclusion, but it can point you towards a conclusion.

SELF-TEST QUESTIONS

Analysis of accounting statements and use of ratios

1 Name three different user groups of financial statements and state the particular interests of each group. (1.2)

Using ratios

2 How do you calculate the return on capital employed for a company? (2.2)

3 Show how two important ratios can be multiple together to give the return on capital employed. (2.4)

Liquidity and funds management

4 What are the two key ratios to assess a company's liquidity? (3.1)

5 How would you asses whether a company's receivables collection procedures were improving or deteriorating? (3.2)

6 Which is the more risky: investment in a company with a low equity to assets ratio or one with a high equity to assets ratio? (3.5)

Investment appraisal

7 What is the formula to calculate the dividend yield? (4.4)

MULTIPLE-CHOICE QUESTIONS

Question 1

An analysis of its financial statements revealed that the receivable collection period of R was 100 days, when 60 days is a reasonable figure.

Which one of the following could NOT account for the high level of 100 days?

A Poor performance in R's credit control department.

B A large credit sale made just before the balance sheet date.

C R's trade is seasonal.

D A downturn in R's trade in the last quarter of the year.

Question 2

Which of the following correctly defines working capital?

A Non-current assets plus current assets minus current liabilities.

B Current assets minus current liabilities.

C Non-current assets plus current assets.

D Share capital plus reserves.

For the answers to these questions, see the 'Answers' section at the end of the book.

PRACTICE QUESTIONS

Question 1: Electrical engineering

You are given summarised results of an electrical engineering business, as below. All figures are in $'000.

You are required:

(a) To prepare a table of the following 12 ratios, calculated for both years, clearly showing the figures used in the calculations:

- current ratio
- quick assets ratio
- inventory turnover in days
- receivables turnover in days
- payables turnover in days
- gross profit %
- net profit % (before tax)
- interest cover
- dividend cover
- return on equity (before tax)
- return on capital employed (ROCE)
- equity to assets ratio. **(12 marks)**

(b) Making full use of the information given in the question, of your table of ratios, and your common sense, comment on the actions of the management. **(8 marks)**

(Total: 20 marks)

Income statement

	Year ending 31.12.X1	*31.12.X0*
Sales revenue	60,000	50,000
Cost of sales	42,000	34,000
Gross profit	18,000	16,000
Operating expenses	15,500	13,000
	2,500	3,000
Interest payable	2,200	1,300
Profit before tax	300	1,700
Tax	350	600
(Loss) profit after tax	(50)	1,100

Dividends paid were 600 in both years.

Balance sheet

	31.12.X1		31.12.X0	
Non-current assets				
Tangible	500		–	
Intangible	12,000		11,000	
		12,500		11,000
Current assets:				
Inventory	14,000		13,000	
Receivables	16,000		15,000	
Bank and cash	500		500	
		30,500		28,500
		43,000		39,500
Capital and reserves				
Share capital	1,300		1,300	
Share premium	3,300		3,300	
Revaluation reserve	2,000		2,000	
Accumulated profits	7,350		8,000	
		13,950		14,600
Long-term liabilities				
Loan notes		6,000		5,500
Current liabilities				
Trade payables		23,050		19,400
		43,000		39,500

Question 2: Ratios – B

The following are the summarised accounts for B, a company with an accounting year ending on 30 September:

You are required:

(a) to calculate, for each year, two ratios for each of the following user groups, which are of particular significance to them:

- shareholders
- trade suppliers
- internal management. **(12 marks)**

(b) to make brief comments upon the changes, between the two years, in the ratios calculated in (a) above. **(8 marks)**

(Total: 20 marks)

Summarised balance sheets

	20X6		20X7	
	$'000	$'000	$'000	$'000
Non-current assets				
Property, plant and equipment at cost less depreciation		4,995		12,700
Current assets:				
Inventory	40,145		50,455	
Receivables	40,210		43,370	
Cash at bank	12,092		5,790	
		92,447		99,615
		97,442		112,315
Capital and reserves				
Equity capital - shares of 25c		9,920		9,920
Accumulated profit		32,605		42,065
		42,525		51,985
Non-current liabilities				
10% loan notes		19,840		19,840
Current liabilities				
Trade payables	32,604		37,230	
Tax	2,473		3,260	
		35,077		40,490
		97,442		112,315

Movement on reserves

Accumulated profit		
At 1 October	25,325	32,605
Profit for year	9,520	11,660
Dividends paid	(2,240)	(2,200)
	32,605	42,065

Summarised income statements

	20X6	20X7
	$'000	$'000
Sales revenue	486,300	583,900
Operating profit	17,238	20,670
Interest payable	1,984	1,984
Profit before tax	15,254	18,686
Tax	5,734	7,026
Profit for the year	9,520	11,660

EXAM-TYPE QUESTION

Brood

The balance sheets of Brood at 30 April 20X0 and 30 April 20X1 are given below

Required:

(a) Calculate the following ratios for each of the two years:

- return on total capital employed
- return on owners' equity
- current ratio
- quick ratio (acid test)
- gearing (leverage).

Use year-end figures for all ratios. **(5 marks)**

(b) Comment briefly on the movements in these ratios between the two years. **(5 marks)**

(Total: 10 marks)

	30 April			
	20X0		*20X1*	
	$000	$000	$000	$000
Assets				
Tangible non-current assets				
Cost or valuation	51,000		63,000	
Accumulated depreciation	(12,500)	38,500	(16,300)	46,700
Current assets				
Inventories	16,400		18,400	
Trade receivables	19,100		20,600	
Prepayments	3,100		4,000	
		38,600		43,000
Total assets		77,100		89,700
Issued share capital		10,000		10,000
Share premium account		5,000		5,000
Revaluation reserve		5,000		5,000
Accumulated profits		8,600		12,300
		28,600		32,300
Non-current liabilities:				
7% loan notes ($20m issue 1 May 20X0)		20,000		40,000
Current liabilities				
Trade payables	11,400		8,400	
Accruals	3,400		4,200	
Overdraft	13,700	28,500	4,800	17,400
		77,100		89,700

The summarised income statements of Brood for the years ended 30 April 20X0 and 20X1, ignoring tax, are:

	Year ended 30 April	
	20X0	*20X1*
	$000	$000
Sales revenue	58,000	66,000
Cost of sales	(43,000)	(49,000)
Gross profit	15,000	17,000
Operating expenses	(10,000)	(10,500)
Profit from operations	5,000	6,500
Interest payable	(1,400)	(2,800)
Net profit for the period	3,600	3,700

For the answers to these questions, see the 'Answers' section at the end of the book.

FEEDBACK TO ACTIVITY **1**

Total capital employed

20X6 $\frac{23+2}{139} \times 100 = 18.0\%$

20X7 $\frac{27+2}{158} \times 100 = 18.4\%$

Equity capital employed

20X6 $\frac{23-2}{99-25} \times 100 = 28.4\%$

20X7 $\frac{27-2}{118-25} \times 100 = 26.9\%$

There is a slight improvement in total ROCE and a falling off in equity ROCE.

A reason for the variation is the revaluation of fixed assets during the year. This has the effect of increasing the denominator in 20X7 relative to 20X6 and creates an unfair comparison as it is likely that the fixed assets were worth more than their book value last year as well.

The differences in returns for equity compared to total capital employed are large. It means that equity shareholders have had a significant increase in their return because the company is using fixed interest finance to enlarge the capital employed in the business.

Chapter 24
THE THEORETICAL AND OPERATIONAL ADEQUACY OF FINANCIAL REPORTING

CHAPTER CONTENTS

This brief chapter reviews the advantages and disadvantages of historical cost accounting, particularly in times of changing prices.

It goes on to review alternatives to historical cost accounting and to outline the work of IASB and IOSCO in this area.

Objectives

By the time you have finished this chapter you should be able to:

- understand some of the limitations of conventional financial reporting
- be aware of the possible means of addressing such limitations
- be aware of the implications of IOSCO's qualified backing for IASs in global capital markets.

1 The limitations of historical cost accounting

1.1 Introduction

KEY POINT

Under **historical cost accounting**, assets are recorded at the amount of cash or cash equivalents paid, or the fair value of the consideration given for them.

Virtually everything you have studied so far in this book has been based on **historical cost accounting**. Under historical cost accounting, assets are recorded at the amount of cash or cash equivalents paid, or the fair value of the consideration given for them.

Liabilities are recorded at the amount of proceeds received in exchange for the obligation. This method of accounting has advantages, but it also has serious disadvantages.

1.2 Advantages of historical cost accounting

1 Records are based on objectively verifiable amounts (actual cost of assets, etc.).

2 It is simple and cheap.

3 The profit concept is well understood.

4 Within limits, historical cost figures provide a basis for comparison with the results of other companies for the same period or similar periods, with the results of the same company for previous periods and with budgets.

4 Lack of acceptable alternatives.

1.3 Disadvantages of historical cost accounting

1 It overstates profits when prices are rising through inflation. Several factors contribute to this. For example, if assets are retained at their original cost, depreciation is based on that cost. As inflation pushes prices up, the true value to the enterprise of the use of the asset becomes progressively more than the depreciation charge.

   This disadvantage can be overcome by revaluing non-current assets. IAS 16 then requires depreciation to be based on the revalued amount.

2 It maintains financial capital but does not maintain physical capital.

If an enterprise makes a profit it must necessarily have more net assets. If the whole of that profit is distributed as dividend by a company, or withdrawn by a sole trader, the enterprise has the same capital at the end of the year as it had at the beginning. In other words, it has maintained its **financial** capital. However, it will not have maintained its **physical** capital if prices have risen through inflation during the year, because the financial capital will not buy the same inventory and other assets to enable the enterprise to continue operating at the same level.

3 The balance sheet does not show the value of the enterprise. A balance sheet summarises the assets and liabilities of the enterprise, but there are several reasons why it does not represent the true value of the enterprise. One reason for this could be that the use of historical cost accounting means that assets are included at cost less depreciation based on that cost rather than at current value. (Another reason is, of course, that not all the assets are included in the balance sheet – internally generated goodwill does not appear.)

4 It provides a poor basis for assessing performance. The profit is overstated as explained in (1), while assets are understated as discussed in (3) above. The result is that return on capital employed is doubly distorted and exaggerated.

5 It does not recognise the loss suffered through holding monetary assets while prices are rising.

   An enterprise holding cash or receivables through a period of inflation suffers a loss as their purchasing power declines.

These factors are developed and illustrated in the next section.

2 The impact of changing prices

2.1 Shortcomings of historical cost accounting

KEY POINT

When prices are not changing, **historical cost accounting** (HCA) does accurately and fairly show profits made by the enterprise and the value of the assets less liabilities to the enterprise.

When prices are not changing, historical cost accounting (HCA) does accurately and fairly show profits made by the enterprise and the value of the assets less liabilities to the enterprise.

When prices are changing, however, there are problems.

The problems of changing prices

Depreciation

Under a system of HCA the purpose of depreciation is simply to allocate the original cost (less estimated residual value) of a non-current asset over its estimated useful life. If depreciation is charged in the income statement, then by reducing the amount which can be paid out as a dividend, funds are retained within the company rather than paid to the shareholders. When the time comes to replace the asset, management must ensure that those funds are available in a sufficiently liquid form.

When inflation is taken into account, we can note that:

1 The depreciation charge is based on the original cost of the asset measured in terms of historical $s, whereas the revenues against which depreciation is matched are measured in terms of current $s. The profit figure we calculate is not meaningful as it ignores price changes which have taken place since the asset was purchased.

2 Although the concept of depreciation ensures that the capital of the enterprise is maintained intact in money terms, it does not ensure that the capital of the enterprise is maintained intact in real terms (see Examples below).

3 The accumulated depreciation at the end of the asset's useful life will fall short of its replacement cost.

Example

An enterprise starts off with $1,000 cash and buys two machines at a cost of $500 each. All profits are distributed to the owners. At the end of ten years the company has no machines and $1,000 cash.

Thus the capital of the enterprise has been maintained intact in money terms. Suppose at the end of ten years the current replacement cost of one machine is $1,000. Therefore the $1,000 cash at the end of the ten years will buy only one machine. In real terms, the capital at the end of the period is half that at the beginning of the period.

Profit has been over-distributed. If profit is a true surplus, the owners should be able to withdraw all the profit and be in exactly the same position as before in real terms.

Inventory and cost of sales

KEY POINT

During a period of inflation the effect of **FIFO** is to overstate the real profit of the enterprise.

Assume a company values inventory on a historical cost basis using the FIFO method. During a period of inflation the effect of this method is to overstate the real profit of the enterprise, since sales (in current terms) are matched with cost of sales (in historical terms). If the company distributed the whole of its historical cost profit, it would not be maintaining the capital of the enterprise intact in real terms.

Example

An enterprise starts off on 1 January 20X7 with $1,000 cash (contributed by the proprietor). On the same day it purchases 500 motors at $2 each. These are sold on 31 March 20X7 for proceeds of $1,650. At this date the replacement cost of an identical motor is $2.20.

Under HCA the profit for the three months is $650 ($1,650 – $1,000). If the proprietor withdraws this profit, the closing balance sheet at 31 March would show capital account $1,000 represented by cash of $1,000.

Although capital has been maintained intact in money terms (it was $1,000 at 1 January), it has not been maintained intact in real terms. At 31 March $1,000 cash will buy only 455 (approximately!) motors.

Comparability of data over time

We saw earlier a need for users of accounts to be able to compare the results of the enterprise over a number of years so that trends could be identified. Thus, if sales were $100,000 four years ago and $130,000 in the current year, we could conclude that sales have increased by 30%. However, in real terms the increase may not be this amount, as price levels may have changed in the previous four years. If price levels have risen by 40% in the last four years, then the sales should be $140,000 in the current year in order to maintain the real value of sales. There has therefore been a real decline.

2.2 How the shortcomings of HCA might be overcome

Alternatives to HCA mainly fall into one of two categories:

Current purchasing power accounting (CPP)

KEY POINT

Current purchasing power accounting (CPP) adjusts the historical cost accounts using a general price index.

This involves adjusting the historical cost accounts using a general price index (e.g. Retail Price Index) so that all items are expressed in $s of year-end purchasing power.

The method has been largely rejected, most notably because many accountants felt it misleading to adjust specific assets such as inventory and non-current assets by means of a general price index which was far more relevant to the spending power of a family than that of a trader.

Current cost accounting (CCA)

KEY POINT

Current cost accounting (CCA) takes account of specific price changes as they affect a particular enterprise.

This involves taking account of specific price changes as they affect a particular enterprise and will result in a separate set of financial statements, distinct from the historical cost financial statements.

Although accountants generally believe CCA is superior to CPP, the profession has yet to agree on any single method of (or indeed, some people would even argue, on the need for) accounting for inflation.

CCA can be argued to be the best solution to the first two problems of HCA involving non-current assets and inventory. By charging the current worth of these items against profits, the amount of operating profit recorded in the income statement will be reduced. Thus the amount of dividends will tend to be reduced due to the lower profits and more sums will be retained in the enterprise to finance the increased replacement price of these assets.

Example

Continuing the example of inventory and cost of sales above, we could measure profit by comparing the sale proceeds with the replacement cost of the inventory at the time of sale.

	$
Proceeds of sale	1,650
Current (or replacement) cost at the date of sale	1,100
Current cost profit	550

Note that the terms current cost and replacement cost mean the same, though the term current cost tends to be used more frequently.

If the proprietor withdrew $550, the closing balance sheet would appear as follows:

	$
Assets – Cash	1,100
Capital account:	
Balance at 1 January 20X6	1,000
Add: Net profit	650
	1,650
Less: Drawings	550
	1,100

This cash is now sufficient to buy 500 motors at the new price of $2.20 per motor. The trader can continue trading at the same level of business – capital has been maintained intact in real terms.

KEY POINT

The comparability of data over a period of time is generally best handled by a CPP approach.

The comparability of data over a period of time is generally best handled by a CPP approach. Financial data from earlier years is uplifted to current price levels by the fraction:

$$\frac{\text{Retail price index in current year}}{\text{Retail price index in year when item originated}} \times \begin{array}{c}\text{Amount at which item stated}\\ \text{in accounts in earlier year}\end{array}$$

Thus sales in the previous example illustrating the problem of lack of comparability of data of $100,000 would be restated at $140,000 in current year price levels.

2.3 The usefulness of historical cost accounting

In terms of examinations at this level, questions are going to concern themselves with HCA accounting and you will only need to appreciate that historical cost accounts do not account for changing prices, as clearly shown by the examples involving non-current assets and inventory.

In practice it is largely accepted that HCA accounts have severe limitations, but it is very difficult to persuade preparers of accounts to take account of changing prices. Attempts to impose a system of current purchasing power and a system of current cost accounting have at best met with indifference, and in most countries at present there is no requirement to prepare either.

Most organisations seem content to prepare HCA accounts, presumably considering that they (and the users of financial statements) are aware of the inherent limitations therein. Indeed, the only regularly adopted relevant practice in financial statements is to revalue land and buildings periodically and include such values in the financial statements.

In conclusion, the debate on accounting for changing prices is likely to continue in years to come, but at this stage students merely need to be aware (in broad outline) of the limitations of HCA.

3 The contribution of the IASB

The International Accounting Standards Board currently has no mandatory accounting standard dealing with changing prices. IAS 15 *Information Reflecting the Effects of Changing Prices* was made non-mandatory in 1989, and you are not required to be familiar with its contents. Instead the IASB has been working to develop a Framework and suite of IASs (its core standards) that prevent serious problems in this area. For example, where a non-current asset is revalued upwards, depreciation is required by IAS 16 subsequently to be calculated on the revalued amount. In 1999 the IASB completed its set of core standards.

The International Organisation of Securities Commissions (IOSCO) in particular has been looking to IASB to publish standards for use in multinational securities offerings, where shares in a company are offered for sale in more than one country simultaneously. The idea is that such a company need only prepare financial statements in accordance with IASs to support such a share offering, rather than have to incur the expense of redrafting the statements to accord with the separate practices of each of the countries concerned.

The IASB duly finished its core standards in 1999 and submitted them to IOSCO for endorsement. In May 2000 IOSCO announced its qualified endorsement, recommending that its members (the major stock exchanges around the world) should allow multinational companies to use IASs in cross-border listings. However, the endorsement fell short of complete acceptance, in that it allowed national and regional regulators scope to disallow aspects of IASs, require additional disclosures and/or reconciliations to national GAAP. Despite this qualified acceptance, real progress in lifting the status of IASs has been achieved, and IASs will now become much more acceptable as the basis for capital raising and quotation purposes in all global stock markets.

Conclusion

The chapter has addressed a number of issues relating to the adequacy of financial reporting. The other approaches to financial statements consist of further statements being produced or financial statements being produced which incorporate the effect of changing prices.

SELF-TEST QUESTIONS

Limitations of historical cost accounting

1 What are the advantages of historical cost accounting? (1.2)

2 What are the limitations of historical cost accounting? (1.3)

Impact of changing prices

3 What does CPP stand for? (2.2)

4 What does CCA stand for? (2.2)

Contribution of IASB

5 What advantage is gained by IOSCO endorsing IASs? (3)

Answers to end of chapter questions

CHAPTER 1

EXAM-TYPE QUESTION

Financial statements

(a) The information in the report is to be communicated to:

- Shareholders – the owners of the company: existing and potential, including persons or groups interested in take-overs and mergers.
- Providers of external finance, long and short term, such as lenders and finance companies, both existing and potential.
- Employees past, present and potential.
- Suppliers of goods and services, and customers, past, present and prospective.
- Tax authorities.
- Trade agencies, environmental pressure groups and any other members of the public who may require such information as is normally and legally contained in the report.
- Analysts and advisers, both of investors (economists, statisticians and journalists) and of employees (trade unions).

(b) The information contained in the report should be:

- Reliable – so that conclusions drawn may be 'true and fair'.
- Understandable – material matters should be disclosed without unnecessary complex detail.
- Complete – if an unbalanced or biased report is presented, readers will be unable to make sound judgements.
- Comparable – the information contained in one period's report should be, as far as possible, calculated and presented on the same bases as in previous periods, so that comparisons are relevant.
- Objective – an unbiased view of the company's affairs, without regard to the interests of particular groups of interested parties, should be put forward.
- Up-to-date – companies normally prepare their reports annually, and this is important from the point of view of investors and those advising them, for evaluation purposes. In many countries a maximum time limit after the balance sheet date is prescribed, before which the report must be distributed.

(c) The kind of information required by two of the groups is:

- Shareholders, who are interested in the future performance of the business but require past figures as a guide to the future. Therefore, all financial information in the report is needed.

  In addition, any general indication given in the report as to future prospects is relevant.

- Tax authorities, who require past figures as a basis for computing tax liabilities.

CHAPTER 2 EXAM-TYPE QUESTION

The Frog Shop

(a) Balance sheets at end of each day:

Balance sheet for Day 1

	$		$
Cash	2,000	Capital	2,000

Balance sheet for Day 2

	$		$
Motor van	1,000	Capital	2,000
Shop fittings	800		
Cash	200		
	2,000		2,000

Balance sheet for Day 3

	$		$
Motor van	1,000	Capital	2,000
Shop fittings	800	Accounts payable	500
Inventory	500		
Cash	200		
	2,500		2,500

Balance sheet for Day 4

	$		$
Motor van	1,000	Capital	2,000
Shop fittings	800	Add: Profit	400
Inventory	250		
Cash	850	Accounts payable	500
	2,900		2,900

Balance sheet for Day 5

	$		$
Motor van	1,000	Capital	2,000
Shop fittings	800	Add: Profit	400
Inventory	250		
Cash	350		
	2,400		2,400

Balance sheet for Day 6

	$		$
Motor van	1,000	Capital	2,000
Shop fittings	800	Add: Profit	400
Inventory	250		
Cash	300		2,400
		Less: Drawings	(50)
	2,350		2,350

Note: the capital could be shown in total as $2,350 without showing how it is made up.

Balance sheet for Day 7

	$		$
Motor van	1,000	Capital	2,350
Shop fittings	800	Accounts payable	1,000
Inventory	1,250		
Cash	300		
	3,350		3,350

Balance sheet for Day 8

	$		$
Motor van	1,000	Capital (2,350 + 300)	2,650
Shop fittings	800	Accounts payable	1,000
Inventory	350		
Accounts receivable	1,200		
Cash	300		
	3,650		3,650

Balance sheet for Day 9

	$		$
Motor van	1,000	Capital	2,650
Shop fittings	800	Accounts payable	1,000
Inventory	350		
Accounts receivable	700		
Cash	800		
	3,650		3,650

Balance sheet for Day 10

	$		$
Motor van	1,000	Capital (2,650 – 100)	2,550
Shop fittings	800	Accounts payable	1,000
Inventory	350		
Accounts receivable	700		
Cash	700		
	3,550		3,550

(b) Income statement for the ten days ended Day 10:

	$	$
Sales revenue (650 + 1,200)		1,850
Purchases (500 + 1,000)	1,500	
Less: Closing inventory	350	
		1,150
Gross profit		700
Wages		100
Net profit		600

Note: the link between the income statement and the balance sheet amount of capital. Capital has moved during the ten days as follows:

	$
Opening capital	2,000
Add: Net profit for the period	600
Less: Drawings	(50)
	2,550

CHAPTER 3

EXAM-TYPE QUESTION

Grace

Balance sheet for Day 1

	$		$
Capital	5,000	Purchases	1,000
Sales revenue	1,200	Fixtures	
Tom	1,900	Wages	100
Sales revenue	500	Eileen	1,500
Trevor	500	Purchases	700
Guy – loan	1,000	Wages	150
		Eric	850
		Premises	
		Wages	150
		Balance c/d	750
	10,100		10,100
Balance b/d	750		

Car

	$		$
Capital	4,500		

Capital

	$		$
Balance c/d	9,500	Cash	5,000
		Car	4,500
	9,500		9,500
		Balance b/d	9,500

Purchases

	$		$
Cash	1,000	Balance c/d	4,050
Eileen	1,500		
Eric	850		
Cash	700		
	4,050		4,050
Balance b/d	4,050		

Sales revenue

	$		$
Balance c/d	4,400	Cash	1,200
		Tom	900
		Trevor	800
		Tom	1,000
		Cash	500
	4,400		4,400
		Balance b/d	4,400

Fixtures and fittings

	$		$
Cash	900		

Eileen – account payable

	$		$
Cash	1,500	Purchases	1,500

Tom – account receivable

	$		$
Sales revenue	900	Cash	1,900
Sales revenue	1,000		
	1,900		1,900

Eric – account payable

	$		$
Cash	850	Purchases	850

Trevor – account receivable

	$		$
Sales revenue	800	Cash	500
		Balance c/d	300
	800		800
Balance b/d	300		

Wages

	$		$
Cash	100	Balance c/d	400
Cash	150		
Cash	150		
	400		400
Balance b/d	400		

Guy – Loan

	$		$
		Cash	1,000

Premises

	$		$
Cash	4,000		

Grace – Trial balance as at 30 June 20X9

Account	*Dr* $	*Cr* $
Cash at bank	750	
Car	4,500	
Capital		9,500
Purchases	4,050	
Sales revenue		4,400
Fixtures	900	
Trevor – account receivable	300	
Wages	400	
Guy – Loan		1,000
Premises	4,000	
	14,900	14,900

CHAPTER **4**

MULTIPLE-CHOICE QUESTIONS

Question 1

The correct answer is **C**. The other three answers contain items which cannot be included in inventory as per IAS 2.

Question 2

The correct answer is **C**.

400 items		$
Cost	400 × $4	1,600
NRV	(400 × $3) – $200	1,000

Therefore use NRV.

200 items		$
Cost	200 × $30	6,000
NRV	(200 × $35) – $1,200 – $300	5,500

Therefore use NRV.

Total inventory figure = $116,400 + $1,000 + $5,500 = $122,900.

CHAPTER 4

EXAM-TYPE QUESTIONS

Question 1: Blabbermouth

Income statement for the year ended 31 March 20X7

	$	$
Sales revenue:		25,375
Less: Cost of goods sold:		
Opening inventory	4,100	
Purchases	17,280	
	21,380	
Less: Closing inventory	5,200	
		16,180
Gross profit		9,195
Less: Expenses:		
Postage and stationery	727	
Rent	500	
Light and heat	100	
Wages	8,237	
		9,564
Net loss		(369)

Note: the expenses of the business exceed gross profit therefore a net loss has been made.

Balance sheet as at 31 March 20X7

	$	$
Non-current assets:		
Fixtures and fittings		2,100
Current assets:		
Inventory	5,200	
Trade receivables	8,250	
Cash	6,078	
		19,528
		21,628
Capital employed:		
Capital at 1 April 20X6	18,250	
Less: Loss for year	369	
	17,881	
Less: Drawings by proprietor	3,500	
		14,381
Current liabilities		
Trade payables		7,247
		21,628

Question 2: Alpha

Income statement for year to 31 December

	$	$
Sales revenue		39,468
Opening inventory	3,655	
Purchases (working 2)	27,101	
	30,756	
Less: Closing inventory	3,123	
		27,633
Gross profit		11,835
Insurance	580	
Plant repairs	110	
Rent	1,782	
Wages	3,563	
Discount allowed	437	
Motor van expenses	1,019	
General expenses	522	
		8,013
Net profit		3,822

Balance sheet as at 31 December

	$	$
Non-current assets:		
Motor van		980
Plant		2,380
Shop fittings		1,020
		4,380
Current assets:		
Inventory	3,123	
Receivables	3,324	
Cash on hand	212	
		6,659
		11,039
Capital:		
Balance at 1 Jan	2,463	
Add: Profit for year	3,822	
	6,285	
Less: Drawings (working 2)	3,040	
		3,245
Current liabilities:		
Payables		4,370
Bank overdraft (working 1)		3,424
		11,039

Workings

(W1) **Trial balance at 31 December**

	Dr	*Cr*
	$	$
Sales revenue		39,468
Insurance	580	
Plant repairs	110	
Rent	1,782	
Motor van	980	
Plant	2,380	
Purchases	27,321	
Wages	3,563	
Inventory at 1 Jan (opening)	3,655	
Discount allowed	437	
Motor van expenses	1,019	
Shop fittings	1,020	
General expenses	522	
Capital account at 1 Jan		2,463
Receivables	3,324	
Payables		4,370
Cash on hand	212	
Personal drawings by proprietor	2,820	
	49,725	46,301
Bank overdraft (balancing figure)		3,424
	49,725	49,725

(W2) **Goods for own use:**

	$
Drawings per list of balances	2,820
Add: Goods for own use	220
	3,040
Purchases per list of balances	27,321
Less: Goods for own use	220
	27,101

Note: if inventory is taken from the business by the proprietor for his personal use, the double entry is to debit drawings and credit purchases. No entry is made in the inventory account.

CHAPTER **5**

EXAM-TYPE QUESTIONS

Question 1: Dundee Engineering

Motor expenses and insurance

20X7/8		$	*20X7/8*		$
1 May	Bal b/d – insurance	290	1 May	Bal b/d – garage bills	478
30 June	Cash	698			
1 Sept	Cash	3,480			
1 Dec	Cash	3,900	30 Apr	Income statement (bal fig)	4,811
30 Apr	Bal c/d – garage bills	356	30 Apr	Bal c/d – insurance (W1)	3,435
		8,724			8,724
1 May	Bal b/d	3,435	1 May	Bal b/d	356

Workings

(W1) **Insurance prepayment**

	$
$3{,}480 \times \frac{4}{12}$	1,160
$3{,}900 \times \frac{7}{12}$	2,275
	3,435

Question 2: Heilbronn Properties

Interest payable

20X4/5		$	*20X4/5*		$
1 Aug	Bal b/d Interest prepaid	8,000	1 Aug	Bal b/d Interest payable	12,000
31 July	Cash paid (bal fig)	51,900	31 July	Income statement	56,000
31 July	Bal c/d Interest payable	14,500	31 July	Bal c/d Interest prepaid	6,400
		74,400			74,400
1 Aug	Bal b/d	6,400	1 Aug	Bal b/d	14,500

Rental income

20X4/5		$	*20X4/5*		$
1 Aug	Bal b/d Rental due	15,000	1 Aug	Bal b/d Rental in advance	3,000
31 July	Income statement (bal fig)	120,500	31 July	Cash received	116,000
31 July	Bal c/d Rental in advance	2,500	31 July	Bal c/d Rental due	19,000
		138,000			138,000
1 Aug	Bal b/d	19,000	1 Aug	Bal b/d	2,500

CHAPTER 6

EXAM-TYPE QUESTION

Harry Evans

Step 1

Write off the bad debt in 20X0.

Dr Bad debts expense account

Cr Receivables account

Bad debts expense

20X0		$	*20X0*		$
31 Dec	Receivables	370			

Step 2

Calculate the allowance required.

Allowance for doubtful debts ((6,570 – 370) × 4%) = $ 248

Step 3

Write up the allowance for doubtful debts account.

Dr Bad debts expense account

Cr Allowance for doubtful debts account

This will be the full amount of the allowance as this is the first year that the allowance has been set up.

Bad debts expense

20X0	$	*20X0*	$
31 Dec Receivables	370		
31 Dec Allowance for doubtful debts	248		

Allowance for doubtful debts

20X0	$	*20X0*	$
		31 Dec Bad debts expense	248

Step 4

Write off the balance on the bad debts expense account to the income statement and carry down the balance on the allowance account into 20X1.

Bad debts expense

20X0	$	*20X0*	$
31 Dec Receivables	370		
31 Dec Allowance for doubtful debts	248	31 Dec Income statement	618
	618		618

Allowance for doubtful debts

20X0	$	*20X0*	$
31 Dec Bal c/d	248	31 Dec Bad debts expense	248
	248		248
		20X1	
		1 Jan Bal b/d	248

Step 5

For 20X1 write off the bad debt to the bad debts expense account and set up the allowance required.

20X1 doubtful debts allowance required ((8,400 – 1,500) × 2%) = $ 138

As the allowance required is a decrease of $110 over the 20X0 allowance, the double entry is:

Dr Allowance for doubtful debts account

Cr Bad debts expense account

Bad debts expense

	$		$
20X1		*20X1*	
		31 Dec Allowance for doubtful	
31 Dec Receivables	1,500	debts	110

Allowance for doubtful debts

	$		$
20X0		*20X0*	
31 Dec Bal c/d	248	31 Dec Bad debts expense	248
	248		248
20X1		20X1	
31 Dec Bad debts expense	110	1 Jan Bal b/d	248

Step 6

Balance off the bad debts expense account transferring the balance to the income statement and carry down the required balance on the allowance for doubtful debts account.

Bad debts expense

	$		$
20X1		*20X1*	
31 Dec Receivables	1,500	31 Dec Allowance for doubtful	
		debts	110
		31 Dec Income statement	1,390
	1,500		1,500

Allowance for doubtful debts

	$		$
20X0		*20X0*	
31 Dec Bal c/d	248	31 Dec Bad debts expense	248
	248		248
20X1		20X1	
31 Dec Bad debts expense	110	1 Jan Bal b/d	248
31 Dec Bal c/d	138		
	248		248
		20X2	
		1 Jan Bal b/d	138

Step 7

Calculate the allowance required for 20X2.

	$
Specific allowance	350
General allowance ((6,250 – 350) × 2%)	118
	468

Step 8

Write up the allowance account and the bad debts expense account. The increase in allowance required is (468 – 138) = $330 and the double entry for this increase is

Dr Bad debts expense account

Cr Allowance for doubtful debts account

Bad debts expense

	$		$
20X2		*20X2*	
31 Dec Allowance for doubtful debts	330		

Allowance for doubtful debts

	$		$
20X0		*20X0*	
31 Dec Bal c/d	248	31 Dec Bad debts expense	248
	248		248
20X1		20X1	
31 Dec Bad debts expense	110	1 Jan Bal b/d	248
31 Dec Bal c/d	138		
	248		248
		20X2	
		1 Jan Bal b/d	138
		31 Dec Bad debts expense	330

Step 9

Transfer the balance on the bad debts expense account to the income statement and carry down the required balance on the allowance account.

Bad debts expense

	$		$
20X2		*20X2*	
31 Dec Allowance for doubtful debts	330	31 Dec Income statement	330
	330		330

Allowance for doubtful debts

	$		$
20X0		*20X0*	
31 Dec Bal c/d	248	31 Dec Bad debts expense	248
	248		248
20X1		20X1	
31 Dec Bad debts expense	110	1 Jan Bal b/d	248
31 Dec Bal c/d	138		
	248		248
20X2		20X2	
		1 Jan Bal b/d	138
31 Dec Bal c/d	468	31 Dec Bad debts expense	330
	468		468

CHAPTER 7

MULITPLE-CHOICE QUESTION

B

$$\frac{\$30{,}000 - \$6{,}000}{4} \times \frac{5}{12} = \$2{,}500$$

CHAPTER 7

EXAM-TYPE QUESTIONS

Question 1: Depreciation 1

Usually, with the exception of land (providing that it is not a mine, quarry or other wasting asset), non-current assets have a limited number of years of useful life. When a non-current asset is purchased and later scrapped or disposed of by the firm, that part of the original cost not recovered on disposal is called depreciation. Depreciation is thus the part of the cost of the non-current asset consumed during its working life. Accordingly, it has been a cost for services in the same way as an expense incurred is a cost for those goods or services received. Depreciation is, therefore, a revenue expense item and will be charged annually in the income statement. The depreciation cost apportionable to each year of the asset's life is estimated in advance of disposal and accounted for by making annual charges to reduce the asset from cost to the written down value, at the end of each year of its life.

An example of a method of computing the annual depreciation of an asset is the *straight-line method* which is outlined below:

$$\frac{\text{Cost} - \text{Residual value}}{\text{Number of years of expected use}} = \text{Depreciation charge per year}$$

$$\text{e.g.} \quad \frac{\$1{,}000 - \text{Nil}}{10 \text{ years}} = \$100 \text{ per year}$$

Question 2: Depreciation 2

Motor cars – cost account

		$			$
20X4			*20X4*		
1 Jan	Cash – Car A	8,000	31 Dec	Balance c/d	20,000
1 Jul	Cash – Car B	12,000			
		20,000			20,000
20X5			20X5		
1 Jan	Balance b/d	20,000	1 Jul	Motor car disposal account (Car A)	8,000
			31 Dec	Balance b/d	12,000
		20,000			20,000
20X6					
1 Jan	Balance b/d	12,000			

Motor cars – accumulated depreciation account

Date	Details	$	Date	Details		$
20X4		$	*20X4*			$
31 Dec	Balance c/d	2,800	31 Dec	Income statement – dep'n charge:		
				Car A	1,600	
				Car B	1,200	
						2,800
		2,800				2,800
20X5			20X5			
1 Jul	Motor car disposal account (accumulated dep'n on Car A (1,600 + 800))	2,400	1 Jan	Balance b/d		2,800
31 Dec	Balance c/d	3,600		Income statement – dep'n charge:		
				Car A	800	
				Car B	2,400	
						3,200
		6,000				6,000
20X6			20X6			
31 Dec	Balance c/d	6,000	1 Jan	Balance b/d		3,600
				Income statement – dep'n charge on Car B		
		6,000				6,000

Motor cars – disposals account

Date	Details	$	Date	Details	$
20X5		$	*20X5*		$
1 Jul	Cost of disposal	8,000	1 Jul	Accumulated dep'n	2,400
	Income statement – profit on disposal	400		Cash account (proceeds)	6,000
		8,400			8,400

Balance sheet (extract) as at 31 December 20X5

Non-current assets	*Cost*	*Accumulated dep'n*	*Net book value*
	$	$	$
Motor cars	12,000	3,600	8,400

Question 3: Grasmere

Motor van – cost

	$		$
20X2		*20X2*	
Cash	2,400	Balance c/d	2,400
	2,400		2,400
20X3		20X3	
Balance b/d	2,400	Balance c/d	2,400
	2,400		2,400
20X4		20X4	
Balance b/d	2,400	Disposals	2,400
	2,400		2,400

Motor van – accumulated depreciation

	$		$
20X2		*20X2*	
Balance c/d	210	Income statement	210
	210		210
20X3		20X3	
Balance c/d	630	Balance b/d	210
		Income statement	420
	630		630
20X4		20X4	
Disposal		Balance b/d	630
		Income statement	105
	735		735

Motor van disposals

	$		$
20X4		*20X4*	
Cost	2,400	Accumulated depreciation	735
Income statement (bal fig)	135	Cash	1,800
			2,535

Workings

Depreciation charge p.a. = $\frac{\$2,400 - \$300}{5}$ = $420 p.a.

Charge for 20X2 = (6m) 6/12 × $420 = $210

Charge for 20X3 = (12m) = $420

Charge for 20X4 = (3m) 3/12 × $420 = $105

Effect on financial statements:

(a) Income statement:

	$
20X2 Depreciation charge (Dr)	210
20X3 Depreciation charge (Dr)	420
20X4 Depreciation charge (Dr)	105
20X4 Depreciation over provided (Cr)	135

Note: the net effect of the two items in 20X4 would be combined with the depreciation charge on other non-current assets.

(b) Balance sheet:

		31 Dec	
	20X2	*20X3*	*20X4*
	$	$	$
Non-current assets			
Motor van – cost	2,400	2,400	–
Less: Accumulated depreciation	210	630	–
Net book value	2,190	1,770	–

CHAPTER 8

EXAM-TYPE QUESTION

Delta

Income statement for the year to 31 December 20X9

	$	$	$
Sales revenue			124,450
Less: Returns			186
			124,264
Opening inventory	8,000		
Add: Purchases	86,046		
Less: Returns	135		
	85,911		
Carriage inwards	156		
Wages	8,250		
		94,317	
Less: Closing inventory		(7,550)	
			94,767
Gross profit			29,497
Discount received			138
			29,635
Salaries		3,500	
Travellers' salaries		5,480	
Travelling expenses		1,040	
Discounts allowed		48	
General expenses		2,056	
Gas, electricity and water		2,560	
Rent (W2)		1,750	
Carriage outwards		546	
Printing and stationery		640	
Bad debts (W4)		485	
Loan interest (W1)		100	
Depreciation (W3)		575	
Bank charges		120	
			18,900
Net profit			10,735

Balance sheet as at 31 December 20X9

	Cost	*Dep'n*	
	$	$	$
Non-current assets:			
Premises	8,000	-	8,000
Plant and machinery	5,500	550	4,950
Furniture and fittings	500	25	475
	14,000	575	13,425
Current assets:			
Inventory		7,550	
Receivables	20,280		
Less: Allowance for doubtful debts (W4)	1,014		
		19,266	
Prepayments		250	
Cash at bank		650	
			27,716
			41,141
Capital: balance at 1 Jan 20X9		20,000	
Add: Profit for the year		10,735	
		30,735	
Less: Drawings by proprietor		1,750	
			28,985
Non-current liabilities:			
Loan – Omega			2,000
Current liabilities:			
Payables		10,056	
Loan interest		100	
			10,156
			41,141

Workings

(W1) **Loan interest**

Accrual required = 5% × $2,000 = $100

Interest payable account

	$		$
Balance c/d	100	Income statement	100
	100		100
		Balance b/d	100

Note: it is not necessary to show the writing up of the ledger account as above where there have been no previous expenses stored up in the ledger account during the year.

It is more important to see the effect of the adjustment – a Dr to the income statement account and a Cr on the balance sheet.

(W2) **Rent**

Rent

	$		$
Cash	2,000	Income statement	1,750
		Prepayment c/d	250
	2,000		2,000
Prepayment b/d	250		

(W3) **Depreciation**

Plant and machinery 10% × $5,500	550
Furniture and fittings 5% × $500	25
	575

Note: as with working (1) it is not necessary to write up the ledger accounts. The effect of the calculations can be inserted into the income statement and the balance sheet.

Dr Depreciation (income statement) = Expense

Cr Accumulated depreciation (Balance sheet) = Reduction in asset

(W4) **Bad debts**

Bad debts account

	$		$
Balance b/d (per list of account balances)		Balance b/d (list of account balances)	
Bad debts	256	Bad debts recovered	45
Allowance for doubtful debts	274	Income statement	485
	530		530

Allowance for doubtful debts account

	$		$
Balance required c/d		Balance b/d (per list of balances)	
5% × $20,280	1,014	Bad debts account	274
	1,014		1,014

Note: no workings/ledger accounts have been shown for inventory as the opening and closing inventory figures can be inserted into the final accounts without further adjustments.

CHAPTER 9

PRACTICE QUESTION

Heale

(a) **Sales journal**

	$
Jones	94
Smith	118
Turnip	141
Clog	235
Foul	353
	941

Purchases journal

	Total $	*Purchases* $	*Telephone* $	*Gas* $
Snell	80	80	–	–
Ryan	100	100	–	–
Ovett	150	150	–	–
Coe	300	300	–	–
Keino	100	100	–	–
Telecom	50	–	50	–
Gas	75	–	–	75
	855	730	50	75

Cash book

	$		$
Jones – sale	30	Petty cash	200
Smith – sale	60	Snell – payables ledger	70
Turnip – sale	110	Ovett – payables ledger	30
Foul – sale	80	Telecom (payables ledger)	50
Sundry income	10	Wages	300
Balance c/d	440	Sundry expenses	80
	730		730
		Balance b/d (overdrawn)	440

Petty cash book

Received $		*Total* $	*Stationery* $	*Postage* $	*Travelling* $	*Sundry expenses* $
200	Cash	–	–	–	–	
–	Stationery	16	16	–	–	–
–	Postage	3	–	3	–	–
–	Travelling	8	–	–	8	–
–	Sundry expenses	12	–	–	–	12
		39	16	3	8	12

(b) **General ledger**

Sales revenue

	$		$
Income statement	941	Sales journal	941
	941		941

Note: the sales revenue account has been closed off by transferring the balance to the income statement. Strictly, this would only be done after a list of balances had been extracted and entries made to put through adjustments for the financial statements. The same applies to all the income and expense accounts set out below.

Purchases

	$		$
Purchase journal	730	Income statement	730
	730		730

Telephone

	$		$
Purchase journal	50	Income statement	50
	50		50

Heating and lighting

	$		$
Purchase journal	75	Income statement	75
	75		75

Sundry income

	$		$
Income statement	10	Cash book	10
	10		10

Wages

	$		$
Cash book	300	Income statement	300
	300		300

Sundry expenses

	$		$
Cash book	80	Income statement	92
Petty cash book	12		
	92		92

Stationery

	$		$
Petty cash book	16	Income statement	16
	16		16

Postage

	$		$
Petty cash book	3	Income statement	3
	3		3

Travelling

	$		$
Petty cash book	8	Income statement	8
	8		8

Accounts receivable ledger

Jones

	$		$
Sales journal	94	Cash book	30
		Balance c/d	64
	94		94

Smith

	$		$
Sales journal	118	Cash book	60
		Balance c/d	58
	118		118

Turnip

	$		$
Sales journal	141	Cash book	110
	141	Balance c/d	31
			141

Clog

	$		$
Sales journal	235	Balance c/d	235
	235		235

Foul

	$		$
Sales journal	353	Cash book	80
		Balance c/d	273
	353		353

Accounts payable ledger

Snell

	$		$
Cash book	70	Purchase journal	80
Balance c/d	10		
	80		80

Ryan

	$		$
Balance c/d	100	Purchase journal	100
	100		100

Ovett

	$		$
Cash book	30	Purchase journal	150
Balance c/d	120		
	150		150

Coe

	$		$
Balance c/d	300	Purchase journal	300
	300		300

Keino

	$		$
Balance c/d	100	Purchase journal	100
	100		100

Telecom

	$		$
Cash book	50	Purchase journal	50
	50		50

Gas

	$		$
Balance c/d	75	Purchase journal	75
	75		75

(c) **Trial balance**

	Dr	*Cr*
	$	$
Accounts receivable ledger balances (total)	661	
Sales revenue		941
Accounts payable ledger balances (total)		705
Purchases	730	
Telephone	50	
Gas	75	
Bank		440
Sundry income		10
Petty cash	161	
Wages	300	
Sundry expenses	92	
Stationery	16	
Postage	3	
Travelling	8	
	2,096	2,096

Note: the trial balance in part (c) has been extracted before closing off the income and expense accounts to the income statement.

CHAPTER **10**

MULTIPLE-CHOICE QUESTION

A The other three lists all contain one item which should appear on the debit side of the account.

CHAPTER **10**

EXAM-TYPE QUESTIONS

Question 1: Excel Stores

(a)

	$	$
	–	+
Balance on control account at 30 June 20X4		84,688.31
Error in deriving closing balance (addition of debit side incorrect)		11,000.00
Items posted to wrong side of account:		
Discount received	2,656.82	
	2,656.82	
Contras	3,049.75	
	3,049.75	
Purchase returns omitted	39.60	
Error in credit side total ($195,461.19 – $195,261.19)		200.00
Transposition error in debit side total ($195,261.19 – $192,561.19)		2,700.00
Petty cash payment omitted	10.22	

	11,462.96	98,588.31
		11,462.96
Amended balance		87,125.35

Note: in this question you must spot the errors in the control account itself.

Given the number of errors in the control account, it would be easier to write it out again! However, the question asked for a statement reconciling the original and correct balances, and the answer has been produced in that format. Normally a ledger account format should be used to emphasise that the adjustments form part of the double entry system.

(b)

	$	$
	–	+
Individual payables at 30 June 20X4		86,538.28
Item:		
1 No effect		
2		30.00
3 584.41 – 548.1436.27		
4		674.32
5 12.56 + 8.1320.69		
	20.69	
6	39.60	
	117.25	87,242.60
		117.25
Amended listing		87,125.35

Question 2: DEF – Accounts receivable ledger

(a) **Accounts receivable ledger control**

	$		$
30.9.X8Balance b/d	12,814	30.9.X8Balance b/d	592
30.9.X8Balance c/d	158	Sales overstated (1)	850
		Returns understated (2)	90
		30.9.X8Balance c/d	11,440
	12,972		12,972
1.10.X8 Balance b/d	11,440	1.10.X8Balance b/d	158

Note: net balance $11,282 ($11,440 – 158).

(b) **Accounts receivable ledger control report – 30 Sept 20X8**

		$	
Balance brought forward		15,438	
Add:	Sales (74,691 – 354)	74,337	(4)
	Repayments made (1,249 + 217)	1,466	(5)
	Adjustments	23	
Less:	Sales returns (2,347 + 354)	2,701	(4)
	Payments received (71,203 – 217)	70,986	(5)
	Bad debts written off (646 + 793)	1,439	(6)
	Accounts payable ledger contra (139 + 474)	613	(3)
	Discounts allowed (4,128 + 57)	4,185	(8)
	Adjustments	58	
Balance carried forward		11,282	

Note: part (ii) is a variation on the normal theme of questions set. Normally the amendments are shown rather than the corrected totals.

(c)

1 The sales figure in the accounting system is overstated by $850.

2 The sales returns figure in the accounting system is understated by $90.

3 The computer individual account summary accounts payable ledger contra, is understated by $474.

4 The individual account is overstated by $354 × 2 = $708.

5 The individual account is understated by $217 × 2 = $434.

6 The computer individual account summary bad debts are understated by $793.

7 The individual accounts need adjusting:

Dr CG $919

Cr EG $919

8 The individual account is overstated by $57.

9 There is no effect on the accounts receivable ledger control as the error affects the accounts payable ledger.

Question 3: Open item accounts receivable ledger system

This is a system whereby each customer's accounts receivable ledger account is held in the form of a record of unpaid items. This contrasts with the system of merely knowing the total balance outstanding at any point in time.

It is a more time-consuming system as each customer's payment has to be related to the clearance of specific invoices. Difficulties can arise when customers, for example, pay monthly but only for those items they have cleared by a given date. Thus their monthly payment may not clear all the items supplied in a given month. Another problem occurs where a customer periodically pays a round sum 'on account'.

The system assists a company to control the amount of credit given because of the clearer view of each customer's indebtedness. At each month-end a listing is produced of all outstanding items instead of a 'balance brought forward', plus current month's items less cash received in the month. This may indicate that some items may be very overdue. Action can then be taken to clear them.

CHAPTER 11 MULTIPLE-CHOICE QUESTIONS

Question 1

C The bank reconciliation should have been calculated as follows:

	$
Overdraft per bank statement	(38,600)
Add deposits not yet credited	41,200
	2,600
Less outstanding cheques	(3,300)
Overdraft per cash book	(700)

Question 2

A Items 3 and 4 relate to timing differences only and would appear in the bank reconciliation.

CHAPTER 11

EXAM-TYPE QUESTION

Spanners

(a) **Cash book adjustments**

Cash book

	$		$
Balance b/d	960	(1) Bank charges	35
(4) Correction of balance b/d	63	(2) Reversal of error 2 × $47	94
		(3) Returned cheque	18
		Balance c/d	876
	1,023		1,023
Balance b/d	876		

(b) **Bank reconciliation at 31 October**

	$	$	
Balance per bank statement (overdrawn)		124	o/d
Add: Unpresented cheques (5) $(214 + 370 + 30)		614	
		738	o/d
Less: Outstanding deposit (6)	1,542		
Cheque charged in error (7)	72		
		1,614	
Balance per cash book (in hand)		876	

CHAPTER 12

MULTIPLE-CHOICE QUESTIONS

Question 1

B The profit will be understated by the following amount:

	$
Amount charged in error to the repairs account	38,000
Less depreciation chargeable on the plant (3/12 × 20% × $38,000)	(1,900)
	$36,100

Question 2

D

	$
Opening balance on suspense account ($836,200 – $819,700)	16,500
Difference remaining after postings to the discount accounts ($5,100 – $3,900)	(1,200)
Difference from cheque incorrectly posted ($19,000 – $9,100)	(9,900)
	$5,400

Question 3

B Items 1 and 3 would result in an imbalance in the trial balance and therefore require an entry to the suspense account. Items 2, 4 and 5 do not affect the balancing of the accounts.

CHAPTER 12 EXAM-TYPE QUESTIONS

Question 1: Journal entries

		Dr	Cr
	Details	$	$
(a)	Motor expenses	150	
	Motor vehicles		150
	Repair cost transferred to correct account		
(b)	Pimple accounts payable ledger account	1,500	
	Pimple accounts receivable ledger account		1,500
	Contra on Pimple's ledger accounts per letter dated …		
(c)	Bad debts	570	
	Black		270
	Allowance for doubtful debts		300
		570	570

Closure of Black's accounts receivable ledger account following notification of bankruptcy and creation of doubtful debts allowance.

Note: as the business does not have control accounts for the accounts receivable and payable ledgers the double entry for receivables and payables is in their individual accounts.

Question 2: February

Suspense account

		$			$
(a)	January – Customer account	9	31 Dec	Trial balance: difference	736
(b)	Discount received	237	(d)	Error in list of balances	268
(c)	Discount received in list of balances (397 + 379)	776	(e)	Bank overdraft in list of balances	18
		1,022			1,022

The correcting journal entry is as follows:

		Dr	Cr
		$	$
Dr	Sales revenue account	500	
Cr	Disposal account		500

Note: as a Dr and Cr had originally been made, the trial balance is not out of balance as a result of this transaction. In order to complete the accounts further entries would be required to transfer the cost and accumulated depreciation on the machine to the disposal account.

		Dr	Cr
(f)		$	$
Dr	April – Customer account	1,000	
Cr	Sales revenue account		1,000

Note: as no Dr and Cr had been made, the trial balance still balances!

CHAPTER 13

EXAM-TYPE QUESTIONS

Question 1: Saavik

MEMORANDUM

To: The Company Accountant

From: Assistant Accountant

Date: x-x-20XX

Subject: Principal features of a spreadsheet financial modelling package

As requested in our recent discussion concerning the development of the accounting system of the company, I set out below the principal features of a spreadsheet financial modelling package.

Principal features of a spreadsheet package

1 Overview

A spreadsheet is a large accounting worksheet comprising a matrix of columns (labelled A, B, C, etc.) and rows. The larger spreadsheets could have up to 256 columns and 65,000 rows. The intersection of each row and column is called a cell. Each cell can contain any of the following:

- a description of an item, e.g. 'sales'
- a value, e.g. '3,000'
- a calculation, e.g. SUM(B3..B6).

By carefully inserting data into the spreadsheet in these cells a model of the business can be created. It is normal to have time periods being represented by the columns and items of income and expenditure being represented by the rows.

2 Storage and viewing of the spreadsheet

The spreadsheet will be stored on disk, and called into the computer's memory by the spreadsheet application program when the user wants to work on the spreadsheet. The VDU, however, cannot show all of the spreadsheet at any one time, and so the spreadsheet can be scrolled up/down and right/left using command keys or the computer's mouse if it has one.

A full picture of the spreadsheet can, though, be printed out as a 'hard copy' whenever this is required.

3 Use of the spreadsheet

When the model of the company has been built up on the spreadsheet, then it will permit 'what if' analysis to be carried out on it. The user of the spreadsheet can alter the variables in the spreadsheet to see what effect this has on other parts of the model. For example, sales value for all product lines could be altered and the results on gross and net profit be seen. This type of analysis would normally take many hours using a manual system and gives a spreadsheet a distinct advantage over purely manual systems.

Criteria to be considered when evaluating a spreadsheet package

1 Size of spreadsheet – is the spreadsheet large enough for the company's requirements?

2 Other applications needed within the spreadsheet – does the spreadsheet need a compatible database?

3 Manual – is there a well-written, easy to use reference manual?

4 Supplier support – does the supplier provide telephone hot-line support to sort out problems?

5 Is the spreadsheet display easy to understand?

6 Does the spreadsheet contain all the arithmetical functions needed?

7 Is there an adequate help facility in the software?

8 Is split screen working allowed?

Note: it is important to make sure that your answer is in the format required, in this case a memorandum.

Question 2: Database

(a) **Database**

Database is the term used to describe a sophisticated management information concept, based on the use of computers. It uses a comprehensive file of data so structured that individual applications, eg receivables ledger, production control, management accounting etc can draw on information from the file and update it but do not themselves constrain the file's design or its contents.

Whereas in conventional systems the programmer is concerned with the structure of files and methods of access, in a database system he can work independently of the file.

Between him and the file is a software interface known as the *database management system* (DBMS) which is responsible for providing the data as and when required by the particular application program.

(b) **Advantages**

Advantages to be gained from using such a system include the following:

1 The total needs of the company are taken into account in the design of the centralised file, in contrast to individual files serving the needs of each application.

2 Reports should be more comprehensive and meaningful because management information is based on all the data available.

3 More effective utilisation of programmers is possible because they are no longer concerned with data management as such. Also, they are no longer constrained by the need to consider file structure, etc.

4 Flexibility is increased because the DBMS can effect changes in the file independently of application programs.

Note: this is a definition question requiring a clear, precise answer.

CHAPTER 14 MULTIPLE-CHOICE QUESTION

D The other three contain items which are not considered to contribute towards reliability.

CHAPTER 14

EXAM-TYPE QUESTIONS

Question 1: Fundamental accounting assumptions

(a) ***Going concern***

The going concern concept assumes the enterprise will continue in operational existence for the foreseeable future. This means in particular that the income statement and balance sheet assume no intention or necessity to liquidate or curtail significantly the scale of operation.

For example, non-current assets are not generally stated at 'break up value', i.e. the value obtainable if there were a forced sale of the assets of the enterprise.

(b) ***Accruals***

The effects of transactions and other events should be recognised when they occur and not as cash is received or paid. Thus they are recorded in the accounting records and reported in the financial statements of the periods to which they relate.

(c) ***Consistency***

There should be consistency of accounting treatment of like items within each accounting period and from one period to the next.

For example, the definition of cost for inventory valuation should be applied to all inventory items in the same accounting period and to subsequent accounting periods.

Question 2: Advertising campaign

Tutorial note: There is no right answer for the carrying forward of advertising costs. The full range of alternatives should be explained. The question does not state the date to which the financial accounts are prepared. The answer assumes it to be a calendar year.

To: Client

From: Accountant

Date:

Subject: Accounting treatment of advertising campaign

There are a number of possible treatments.

1 Write off the whole amount in 20X7

This approach may appear to be justified due to the concept of prudence – all costs should be written off unless it is foreseeable that sufficient revenues will be generated in future accounting periods to cover the costs in question and any further anticipated costs.

However, the payment of $10,000 is in advance of the receipt of the service – i.e. the advertisements on the local radio stations. Thus the payment is a prepayment and should be shown as such in the 20X7 financial statements. This is an example of the accruals concept. The costs are costs of the 20X8 period at the earliest as this is the period in which the service is provided to you.

2 Carry forward part to 20X9

The accruals and matching concepts require the carry forward of costs to match against the revenues which the costs generate. Thus 40% of the costs could be carried forward.

However, prudence would suggest that the benefits are difficult to quantify precisely in this area; thus the costs should not be carried forward.

3 Write off in 20X8

For the reasons stated in (1) and (2) above, the write-off of the expenditure in 20X8 appears the best alternative. In suggesting this alternative, it is presumed that other accounting concepts do not affect matters. In particular:

- **The consistency concept**. If similar payments have been made in earlier years, the same accounting treatment should be followed.
- **Materiality**. If the amounts involved are immaterial in relation to the financial statements as a whole, then the accounting treatment of this particular item is not important.

Users of published accounts

The needs of the different users of accounts vary and as a result they may prefer alternative accounting treatments.

A shareholder would be primarily interested in the profit trends of the company. Thus, spreading costs forward to match with anticipated revenue may present the fairest trend for profits. On the other hand, a lender may have more regard to the asset position and may only wish tangible assets to be recorded.

Question 3: Cost concepts

(a) **Historical cost convention**

Under the historical cost convention, assets are stated in the balance sheet at their purchase price at the date of acquisition (less any amounts written off in respect of depreciation or impairment in value). Capital is simply the difference between assets and liabilities, and profit is calculated as revenues less original cost of resources used. If prices are rising, it is possible for a company to show a profit in its historical cost financial statements despite having identical physical assets and owing identical liabilities at the beginning and end of its accounting period.

Going concern convention

The going concern convention assumes that an enterprise will continue in operational existence for the foreseeable future. This means, in particular, that the financial statements are drawn up on the assumption that there is no intention or necessity to liquidate or curtail significantly the scale of operation.

(b) As stated above, the historical cost convention records assets at their original cost. However, to the extent that an asset is worth less to the business on a going concern basis, then the asset is stated at net realisable value.

For example, inventory is normally stated at cost as it is expected to be sold at a higher price in the normal course of business. Slow-moving inventory items effectively reflect a poor purchasing decision by the enterprise and may need to be sold at less than cost. It is thus valued at net realisable value.

If the going concern basis did not apply in the previous paragraph, it is likely that more inventory would have to be sold at less than cost on a 'forced sale' basis. Thus, the historical cost convention still requires the going concern concept to apply so that most items can be stated at original cost.

It could be argued, however, that the going concern convention is less important to the historical cost convention that to the current cost convention, as the current cost convention tends to result in assets being revalued upwards to show their current value. The absence of the going concern convention may result in more reductions from current values to low values that would apply if it is assumed that the enterprise would have to sell its assets quickly.

Question 4: Accounting concepts

(a) **Materiality**

The IASB's *Framework for the Preparation and Presentation of Financial Statements* defines materiality as follows:

> 'Information is material if its omission or misstatement could influence the economic decisions of users taken on the basis of the financial statements.'

Example: The amount of a trade receivable written off as irrecoverable would be disclosed by note only if material.

(b) **Substance over form**

This concept means that when there is a difference between the legal form an item or transaction and its real nature, the real nature (substance) should be recognised whenever legally possible.

Example: An asset being acquired on hire purchase terms should be recognised as an asset when the contract begins, regardless of the fact that ownership does not pass until the end of the contract.

(c) **Money measurement**

The money measurement concept is that financial accounting can only deal with items capable of being expressed in monetary terms. This concept is relevant in deciding whether or not an asset can be recognised – if it cannot be valued with reasonable accuracy it cannot be included in the balance sheet.

Example: The expertise of the research staff of an enterprise may be a vital contributor to its success, but it cannot be recognised in the financial statement because it is almost impossible to value it.

CHAPTER 15 MULTIPLE-CHOICE QUESTION

D Statements 2, 3 and 5 are correct.

CHAPTER 15 EXAM-TYPE QUESTION

Research and development expenditure

(a) **Research**

Original and planned investigation to gain new scientific or technical knowledge or understanding.

Development

The use of scientific or technical knowledge to produce new or substantially improved products.

(b) The two accounting concepts which are particularly relevant here are the accruals concept and the prudence concept.

The accruals concept requires costs to be matched with the relevant revenue. This implies that costs which have been incurred but have not resulted in sales should be carried forward as assets at the year end so that they can be matched with sales when they do arise.

Under this concept all development costs would be carried forward.

The prudence concept, however, requires costs to be written off unless it is reasonably certain that sales will be made in the future which will fully cover those costs.

Under this concept research expenditure would be written off as there is no clear link between the expenditure and the commercial sale of a product. Some development expenditure would also be written off if by the end of the accounting period it is not reasonably certain that profitable production will ensue. Only part of development expenditure would thus be carried forward.

IAS 38 requires development costs to be capitalised if and only if certain conditions are met.

CHAPTER 16 MULTIPLE-CHOICE QUESTION

B The other lists contain adjusting items.

CHAPTER 16 EXAM-TYPE QUESTIONS

Question 1: Events

(a) IAS 10 *Events after the Balance Sheet Date* offers the following definitions of events occurring between the balance sheet date and the date on which the financial statements are authorised for issue:

1 Those which require adjustment in the financial statements – events that provide additional evidence to assist with the estimation of amounts relating to conditions existing at the balance sheet date.

2 Those which require disclosure by note – events that do not affect the condition of assets and liabilities at the balance sheet date, but are of such importance that non-disclosure would affect the ability of users of the financial statements to make proper evaluations and decisions.

(b) Any two from the following lists:

Events which should be adjusted for

The following are examples of post balance sheet events for which the financial statements should normally be adjusted:

Non-current assets. The subsequent determination of the purchase price or of the proceeds of sale of assets purchased or sold before the year end.

Property. A valuation which provides evidence of an impairment in value.

Investments. The receipt of a copy of the financial statements or other information in respect of an unquoted company which provides evidence of an impairment in the value of a long-term investment.

Inventories and work-in-progress

1 The receipt of proceeds of sales after the balance sheet date or other evidence concerning the net realisable value of inventories.

2 The receipt of evidence that the previous estimate of accrued profit on a long-term contract was materially inaccurate.

Receivables. The renegotiation of amounts owing by customers, or the insolvency of a customer.

Tax. The receipt of information regarding rates of tax.

Claims. Amounts received or receivable in respect of insurance claims which were in the course of negotiation at the balance sheet date.

Discoveries. The discovery of errors or frauds which show that the financial statements were incorrect.

Events which should be disclosed by note

The following are examples of post balance sheet events which normally should be disclosed by note to the financial statements:

Mergers and acquisitions.

Reconstructions and proposed reconstructions.

Issues of shares and loan notes or bonds.

Purchases and sales of non-current assets and investments.

Losses of non-current assets or inventories as a result of a catastrophe such as fire or flood.

Opening new trading activities or extending existing trading activities.

Closing a significant part of the trading activities if this was not anticipated at the year end.

Decline in the value of property and investments held as non-current assets, if it can be demonstrated that the decline occurred after the year end.

Government action, such as nationalisation.

Strikes and other labour disputes.

Augmentation of pension benefits.

Question 2: Jurien

To: The Directors of Jurien

From: Financial Adviser

Date: x-x-20xx

Re: Accounting treatment of items in current financial statements

You have asked me for advice on three matters, and I set out my response below.

1 IAS 37 *Provisions, Contingent Liabilities and Contingent Assets* will require a provision to be recognised for the best estimate of the amount needed to settle the obligation, because there is a probable present obligation arising from a past event.

2 In accordance with IAS 10 *Events after the Balance Sheet Date*, the criterion is whether the discovery of the financial difficulties provides evidence that the debtor had difficulties at the balance sheet date. Unless there is clear evidence that there were no difficulties at the balance sheet date, an allowance should be made.

3 IAS 2 *Inventories* contains reasonably clear rules on the allocation of overheads to inventories of finished goods:

- only overheads relating to production may be included
- the allocation of fixed production overheads must be based on the normal level of activities in the period.

Two examples of overheads to be excluded:

- selling costs
- administrative overheads not contributing to bringing inventories to their present condition and location.

Financial Adviser

CHAPTER 17 MULTIPLE-CHOICE QUESTIONS

Question 1

A The sales figure must be reconstructed as follows:

	$
Cash received from credit customers	381,600
Expenses paid out of cash from credit customers	6,800
Cash sales	112,900
Bad debts (i.e. the sale was actually made)	7,200
Discounts allowed to customers	9,400
Less refunds to credit customers	(2,100)
Less opening receivables	(29,100)
Plus closing receivables	38,600
	525,300

Question 2

D

	$
Opening inventory	17,000
Purchases	91,000
Closing inventory	(24,000)
Cost of sales	84,000

Sales = $84,000 × 100/60 = $140,000

Question 3

A The rent expense for the year should be:

5/12 × $24,000 + 7/12 × $30,000 = $27,500

Question 4

B

Cost of sales = 70% × $64,800 = $45,360

	$
Opening inventory	28,400
Purchases	49,600
Cost of sales	(45,360)
Loss of inventory	32,640

CHAPTER 17 PRACTICE QUESTION

B Letitslide

Income statement for year ended 31 December 20X5

	$	$
Credit sales (W2)		1,560
Cash sales (W2)		4,317
Sales revenue		5,877
Opening inventory	1,310	
Add: Purchases (W3)	3,133	
	4,443	
Less: Closing inventory	1,623	
		2,820
Gross profit		3,057
Expenses (W4)	1,090	
Bad debts (W6)	49	
Depreciation (W7)	60	
		1,199
Net profit		1,858

Balance sheet as at 31 December 20X5

	$	$	$
Non-current asset:			
Delivery van, at cost		900	
Less: Depreciation (W7)		60	
			840
Current assets:			
Inventory		1,623	
Receivables	382		
Less: Allowance for doubtful debts (W6)	19		
		363	
Cash at bank		572	
Cash in hand		29	
			2,587
			3,427
Capital account:			
At 1 Jan 20X5 (W1)		1,652	
Add: Profit for year		1,858	
		3,510	
Less: Drawings (W5)		1,100	
			2,410
Current liabilities:			
Trade payables		914	
Accruals		103	
			1,017
			3,427

Note: as the cash account and bank account have already been summarised it is only necessary to post the other side of the cash and bank entries to the relevant accounts. Some information may be inserted immediately into the financial statements, so leave two pages for them. Information can then be inserted as soon as it is available. For example, opening and closing inventory can be put straight to the financial statements.

Workings

(W1) **Calculation of opening capital**

	$
Inventory	1,310
Receivables	268
Cash	62
Bank	840
	2,480
Less: Payables ($712 + 116)	828
Capital at 1 Jan 20X5	1,652

Note: there is no need to complete this working before proceeding to post the transactions for the year. It is better to add the items as and when you find them in the question.

(W2) **Accounts receivable control**

	$		$
Receivables b/d	268	Cheques for sales	1,416
Sales for year (bal fig)	5,877	Bad debt written off	30
		Cash takings	4,317
		Receivables c/d	382
	6,145		6,145
Balance b/d	382		

Note: the accounts receivable control account has been used to find total sales. An alternative approach would be to post the 'shop takings' straight to the income statement as cash sales and the balancing figure in the receivables control account would then be $1,560, i.e. the credit sales.

(W3) **Accounts payable control**

	$		$
Cash	316	Balance b/d	712
Bank	2,715	Drawings	100
Balance c/d	914	Purchases	3,133
	3,945		3,945
		Balance b/d	914

(W4) **Expenses**

	$		$
Cash	584	Balance b/d	116
Bank	519	Income statement	1,090
Balance c/d	103		
	1,206		1,206
		Balance b/d	103

(W5) **Drawings**

	$
Purchases	100
Cash account	600
Bank account	400
	1,100

(W6) **Bad debts account**

	$		$
Bad debt		Income statement	49
Accounts receivable control account	30		
Allowance for doubtful debts account 5% × 382	19		
	49		49

Note: as there is no opening allowance for doubtful debts, there is no need to show that account. The $19 can be inserted into the balance sheet.

(W7) **Depreciation**

20% × 900 × 4/12 = $60.

CHAPTER 17

EXAM-TYPE QUESTION

Ben White

Note: where a gross profit or mark-up is used to compute information for accounting purposes, the gross profit calculation in the income statement is an integral part of the workings (as well as the solution). The missing information may be any item.

Write up the statement with the information immediately available – in this question opening and closing inventory – and insert further information when it becomes available through writing up the accounts receivable and payable control accounts. In the question the purchases figures become available. The income statement can then be used to compute sales.

(a) **Income statement for year ended 30 June 20X6**

	$	$	%
Sales revenue $\frac{125}{100} \times \$12{,}000$		15,000	125
Opening inventory	3,825		
Add: Purchases (W5)	12,175		
	16,000		
Less: Closing inventory	4,000		
Cost of sales		12,000	100
Gross profit 25% × $12,000		3,000	25
Depreciation (10% × $5,000)		500	
Net profit		2,500	

(b) **Balance sheet as at 30 June 20X6**

	Cost $	*Dep'n* $	$
Non-current assets:			
Plant and machinery	5,000	500	4,500
Motor van	700	–	700
	5,700	500	5,200
Current assets:			
Inventory		4,000	
Receivables		7,000	
Cash		1,950	
			12,950
			18,150
Capital account:			
Balance at 1 Jul 20X5 (W1)		13,200	
Legacy introduced		300	
Net profit for year		2,500	
Drawings (W7)		(2,850)	
			13,150
Non-current liabilities:			
Loan (W6)			1,500
Current liabilities:			
Payables			3,500
			18,150

Workings

(W1) **Calculation of opening capital**

	$	$
Assets:		
Plant and machinery		5,000
Inventory		3,825
Receivables		7,175
Cash at bank		2,200
		18,200
Less: Liabilities:		
Payables	3,000	
Loan	2,000	
		5,000
Capital at 1 July 20X5		13,200

(W2) **Bank**

	$		$
Balance b/d	2,200	Purchases	11,675
Capital – legacy	300	Loan	500
Cash (bal fig (i))	13,885	Van	700
		Drawings ($80 × 12)	960
		Drawings – income tax	600
		Balance c/d	1,950
	16,385		16,385
Balance b/d	1,950		

(W3) **Cash**

	$		$
Sales control	15,175	Bank	13,885
		Drawings (bal fig (iii))	1,290
	15,175		15,175

(W4) **Accounts receivable control**

	$		$
Balance b/d	7,175	Cash (bal fig (ii))	15,175
Income statement – sales (calculated using GP percentage)	15,000	Balance c/d	7,000
	22,175		22,175
Balance b/d	7,000		

(W5) **Accounts payable control**

	$		$
Cash	11,675	Balance b/d	3,000
Balance c/d	3,500	Income statement – purchases	12,175
	15,175		15,175
		Balance b/d	3,500

(W6) **Z Loan**

	$
Sum owing	2,000
Less paid in year	500
	1,500

(W7) **Drawings**

	$
Bank account	960
Bank account – income tax	600
Cash account	1,290
	2,850

Note re sequence of entries:

1. Cash paid into bank is calculated as a balancing figure in the bank account ($13,885).
2. Total sales for the year is calculated from the income statement (cost of goods sold can be converted to sales by addition of 25% onto cost).
3. Cash collected from sales is calculated as balancing figure in accounts receivable control account ($15,175).
4. Drawings of $1,290 is balancing figure in the cash account.

CHAPTER 18 MULTIPLE-CHOICE QUESTION

A

	D	*E*	*F*	*Total*
	$'000	$'000	$'000	$'000
First 6 months' profit				240
Salaries		12	12	(24)
Balance in psr(5:3:2)	108	64.8	43.2	216
Second 6 months' profit				240
Salaries		18	12	(30)
Balance in psr (3:1:1)	126	42	42	210
Total profit shares	234	136.8	109.2	

CHAPTER 18 PRACTICE QUESTION

Oliver and Twist

(a) **Trial balance as at 31 December**

	Dr	Cr
	$	$
Capital account:		
Oliver		9,000
Twist		10,000
10% loan account:		
Twist		5,000
Williams		6,000
Current account balance on 1 January:		
Oliver		1,000
Twist		2,000
Drawings:		
Oliver	6,500	
Twist	5,500	
Sales revenue		113,100
Sales returns	3,000	
Closing inventory	17,000	
Cost of goods sold	70,000	
Accounts receivable ledger control account	30,000	
Accounts payable ledger control account		25,000
Operating expenses	26,100	
Non-current assets at cost	37,000	
Accumulated depreciation		18,000
Bank overdraft		3,000
Suspense (bal fig)		3,000
	195,100	195,100

Tutorial note: the question requires a trial balance to be drawn up before any adjustments are made. Many candidates may have attempted to make adjustments before the extraction of the trial balance but this was not what was required.

The information in the question refers to 'closing inventory' and 'cost of goods sold'. Both of these imply that the year-end adjustments for inventory have already been made. This is a very important point to look out for in more advanced questions on the preparation of financial statements.

(b) ***Tutorial note:*** there is no set format per part (b). The key thing to remember is that parts (b) and (c) of the question are the normal parts of an accounts preparation from a trial balance question.

Adjustments to trial balance

Ref to question			Dr	Cr
			$	$
(i)	(a)	Sales returns	100	
		Accounts receivable ledger control		100
	(b)	Accounts payable ledger control	200	
		Accounts receivable ledger control		200
	(c)	Accounts receivable ledger control	1,800	
		Sales revenue		1,800

(ii)	Disposal	5,000	
	Non-current asset cost		5,000
	Accumulated depreciation	5,000	
	Disposal		5,000
	Suspense	1,000	
	Disposal		1,000

Tutorial note: The last entry arises as the transaction was originally inserted into the books as a one-sided transaction (Dr Bank). The missing credit entry must therefore make up part of the $3,000 suspense account balance.

(iii)	Expenses	500	
	Drawings – Twist		500
	Drawings – Oliver	1,000	
	Cost of goods sold		1,000
(iv)	Interest expense	1,100	
	Interest accrual		1,100

(c) **Income statement for the year ended 31 December**

	$	$
Sales revenue (113,100 + 1,800)		114,900
Less: Returns (3,000 + 100)		(3,100)
		111,800
Cost of sales (70,000 – 1,000)		(69,000)
Gross profit		42,800
Operating expenses (26,100 – 1,000 + 500)	25,600	
Loan interest	1,100	
		(26,700)
Net profit for year		16,100

	Oliver	*Twist*	
	$	$	
Interest on capital	900	1,000	
Salary	5,000		
Balance of profit equally	4,600	4,600	
	10,500	5,600	16,100

Balance sheet as at 31 December

	$	$	$
Non-current assets:			
Cost (37,000 – 5,000)		32,000	
Depreciation (18,000 – 5,000)		13,000	
			19,000
Current assets:			
Inventory		17,000	
Receivables (30,000 – 100 – 200 + 1,800)		31,500	
			48,500
			67,500
	Capital	*Current*	*Total*

	$	$	$
Oliver (see working)	9,000	4,000	13,000
Twist (see working)	10,000	2,600	12,600
	19,000	6,600	25,600
Long-term liability – loan			11,000
Current liabilities:			
Payables		24,800	
Interest		1,100	
Bank overdraft		3,000	
			28,900
Suspense account			2,000
			67,500

Working

Current accounts

	Oliver	Twist		Oliver	Twist
	$	$		$	$
Drawings	6,500	5,500	Balance b/d	1,000	2,000
Adjustment to drawings	1,000		Adjustment to drawings		500
Balance c/d	4,000	2,600	Interest on capital	900	1,000
			Salary	5,000	
			Profit	4,600	4,600
	11,500	8,100		11,500	8,100

CHAPTER **19**

MULTIPLE-CHOICE QUESTION

C

Share capital	$'000
Opening 1,000,000 shares of 50c	500
Issue of 200,000 shares of 50c	100
Bonus issue 1,200,000/4 = 300,000 shares of 50c	150
	750

Share premium	$'000
Opening share premium	300
Issue of 200,000 shares at premium of 80c	160
Charge for bonus issue	(150)
	310

CHAPTER **19** EXAM-TYPE QUESTION

Floyd

Income statement for year ended 31 March 20X5

	$
Sales revenue	998,600
Cost of sales (W1)	830,740
Gross profit	167,860
Administrative costs (W1)	100,741
Loan interest (9% × 75,000)	6,750
Profit before taxation	60,369
Tax	31,200
Profit for year	29,169

Balance sheet as at 31 March 20X5

	Cost $	*Dep'n* $	$
Non-current assets:			
Plant (W3)	307,400	115,340	192,060
Current assets:			
Inventory		61,070	
Receivables	52,030		
Less: Allowance	2,601		
		49,429	
Cash at bank		41,118	
Cash in hand		126	
			151,743
			343,803
Capital and reserves:			
Share capital: 25c ordinary shares		100,000	
Share premium		20,000	
Accumulated profit		72,579	
			192,579
Non-current liabilities:			
9% loan notes			75,000
Current liabilities:			
Trade payables		38,274	
Taxation		31,200	
Loan interest		6,750	
			76,224
			343,803

Statement of reserve movements

	Accumulated profit	*Share premium*
	$	$
Balance at 1 April 20X4	57,910	20,000
Profit for year	29,169	
Dividends paid	(14,500)	
Balance at 31 March 20X5	72,579	20,000

Workings

(W1)

	Cost of sales	*Administrative costs*
	$	$
Per question	800,000	100,000
Bad debts (W2)		741
Depreciation (W3)	30,740	
	830,740	100,741

(W2) **Allowance for doubtful debts account**

	$		$
Balance c/d 5% × 52,030	2,601	Balance b/d	1,860
		Income statement	741
	2,601		2,601

(W3) **Accumulated depreciation account**

	$		$
Balance c/d	115,340	Balance b/d	84,600
		Income statement:	
		Cost of sales	
		10% × 307,400	30,740
	115,340		115,340

CHAPTER 19 PRACTICE QUESTION

Nimrod

Income statement for year ended 30 September 20X7

	$	$
Sales revenue		240,000
Less: Returns		1,116
		238,884
Inventory at 1 October 20X6	42,744	
Purchases	131,568	
	174,312	
Less: Closing inventory at 30 September 20X7	46,638	
		127,674
Gross profit		111,210
Discount received		5,292
		116,502

Rent	6,372	
Wages and salaries (W2)	24,840	
Insurance (W1)	5,388	
General expenses	1,308	
Bad debts (W4)	1,476	
Depreciation: Buildings (W3)	11,400	
Fixtures and fittings (W3)	7,200	
Loan interest (W5)	2,400	
		60,384
Profit before tax		56,118
Tax		20,000
Profit for year		36,118

Nimrod Balance sheet as at 30 September 20X7

	Cost $	*Depn* $	$
Non-current assets:			
Land	54,000	-	54,000
Buildings	114,000	29,400	84,600
Furniture and fittings	66,000	37,200	28,800
	234,000	66,600	167,400
Goodwill	49,200	–	49,200
			216,600
Current assets:			
Inventory		46,638	
Receivables	37,920		
Less: Allowance (W4)	1,896		
		36,024	
Prepayments (W1)		300	
Cash in hand		696	
			83,658
			300,258
Capital and reserves:			
Share capital:			
60,000 $1 ordinary shares		60,000	
60,000 6% $1 preference shares		60,000	
Share premium		3,000	
General reserve (30,000 + 24,000)		54,000	
Accumulated profit		16,318	
			193,318
Non-current liabilities:			
5% bonds			48,000
Current liabilities:			
Bank overdraft		18,000	
Trade payables		18,900	
Accruals (W6)		2,040	
Tax		20,000	
			58,940
			300,258

Note: The company proposes to pay the preference dividend for the second half of the year to date ($1,800) and an ordinary dividend of 6% ($3,600).

Statement of changes in equity (reserve movements only)

	Accumulated profit	*General reserve*	*Share premium*
	$	$	$
Balance at 1 October 20X6	10,800	30,000	3,000
Profit for year	36,118		
Dividends paid:			
Preference	(3,600)		
Ordinary	(3,000)		
Transfer	(24,000)	24,000	
	16,318	54,000	3,000

Workings

Note: there is a lot of information to be inserted into the final accounts but some of the balances per the list of balances need adjustment. Work through the additional information, removing the relevant balances from the list of balances into the workings. Balances not requiring adjustment can then be inserted into the financial statements.

(W1) **Insurance account**

	$		$
Balance per list of balances	5,688	Income statement	5,388
		Balance c/d – prepayment	300
	5,688		5,688

(W2) **Wages account**

	$		$
Balance per list of balances	24,000	Income statement	24,840
Balance c/d – accrual	840		
	24,840		24,840

(W3) **Accumulated depreciation account**

	Buildings	*Furniture*		*Buildings*	*Furniture*
	$	$		$	$
Balance c/d	29,400	37,200	Balance per list of balances	18,000	30,000
			Income statement:		
			10% × 114,000	11,400	
			20% × (66,000 – 30,000)		7,200
	29,400	37,200		29,400	37,200

(W4) **Bad debts account**

	$		$
Per list of balances	2,028	Allowance for doubtful debts account	552
		Income statement	1,476
	2,028		2,028

Allowance for doubtful debts account

	$		$
Bad debts account	552	Per list of balances	2,448
Balance c/d 5% × 37,920	1,892		
	2,448		2,448

(W5) **Loan interest account**

	$		$
Per list of balances	1,200	Income statement	2,400
Balance c/d – accrual	1,200		
	2,400		2,400

(W6) **Accruals**

	$
Wages (W2)	840
Loan interest (W5)	1,200
	2,040

CHAPTER 20 PRACTICE QUESTION

General Warehouses

General Warehouses
Balance sheet as at 31 December 20X3

	$m	$m
Non-current assets		
Plant and machinery		22
Goodwill		45
		67
Current assets		
Inventory	50	
Receivables	165	
Cash	30	
		245
		312
Capital and reserves		
Issued share capital	150	
Share premium	10	
Contingency reserve	10	
Accumulated profits	87	
		257

Current liabilities		
Trade payables	30	
Taxation	25	
		55
		312

General Warehouses
Income statement for the year ended 31 December 20X3

	$m	$m
Sales revenue		486
Cost of sales		242
Gross profit		244
Distribution costs	115	
Administrative expenses	50	
		165
Profit from operations		79
Income from investments		8
Profit before tax		87
Income tax expense		25
Profit after tax		62

Statement of changes in equity

	Share capital	*Share premium*	*Contingency reserve*	*Accumulated profit*	*Total*
	$m	$m	$m	$m	$m
Balance at 1 January 20X3	150	10	10	25	195
Net profit for year				62	62
Balance at 31 December 20X3	150	10	10	87	257

Working

	Cost of sales	*Distribution costs*	*Admin expenses*
	$m	$m	$m
Opening inventory	30		
Purchases	270		
Purchases returns	(13)		
Carriage outwards		14	
Warehouse wages		40	
Salespersons' salaries		30	
Administrative wages			20
Delivery vehicle hire		10	
Distribution expenses		5	
Administrative expenses			15
Directors' salaries			15
Closing inventory	(50)		
Depreciation		16	
Amortisation of goodwill	5		
	242	115	50

Tutorial note: This three column working will be needed in almost all questions requiring this format. It is a very fast way of getting the three totals in which all the expenses except interest have to be included. Note that all you need to do is list the items from the list of balances, then add any end of year adjustments. Negatives go in brackets, and you have the three totals you need. Amortisation of goodwill has been included in cost of sales. Alternatively, it may be shown under 'other operating expenses' after administrative expenses.

EXAM-TYPE QUESTIONS

Question 1: Board of Directors

General Warehouses
Income statement for the year ended 31 December 20X3

	$m	$m
Sales revenue		486
Increase in inventory of goods for resale		20
		506
Purchases of goods for resale		257
		249
Staff costs	90	
Depreciation (16 + 5)	21	
Other operating charges (working)	59	170
Profit from operations		79
Income from investments		8
Profit before tax		87
Tax		25
Profit for year		62

Working

The figure for other operating charges is as follows:

	$m
Carriage outwards	14
General distribution expenses	5
Vehicle hire	10
General administrative expenses	15
Directors' salaries	15
	59

Question 2: Ople

Income statement for the year ended 31 March 20X2

	$'000	$'000
Sales revenue		8,500
Cost of sales (working)		(5,270)
Gross profit		3,230
Distribution costs (working)		(1,490)
Administration expenses (working)		(630)
Operating profit		1,110
Income from investments		240
Profit before tax		1,350
Tax: based on profit for year	380	

Over-provision for previous year	(30)	
		(350)
Profit for year		1,000

Working

Analysis of costs

	Cost of sales	Distribution	Admin.
	$'000	$'000	$'000
Purchases (500 + 4,400 – 700)	4,200		
Audit			50
Depreciation	85	40	20
Salaries			95
Distribution		425	
Factory expenses	970		
Hire	15		
Office expenses			190
Legal expenses			35
Warehouse rent		65	
Wages 0 : 80 : 20		960	240
	5,270	1,490	630

Question 3: Small

Balance sheet as at 31 March 20X5

	$	$
Non-current assets:		
Land and buildings (W3)	120,000	
Plant and machinery (W3)	37,760	
		157,760
Current assets:		
Inventory	160,000	
Receivables	100,000	
Prepayments	80,000	
Cash	90,000	
		430,000
Total assets		587,760
Capital and reserves:		
Issued capital	200,000	
Accumulated profits	157,760	
		357,760
Non-current liabilities:		
Loan notes		50,000
Current liabilities:		
Trade payables	170,000	
Loan notes	10,000	
		180,000
Total equity and liabilities:		587,760

Tutorial note: as some of the loan notes are payable within one year of the balance sheet date, that part of the liability has been shown under current liabilities.

Workings

(W1) **Depreciation**

	$	$
Factory 2% of $200,000		4,000
Plant and machinery		
NBV b/f	50,000	
Additions	10,000	
Disposals at NBV	(12,800)	
Depreciation 20% ×	47,200	=
		9,440
		13,440

(W2) **Disposal of plant**

	$	$
Proceeds		12,000
Cost	16,000	
Less: Depreciation	3,200	
		12,800
Loss on sale		800

(W3) **Property, plant and equipment**

	Land and buildings $	*Plant and machinery* $
Cost:		
At 1 April 20X4	200,000	80,000
Additions	-	10,000
Disposals	-	(16,000)
	200,000	74,000
Aggregate depreciation:		
At 1 April 20X4	76,000	30,000
Eliminated on disposals		(3,200)
Amount provided	4,000	9,440
At 31 March 20X5	80,000	36,240
Net book value at 31 March 20X5	120,000	37,760

(W4) **Profit for year**

	$	$
Profit for year per trial balance		111,000
Less: Depreciation (4,000 + 9,440)	13,440	
Loss on sale (W2)	800	
		14,240
		96,760

(W5) **Accumulated profit**

	$
Balance at 1 April 20X4	61,000
Profit for year (W4)	96,760
	157,760

Question 4: Pride

Balance sheet as at 31 March 20X1

	Cost	*Accumulated Depn.*	
	$'000	$'000	$'000
Assets			
Non-current assets:			
Land	210		210
Buildings	200	124	76
Plant and equipment (W1)	300	136	164
	710	260	450
Current assets:			
Inventory		180	
Receivables (146-12)		134	
Prepayments		8	
Cash		50	372
Total assets			822
Equity and liabilities			
Capital and reserves:			
Issued capital			
700,000 ordinary shares of 50c each		350	
Share premium account		240	
Accumulated profits		34	624
Non-current liabilities:			
10% loan notes			100
Current liabilities:			
Payables		94	
Accruals		4	98
Total equity and liabilities			822

Workings

(W1)

Plant and equipment

	Cost	*Accumulated depreciation*
	$'000	$'000
At 1 April 20X0	318	88
Less: Disposal	18	12
	300	76
		60
Depreciation for year		136

CHAPTER 21

MULTIPLE-CHOICE QUESTIONS

Question 1

B

	$	$
Cost of shares acquired		160,000
Net assets acquired		
Share capital	100,000	
Reserves	40,000	
	140,000	
Proportion acquired	80%	
		112,000
Goodwill acquired		48,000
Amortised to date (3/5 × $48,00)		(28,800)
Net book value		19,200

Question 2

D Minority interest = 40% × ($100,000 + 180,000) = $112,000

Question 3

C

	$
H Profits	480,000
Share of S's post-acquisition profits 75% × ($180,000 – $120,000)	45,000
Less: Good will fully amortised $280,000 – 75% ($200,000+$120,000)	(40,000)
	485,000

CHAPTER 21

EXAM-TYPE QUESTIONS

Question 1: Park and Gate

Park and its subsidiary
Consolidated balance sheet as at 31 December 20X4

	$
Freehold property	99,000
Other non-current assets	217,300
	316,300
Current assets	130,100
	446,400
Share capital	200,000
Accumulated profits	78,300
	278,300
Minority interest	58,400
Non-current liabilities – unsecured loan	30,000
Current liabilities	79,700
	446,400

Cost of control

	$		$
Shares in Gate	72,000	60% share capital	48,000
		60% pre-acquisitions reserves	22,500
		Balance: goodwill written off	1,500
	72,000		72,000

Minority interest

	$		$
Balance to CBS	58,400	40% share capital	32,000
		40% accumulated profits	26,400
	58,400		58,400

Accumulated profits

	$		$
Minority interest: 40% × $66,000	26,400	Park	62,700
Cost of control: 60% × $37,500	22,500	Gate	66,000
Cost of control: goodwill written off			
Balance to CBS	78,300		
	128,700		128,700

Question 2: Rich and Poor

Rich and its subsidiary
Consolidated balance sheet as at 30 June 20X8

	$	$
Non-current assets:		
Intangible assets – goodwill	2,800	
Tangible assets	360,000	
		362,800
Current assets		456,000
		818,800
Capital and reserves:		
Issued share capital		200,000
Accumulated profits		191,100
		391,100
Minority interest		65,700
		456,800
Current liabilities		362,000
		818,800

Cost of control account

	$		$
Shares in Poor:		Share capital:	
Ordinary	140,000	Ordinary (70%)	91,000
		Accumulated profits	35,000
		Accumulated profits – goodwill written off: 20% × $14,000 × 4	11,200
		Balance carried down	2,800
	140,000		140,000

Minority interest account

Consolidated balance sheet	65,700	Share capital:	
		Ordinary (30%)	39,000
		Accumulated profits	26,700
	65,700		65,700

Accumulated profits

	$		$
Cost of control account:		R	175,000
(70% × $50,000 pre-acquisition)	35,000	P	89,000
Minority interest account:			
(30% × $89,000)	26,700		
Cost of control: goodwill written off	11,200		
Balance to CBS	191,100		
	264,000		264,000

Note

As the shares were acquired four years before the current balance sheet date, it is necessary to include four years' amortisation of the $14,000 goodwill arising. For convenience the whole amortisation to date is shown as a single figure in the Cost of control account.

CHAPTER **22**

MULTIPLE-CHOICE QUESTION

B

All other lists contain one or more items that would not appear in the calculation of net cash from operating activities.

CHAPTER 22

PRACTICE QUESTIONS

Question 1: Bogdanovitch

Cash flow statement for the year ended 31 December 20X9

	$	$
Cash flows from operating activities		
Net profit before taxation	1,381	
Depreciation (111 + 351)	462	
Gain on sale of plant (W1)	(19)	
Loss on sale of fixtures (W2)	5	
Operating profit before working capital changes	1,829	
Increase in inventory	(660)	
Increase in receivables	(323)	
Increase in payables	4	
Cash generated from operations	850	
Dividends paid	(300)	
Tax paid (W3)	(255)	
Net cash from operating activities		295
Cash flows from investing activities		
Purchase of non-current assets (312 + 366) (W2)	(678)	
Proceeds of sale of non-current assets (203 + 95)	298	
Net cash used in investing activities		(380)
Cash flows from financing activities		
Issue of shares	400	
Net cash from financing activities		400
Net increase in cash and cash equivalents		315
Cash and cash equivalents at 1 January 20X9		197
Cash and cash equivalents at 31 December 20X9		512

Cash and cash equivalents

	31 December	
	20X8	*20X9*
	$	$
Balance at bank	197	512

Workings

(W1) **Plant and machinery (NBV)**

	$		$
Balance b/d	2,086	P & M – disposal	184
Bank – purchase	312	Depreciation (bal fig)	111
		Balance c/d	2,103
	2,398		2,398

Plant and machinery – disposal

	$		$
P & M (NBV)	184	Bank – proceeds	203
Gain on disposal	19		
	203		203

(W2) **Fixtures and fittings (NBV)**

	$		$
Balance b/d	1,381	F & F – disposal	100
Bank – purchase (bal fig)	366	Depreciation	351
		Balance c/d	1,296
	1,747		1,747

Fixtures and fittings – disposal

	$		$
F & F – NBV	100	Bank – proceeds	95
		Depreciation – loss on disposal	5
	100		100

(W3) **Taxation**

	$		$
Bank – tax paid (bal fig)	255	Balance b/d	257
Balance c/d	312	Income statement	310
	567		567

Question 2: Algernon

(a) **Cash flow statement for the year ended 31 December 20X7**

	$	$
Cash flows from operating activities		
Cash receipts from customers (W1)	190,000	
Cash paid to suppliers and employees (W2)	(155,000)	
Cash generated from operations	35,000	
Interest paid	(13,000)	
Dividends paid	(20,000)	
Net cash from operating activities		2,000
Cash flows from investing activities		
Purchase of tangible non-current assets (1,000 + 40,000)	(41,000)	
Purchase of investments	(30,000)	
Net cash used for investing activities		(71,000)
Cash flows from financing activities		
Issue of shares	12,000	
Loan notes	50,000	
Net cash from financing activities		62,000
Net decrease in cash and cash equivalents		(7,000)
Cash and cash equivalents at 1 January 20X7		3,000
Cash and cash equivalents at 31 December 20X7		(4,000)

Cash and cash equivalents

	31 December 20X6	*31 December 20X7*
	$	$
Balance at bank	3,000	(4,000)

Workings

(W1) **Receipts from sales**

Receivables control

	$		$
Balance b/d	40,000	Cash receipts (bal fig)	190,000
Sales revenue	200,000	Balance c/d	50,000
	240,000		240,000

(W2) **Payments**

Payables and wages control

	$		$
Cash paid (bal fig)	155,000	Balance b/d	40,000
Depreciation	2,000	Purchases re cost of sales (W3)	130,000
Balance c/d	60,000	Expenses	47,000
	217,000		217,000

(W3) **Cost of sales**

	$		$
Opening inventory	55,000	Cost of sales	120,000
Purchases and wages	130,000	Closing inventory	65,000
	185,000		185,000

Tutorial note: Little information has been given as to the nature of the costs of the company; for example, no information is supplied on wages and salaries. The payments figure thus includes all cash outflows relating to trading activities. Depreciation would have been charged in either cost of sales or expenses and this needs to be adjusted for. It does not matter whether the adjustment is shown in the payables control or the cost of sales accounts.

(b) Algernon has invested substantially in buildings, investments, inventory and receivables in the year. The finance has come from new share capital in part but mainly from loans. The equity to assets ratio of the company has thus decreased. The working capital has been financed by an equal increase in trade payables

The profits have been fully distributed as dividends despite the halving of profits from last year. It might have been wiser to cut back on dividends in the period of expansion until the benefits of the expansion are seen in the form of higher profits.

CHAPTER 22 EXAM-TYPE QUESTION

Crash

	$	$
Net profit (555 – 150 interest)	405	
Adjustments for:		
Depreciation	1,500	
Profit on sale of non-current asset	(75)	
Interest expense	150	
Operating profit before working capital changes:	1,980	
Increase in inventories	(135)	
Decrease in receivables	60	
Increase in payables	90	
Cash generated from operations:	1,995	
Interest paid	(150)	
Net cash from operating activities		1,845
Cash flows from investing activities:		
Purchase of property, plant and equipment (W1)	(2,700)	
Proceeds from sale of non-current asset	375	
Net cash used in investing activities		(2,325)
Cash flows from financing activities		
Proceeds from issuance of share capital	1,200	
Repayment of loan notes	(750)	450
Decrease in cash		(30)
Net overdraft at beginning of period (60–195)		(135)
Net overdraft at end of period (105–270)		(165)

Movement in non-current assets

Working

(W1)

Non-current assets – cost/valuation

	$'000		$'000
Opening balance	9,000	Transfer disposal	1,500
Revaluation	750	Closing balance	10,950
Net assets purchased	2,700		
	12,450		12,450

Non-current assets – depreciation

Non-current assets – depreciation

	$'000		$'000
Transfer disposal	1,200	Opening balance	3,300
Closing balance	3,600	Income statement	1,500
	4,800		
	4,800		4,800

Non-current assets – disposal

	$'000		$'000
Transfer cost	1,500	Transfer depreciation	1,200
Income statement – profit	75	Proceeds of sale	375
	1,575		1,575

CHAPTER **23**

MULTIPLE-CHOICE QUESTIONS

Question 1

D

Question 2

B

CHAPTER **23**

PRACTICE QUESTIONS

Question 1: Electrical engineering

Tutorial note: Fairly straightforward ratio analysis question. Ensure that your calculations are shown clearly.

For part (b) comment on the liquidity position of the company, the declining profitability, the equity to assets ratio and interest payable.

(a)

	20X1	*20X0*
Current ratio	30,500: 23,050 = 1.3:1	28,500: 19,400 = 1.5:1
Quick ratio	16,500: 23,050 = 0.7:1	15,500: 19,400 = 0.8:1
Inventory turnover in days	$\frac{14,000}{42,000} \times 365 = 122$ days	$\frac{13,000}{34,000} \times 365 = 140$ days
Receivables turnover in days	$\frac{16,000}{60,000} \times 365$ days $= 97$ days	$\frac{15,000}{50,000} \times 365 = 110$ days
Payables turnover in days (assume operating expenses incurred on credit terms)	$\frac{23,050}{42,000+15,500} \times 365$ = 146 days	$\frac{19,400}{34,000+13,000} \times 365$ = 151 days
Gross profit %	$\frac{18,000}{60,000} \times 100 = 30\%$	$\frac{16,000}{50,000} \times 100 = 32\%$
Net profit % (before tax)	$\frac{300}{60,000} \times 100 = 0.5\%$	$\frac{1,700}{50,000} \times 100 = 3.4\%$
Interest cover	$\frac{2,500}{2,200} = 1.1$ times	$\frac{3,000}{1,300} = 2.3$ times
Dividend cover	$\frac{(50)}{600} = (0.8)$ times	$\frac{1,100}{600} = 1.8$ times
Return on equity (before tax)	$\frac{300}{13,950} \times 100 = 2.2\%$	$\frac{1,700}{14,600} \times 100 = 11.6\%$
ROCE	$\frac{2,500}{13,950+6,000} \times 100 = 12.5\%$	$\frac{3,000}{14,600+5,500} \times 100 = 14.9\%$
Equity to assets ratio	$\frac{13,950}{43,000-23,050} \times 100 = 69.9\%$	$\frac{14,600}{39,500-19,400} = 72.6\%$

(b) There has been a decline in the liquidity position of the business. The 'weak' position in 20X0 where quick assets (receivables and bank) do not cover the immediate liabilities has deteriorated even further in 20X1. If this trend were to continue the going concern ability of the business would probably be in question. In addition the cover provided by profits over interest payable has more than halved; this would be considered a poor indicator by the interest bearing creditors. Such creditors may question the decision to declare the same level of dividend for 20X1 as for 20X0, even though the business made an after tax loss.

The business's profitability shows only a small 2% drop at the gross profit level but because of the significant levels of operating expenses and interest payable the net profit percentage in 20X1 is only one seventh of its 20X0 level. Clearly improvements are required if the business is to continue to report positive profit after tax figures.

Finally, management has increased the level of non-current assets; with such poor trading results they should be asked if such expansion was necessary and when the benefits from the use of such resources can be expected to accrue.

Question 2: Ratios – B

(a) (i) **Ratios of particular significance to shareholders**

	20X6	*20X7*
Earnings per share	$\frac{9,520}{39,680} \times 100 = 23.99c$	$\frac{11,660}{39,680} \times 100 = 29.39c$
Dividend cover	$\frac{9,520}{2,240} = 4.25$ times	$\frac{11,660}{2,200} = 5.3$ times

Tutorial note

$$\text{Earnings per share} = \frac{\text{Net profit for year after tax}}{\text{No of equity shares in issue}}$$

$$\text{Dividend cover} = \frac{\text{Profit for the financial year}}{\text{Ordinary dividend}}$$

(ii) **Ratios of particular significance for trade creditors**

	20X6	*20X7*
Current ratio	$\frac{92,447}{35,077} = 2.64$	$\frac{99,615}{40,490} = 2.46$
Quick ratio	$\frac{92,447 - 40,145}{35,077} = 1.49$	$\frac{99,615 - 50,455}{40,490} = 1.21$

Tutorial note

$$\text{Current ratio} = \frac{\text{Current assets}}{\text{Current liabilitie s}}$$

$$\text{Quick ratio} = \frac{\text{Current assets excluding inventory}}{\text{Current liabilitie s}}$$

(iii) **Ratios of particular significance for internal management**

	20X6	*20X7*
Return on capital employed	$\frac{15,254}{42,525} \times 100\% = 35.9\%$	$\frac{18,686}{51,985} \times 100\% = 35.9\%$
Sales revenue/Non-current assets	$\frac{486,300}{4,995} = 97.36$ times	$\frac{583,900}{12,700} = 45.97$ times

Tutorial note

$$\text{Return on capital employed} = \frac{\text{Profit before tax}}{\text{Share capital and reserves}}$$

It can also be calculated as:

$$\frac{\text{Profit before interest and tax}}{\text{Share capital and reserves and long - term liabilitie s}}$$

$$\text{Sales revenue/Non-current assets} = \frac{\text{Sales revenue}}{\text{Tangible non-current assets (NBV)}}$$

Other management ratios include Operating profit/Sales and Receivables/Sales.

(b) Earnings per share has increased by 22.5% due to improved profits. There has been no change in share capital. The dividend cover (the number of times the ordinary dividend is covered by the available profits) has increased because the percentage of profits paid out as a dividend has decreased. The dividend itself hardly changed which is clearly out of line with the earnings improvement. The company is adopting a cautious policy but the dividend looks secure.

The current ratio is decreasing, but it is still at an acceptable level. The quick ratio (measure of the company's liquidity) is also decreasing and at a faster rate, due to the increasing investment in inventory (current ratio is down approximately 7% and the quick ratio about 19%). The quick ratio is above the generally desired level of 1, but the company should watch this area carefully.

Return on capital employed has remained constant. The ratio of sales revenue to non-current assets has reduced dramatically, due to the high investment in non-current assets. These should help increase sales revenue and profitability in future years.

CHAPTER 23 EXAM-TYPE QUESTION

Brood

(a) **Ratios of particular significance for internal management**

				30 April	
				20X0	*20X1*
1	Return on total capital employed	5,000/48,600	6,500/72,300	10.3%	9.0%
2	Return on owners' equity	3,600/28,600	3,700/32,300	12.6%	11.5%
3	Current ratio	38,600/28,500	43,000/17,400	1.35:1	2.47:1
4	Quick ratio	22,200/28,500	24,600/17,400	0.78:1	1.41:1
5	Gearing	20,000/48,600	40,000/72,300	41.2%	55.3%

Alternative methods of calculation marked on their merits.

(b) The return on capital employed and the return on owners' equity both show a decline during the year. Gross profit has remained steady and expenses have not risen in line with increased sales revenue, so the cause is probably that the new capital raised by the loan note issue has not yet been deployed to increase profit.

The current ratio and the quick ratio were somewhat low at 30 April 20X0, because of the high bank overdraft. About half of the funds raised by the loan note issue have been used to reduce the overdraft, resulting in a movement to seemingly high ratios by 30 April 20X1. Expansion of the business as funds are deployed in the future development of the business should mean that these ratios return to a lower level.

The gearing ratio has risen from a fairly high level to a very high level as a result of the loan note issue. This means that the business is vulnerable to a downturn in profits as almost half of the current operating profit is absorbed by interest.

Index

U

V

W

FOULKS LYNCH
PUBLICATIONS

TEXTBOOK REVIEW FORM

Thank you for choosing the Official Text for the ACCA professional qualification. As we are constantly striving to improve our products, we would be grateful if you could provide us with feedback about how useful you found this textbook.

Name: ....

Address: ....

....

Email: ....

Why did you decide to purchase this textbook?

Have used them in the past	☐
Recommended by lecturer	☐
Recommended by friend	☐
Saw advertising	☐
Other (please specify)	☐

Which other Foulks Lynch products have you used?

Examination kit	☐
Distance learning	☐
Lynchpins	☐

How do you study?

At a college	☐
On a distance learning course	☐
Home study	☐
Other	☐

Please specify ....

Overall opinion of this textbook

	Excellent	*Adequate*	*Poor*
Introductory pages	☐	☐	☐
Syllabus coverage	☐	☐	☐
Clarity of explanations	☐	☐	☐
Clarity of definitions and key points	☐	☐	☐
Diagrams	☐	☐	☐
Practice questions	☐	☐	☐
Self-test questions	☐	☐	☐
Layout	☐	☐	☐
Index	☐	☐	☐

If you have further comments/suggestions or have spotted any errors, please write them on the next page.

Please return this form to: Veronica Wastell, Publisher, Foulks Lynch, FREEPOST 2254, Feltham TW14 0BR

Other comments/suggestions and errors

ACCA Order Form

4 The Griffin Centre, Staines Road, Feltham, Middlesex, TW14 0HS, UK.
Tel: +44 (0) 20 8831 9990 Fax: + 44 (0) 20 8831 9991
Order online: www.foulkslynch.com Email: sales@ewfl-global.com

Examination Date: **Jun 04** ☐ **Dec 04** ☐ (please tick the exam you intend to take)	**Textbooks** **£20.95**	**Revision Series** **£11.95**	**Lynchpins** **£6.50**	**Distance Learning Courses** **£95.00**
Part 1				
1.1 Preparing Financial Statements (UK)	☐	☐	☐	☐
1.1 Preparing Financial Statements (International)	☐	☐	☐	☐
1.2 Financial Information for Management	☐	☐	☐	☐
1.3 Managing People	☐	☐	☐	☐
Part 2				
2.1 Information Systems	☐	☐	☐	☐
2.2 Corporate & Business Law	☐	☐	☐	☐
2.2 Corporate & Business Law (Scottish)	☐			
2.3 Business Taxation – FA 2003	☐	☐	☐	☐
2.3 Business Taxation – FA 2003 (Hong Kong)	☐			
2.4 Financial Management & Control	☐	☐	☐	☐
2.5 Financial Reporting (UK)	☐	☐	☐	☐
2.5 Financial Reporting (International)	☐	☐	☐	☐
2.6 Audit & Internal Review (UK)	☐	☐	☐	☐
2.6 Audit & Internal Review (International)	☐	☐	☐	☐
Part 3				
3.1 Audit & Assurance Services (UK)	☐	☐	☐	☐
3.1 Audit & Assurance Services (International)	☐	☐	☐	☐
3.2 Advanced Taxation – FA 2003	☐	☐	☐	☐
3.2 Advanced Taxation – FA 2003 (Hong Kong)	☐			
3.3 Performance Management	☐	☐	☐	☐
3.4 Business Information Management	☐	☐	☐	☐
3.5 Strategic Business Planning & Development	☐	☐	☐	☐
3.6 Advanced Corporate Reporting (UK)	☐	☐	☐	☐
3.6 Advanced Corporate Reporting (International)	☐	☐	☐	☐
3.7 Strategic Financial Management	☐	☐	☐	☐

Postage, Packing and Delivery:

Textbook & Revision Series	*First*	*Each Extra*	*Lynchpins*	*First*	*Each Extra*	*Distance Learning (Per subject)*	*Each*
UK	£5.00	£2.00		£2.00	£1.00		£6.00
Europe (incl ROI and CI)	£7.00	£4.00		£3.00	£2.00		£15.00
Rest of World	£22.00	£8.00		£8.00	£5.00		£40.00

Product Sub Total £............... | **Post & Packing £...................** | **Order Total £...................** | **(Payment in UK £ Sterling)**

Customer Details

☐ Mr ☐ Mrs ☐ Ms ☐ Miss Other ....

Initials:.................................. Surname: ....

Address: ....

....

....

Postcode: ....

Telephone: ....

Fax: ....

Email address: ....

Delivery Address – if different from above

Address: ....

....

Postcode: ....

Telephone: ....

Payment

1 I enclose Cheque/Postal Order/Bankers Draft for £.......................
Please make cheques payable to '**Foulks Lynch**'.

2 Charge MasterCard/Visa/Switch card number:

Valid from: Expiry date:

Issue no: (Switch only)

Signature: .... Date: ....

Declaration

I agree to pay as indicated on this form and understand that Foulks Lynch Terms and Conditions apply (available on request).

Signature: .... Date: ....

For delivery – please allow:	United Kingdom	– 5 working days
	Eire & EU Countries	– 10 working days
	Rest of World	– 10 working days

Notes: All orders over 1kg will be fully tracked & insured. Signature required on receipt of order. Delivery times subject to stock availability. A telephone number or email address is required for orders that are to be delivered to a PO Box number.

Notes: Prices are correct at time of going to print but are subject to change

FOULKS LYNCH PUBLICATIONS

ACCA Official Publisher